Crossing Borders

Crossing Borders

The Life and Work of Peder Borgen in Context

TORREY SELAND

Foreword by Paul N. Anderson

WIPF & STOCK · Eugene, Oregon

CROSSING BORDERS
The Life and Work of Peder Borgen in Context

Copyright © 2022 Torrey Seland. All rights reserved. Except for brief quotations in critical publications or reviews, no part of this book may be reproduced in any manner without prior written permission from the publisher. Write: Permissions, Wipf and Stock Publishers, 199 W. 8th Ave., Suite 3, Eugene, OR 97401.

Wipf & Stock
An Imprint of Wipf and Stock Publishers
199 W. 8th Ave., Suite 3
Eugene, OR 97401

www.wipfandstock.com

PAPERBACK ISBN: 978-1-6667-3793-6
HARDCOVER ISBN: 978-1-6667-9805-0
EBOOK ISBN: 978-1-6667-9806-7

09/16/22

Biblical quotations are from the New Revised Standard Version Bible (NRSV), copyright © 1989 by the Division of Christian Education of the National Council of the Churches of Christ in the United States of America. Used by permission. All rights reserved.

The picture on the front leaf is used by permission of Studio OSKAR, Lillestrøm, Norway.

The picture on p. 35 is used by permission of Akershusbasen/MiA, Norway.

The picture on p. 159 is used by permission of Ole-Einar Andersen, Trondheim.

The epigraph on p. v is adopted and translated from Danish by me (TS). I am grateful for the permission of Birgitte Possing to use this saying of hers. The original saying is found in an interview published at https://www.information.dk/moti/2015/02/laeserne-spoerger-birgitte-possing.

"Biographies humanize history, are a reflective mirror for ourselves and narrative entrances to think about our roots."

BIRGITTE POSSING (2015)

Contents

Foreword by Paul N. Anderson	ix
Preface	xv
Acknowledgments	xvii
List of Abbreviations	xix
Introduction	1
1 Family Background and Childhood	13
2 Formative Years in College and University	37
3 Further Studies on Luke and Eschatology (USA, 1953–56)	59
4 Borgen as a Pastor (1956–58)	65
5 Searching for Bread from Heaven: Research Fellow (1958–62)	73
6 Peder and Inger	86
7 Crossing into the Diaspora of the USA (1962–66)	92
8 The *Bread from Heaven* Disputation (1966)	104
9 Borgen in Bergen (1967–73)	120
10 In the Middle of Norway: Professor in Trondheim (1973–93)	154
11 Borgen on the Issue of Church-State Relations	184
12 Peder Borgen, a Struggling Ecumenist from a Minority Church	198
13 A Busy Senior Research Scholar (1993–99)	225
14 Biblical Studies in Trondheim: A Review	239
15 Returning Home: Back to Lillestrøm	264
16 A Life of Border Crossings: Outlook and Conclusions	278
Appendix: Bibliography of Peder Borgen's Works (1956–2021)	285
Bibliography	305

Foreword

Paul N. Anderson[1]

THE LIFE AND CONTRIBUTION OF PEDER BORGEN—A ROYALLY DISTINGUISHED BIBLICAL SCHOLAR

So, how many biblical scholars receive a royal knighthood from the King of Norway, become the chair of the Royal Norwegian Society of Sciences and Letters (receiving also its Gunnerus Medal, its highest honor), get elected president of the Society of New Testament Studies (the most prestigious religious society in the world), have two Festschrifts gathered in their honor, serve as editor of *Novum Testamentum* and as chief editor of the journal's monograph series, provide international and national ecumenical leadership, serve in pastoral leadership, get offered teaching positions at top academic institutions in America and Europe, have their works included in collected essays and a distinguished monograph series, and have their life story published by one of their leading students?

Such is the case for Peder Borgen, and in this fine overview of his life, service, and scholarship, Torrey Seland—Borgen's first doctoral student at Trondheim—not only honors his professor and friend; he also serves well the interests of biblical scholarship and religious leadership worldwide. As a thorough and thoughtful overview of the life of Peder Borgen,

---

1. Paul N. Anderson serves as Professor of Biblical and Quaker Studies at George Fox University in Newberg, Oregon, and as Extraordinary Professor of Religion at the North-West University of Potchefstroom, South Africa.

Crossing Borders: The Life and Work of Peder Borgen in Context documents his personal sojourn and contributions to church and society, in addition to covering the scholarly contribution of a world-class biblical scholar and theologian. Too rarely is a scholar's personal story considered as the backdrop, or even the foreground, of one's academic work. In that sense, Torrey Seland's detailed biography is inextricably linked to Borgen's bibliography: a multitude of connections that contextualize the intrigue and significance of an exemplary scholar's work.

That being the case, Borgen's upbringing within and lifelong commitment to the Methodist Church—a minority and sometimes disparaged denomination by the state Church of Norway (Lutheran)—is significant for understanding his scholarship and contributions. Participating at the formation of the World Council of Churches in 1947 and beyond, as well as in ecumenical conversations in Norway and internationally, Peder Borgen always possessed and championed a larger vision of the larger body of Christ, served by its component parts but not limited to any of them. This gave rise to his challenging state-church approaches to Christian discipleship, calling for the following of Jesus as the first priority of authentic believers.

Indeed, with his being steeped in the New Testament writings, Christ being the head of the church is the center of ecclesial organization and concern, and that witness bore fruit in Norway and beyond. As Ernst Käsemann shared with me in personal correspondence nearly three decades ago, it was the lordship of Christ that also posed the biblical basis for the Barmen Declaration in 1934, and attending, discerning, and minding the leadership of Christ is the high calling of every Christian leader and movement.[2] Peder Borgen also served the church well with his pastoral and teaching work, and that vocation provided direction for his biblical studies, and vice versa.

As a biblical scholar, the exegetical work of Peder Borgen is also without parallel in the Scandanavian nations and beyond. Inspired by Nils Alstrup Dahl and other Scandanavian scholars, Borgen played a major role in wresting the socioreligious backdrop of the New Testament writings away from Continental infatuation with second-century Gnosticism, showing the pervasively Jewish character of the writings of John and Paul and other New Testament texts. In particular, the works of Philo and the Babylonian Talmud help one appreciate the ways Jesus and his ministry were engaged by contemporary Jewish leaders in Palestine, as well as among other settings

---

2. Correspondence with Professor Käsemann, 1994; see Paul N. Anderson, "John 17—The Original Intention of Jesus for the Church, a Foreword by Paul N. Anderson," in *The Testament of Jesus*, by Ernst Käsemann, translated by Gerhard Krodel, Johannine Monograph Series 6 (Eugene, OR: Wipf & Stock, 2017), xxxvi n. 76. See also my book *Following Jesus: The Heart of Faith and Practice* (Newberg, OR: Barclay, 2013).

in the larger Mediterranean world. Pivotal in his own development, and a subject to which he continually returned throughout his career, was the midrashic debate between Jesus and Jewish leaders in John 6.

Challenging the diachronic fragmentation of John 6 by Rudolf Bultmann, who inferred no fewer than four major and distinctive literary sources underlying John 6,[3] Borgen was able to demonstrate compellingly the textual and thematic unity of the chapter. Like the proem text of a midrashic sermon, or a text-based argument by Philo, Borgen demonstrated the linguistic continuity and development of John 6:31–54 as a unity, arguing against a complex history of textual displacement, reordering, additions, and expansions upon alien documents posed by Rudolf Bultmann. In personal correspondence with me, he shared how he discovered the continuity of word patterns in Exodus 16:4 as played out within John 6, while passing time during a long wait in the Main Train Station of Copenhagen. He later found similar patterns in treatments of the manna motif in the writings of Philo, which led to further inquiry.[4] The monumental significance of his *magnum opus* demonstrated the textual unity and Jewish character of the Fourth Gospel with considerable implications for understanding its origin, character, and development.

When I first came to Glasgow for my doctoral work, diving into top Johannine studies in investigating the Christology of the Fourth Gospel, my advisor, John Riches, assigned me to thoroughly engage the great commentaries of Rudolf Bultmann, Rudolf Schnackenburg, C. K. Barrett, Raymond Brown, Barnabas Lindars, and others, as well as to look into the works of Ernst Käsemann, John Ashton, J. Louis Martyn, Wayne Meeks, and others, including, of course, Peder Borgen. This was just after his hosting of SNTS at Trondheim, and his *Bread from Heaven* and other works were already making a stir, internationally. In my work on John 6, I followed Borgen's lead and spent several months looking up all the manna-related midrashim in Philo and the Babylonian Talmud. There, I concurred with his overall treatment of the motif (noting also Psalm 78:24–25 as a significant link, as well as Exodus 16:4), but found that in most of the cases (about 85 percent of them) manna references served as a secondary text—a "rhetorical trump card," taking all hands—in the ways the motif was used. When applied to John 6,

---

3. For an extensive analysis of Bultmann's diachronic Johannine theory, see Paul N. Anderson, *The Christology of the Fourth Gospel: Its Unity and Disunity in the Light of John 6* (WUNT 2.78, 1996; third printing, Eugene, OR: Cascade, 2010), 33–169.

4. Paul N. Anderson, "Peder Borgen's *Bread from Heaven*—Midrashic Developments in John 6 as a Case Study in John's Unity and Disunity, a Foreword by Paul N. Anderson," in Peder Borgen, *Bread from Heaven*, Johannine Monograph Series 4 (Eugene, OR: Wipf & Stock, 2017), iii–iv.

this is what the crowd and the religious leaders argued: "What must we do to *get* the works of God (i.e., more bread—the main interest)?" bolstered by a reference to what Moses gave: manna from heaven (John 6:28–31). And, in my view, I would not be surprised if actual conversations and challenges like that (couched in the form of the Johannine temptation narrative) might have actually happened—a form of real-life midrashic debate—within the Capernaum synagogue. It could also have played well within a synagogue debate among the Gentile mission settings of Asia Minor or elsewhere.

Having met Professor Borgen at the 1987 Göttingen SNTS meetings, our paths crossed again at the 1993 University of Chicago SNTS meetings. This was the last year the Johannine Seminar was working on John 6, and Raymond Brown had withdrawn his paper, as he'd moved on to the Passion Narratives Seminar. This allowed me to offer a paper on the Sitz im Leben of the Johannine Bread-of-Life Discourse, accepted graciously by John Painter. In that expansive essay (twenty-eight thousand words), I attempted with John 6 what Lou Martyn had achieved with John 9, connecting the narrative with four additional audience-related issues, besides the Johannine-Jewish engagements.[5] There I described the importance of Borgen's work, while also noting the use of manna as secondary text. By then, Professor Borgen was taking leadership in the Philo Seminar, but he'd heard about my paper, and when we met up, he confronted me directly: "So, you've said my monograph on John 6 is the most important book on that chapter, and then you do everything you can do to dismantle my argument!" "Let's talk," I replied. We engaged a bit there, at the University of Chicago, and when we ran into each other at the Washington, DC, SBL meetings in November, we took our conversation further.

We agreed to meet in the lobby of the Washington Hilton, and we had a first-rate disciplinary debate over the use of manna rhetoric in Philo, the ancient midrashim, and John 6. Professor Borgen challenged: "What do you mean by 'a rhetorical trump card'? That's not a technical category used by biblical scholars." I replied, "Yes, I'm aware of that; it's a fitting term I've devised, describing the way manna is used—especially in Philo—where the highest trump card played takes all other cards in the hand." (As a Methodist, of course, he might not have been familiar with card-playing terms. . . not that all Quakers would have understood it either.) As our engagement continued, discussing a variety of Jewish homiletical patterns used in Second Temple Judaism, Jacob Neusner—the leading authority on Jewish

---

5. Paul N. Anderson, "The *Sitz im Leben* of the Johannine Bread of Life Discourse and its Evolving Context," in *Critical Readings of John 6*, edited by Alan Culpepper, Biblical Interpretation Supplemental Series 22 (Leiden: Brill, 1997; reprinted, Atlanta: SBL, 2006), 1–59.

interpretive texts—walked up and said, "Hello, Peder, how are you doing?" After they exchanged greetings, Peder introduced me to this scholar with whose works I was familiar. After saying hello, I said, "We're so glad you showed up just now, Professor Neusner; we've been discussing whether or not there is one, primary homiletical pattern that was used in ancient midrashic debates." He insisted, "Absolutely not! The only determining factor is the interpretive interest of the midrashist, serving his rhetorical purpose." I turned to Professor Borgen and said, "See?" We both laughed and thanked Professor Neusner for his input.

My good engagement with Peder Borgen continued over the years, in constructive, friendly ways. He reviewed *The Christology of the Fourth Gospel* when it was published three years later,[6] and I invited him to contribute on aspects of historicity in John 5–9 at the 2010 SBL meetings, published later in the third central volume of the John, Jesus, and History Project.[7] When Alan Culpepper and I envisioned the value of the Johannine Monograph Series over a decade ago, we led off with Bultmann's commentary on John, including four other volumes following in its wake.[8] These included the monographs of Moody Smith, Wayne Meeks, Peder Borgen, and Ernst Käsemann, each in their own ways furthering the interest of Nils Alstrup Dahl—Professor at Oslo and Yale—in showing the Jewish and ecclesial thrust of the Fourth Gospel against Bultmann's Hellenistic and diachronic approach.

As I've edited the ninth volume overall emerging from the John, Jesus, and History Project, focusing on archaeology, John, and Jesus,[9] Borgen's important work continues to come to mind in relation to several of the essays. Given the Jerusalem temple links with the Migdal Synagogue stone and likely presence of Judean leaders in the Capernaum synagogue, Borgen's midrashic analysis of John 6 indeed resembles the sort of midrashic debate that may actually have occurred in the region, following a feeding event and Passover messianic hopes of a political uprising associated with nationalistic

---

6. Peder Borgen, review of "The Christology of the Fourth Gospel," *Journal of Theological Studies* 49 (October 1998) 751–58. See my response, Paul N. Anderson, "Epilogue: Responses to *The Christology of the Fourth Gospel*," *Christology* (2010), 347–49.

7. Peder Borgen, "Observations on God's Agent and Agency in John 5–9: Tradition, Exposition, and Glimpses into History," in *John, Jesus, and History*, vol. 3, *Glimpses of Jesus through the Johannine Lens*, edited by Paul N. Anderson, Felix Just, and Tom Thatcher, Early Christianity and Its Literature 18 (Atlanta: SBL, 2016), 423–38.

8. Rudolf Bultmann, *The Gospel of John: A Commentary*, Johannine Monograph Series 1 (Eugene, OR: Wipf & Stock, 2014).

9. Paul N. Anderson, *Archaeology, John, and Jesus: What Recent Discoveries Show Us about Jesus from the Gospel of John* (Grand Rapids: Eerdmans, forthcoming, 2023).

typologies of Moses and Elijah.[10] In that sense, Borgen's contribution bears considerable implications historically, in addition to addressing John's literary and theological riddles.[11]

As Torrey Seland's expansive overview of Peder Borgen's life of biblical scholarship and Christian leadership documents, his additional contributions to Philonic and Pauline studies are also worth noting. I think it would be fair to say that Philonic New Testament studies would not have developed in the ways they did were it not for the lifelong contributions of Peder Borgen. Likewise, understandings of Paul's uses of Hebrew Scripture in Galatians and his other writings, and appreciation for John's autonomy over against the Gospels of Matthew and the other Synoptics, are likewise indebted to his numerous contributions over the years. For these and other reasons, Peder Borgen's membership and leadership as chair (1996–1999) within the Royal Norwegian Society of Sciences and Letters—receiving also its Gunnerus Medal (2003), its highest honor, in appreciation for his rigorous academic work—is appreciated. It is also fitting that he was awarded Knight First Class of the Norwegian Order of Saint Olav by King Herald V, a royal tribute to his academic, biblical, ministerial, and ecumenical work. In addition to authoring no fewer than nine books and numerous peer-reviewed essays, the two Festschrifts gathered in his name represent but a small tribute to his work over the years by top biblical scholars internationally.[12] Not only has Peder Borgen crossed many borders in his international travels, but his work has also crossed borders between academic disciplines, between denominations, between church and state, and between academic and general audiences. He is truly a royally distinguished biblical scholar, and Torrey Seland is to be thanked for this monumental contribution covering the life and scholarship of Peder Borgen.

---

10. D. Moody Smith, *The Composition and Order of the Fourth Gospel*, Johannine Monograph Series 2 (Eugene, OR: Wipf & Stock, 2015); Peder Borgen, *Bread from Heaven*, Johannine Monograph Series 4 (Eugene, OR: Wipf & Stock, 2017); Wayne A. Meeks, *The Prophet-King*, Johannine Monograph Series 5 (Eugene, OR: Wipf & Stock, 2017); Ernst Käsemann, *The Testament of Jesus*, Johannine Monograph Series 6 (Eugene, OR: Wipf & Stock, 2017).

11. Paul N. Anderson, *The Riddles of the Fourth Gospel: An Introduction to John* (Minneapolis: Fortress, 2011).

12. *Context: Essays in Honor of Peder Borgen*, edited by Peter Wilhelm Böckman and Roald E. Kristiansen (Trondheim: Tapir, 1987); *Neotestamentica et Philonica: Studies in Honor of Peder Borgen*, edited by D. E. Aune, T. Seland, and J. H. Ulrichsen (Leiden: Brill, 2003).

Preface

WHEN I STARTED AS a young pastor in the parish of Bakklandet, Trondheim, Norway, in 1978, I had some expectations of also being able to continue studying the New Testament and early Christianity. In fact, I did not see myself as a parish pastor for the rest of my life but had already been looking for some opportunities for further studies. As part of my continuing search, I one day paid a visit to the professor in "the New Testament and its world" at the University of Trondheim, Peder Borgen. I did not know him then. In fact, I do not remember if I had ever seen him before or read anything of what he had published. Nevertheless, Professor Borgen received me in a way that gave me the impression that he supported my intentions of further studies 110 percent and he gave me an introduction to what he was working on.

As I became better acquainted with Peder Borgen, I soon realized that I was dealing with a non-Lutheran, in his case a Methodist. As I myself grew up in a Baptist family, we had some comparable childhood and early youth experiences. However, while I later became a member of the Church of Norway, which is Lutheran, he has stayed a Methodist all his life. Peder Borgen was and is a Methodist. Those who got to know him would probably realize that denominational affiliation too. Nevertheless, not all who know his scholarly works know his love for Methodism and the Norwegian Methodist Church. Hence, I presume some will be surprised by the number of pages spent here on his commitment to Methodism and his work in ecumenical contexts. However, it would not be a description of the "historical Peder Borgen" if these sections of his life were not given their proper place in a biography like this. Sometimes I get the impression that those who know him as a Methodist do not know much of his scholarly achievements as a New Testament scholar, not to say an expert on Philo of Alexandria. And those who know him as a biblical and Philo scholar do not know much about his work in the context and service of his church. Hopefully, readers of this volume may find that it does bring these two fields together, providing a more comprehensive picture than what they knew before they opened this book.

The biography is a revised and translated version of the Norwegian edition, published in December 2020: *Peder Borgen. Metodist—Økumen—Professor i en brytningstid* (Cappelen Damm: Oslo, 2020). The revisions carried out have been twofold: on the one hand, some issues and events related to Borgen's life in the Norwegian context have been abbreviated; on the other hand, some specific aspects of Norwegian church life and structures have been expanded to make the context of Peder Borgen's life as a Methodist more understandable for those without knowledge of the Norwegian ecclesiastical landscape. These issues are most often related to the fact that the majority church in Norway was a state church up to 2012 and is still a church with close relations to the state. As Borgen was a Methodist, in a Norwegian setting that means that he belonged to a minority, a member of a free church; that is, in a Norwegian context a "dissenter." To understand the impact of such social constructions, a reader must know the Norwegian ecclesiastical landscape, including the dominating role of the Church of Norway, the variety of the Norwegian free churches, and the Christian societies like the lay mission movements so typical of a Nordic country.

In the present volume, the sections dealing with the research of Peder Borgen have also been considerably expanded compared to the Norwegian edition. This is a choice made based on the presupposition that readers of this version will probably, to a larger extent than the readers in Norway, not only be interested in his life but also in his scholarly achievements. However, the reviews given here are not meant to be extensive discussions of his ideas and results but brief descriptive reviews of the central tenets of his research. Only in a few cases have the *Wirkungsgeschichte* of some of his ideas been dealt with. Otherwise, the volume would have been much more extensive and probably not written by me either.

Finally, the volume probably has a much longer introduction than typical in similar biographies. This feature is grounded in my own efforts to understand what a biography really is, that is, how it is to be understood as a *genre*. Hence, I here describe some of what I have found. I also provide some comments on what kind of sources I have used. I hope both these features may be found profitable to the reader.

Torrey Seland
Kvinesdal, Norway, May 2022

Acknowledgments

As this volume is a translated and revised version of a Norwegian edition,[1] I am grateful to its publisher, Cappelen Damm Akademisk, for the permission to translate, reuse, and revise this work in the present volume.

Accordingly, as I am reusing the material applied in the Norwegian volume, I would also like to reexpress my gratitude to the following persons that served as informers for the Norwegian version: Roar G. Fotland, Ivar Granum, Lars-Erik Nordby, Thor Bernhard Tobiassen, Lars Østnor, and Per Magne Aadnanes. Thanks also to Jan Ove Ulstein for his willingness to accept the Norwegian edition for publishing in the series he has edited for so many years: Kyrkjefag Profil (now: Religionsfag Profil).

Furthermore, I am grateful for the help offered by the Library of the Methodist Historical Society in Oslo, and especially by the National Library in Oslo, Norway.

I also want to express my thanks to the staff at Wipf and Stock for the efforts they have put into action in order to make this volume getting published in an American context. I am also grateful to Professor Paul N. Anderson, who has written an interesting essay as a foreword to this edition.

And then again, I owe a ton of gratitude to Peder and Inger Borgen, the main characters in this story, for accepting me into their stories. Thank you for the interviews, the lunches, the conversations and hard discussions, the fellowship over forty years, and your contribution in support of the expenditures of printing and publishing.

Last, but not least, a big hug to my wife for over fifty two years, Anne Margrete. I know she wants me to slow down and may be even stop studying. OK, I will slow down, but can I stop studying, that is: reading books? *Non, ma chérie. Ce n'est pas possible!*

---

1. *Peder Borgen. Metodist—Økumen—Professor i en brytningstid* (Cappelen Damm Akademisk: Oslo, 2020).

List of Abbreviations

SEVERAL ABBREVIATIONS ARE USED only a couple of times, and they are explained in their immediate context. Hence, they are not included in this list. Furthermore, biblical references are not given here; they are used following *The SBL Handbook of Style* (2nd ed., Atlanta: SBL, 2014).

Ant.	*Antiquitates Judaica* / *Jewish Antiquities* (Josephus)
DKNVS	Det Kongelige Norske Videnskabers Selskab / Royal Norwegian Society of Sciences and Letters
IMC	International Mission Council
MF	Menighetsfakultetet
MUO	Methodist Church's Education and Information Council
NAVF	Norges Almenvitenskapelige Forskningsråd / Norwegian Research Council for Science and the Humanities
NLHT	Norges Lærerhøgskole / Norwegian College of Teaching
NMC	Norwegian Mission Council
NOU	Norges Offentlige Utredninger
NRK	Norsk Rikskringkasting / Norwegian Broadcasting Company
PC	personal computer
SBL	Society of Biblical Literature
SNTS	Studiorum Novi Testamenti Societas
St.mld	*Stortingsmelding* /a ministry's report to the Parliament
TF	Teologisk Fakultet
TS	Torrey Seland
UMC	United Methodist Church

USA	United States of America
WCC	World Council of Churches

PHILO OF ALEXANDRIA

Conf.	*De confusion linguarum* / On the Confusion of Tongues
Flacc.	*In Flaccum* / Against Flaccus
Legat.	*Legatio ad Gaium* / On the Embassy to Gaius
Leg.	*Legum allegoriae* / Allegorical Interpretation
Mos.	*De vita Mosis* / On the Life of Moses
Mut.	*De mutatione nominum* / On the Change of Names
QE	*Questiones et solutiones in Exodum* / Questions and Answers on Exodus
Spec.	*De specialibus legibus* / On the Special Laws
Virt.	*De virtutibus* / On the Virtues

Introduction

AUGUST 25, 1953: A tall and slender dark-haired young man—twenty-five years of age—entered the Norwegian ocean liner S/S *Stavangerfjord* in Oslo. Destination: New York, United States of America.

The ship had a prestigious thirty-six-year history in her transatlantic route, carrying passengers between North America and Scandinavia. Eleven years later, she was scrapped in Hong Kong. The airplanes took over.

The young man entering the ship was Peder Johan Borgen. He was at the beginning of his career, a career that would bring him to the United States repeatedly for several decades to come.

But, unlike many others on that ship in 1953, he was not immigrating to the USA to get a job "over there" as, e.g., a carpenter, to earn some money to improve his living in Norway. When he arrived at Ellis Island, he proceeded immediately to a university in New Jersey, where he was to study for the next three years, hoping to achieve a PhD degree in New Testament studies.

Peder had graduated from his theological studies at the University of Oslo earlier that year. In June, he left the university as a *candidatus theologiae*. His diploma demonstrated solid years of studying, and his good grades made him hope for opportunities for further studies. But there were some obstacles; he was not a Lutheran! His applications were turned down for church denominational reasons.

In the Norwegian ecclesiastical landscape of these days, the Church of Norway was a *state church* with many privileges and prerogatives. The state had an over four hundred years long history of favoring the Lutheran church. Even though many things had changed since the introduction of the Lutheran Reformation in Norway in 1536/37, and with that, the political dominion of the majority church as a state church, there were still some obstacles in vogue for those belonging to "the dissenters," that is, the non-Lutheran minority churches. One of these obstacles was represented by the fact that theological scholarships at the University of Oslo were only available to Lutheran applicants. And Peder was not a Lutheran; he was a Methodist, having no thoughts of changing that identity.

Accordingly, when he entered the S/S *Stavangerfjord*, the money he had in his pocket did not derive from any Norwegian institution but from abroad. He knew the restrictions laid upon the Norwegian scholarships. Hence, he had been looking around for some other sources. He applied to the American Fulbright Fund, to the World Council of Churches in Switzerland, and to a program within the Methodist Church (USA) called Crusade Scholarships. And he received scholarships from all three! Through the World Council of Churches scholarship, he was admitted to Drew University, Madison, New Jersey, which was affiliated with the Methodist Church.

On September 4, he could enter the immigrant inspection station at Ellis Island, and from there, proceed to Drew University in New Jersey. Less than three years later, he received his PhD diploma and returned to Norway.

Peder Johan Borgen, probably better known as just Peder Borgen, was to become one of the internationally best-known Norwegian biblical scholars of the latter half of the twentieth century. Along with scholars like his teachers Sigmund Mowinckel and Nils Alstrup Dahl, and to some extent also his contemporary Jacob Jervell, he enjoyed a respect and fame hardly matched by any other Norwegian biblical scholars in the guilds of international scholarship.

In a Norwegian lexicon, Borgen is described thus (my translation):

> Peder Johan Borgen is a Methodist and professor of New Testament theology. He has been a pioneer[1] in the theological, scholarly environment in Norway and was the first Methodist and first member of a Norwegian Free Church to obtain the degree of Doctor Theologiae at a Norwegian university.[2]

It is Jon Arne Lund, former editor of the Norwegian newspaper *Vårt Land* and one of the authors of the *Norsk Biografisk Leksikon* (*Norwegian Biographical Encyclopaedia*), who characterizes Peder J. Borgen in this way. Moreover, he adds that Borgen was also the first free church theologian to receive a theological teaching position at a Norwegian university. And in 1998, he was the first free church theologian to be appointed Knight of the First Class of the Order of St. Olav "for the merit of theological research."

In the *Norwegian context*, he is also known as a person who has played a vital role in highlighting Methodist identity and a tireless advocate for the

---

1. The expression used here is almost impossible to translate. Norwegian: *banebrytende murbrekker*; Eng., literally: groundbreaking brick breaker. Hence: "pioneer."
2. See https://nbl.snl.no/Peder_Borgen.

rights and demands of the free churches in a country in which the majority church, called the Church of Norway, had been a Lutheran state church since the sixteenth century. Furthermore, in the Norwegian context, his denominational affiliation made him an ecclesiastical "dissenter" and an advocate for religious freedom in a broad sense with both a view to inter-church cooperation in what we call ecumenical work, and concerning the relations between state and church.

In *Biblical research*, his name is internationally known and respected, primarily as related to the research of the Gospel of John and the ancient Jewish scholar, theologian, politician, and philosopher Philo of Alexandria, who lived at approximately the same time as Jesus and Paul. But Borgen also worked extensively on several of the other New Testament scriptures. Besides, he has published several studies related to the history of Methodism in Norway.

Many threads need to be woven together to get a recognizable picture of him. Thus, this biography represents an attempt to present such a tapestry.

But what actually is a *biography*?

WHAT IS A BIOGRAPHY?: SOME THEORETICAL PERSPECTIVES

It might be profitable to consider for a moment the question, what is a biography? The term "biography" itself is composed of the Greek words *bios* (life) and *graphein* (to write); that is, a biography is a description or depiction of a life. However, biography as a genre may be divided into two main types: *autobiographies* and *secondary biographies*. An autobiography is written by the protagonist; a secondary or second-hand biography is written by another person, either while the protagonist is still alive or—and this is perhaps the most common procedure—after the protagonist's death. If it happens while the protagonist is alive, he or she may also approve the biography; then we get close to the autobiography, and we get an "authorized biography," which perhaps should preferably be classified as a subgroup under autobiographies. This book is not an autobiography, nor is it an authorized biography, even though the main character was alive while the book was being researched and written. In the following, I will provide a somewhat more comprehensive presentation of what kind of biography you are currently reading.

The Norwegian author and biographer Knut Olav Åmås once reflected in a chapter on "The Theory and Method of Biography"—a chapter which is placed at the end of his significant biography on the Norwegian poet Olav H. Hauge—thus: "How to write about a literary life like that of the poet Olav H. Hauge, which was often quite stagnant and little eventful, outward-looking?"[3]

That is a question someone might also want to raise when it comes to writing about a theological scholar like Peder Borgen; that is, about a person who loves books, who loves to study the New Testament and the scriptures that belong in its contemporary and broader cultural context, and to write and publish articles and books that discuss complicated issues with other scholars. Could that be something to deal with in a biography? Could it be interesting to anyone else than his colleagues?

Tim Grass is reflecting on similar issues when he comments on the prospects of writing a biography of F. F. Bruce: "But why write a biography of such a man? Indeed, given that so much of his life was about thought rather than action, is the enterprise even possible?"[4]

Now, I would probably say that Borgen's life and work were quite different from Hauge's, and even Bruce's, life; maybe they can hardly be compared. But Hauge's life as a writing poet had some similarities to that of a theological scholar like Borgen. They were both deep thinkers and researchers, each in their own field, and they wrote and published, and their works were weighed and measured. In that sense, there are similarities. But Borgen did not write poems and was concerned with so much more than biblical research, even though that research runs like a red thread throughout his life. Borgen's life is a tapestry with many different threads of different colors, and the image that emerges is different from Hauge's. To some extent the same can be said about F. F. Bruce. And it is these threads of Borgen's tapestry that are focused here. While Åmås calls his biography a "literary biography," and Grass calls his biography of Bruce for "an intellectual biography,"[5] we might characterize this biography of Borgen as a "theological biography"; a biography in which a person's life story becomes part of both a person's theological development[6] and research efforts, but one which also represents a part of a country's church history; and especially as here a part of a small church denomination's history (in a Norwegian context) in the form of a *minority story*.

The present biography's focus on a representative from a denomination that—again in its Norwegian context—was, and was perceived as, a

3. Åmås, *Mitt liv*, 547.
4. Grass, *Life*, xii.
5. Grass, *Life*, xii. This is also the characterization used by Niehoff in her biography of Philo of Alexandria (see Niehoff, *Philo of Alexandria*, 1–3).
6. Compare, to some extent, Smidt, *John Wesley*, 10. In general, however, Smidt's biography is of a more hagiographic nature.

religious minority, is a phenomenon that is not widely found in Norwegian historical literature. The present biography will thus fill a gap both in our general history and as part of recent Norwegian church history. Hopefully, it will also provide an interesting insight into the Norwegian cultural and ecclesiastical history for non-Norwegians, especially those who know Borgen primarily as a biblical scholar, and who are interested in not only his scholarly achievements, but also the person behind these accomplishments.

In recent years, several biographies have been published about New Testament scholars and other theologians.[7] They contain, however, very few historiographic deliberations on what a biography really is; what its characteristics are, and how it should be understood as a *genre*. As a Scandinavian scholar, living in Norway, I have found a recent work by the Danish literary scholar Birgitte Possing extremely helpful.[8] In her interesting volume, she discusses several distinct types of biographies, principles of source use, and other aspects relevant for understanding the biography genre.[9]

Birgitte Possing suggests that the phenomenon or genre of biography can be divided into eight diverse types, or "archetypes" as she calls it, and since the typology she presents has been useful to me as an author, it may also be useful to my readers. It should, therefore, be briefly presented and characterized further here.

There is a certain historical progression in Possing's presentation as she begins with the oldest and ends up with the more recent biography types: "They each stem from their individual specific historical epoch, but by and large they are still around and in the best of health today."[10]

Eight archetypes

Possing labels and characterizes eight biographical archetypes as follows (numbers in the text are page references to the English version):

---

7. To mention just a few recent biographies, see e.g., Grass, *A Life*, (on F. F. Bruce, 2011); Hammann, *Rudolf Bultmann* (2013); Bach, *Leon Morris* (2016); Hughes, *Jacob Neusner* (2016), and Falcetta, *Daily Discoveries of a Bible Scholar* (on J. Rendel Harris, 2018). A couple of recent autobiographies might also be mentioned: Van Seters, *My Life*; and Johnson, *Mind in Another Place*.

8. Possing, *Ind i Biografien*. I have here used the English translation: Possing, *Understanding Biographies*.

9. Besides, there are now also some other Norwegian academic biographies that contain good reflections on the nature of a biography. See, e.g., Åmås, *Mitt Liv*, 545–604, 679–704 (notes); Jølle, *Innledning*, 1–101; Skre, *Tilnærmingar, metode, drøftingar og val*.

10. Possing, *Understanding Biographies*, 69.

1. *Mirror biography.* This type is "so named because by canonizing the protagonist it might serve as a mirror for grand human endeavor, or because by vulgarizing the protagonist it might serve to mirror the opposite, the unsympathetic human features. The mirror biography can also be called the didactic biography..." (70). Possing mentions works of the Greek historian and biographer Plutarch (45–120 CE), and the Roman historian Gaius Suetonius (69–122 CE) as early examples of this genre. And I might add another person from antiquity—and one which is very familiar to Peder Borgen—the Jewish theologian, philosopher, politician, and biographer Philo of Alexandria (20 BCE–ca. 50 CE), and his biography of Moses (*De vita Mosis* I–II). Hence, in such biographies, the readers "are to look in the mirror, be inspired or pass judgement" (71).

2. *The hagiography.* This type can be considered an offshoot of the former but represents a much more direct applauding description of the biographee. Possing suggests the type as such stems from the early centuries of the Christian church: "Using a mixture of fact and myth, it was designed to glorify and honour the saints, heroes or individuals who were to be idealized for their deeds" (71). Even today, many biographical descriptions of Christian leaders and preachers display not a few hagiographic traits. An academic biography, however, must evade such pitfalls. According to Possing, furthermore, "In modern times, the hagiography has mainly been manifested in its opposite form, also structured around a mixture of myth and fact: the *villainography*..." Hence, "acclaim or disdain, rather than mirroring, is the intention of this archetype" (72).

3. *The personality portrait.* As an archetype, according to Possing, "this focuses on the characteristic features of the personality, analysing its way to an impartial characterisation of a nuanced, multi-layered and perhaps ambiguous individual who changed over the course of a lifetime. This archetype is concerned with the individual—who might indeed be placed in a context—and the biographer's agenda is to trace that protagonist's character traits" (73). Possing believes that this archetype made its mark as a genre at the end of the eighteenth century and is thus representative of the era when critical historical studies were born. It represents thus part of a paradigm shift because of its use of a wide range of source material and a critical attitude to the sources. Hence, "The purpose of the personality portrait is to reach an understanding of the character and the deeper strata working as motive and compass of a well-known personality" (76).

4. *The interpretive biography.* This type is very close to the preceding but has a somewhat different focus: "The idea was to get behind the myths about the central characters and to pave the way for biographies that demythologised real-life men and women" (77). The interpretations became here particularly important and were emphasized in the narrative. Possing summarizes this type thus: "The purpose of the interpretive biography is to expose conventions, reveal and display new truths, demythologise, analyse and apply new thinking to portraits and biographies of historical personalities" (78).

5. *The prism biography.* "Although portraying a historical person, the keenly interpretive prism biography uses him or her as a lever for analysis of something other than the protagonist: for example, the focus is on a type, a class, a culture, a gender, a race or a minority. This archetype has proven to be a forum for social critics, historians or anthropologists, rather than literary scholars and journalists" (79).

6. *The life-and-times biography.* A key feature of this type is that the biography writer here attempts to place the protagonist in a larger context and will examine the dynamic relationship between the protagonist and his or her temporal and societal context. A keyword here thus becomes *contextualization*; it becomes important to see the main person in the light of both his or her past (e.g., parents/grandparents and their social positions, etc.) and the main character's life and society. It is also important to see how a person is influenced by both the past and present, but also how he or she can influence his or her own time. The purpose, according to Possing, of the life-and-times biography is "to understand and explain how a notable individual could become both 'carrier' of and 'redeemer' of a major need in his/her day—and by so doing became a figure worthy of remembrance" (81).

7. *The polyphonic biography.* A polyphonic (multi-voiced) biography might be written by one or several authors, but its main characteristics are that it reconstructs a person's life from various perspectives based on various sources, and in various situations. Past and present do not have the same explaining role as the preceding archetype dealt with here. The genre is quite recent and belongs to our postmodern era. Possing describes its purpose thus: "The purpose of the polyphonic archetype is to tell a life and work from several angles and in several voices, supplementing and contradicting one another, so the narratives invite the reader into the biography" (83).

8. *The prosopography*. In contrast to the other archetypes dealt with here, this genre deals not with one person only but comprises several. It is the collective genre; it is used to investigate the common traits of a group of persons. Its purpose is "to tell about the life of a group and the narratives stemming from their configuration as a group" (84).

These archetypes are presented here because they are not only important and useful for a writer of biographies, but also to the readers. However, one should keep in mind that there are no waterproof walls between the diverse types; many biographies apply several perspectives and provide different viewpoints. But as archetypes they demonstrate that life is always life lived in contexts, and that it contains contrasts of diverse kinds and many different influences and choices, and that it both shapes and is shaped by its surroundings. In this way, it is also important to use various sources in one's exposition.

This book about Peder Borgen belongs to the type of *life-and-times biography*. Hence, I will present this type somewhat more fully below.

A life-and-times biography; some further characterizations

This biography belongs primarily to the sixth archetype: the *life-and-times biography*. I take as a starting point that Peder Borgen's genealogy and immediate family represented crucial inputs in his life and will try to explain these features in the following presentation. Moreover, we will see that the fact that he grew up within a *minority group* in Norway, namely, the Norwegian Methodist Church, and that he continued to be a member of this church, also influenced several aspects of his life and ministry, and thus are prominent issues for our interpretation of his life.

The specific lenses used in this study

Two issues might legitimize further a *minority focus* on Peder Borgen's life and work. Firstly, it is once again necessary to point out that in the Norwegian church-life and cultural landscape, the individual church communities and denominations outside the majority church, i.e., outside the Norwegian Lutheran state church—the Church of Norway—have always had the characteristics of being *minority communities*. Statistically, this is a correct observation: there has always been a significant difference between the Church of Norway and the other denominations in Norway regarding the number of members.[11] This fact influenced both how the free churches have been understood and treated, and how they experienced themselves; they were minority churches.

Secondly, inherent in the experience of being a minority, there can sometimes also be a sense of *inferiority*. The term that has been used for members of non-Lutheran denominations for a long time, the Norwegian term "dissenter" (a dissenting person), can be considered an indicator of such an understanding by the larger community, and possible not at least by the majority church, the Church of Norway. It should also be considered a consequence of the dominant role the Church of Norway—often called the *state church*—has held in Norway as a majority church with a great number of state privileges. A prism biographical aspect (see type 5 above in Possing's list) will therefore also be inherent in my presentation.

In this book, a portrait of Peder Johan Borgen, his life and work, will be drawn by focusing on *three main lines of his life*. These are not chronologically distinct lines; they often intervene and are bound together in both time and space. They will therefore not be cultivated as separate lines, but will be recognized in the presentation as relevant and central features of his life and work:

- Peder Borgen as a Methodist and churchman
- Peder Borgen as a theologian and New Testament scholar
- Peder Borgen as a university teacher

Accordingly, when I focus on these three main lines in my narrative, it means that these are the areas I consider he has been most concerned with in his life, and in which he has spent much of his time, efforts, and energy. But I would also insist that in the present biography, this procedure can be justified methodologically. This does not mean that other lines will be neglected and omitted, but that these areas are where I find some of the most central issues, and they will thus constitute the *skeleton* around which the biography is built. However, as a skeleton is not visible on the outside of a body, these three main fields will not be as visible in my outline as might be expected.

---

11. Cf. the following self-representation of the Church of Norway: "The Church of Norway has represented the main expression of religious belief in Norway for a thousand years. It has belonged to the Evangelical Lutheran branch of the Christian church since the 16th century and has been a state church since then until 2012. Around 70 per cent of Norway's population are currently baptized members." https://kirken.no/nb-NO/church-of-norway/.

In general, I will adopt a chronological arrangement. However, based on these methodological considerations, the *lenses* applied in my presentation can be further formulated thus:

- As a given historical point of departure, we may consider it as a fact that Peder Borgen's family background as Methodists positioned them as a religious *minority group* in Norway.[12]

- At the same time, in this specific denomination, they were well aware that, though being a national free church, they also belonged to the large *international Methodist Church family*. Hence some *border crossings* were inherent in the structures of the Methodist Church.

- Borgen's minority background and personal experiences of being a minority, coupled with some experiences of *discrimination*, provide a central key to understanding several aspects of his life and work. In particular, it had a substantial impact on his attitude to Norwegian church life and ecumenical work, but some impact can also be found in his research interests and works. It soon turned out that he had to do some *border crossings* both in his personal life and in his research.

- Hence, in this volume, I will argue that the issues of belonging to a *minority*, coupled with some explicit experiences of *discrimination* and the need for some *border crossings*, have been an underlying and *intriguing impetus* to several aspects of his research—not least to his understanding of early Christianity; the Jewish theologian, philosopher, and politician Philo of Alexandria; and to Borgen's later interest in the *Sami minority situation* in his own country.

More on the sources used

The present study is based on a variety of sources. Peder Borgen himself has partly organized and then handed over a large amount of material from his life to the National Library in Oslo. The library now has a total of fifty-five boxes of such material. Included here are letters of correspondence, manuscripts for lectures, sermons, newspaper articles, seminar papers, and some preliminary material for studies he worked on and later published. In addition, there are many items from various conferences he attended, including items from his work as president of the Studiorum Novi Testamenti Societas, from his work as a member of the board of the Royal Norwegian

---

12. As a denomination comprising only about eleven thousand members, the Methodists were clearly a religious minority group in Norway.

Society of Sciences and Letters in Trondheim, and as a pro-rector at the Almenvitenskapelige Høgskolen at the University of Trondheim. The material extends from his early years as a theological student in Oslo, and up to his work as a retired but still active professor emeritus, living in his hometown of Lillestrøm. General access to this material is restricted, but by the kind permission of Peder Borgen, I have had access to the entire material through the National Library's special Reading Room.[13]

Borgen still has some material in his private home archive; there is, however, no record of what it covers, but Borgen has made at least parts of it available to me.

Another widely used source is *newspaper articles* and announcements; both articles written by Borgen and those about him. Newspaper articles are an invaluable source of contemporary perceptions of events and people; they are not reflections in retrospect, but reactions in real time and thus highly informative concerning reactions to the contemporary issues dealt with in the biography.

Last, but not least, I have carried out a series of *interviews*: these are primarily interviews with the main character, recorded in the years 2016–18. The interviews were digitalized but are transcribed and kept in my archives. I have also interviewed or had conversations with some other people who have been in contact with Peder Borgen in one or more phases of his life, and/or who know various aspects of his life. These range from people in his immediate family to others who may have read only some of his literary production.

The role of the author

In all literature, whether in that of the entertaining genres or of the stricter historical representations of past persons and events, the author is not a neutral observer or hidden figure in the text. Not even in scholarly works. He or she observes and evaluates, selects, and deselects material, disposes and adopts, and creates lines, focuses, and profiles. The author consciously and instinctively characterizes his/her material and presentation. In recent literary studies, as well as in much other recent research, it has become

---

13. Some of this stuff represents problems of their own. The letters included are extensive, but they are not arranged chronologically, but alphabetically. This makes it very time consuming to find one's way through the material. In many cases, the material represents only letters from one part; often we do not know, for example, whether Borgen replied to the letters sent to him, or how he responded. Hence, we often lack his responses. When it comes to family or private correspondence, it is rather sparse, and in most instances the responses come from his wife, Inger Borgen more than from Peder.

increasingly clear that if it is true that the author always plays a part in what s/he writes, it is useful and necessary for the author to appear in the text as what he or she is: an *observer, collector,* and *commentator.* Besides—and here appears an additional issue relevant in this book—when entering the 1980s, the present author is also a participating part in some of the events narrated. Accordingly, he must write himself into the text in a way that shows the reader where he is and what he does and says as an actor, and not just as an observer. This is not easy, but I hope I have succeeded. The problems have at least been acknowledged along the way.

Peder Borgen has given me complete freedom to present the material in the ways I found best and to present the various interpretations of the material that I believed to be the most relevant. It has never been the case of having him approve the product; this is not a so-called authorized biography in the sense that here the author is presenting a life story on behalf of and as a voiceover for the protagonist. We have had several conversations along the way—even some discussions—in addition to the direct interviews that have been digitally recorded and transcribed by me, but Borgen has in our conversations strongly emphasized that "this is your book, Torrey." In this way, Borgen has acted in an exemplary manner by primarily arranging material he may have, and occasionally pointing to other sources. The selection, interpretations, finding my pattern or plot, and finding the peculiar form has been my task and work, and is my responsibility alone.

To what extent I have succeeded, those engaging themselves with the book must decide in the interplay between a reader and the text that we call reading.

1

Family Background and Childhood

FAMILY BACKGROUND

Peder's father: Omar Emil Borgen

ONE DAY IN 1924—THE exact date is now no longer known—a young man came to the then small Norwegian town named Lillestrøm. He was planning to start a business, more specifically, a meat shop, and was looking for an appropriate location. For some time, he had scrutinized several advertisements and had researched premises in Oslo but found nothing that appealed to him. But now he had discovered an advertisement for a location in Lillestrøm that looked interesting. Actually, he was on his way home from Oslo to Sarpsborg by train when he saw the advertisement in the newspaper *Aftenposten*. It caused him to get off the train at Ski and return to Oslo. After contacting a broker, they both traveled to Lillestrøm. At first, it seemed that that journey would fail too. The advertised site did not meet his expectations. Nor did he find another location he checked suitable. But then he was told that a building at the town square in the center of the small town was for sale—Torvet 1. Further investigations convinced him: he liked the place and its location. After many considerations and financial negotiations, the property was purchased, and on October 24, 1924, at the age of twenty-four, he was able to open a business of his own: O.E. Borgen Kjød og Flæsk (O.E. Borgen Meat and Pork)!

This young man was named Omar Emil Borgen, and a few years later, in 1928, he, for the second time, became the father of a boy; this time to a boy to be named Peder Johan, the protagonist of this book.

Omar Emil Borgen was born on November 16th, 1900, in Midtre Klavestad in Skjeberg, in Østfold county, located in the south of the eastern part of Norway. His parents were Ole Edvard Andersen (Greaker) and Elisabeth Andersdatter Helgesen. He was number four in a sibling group, which later increased to six,[1] and was baptized at Skjeberg church on Second Christmas Day 1900.

The family lived at Klavestad until Omar Emil was approximately six years old; then, after a year's stay on a farm called Borgen, they moved on to Torp in Rakkestad, where Omar Emil spent the rest of his childhood and adolescence. While living at Borgen, they took Borgen as their family name.

The Borgen Family at Torp, Rakkestad

When Omar Emil attained the age of mid-sixties, he wrote—on the invitation of his second oldest son, Peder Johan—a small booklet containing some of his memories. These were copied and made available to family and friends on his seventieth birthday, November 16, 1970. The booklet, named *Letters to a Friend—Memories*, is a valuable source both to Omar Emil's upbringing and to his adult life, his work, thoughts, and ideals, as he remembered these in his old days.

The Haugian forms of Christianity in Rakkestad

In his booklet Omar Emil characterizes his grandfather as a "Haugian," but he does not use this term for his own parents. However, Peder Borgen later emphasized that his father Omar

> grew up in an environment where they had meetings in the Haugian style, or the style of the *Inner Mission* [*indremisjonen*] you might say, in their homes. There was no Prayer house [*bedehus*] in their neighborhood, but there was a society for mission that held gatherings in the vicinity. And it is obvious that both the presence of these lay gatherings, and other Christian people that he met make it likely to say that both his upbringing and the

---

1. The other children were Johan Arthur (May 23, 1891—November 3, 1918), Harald Olaf (February 3, 1894—June 13, 1974) and Anders Marensius (April 14, 1896—October 1974). Then, after Omar Emil, Sigurd Hjalmar was born on December 23, 1903 (died May 13, 1993); and Jenny Antonie (January 13, 1908—May 19, 1995).

form of the particular form of Christianity he adopted caused him to be characterized by an element of Haugianism.²

Many local communities in the country sides of Norway, not at least in the county of Østfold, where Omar Emil Borgen had his upbringing, were greatly influenced by various Christian lay movements. The most famous of these in the nineteenth century was probably the movement started by a man from Tune in Østfold, named Hans Nielsen Hauge (1771–1824):³

> Hans Nielsen Hauge was a 19th-century Norwegian Lutheran lay minister, spiritual leader, business entrepreneur, social reformer, and author. He led a noted Pietism revival known as the Haugean movement. Hauge is also considered to have been influential in the early industrialization of Norway . . .

It is generally agreed that Hans Nielsen Hauge had a profound influence on both secular and religious history in Norway. Hauge's message emphasized the type of spirituality he felt originated with Martin Luther. He led charismatic meetings, and his organization became an informal network that in many ways challenged the establishment of the state church. As a result, he and his followers were persecuted in several ways. Hauge was imprisoned on several occasions, spending a total of nine years in prison.

> Over time the Haugean movement increased its influence throughout the country. . . . It is not an exaggeration to state that he revived the faith in most of Norway . . .

When Peder Borgen's father, Omar Emil, grew up, Hauge had been dead for over eighty years. But the movement he started was still strong in many parts of Norway. As a teenager, Omar Emil lived for a while at an aunt of his father, whom he later characterized as "a strange Haugian woman—the family's godly intercessor and benefactor."⁴ Obviously, there was something in the way Christianity was carried out in day-to-day life that made him characterize it as "Haugian." His description of a specific meeting held in his home of Torp is also telling. Unfortunately, no date is given, but it must have happened before 1918, probably late in 1917, since

---

2. Peder Borgen, interview by the author, September 14, 2016.

3. There is an easily accessible presentation of Hans Nielsen Hauge and his work at https://en.wikipedia.org/wiki/Hans_Nielsen_Hauge, and I quote from this article here. For a further presentation of Hans Nielsen Hauge and the movement he initiated, see these Norwegian texts: Aarflot, *Norsk kirkehistorie* II, 231–74; Molland, *Norges kirkehistorie* I, 52–95.

4. O. E. Borgen, *Brev til en venn*, 11.

he describes that year in the subsequent text. The meeting became crucial to Omar Emil's attitude to and development of his Christian faith:

> First Sunday of Advent, there was a meeting at my home. Lars Lofthus was there—and several friends from Rakkestad station . . . . It became a warm and significant meeting that night. My older brother (Harald) sat by the stove in the living room—I sat in the adjoining room. Suddenly during the meeting, Harald fell to his knees by his chair and broke out in prayer and crying. There was a strange heavenly atmosphere in the rooms; the congregation was kneeling—and for the first time, I bowed my knees and earnestly prayed to God for forgiveness and help. And thus, a new period began in our lives. That evening, Harald and I worked in the stable, feeding the horses. There and then, we held each other's hands and promised to help each other endure and keep our promises of faith.[5]

There is no doubt that this was a crucial event in Omar Emil's life. He even characterizes it as "a new period began in our lives." He and his brother Harald lived together in the small cottage on the farm that winter, and they read the Bible and prayed together every night. The meeting described above undoubtedly influenced Omar Emil for the rest of his life; it was his basic and decisive conversion experience.

What is indicated by labeling several members of the family as "Haugians"? Neither Peder Borgen nor his father define this term but they take it for granted. But the Haugians were known for placing great emphasis on the "fellowship of the believers." Furthermore, they wanted to have a good relationship with the local pastor of the state church and his ministry; they were earnest in their earthly calling, and many were pioneers in agriculture, industry, and various crafts. Several were also active in witnessing and preaching. And we might add: they emphasized a pietistic kind of lifestyle, with a strong distinction between what they perceived as negative worldly activities, and what a Christian could and should be involved in. For instance, Omar Emil recalled that once, in his youth, a colleague at work asked him to go to Borregaard's Liquor Store to make some purchases, which he did; but he added: "Luckily, it happened only once."[6]

In retrospect, one might say that Omar Emil's later openness to Methodism can be understood in light of his Haugian background. The Norwegian church historian E. Molland has pointed out that the conversion experience of Hans Nielsen Hauge in 1796 is comparable to the experience

---

5. O. E. Borgen, *Brev til en venn*, 14.
6. O. E. Borgen, *Brev til en venn*, 12.

John Wesley had in 1738.[7] Both were pious and conscientious Christians who suddenly had an experience that gave them new certainty and power. Admittedly, there are also quite a few similarities between the experiences of these two major figures, and the experience Omar Emil describes for his part from the year 1917. His description, however, is much later and thus also characterized by what was typical descriptions concerning a radical conversion in his milieu. His son Peder mentioned several times in my interviews with him that there are similarities between the Haugian and Methodist patterns of faith and life, and that he finds this confirmed in his own extended family history.[8]

Leaving home for work

Omar Emil was given some additional schooling after primary school, and he attended an agricultural school in Oslo during the winter of 1919–20. It was a one-and-a half-year curriculum, but he was impatient, and graduated after only one year. Before entering the school, he had already been working on a farm for some time, a farm he had administered after his brother Arthur died in the late fall of 1918.

Then, after finishing the agricultural school, he applied for a job as a leaseholder, and got a job at farmer Ole Eid in Ytre Sandsvær in Buskerud. Here he worked for three years as a tenant. He had a very good relationship with the owner of the farm and enjoyed the work: "These years have always represented good memories throughout my life," he later wrote in the autobiographical booklet called *Letter to a Friend*.[9] He made new Christian friends, and he was able to save some money so that he could build up a basic fund for himself.

In Hvittingfoss, close by, there was also a small Methodist church, which Omar Emil joined:

> I got to know a bunch of Christian friends at the little Methodist chapel at Hvittingfoss. I joined and became engaged in founding a youth association there—I was a member of its board and accompanied a group of singers with my violin. . . . Then I got to know Harda Pytte, and she became my companion for life.

---

7. Molland, *Norsk Kirkehistorie* (Norwegian Church History in the Nineteenth Century), 1:56.

8. Peder Borgen claims that T. B. Barratt too, who was a Methodist before he became the main Pentecostal leader in Norway, argued that Methodism should carry on the work Hauge initiated in Norway. See Borgen, *Vei utenfor Allfarvei*, 16.

9. O. E. Borgen, *Brev til en venn*, 20.

After the leasing period was over, he spent another year in the vicinity. His father-in-law to be, Peder Pytte, had bought a farm in Våle in Vestfold, and Omar Emil ran it for a year. But he did not thrive in Våle, and after a year he moved back home to Torp in Rakkestad in the summer of 1924. There he stayed all summer and helped out on the farm. But he was restless. He had to find a way for himself, and now Harda was in Ytre Sandsvær waiting for him. They had agreed to marry.

Harda Pytte, the mother of Peder Borgen

Harda Pytte (born August 24, 1901), was a third-generation Methodist. Her grandparents, Ole Halvorsen Engrønningen Pytte (1825–1908) and Maren Andrine (born Reiersdatter; 1842–1901), had joined a new Methodist congregation in 1876–78. At that time, there was a Methodist revival in that area.[10] The grandparents were among the first to join the new Methodist congregation that was established, and when a congregational house was built; it was built on the Pytte farm in 1893. Harda called it the "House of Prayers" (Bedehus), but in fact it served as a Methodist chapel.

Harda's parents were Peder Johan Olsen Pytte (1874–1955) and Hanna Gunelia (born Antonsdatter Bakke; 1874–1938). She grew up in what she experienced as a secure and good Christian home. The fact that there was a chapel on the farm became important for her as a child. Here she went to Sunday school, run by her father, Peder, and an uncle named Reidar. As she grew up, she became an active member of the Methodist congregation at Hvittingfoss.

At this time, Hvittingfoss gradually expanded and became the center of the local municipality. A Methodist congregation was established there in 1910 with Peder Pytte as its principal; the prayer house at Pytte farm was moved from the farm and to Hvittingfoss two years later. It was named Elim, and this was the Methodist chapel in which Omar and Harda met in the early 1920s, and where they participated in the youth congregational work. Their relationship developed, they got engaged, and plans were made for a wedding on December 30, 1924, in the Elim chapel.

Thus, we are by now back to where this chapter began: a young man named Omar Emil was looking for a house where he could start a meat business. He found that location in Lillestrøm in 1924.

By the end of 1924, December 30, the wedding was celebrated in Ytre Sandsvær, in the Elim Methodist chapel. Early next year they moved to

---

10. Haddal, *Vær fra Vest*, 93.

Lillestrøm and started a new life together at Torvet 1, Lillestrøm, which was to be their address for many years to come.

Towards the end of that year, on November 8, their first child was born; a boy. He was named Ole Edvard, after Omar Emil's father. Three years later, on January 26, 1928, their next child was born. He was named Peder Johan, after Peder Johan Pytte, the grandfather at the Pytte farm. In 1931 they had a daughter named Ester Helene, and then the last child, to be named Arne Johannes, was born in 1933. A new family was established and settled in Lillestrøm, and thrived in the daily run of work, leisure, school, and church attendances. Harda and Omar Emil established themselves from the beginning as active members of Lillestrøm Methodist church, a small local congregation of approximately fifty members. Hence, we might take a closer look at the distinctive character and place of the Methodist church in the Norwegian church landscape to understand better how such a church community functioned in that setting.

IMPORTANT ASPECTS OF THE NORWEGIAN CHURCH SETTINGS

In order to understand several issues in the life of the Borgen family, particularly in the life of Peder Borgen, it is both necessary and vital to have some insight into the denominational geography of the Norwegian church landscape.

The majority church, the Lutheran Church of Norway

The Church of Norway[11] is by far the largest denomination in Norway. It can trace its origins to the ninth century, when Christianity was introduced in Norway via influences from the British Isles by several Norwegian kings and Catholic missionaries from the Continent. If a date is sought, July 29, 1030, is usually considered the pinpoint in Norway's Christianization. In the following years, the church was a Catholic church for several centuries

11. There is an easily accessible brief, but precise presentation of the history and characteristics of the Church of Norway in *Wikipedia*: https://en.wikipedia.org/wiki/Church_of_Norway. For the church's self-presentation on the internet, see https://kirken.no/nb-NO/church-of-norway/. For some further literature, especially concerning the church's relation to the state, and to other denominations in Norway, one might point to the following literature (as a few examples of relevant literature): Oftestad, *Den norske statsreligionen*. For a description of the church in its relation to other denominations in Norway, one might consult the following works: Øverland, ed., *Norske Frikirker*.; Øverland, ed., *Norges kristne kirkesamfunn*; and especially Tjørhom, ed., *Kirkesamfunn i Norge*.

until the Lutheran Reformation was introduced in Norway by the Danish king in 1536–37, as Norway was then in union with Denmark.

The introduction of the Reformation did not only imply a change in doctrine, but also in the ideology of state and of ways of ruling, as the political power so far held by the pope was taken over by the king: "The King appointed bishops (initially called superintendents). This brought forth tight integration between Church and State. After the introduction of absolute monarchy in 1660, all clerics were civil servants appointed by the King, but theological issues were left to the hierarchy of bishops and other clergies."[12] This practice remained until 1997. When Norway gained national independence from Denmark in 1814 and established its own constitution (*grunnlov*), and during the years in union with Sweden (1814–1905), the church was regarded as a state church. The close association with the state was visible in several areas, but for the church, it was most important that the bishops and the clergy were both elected and paid by the state.

The close association of the church with the state was challenged when in the late eigtheenth and early nineteenth centuries, several representatives from various denominations tried to establish themselves in Norway. In fact, until the mid-nineteenth century, the Church of Norway ". . . was the only legal church in Norway, membership was mandatory for every person residing in the kingdom, and it was forbidden for anyone other than the official priests of the State Church to authorize religious meetings."[13] However, due to several influences from both within and from outside of Norway, the years of 1842 and 1845 represent two important changes in Norwegian laws concerning church life. In 1842, due to not at least several lay movements in Norway as the Haugian movement, "lay congregational meetings were accepted in church life, though initially with limited influence."[14] Three years later, in 1845, another law with even greater relevance for the establishment of non-Lutheran denominations was the so-called Dissenter Law, which opened up for the establishment of non-Lutheran churches. Until then, the Church of Norway "was the only legal, religious organization in Norway, and it was not possible to end membership in the Church of Norway."[15] In the following decades, several other church denominations established themselves in Norway, including the Methodist Church in the 1850s.

In 1950, when Peder Borgen was a student in Oslo, the total population of Norway was approximately 3.1 million. The three largest denominations,

---

12. https://en.wikipedia.org/wiki/Church_of_Norway
13. https://en.wikipedia.org/wiki/Church_of_Norway
14. https://en.wikipedia.org/wiki/Church_of_Norway.
15. https://en.wikipedia.org/wiki/Church_of_Norway.

Methodists, Baptists, and Pentecostals, represented 11570, 7788, and 7856 persons, respectively. A total of 97459 persons of the population were not members of the Church of Norway (about 2.9 percent). Some other figures may illustrate further the size and influence of the majority church: in 1960, 96.8 percent of the population were baptized in the Lutheran Church of Norway, and 85.2 percent of the weddings found place in that church. These figures have, however, changed drastically in more recent decades.[16]

In the twenty-first century, the Church of Norway has initiated several revisions of its internal structure and organization and its role and place as a state church, and in 2012 the Norwegian Parliament passed a constitutional amendment that granted the Church of Norway increased autonomy. The decision cut loose much of the historical ties between the state and the Church of Norway, which had been considered a state church since the sixteenth century. A new church law is currently being developed, representing significant changes in several of the church's relations to the state, but not all. One great benefit to the church in its relationship to the state may be mentioned; the state still funds the majority church, and some other prerogatives remain too.

The Methodist Church; the church settings of the Borgen family

Methodism did not come to Norway from England, but from the United States of America. Here the Methodists established themselves as a separate denomination in 1784 as the Methodist Episcopal Church, a church that had bishops, something one did not have in English Methodism. This church order was also carried over to Norway when Methodism was transferred there and in several other parts of the world.

The beginning of Methodism in Norway is particularly related to a Norwegian sailor named Ole Peter Petersen.[17] He had been to America, met Methodism there, and received lasting impressions. When he returned to

16. In 2019 only 51.4 percent were baptized in the Church of Norway, and only 31.3 percent got married in that church. That does not mean that the "dissenters" have taken over, but the decline is due to secularization and migration. "A survey conducted by Gallup International in 65 countries in 2005 found that Norway was the least religious among the Western countries surveyed, with only 36% of the population considering themselves religious, 9% considering themselves atheist and 46% considering themselves "neither religious nor atheist." http://www.klassekampen.no/31940/mod_article/item. In recent years the figures have declined even more.

17. Peder Borgen himself has contributed to the history writing of the Norwegian branch of Methodism by publishing several articles in Norwegian: see here especially his "Kirkebevegelse og foreningsbevegelse," "Metodistkirken, en tverrnasjonal Kirke," and "Metodistkirken." See also Hassing, *Religion and Power*, 19–42.

Norway (Fredrikstad) in 1849, he talked about his conversion and new life both in private contexts and by organizing public meetings. This activity resulted in several persons joining him, and it looked like the beginning of a revival in the city. However, Petersen returned to the United States after only a few months (May 1850), and what could have become a greater revival under his leadership became a newborn movement left without any leadership, and this situation soon had several unfortunate consequences. Requests were then made to the United States for Petersen to return, but this wish was not fulfilled until 1853. By then—in fact already in 1851—Petersen had been authorized as a local pastor in the American Episcopal Methodist Church and served as a pastor with special responsibility for the Norwegian immigrants. In 1853 he was ordained a pastor, and in the fall of that same year he returned to Norway with his family as a missionary authorized by the Episcopal Methodist Church with the stated goal of founding Methodist churches in Norway. After some years of work, partly under opposition, the first Methodist congregations were officially registered in 1856; one in Sarpsborg and one in Halden, both located in Østfold county.

However, resistance continued throughout the following years, both from the majority church (the state church, the Church of Norway) and partly on a grassroots level in the local communities. Although an infamous Norwegian law, the so-called *Konventikkelplakat*, which denied non-Lutheran activities in the country, had been abolished in 1842, and a new law concerning the "dissenters" (*Dissenterloven*) opened up for non-Lutherans to establish congregations in the country had been introduced in 1845, many free churches experienced somewhat unfavorably attitudes and conditions in the second half of the nineteenth century. Some of these might be characterized as persecutions, carried out not by physical violence but by words of counter-agitations.

Nevertheless, the Methodists eventually established themselves with congregations throughout the country, though primarily in urban environments along the coast of Norway. After the first Methodist churches in Norway were established in the towns of Sarpsborg and Halden in the southeastern part of Norway, other churches were established in the neighboring town of Fredrikstad, then in Porsgrunn, Høland, and Christiania (1865; Grünerløkka, now Oslo). In the 1860s there was some stagnation, but in the 1870s they had greater progress. Then they also started their own magazine and opened a small seminary for pastors. But the resistance persisted during these years as well. Many pastoral meetings in the majority church discussed the teachings of the Methodists, and in Stavanger a Lutheran pastor even held sixty-eight public lectures against them at this time.[18]

The Methodist Church in Norway is thus a result of extended missionary activity from the United States; it received the first missionaries from the USA, and they were authorized by the Methodist Episcopal Church, and bishops from America traveled to Norway to oversee the work. However, many methodists also emigrated to the United States. Hassing states this latter aspect thus: ". . . converting to Methodism either stimulated the thought of emigration, by being an American church and thus providing a foretaste of American religious life or that Methodism attracted to itself persons who were already open to emigration and for whom conversion to Methodism was the first step, however unconsciously, in becoming an American."[19] It must be admitted that the emigration to America was great in these days, whether being Methodist or not.[20] On the other hand, it is a fact that emigration worked negatively for some of the new Methodist churches, which in this way lost members.

After thus having been a part of an American mission field in Norway, the new churches consolidated their positions in the 1870s, and the ground were laid for further expansion in the next two decades. In 1876 the Norway Mission became the Norway Annual Conference,[21] a central feature of Methodist organization. Having thus proceeded from a *man* to a *movement*, Methodism in Norway entered the next step by becoming more institutionalized. And with institutionalization followed clericalism, an aspect not cherished by all members as it represented a feature they knew too well from the majority church, the Church of Norway. Some even lamented the use of "pastor" on the one hand and "layman" on the other.[22] This clericalization was also visible by the fact that laymen had no seats in the Annual Conference until 1932.[23] Peder Borgen's father, Omar Borgen, was one of those who worked for better recognition of the laity in the Methodist Church in Norway.

Today (2022), there are close to fifty Methodist churches in Norway and a total membership of approximately eleven thousand; if only full members are counted, the membership is on the level of four thousand. The

18. Molland, *Norges Kirkehistorie*, 1:240.

19. Hassing, *Religion and Power*, 48–49.

20. In the years 1879–1893, a quarter of a million Norwegians emigrated to the United States, and that from a land that numbered only two million in 1880. "Only Ireland experienced a higher rate of emigration." Hassing, *Religion and Power*, 53.

21. Hassing, *Religion and Power*, 50.

22. Hassing, *Religion and Power*, 84, note 133.

23. Cf. Haddal, *Vær fra vest*, 148–54. Hassing, *Religion and Power*, 104–5.

Nordic and Baltic countries have a *bishop* in common. Under the bishop, there are two supervisor/superintendent districts in Norway. The two overseers have overall staff responsibility for the pastors and the oversight of the congregations.

Of the several Methodist churches worldwide, the Methodist Church in Norway[24] is now an integral part of the worldwide United Methodist Church,[25] which has approximately fourteen million members; the Methodist Church in Norway may thus be labeled the United Methodist Church in Norway.[26] The total number of Methodists in the world is more than eighty million. Most of these churches are members of the World Methodist Council.[27] The Methodist Church in Norway is a member of the World Council of Churches, the Conference of European Churches,[28] and the Christian Council of Norway,[29] and has an agreement on mutual recognition with the Church of Norway and a cooperation agreement with the Norwegian Baptist Church (Det norske Baptistsamfunn). The Methodist Church is also part of the Community of Protestant Churches in Europe (CPCE), also called the Leuenberg Churches.[30]

THE EARLY FORMATIVE YEARS

The establishment of the new family

Harda and Omar Emil Borgen thus became involved in the Methodist Church from the beginning of their life in Lillestrøm. The local Methodist congregation was founded on September 3, 1899. The Borgen family played a significant role in the church for many years to come. They participated in its many activities, such as the various congregational societies, Sunday school, scouting, and in the fields of singing and music.

24. Cf. http://www.metodistkirken.no/hoved.

25. Established in 1968 by a merger of several Methodist churches; cf. http://www.umc.org.

26. This is not the term usually used in Norway, but it is the terminology used in the English version of the final report from the conversations between Church of Norway and the Methodist Church in Norway ("Fellowship of Grace"), published in 1994. The Norwegian version has *"Metodistkirken i Norge"* (The Methodist Church in Norway), the English version has the "United Methodist Church in Norway." See https://kyrkja.no/globalassets/kirken.no/church-of-norway/dokumenter/fellowship_of_grace_1994.pdf.

27. Cf. https://worldmethodistcouncil.org.

28. Cf. https://www.ceceurope.org.

29. Cf. https://norgeskristnerad.no/english/.

30. Cf. http://www.leuenberg.net.

When Harda and Omar settled down in Lillestrøm in 1925, the church's music society was down. Hence, they got engaged in this work and reestablished the choir and a group of musicians. Soon they had several instruments in use, such as cello, violins, guitars, and piano. Their son Peder later also learned to play the violin. Omar played the piano, but he could also play some violin. Eventually, Omar was given several leadership positions in the congregation, from Sunday school to leadership functions in the national church. In 1935 he was a secondary deputy delegate to the General Conference in the United States, and when the primary elected delegate could not go, Omar Emil started some private studies in English and was able to participate in the General Conference that year.

Omar Emil himself extended his time and service to several arenas. He was not only engaged in his own business and the Methodist church but also participated actively in local politics. He was instrumental in establishing the local group of the Christian Democratic Party (Kristelig Folkeparti–KrF), and he became the chairman of the first local board of Skedsmo KrF. In 1945 he and two others were elected as the first representatives in Skedsmo municipality council for KrF, a function he had for sixteen years until he was transferred to Lillestrøm. Once he was also close to being elected as a representative to the Norwegian Parliament but lost by only a few votes.

Omar Emil was young, but nevertheless a mature man when he—at the age of twenty-four—in the fall of 1924, was able to start his own business in Lillestrøm. His further personal development and his active life in the family, church, and municipal work show us a man of initiative and drive. In his little biographical booklet mentioned above, we also meet a devout Christian, a man who wanted to be guided by God in his challenges and decisions. His son Peder describes him as a man who was eager to promote the roles of the laymen in the church and as one who "tried to imprint 'a burning heart' which was active and consecrated."[31] Peder describes him also as "stern but warm."[32] When Peder was about to start at the Faculty of Theology in Oslo, his father had his doubts, but he realized that—due to the denominational situation in Norway—Peder had no other choice when it came to where to study theology in Norway,[33] and he encouraged him. And he funded the entire study. Nevertheless, he repeatedly mentioned that

31. Borgen, interview by the author, September 14, 2016.
32. Borgen, interview by the author, August 22, 2017.
33. In Norway at this time, there were two theological institutions of education: The Theological Faculty at the University of Oslo, run by the state; and the Free Faculty of Theology (Menighetsfakultetet) in Oslo. The former was considered by many to be more liberal theological institution than the latter. The latter paid also more attention to Lutheranism.

it was important "not to lose the burning heart"; the fire of a personal Christian faith was significant.

In our times, several decades later, he might have been labeled a "pietist," although that is not a good characterization. But he was, for example, strongly opposed to sports competitions on Sundays. Peder had a long, intense, and emotional dispute by mail with him about this and several other issues in the fall of 1955, and they disagreed very much. It seems that Peder was trying to get along with his father in this exchange of letters.[34] But he found his father to be too old-fashioned; his ideals were far too much of the past. Likewise, when their new church was consecrated in 1974, the Methodist periodical *Kristelig Tidende* had an interview with Omar Emil. Here he expressed great admiration for the revivals of former times, and he suggests that the preaching of the present day had become too cautious:

> One does not hear much today about the fact that there are only two ways to choose; one to heaven and one to perdition. That is why not so many people are in personal agony over their sins, and regrets and repentances from sin are rare. It was more of both tears and hallelujahs in the past, said Omar Borgen with a certain sadness in his voice.[35]

Omar was a layman and a very dedicated Christian and Methodist, and Peder sometimes found him too strict but respected him as a father and a devout Christian.

When Peder describes his mother Harda's influence in his childhood home, he uses two words: "positive" and "calm." He experienced her as quiet and calm and as a "woman of the home and church." But it happened that she intervened if she thought Omar Emil was too strict. Peder once recalled, with a smile on his face, that when he, as a thirty-one-year-old research fellow, wanted to visit Russia with some friends, his father said: "No, that is too dangerous." But Harda intervened and said: "Peder has probably by now reached the age in which he must be allowed to decide this for himself."[36]

---

34. Without getting involved in a psychological analysis of Peder's relationship with his parents, and his father in particular, it is nevertheless a bit thought-provoking to read a sermon he held during his time in Trondheim. Here he uses psychological thoughts quite intensively. And one of his themes in this speech is about "the importance of forgiving our parents": "Even with the best parents, all children are subjected to a treatment they sometimes experience as unreasonable and unjust, and which they must nevertheless tolerate . . . No parents are perfect. They are either too kind or too strict, either too generous or too restrained. But it is necessary to forgive them. Unless you forgive them, you cannot be free." Sermon in Trondheim, undated.

35. *Kristelig Tidende* 25:103 (1974) 4–5, 7.

36. Borgen, interview by the author, August 22. 2017.

A woman of home and church, she played guitar and participated in several of the church's various duties and events. Furthermore, when she sometimes feared there might be too little attendance at evening meetings, she said: "I have to go to the evening meeting because I think there will be few people there tonight."

These features, too, are parts of the heritage that Peder Borgen received from his childhood home. In the following chapters, Peder is to be the main character of our story.

Peder's childhood years in Lillestrøm, 1928–36

The Borgen family lived on the second floor of Torvet 1 until the summer of 1936. Peder thus spent his first years as a small-town boy in Lillestrøm. Lillestrøm was a relatively small village these days and did not have the formal status of a town. That status was not obtained until 1998. When Peder started running around in the streets in the early 1930s, Lillestrøm had approximately seven thousand inhabitants; 27.7 percent were fourteen years or younger, and 56.9 percent were under thirty years. Only 3.6 percent were seventy years or older. Lillestrøm was thus a place with great potential for population growth. But the population increase that had occurred and still occurred during his early years was not only due to a birth surplus, but also to substantial immigration from other areas in Norway because of the possibilities for work in Lillestrøm. Hence Peder's family did not stand out as "migrants," and Lillestrøm grew steadily in these years.

His father, Omar Emil, later wrote in his memoirs that the children "grew up as healthy and active children. There were problems keeping track of them in the dense center of the town."[37] He does not comment on this any further, but it is conceivable that several factors contributed to the conclusion that he eventually wanted to move out of the village; pivotal among these factors was that he intended to let his children grow up in a more rural environment, perhaps even on a farm.

At the appropriate age, Peder joined the church's Sunday school. Moreover, the children were supposed to attend the main service too. Thus, children and the adults went to church together as a family as soon as the children reached the appropriate age. Once, when Peder was approximately seven years old and his little brother Arne was only two, staying at home with a nanny during service time, an accident occurred that could have had a terrible outcome. Arne got a large pot of hot water over his back. He got so severely burned that they were anxious about whether he would overcome.

---

37. O. E. Borgen, *Brev til en venn*, 27.

The years at the elementary school (1935–41)

In the autumn of 1935, Peder was enrolled in the local primary school. This school, Volla Elementary School, was then the oldest school in Lillestrøm, established in 1922. Its building is still in use as a primary school. Peder thrived at Volla but thought they had a relatively strict female teacher. As a typical boy's memory, he still remembered in his old days an episode where he thought she was utterly unreasonable: There was a bit of noise and fighting once when everyone was going out into the hallway, leaving the school for the day. The teacher then became so angry that she decided that the whole class should remain in the classroom for some time as a kind of punishment. Peder, who was sitting on the last bench and had not yet reached the door when the fighting started, found this quite unreasonable as he had not managed to get out into the hallway yet. "Then I was very angry with her," he chuckled eighty-two years later.[38]

In general, however, Peder enjoyed himself very much at school: "I found it very interesting to be diligent, not only to be diligent, but I was simply a little excited by learning," he said many years later. It is here probably the aging professor who looks back and remembers his first school years. And he remembered it as a time characterized by the joy of learning. He continued to enjoy learning all his life.

Peder spent only one year at Volla school. His father, Omar Emil, bought a small farm called Furua in Skedsmo, and in 1936 they moved from Torvet 1 to Brånåsdalen, where the farm was located. Peder's father grew up on a farm and worked for several years as a tenant, and now he got the chance to continue as a farmer while also carrying on his business in Lillestrøm. Later he said that "we got a cozy place in the countryside, which both the children and we longed for."[39] Furthermore, it turned out later that when World War II set the scene, it was good for them to live in the countryside. During the years of war, they were able to be self-sufficient in a way that would have been impossible in Lillestrøm center. They rented an additional forty to fifty acres of land so that they could grow vegetables etc., and otherwise become independent farmers during the war. However, after

---

38. Borgen, interview by the author, September 14, 2016.
39. O. E. Borgen, *Brev til en venn*, 31.

a while, Omar Emil found it too challenging to live in Skedsmo and run the business in Lillestrøm because his absence made his wife Harda much alone with the children, who were then three, five, eight, and ten years old. From 1937, therefore, the butcher business was rented out. This lasted until the spring of 1945, when Omar Emil took over the operation again.

The move out of Lillestrøm, however, resulted in the fact that Peder had to change school. On the one hand, the change was relatively unproblematic; but on the other hand, it resulted in that he got a much longer way to walk to get to the school. He was first supposed to go to Sten school close to Skedsmo church. But Sten had a relatively small school building, and it turned out that they did not have room for the second-grade class the year he was supposed to start. The solution was that the school authorities rented a barracks at Kjeller for this class. Peder thus got a longer way to school than he otherwise would have had. And he had to go there alone because his brother Ole was to go to Sten school. Peder himself remembers it as a demanding situation, and he described it later with some mixed feelings:

> And then I walked—in the fimbul winter, in the darkness— alone for almost three kilometers, all winter. It was a challenging time for me. But amazingly, I managed to walk alone in the dark both in the morning and after school during the whole winter. We also had a somewhat simple school location without a room for physical exercise, but the classroom was good. We had a teacher named Ms. Nøkleby, and I still enjoyed school. Hence, after all, it was a good year. But sometimes, both physically and mentally somewhat hard for me because of the distance I had to walk every day. It was a hard time for me.[40]

"In the fimbul winter," "in the darkness," "alone for almost three kilometers," "all winter." "It was a hard time for me." These expressions reveal that it was well remembered over eighty years later as a difficult school road. Nevertheless, "I managed to walk alone in the dark." It shows a boy who also had accumulated a certain stubbornness. Peder struggled through a long school year as a second-grade schoolboy.

Then he continued at Sten school. However, there he came up with something out of the ordinary. It was a school with seven class levels, but the third and fourth grades merged in the classroom. Peder decided to take both grades in parallel during his first year at Sten. He finished relatively quickly the third-grade curriculum, and then took the fourth grade, and completed it and got solid scores. This was a rather unusual choice, and in retrospect, he was not quite sure if that combination of the school years was

40. Borgen, interview by the author, September 14, 2016.

smart. However, there and then, he later claimed, he was curious enough to get away with it.

It also led to the fact that when he finished primary school after seven years, he stayed at home for one year (1941–42) before continuing with high school. In part, during that year, he was ill; he got gastritis. The principal is said to have suggested that it may have been psychosomatic. Peder later wondered if it had to do with the fact that he took the third- and fourth-grade curriculum in one year and that it led to too much stress in a boy who was one year too young for the grade levels that followed (fifth through seventh grade). Maybe it was also a warning of something to come later? Thus, his stay at home had a rationale in the fact that he was considered a little too young to start high school. He simply needed a year of maturation and rest and struggled a bit with physical ailments. So instead of going to school, he helped out at home. There they had a fox farm where they were breeding silver foxes, and they had a horticulture. Peder thus tended the foxes, and otherwise worked on the farm.

High school years (1942–44)

The Norwegian school system was and is not directly comparable to the USA system of high school and college. In Norway, elementary (or primary) school, which at this time was attended from age seven, lasted for seven years. Then one might attend the *realskole*, which lasted for three years, and one might proceed to the *gymnas* for another three years. While the curriculum of the *realskole* was fairly general, the *gymnas* offered several more specialized courses: one might choose among a curriculum focused on languages (most often English, with French and German), a mercantile curriculum, or science (*realfag*; with an emphasis on mathematics, physics, and chemistry).

There was no question whether or not Peder should continue his schooling and start on the *realskole* level. Loving learning and clever at school as he was, it went without saying that he was to continue. The question was eventually rather about which school he should attend. Geographically, it would have been most natural for him to start at the local *realskole* in Lillestrøm. But as they now lived in Brånåsdalen, outside Lillestrøm, there was actually a better bus connection from there and into Oslo than to Lillestrøm. The reason was that there were buses from both Nannestad and Gjerdrum further north of Lillestrøm that passed close to Peder's home on their way to Oslo. Thus, he chose the *realskole* at Grorud, Oslo. He attended this school in the years of 1942–44, at what was then a relatively new high school campus. Peder had good times there.

During these years, however, his time at the *realskole* was daily affected by World War II in several ways. Peder most often used to go to school by bus. However, there were problems getting hold of an ordinary bus; the relevant bus to Oslo was driven by "knob." It had a generator built on the back and up the hills from Lillestrøm via Gjelleråsen it went very slowly, almost crawling. Hence Peder sometimes went to school by his bicycle.

He experienced his years in the *realskole* as good and pleasant; he had some fellow students he knew from Lillestrøm, and some from the area where he lived. But eventually, he looked forward to starting at Kristelig Gymnasium (Christian Gymnasium—KG); he had decided that he would study theology as his further education. Hence, instead of taking the third year, he therefore switched to the Gymnasium after having finished the second year in the *realskole*.

The awakening of a sense of minority

But not everything was always simple and easy to cope with. As a Methodist, he not only stood out as a Christian, but he was even a "dissenter." Not everyone knew what that indicated. When asked if he experienced any bullying because of this, he was a bit reluctant. He admitted that there was a bit of antagonism in Skedsmo during the war. But even though they went to Lillestrøm on Sundays for worship in the Methodist church there, he participated with other youngsters at the local Bedehus (a local congregational—but Lutheran—institution) during the weekdays. And he thinks that local engagement had a mitigating effect. Nevertheless, he admitted that he had to deal with some negative attitudes during his high school years at Grorud:

> But it turned out that together with another student in the class, it eventually became us two who became dominant because we played handball, and we generally functioned well. And I raised my head, it is something I have done all the way, and I put a cross on my lapel, raised my head, and was proud.[41]

There are many emotional experiences inherent in the statement that "I raised my head; it is something I have done all the way." It represented minority and discrimination experiences. However, Peder gradually grew and became bigger than many of his fellow students and used this physical prerogative to assert himself in sports. Many other young persons have

41. Borgen, interview by the author, September 14, 2016.

experienced that if you are bullied in one area, it helps to compensate by asserting yourself in another. Peder used sport activities. But the quote above also demonstrates two other areas we will meet several times in his life story: On the one hand, the fact that there were arenas where he got to know that he was different; he was a "dissenter," he did not belong to the main church most other Norwegians belonged to, he did not belong to the majority church, and he did not share its teachings. Moreover, on the other hand, his determination and ability—some might say stubbornness—to raise his head and go on was strengthened: I am a Christian; I am a Methodist. Cross on the lapel! Raised head! His awareness of belonging to a minority had been awakened.

Throughout all this, both during the *realskole* and *gymnas* and during his theological studies, Peder was active in the Methodist church in Lillestrøm. We shall return to these activities, but first take a somewhat closer look at what also characterized a large part of his life in the early forties: the Second World War and his experiences during these years. These experiences represented events that he also investigated further as a local historian after retiring and settling down at Lillestrøm in 1999, more than fifty years later.

Experiences during World War II (1940–45)

In the times before the German invasion, Norway had tried to stay neutral, as they did in the First World War. However, during the winter of 1939-40, it became increasingly more difficult. Furthermore, German leader Adolf Hitler realized that Norway could be valuable in his plans and strategies and started to prepare for an invasion. On April 9, 1940, then, Norway was invaded. The Germans took all the major cities and proceeded from these as their major hubs. After a brief time of resistance to the overwhelmingly larger German troops, Norway signed the capitulation on June 10. The king and his government managed to get over to England; the queen and her children were sent to the United States, where they stayed during the war.

The Borgen family lived some fifteen miles north of Oslo. Their location as such was not that much attractive to the Germans, but there was an airport close to Lillestrøm, at Kjeller, which caught their attention. This location became essential to the Germans as they started using it as a facility for repairing their airplanes. Hence it became important both for the Germans and the Allied forces.

On the morning of April 9, Peder Borgen and his brother Ole were getting ready for a new day at school. Since Peder had taken the third and fourth grades in one year, there was now only one school year between the two brothers; Peder was in sixth grade, and Ole was in the seventh and ready for this spring's completion of primary school. Around seven o'clock in the morning, the first German planes came thundering at low altitude in the direction of Lillestrøm and Kjeller. Peder and Ole heard and saw the planes coming in. Soon, they could see the bombs falling from the fuselages, but they could not see the impact on Kjeller because there was too much forest hindering their view. They heard, however, the explosions and understood what was happening.

At school, they got some more information about what was about to happen. The sad truth eventually dawned on everyone, and schools were closed for several days.

Peder and Ole did not go to Lillestrøm that day; hence they did not get a personal view of what happened there. But some most critical situations arose there that day. People in Lillestrøm were naturally shaken by what happened, and many fled out of town. The municipality sent out an order for evacuation in the morning, but people were already on their way out. The majority of those who left ran to the neighboring areas of Sørum, Enebakk, Fet, ahd Rælingen. A few days later, on April 12, the first German soldiers came to Lillestrøm and settled down there. Now the Borgen family realized what benefits they could enjoy because they had moved out of town and to a place where they could run their own farm. To many people in the more urban areas, it became difficult to obtain a variety of food during the five years of war; much food and other products were restricted, and access to even more was controlled. Fruit was scarce, and flour, bread, meat, and fish became difficult to obtain. When Omar Emil rented some additional land, they had better opportunities for growing various crops. Nevertheless, several kinds of food had to be rationed; for example, there was no question of throwing away small potatoes—they were to be eaten. Peder remembered that he once ate twenty very small potatoes for dinner.

After a few days, however, schooling was resumed, and life went on with the restrictions that the occupation required. Peder completed primary school in 1941, and in late spring of the following year he was confirmed in the Methodist church in Lillestrøm. Friends and relatives from Skedsmo and Oslo, Rakkestad, and Sandsvær came to celebrate the event. They all had to travel as best they could by bus or train. Not many people had the privilege of having a private car; Omar Emil's car, a Ford V-8, had already been confiscated by the Germans.

In the fall of 1942, Peder was enrolled at a *realskole* in Oslo, at the Grorud Realskole.

There were several other air raids at Kjeller, and these inflicted Lillestrøm even more severely. On November 18, 1943, Kjeller was attacked by Allied (American) planes. Peder took his turn as an observation guard on the roof of the Grorud school and saw an armada of approximately one hundred large bombers on their way to Kjeller. This time several bombs also struck in Nittedal, Lillestrøm, and Rælingen, but Kjeller was the primary target. The Germans had planned an extensive exercise there, and all the Norwegian civilians who worked there had been sent home. But several of the Germans who remained there were killed. Kjeller was not a large or central airport, but "Kjeller was the main workshop for Luftwaffe and Luftflotte 5 in Norway and Finland."[42] However, the airport and the workshops were not wholly damaged; the Germans had it repaired relatively quickly, and before the end of the year, they took in aircrafts for repair. Therefore, the Allies (this time it was British airplanes) launched a new attack on the night of April 29, 1944. This attack struck much harder in Lillestrøm; several civilians were killed, and many became homeless.

Not long after, Peder and Ole were searching one of the places where several soldiers had been killed. The bodies were already removed, but some remnants remained. In a later conversation about this incident, Peder did not want to specify what kind of remains they saw, but it made a lasting impression on him. He and Ole gathered some pieces of equipment that they found, a piece of a belt, and some pieces of bombs.

However, Peder and his brothers also got familiar with another consequence of war. In their neighborhood, at some localities called Bergli, a prisoner of war camp for Soviet prisoners was established. This was located only approximately ten minutes from their home in Brånåsdalen. There was a high barbed wire fence around the whole camp, and armed guards patrolled the area and the fences. The camp consisted of barracks where the prisoners lived, but during the day they worked at Skedsmokorset in a German military camp set up there (Prestegårdshagen). Peder and his brothers several times brought some small food packages to the prisoners:

> Hiding outside the camp, they watched the guards from the edge of the forest outside the high barbed wire fence (Peder Borgen took care of a piece of the barbed wire fence for several years). They approached the fence, giving small packages of food to the prisoners through the fence. Some of the prisoners had picked up a few Norwegian and English words so that the boys

---

42. See "Amerikansk bombeangrep på Kjeller 1943," https://lokalhistoriewiki.no/index.php/Amerikansk_bombeangrep_p%C3%A5_Kjeller_1943. Kjeller Aircraft Factory carried out major inspections and structural repairs on the fighter aircrafts, but in addition, BMW and Daimler Benz had overhaul workshops for their aircraft engines at Kjeller, and it was primarily the engine workshops that were considered a strategic bomb target.

could communicate a little with them. It was primarily words of thanks, names, and the like. The brothers knew that what they were doing might be dangerous, but they only gave them food, and the guard seemed to accept that they were coming.[43]

Peder and others who provided these prisoners with some food received several gifts of thanks in return, small things that they had cut out of wood in the evenings. Peder has taken care of several of the things he got, including a clog with a beautiful pattern and the name of the donor engraved and the year 1943.

Peder Borgen, in his eighties, shows the things he was given by the prisoners of war during the 1940s.

Many years later, when Peder had retired and had moved back to Lillestrøm, he became involved in clarifying and describing more about the

43. See https://lokalhistoriewiki.no/index.php/Tyske_fangeleire_i_Skedsmo.

prison camps in this area. It turned out that there had been several others in the proximity, including one at Kjeller and one at Leiraveien. Information about these was almost forgotten, but much information is now presented in an article on Lokalhistoriewiki.no.

When the days of peace came in 1945, Peder was a student at Kristelig Gymnasium. Due to the celebration of the German capitulation on May 7, there was not much schooling for a while. Peder went to Oslo to observe the events there. At first, there was a bit of turmoil because people did not quite know if it was really true that freedom had come. Peder observed that some of the Germans and their conspirators fled and that Norwegian resistance groups returned from their secret hiding places. Some Norwegian military personnel came back home from Sweden. But he also saw groups of flight crews returning from England. And there was great excitement and rejoicing when Crown Prince Olav arrived on May 13.

On June 7, the king and the royal family returned to Norway. Peder had arranged it so that he would then sell the underground paper called *Griniposten*,[44] and in order to be able to move more freely around, he also wore a scout suit—it gave him access to suitable and various locations. He was first down by the harbor, at the pier close to the city hall, and saw King Haakon VII coming ashore. When the king then drove away from the ship, Peder and others ran along the streets up to the main street, called Karl Johan Street, and could then watch the royal family as they drove further up to the castle at the end of that street. There were huge crowds of people out in the streets, waving flags and cheering. King Haakon VII had received great admiration and love from the people because of his stern attitude to the demands of the German occupants. He had been one who stood firm both during the transition period when the Germans moved into the country, and during his exile in England. And now, the people praised him for his attitudes and efforts during these heavy years of war.

---

44. Griniposten was a small newspaper that was originally smuggled in among the prisoners at Grini Prison Camp, but on May 8, 1945, a separate printed edition was published by Grini Press. The newspaper cost NOK 1, and was sold on the occasion of the return of the king. The proceeds were to go to the "Grinifangenes Kulturfond." The issue had the following date on the front page: "Grini, May 8th, 1945—the day after the victory." See https://digitaltmuseum.no/011024286403/grini-posten.

2

Formative Years in College and University

COLLEGE YEARS AND THEOLOGICAL STUDIES

WHILE HE WAS IN the *realskole* (partly equivalent to USA high school, hence sometimes here called "high school"), Peder decided that he wanted to take further gymnasial education and that he then wanted to study theology. He therefore chose—as was not an uncommon procedure in those days—not to finish high school as such, but to skip the third year and go directly to the *gymnas* (partly equivalent to USA college, hence I may here also call it "college"). It was pretty common for those who wanted to continue at a college level to take only two years at the *realskole*. In addition, Peder was so convinced that he would pursue a degree in theology after college that he chose the program that gave him the most credit for his further studies, namely, a curriculum that comprised both the old Latin and Greek languages. Such a procedure would save him one year in his later study of theology. For his college studies, he chose the Christian college in Oslo, in Norwegian named Kristelig Gymnasium (KG).

Studies at Kristelig Gymnasium 1944–47

He started his studies at Kristelig Gymnasium in August 1944. However, he did not move from Lillestrøm to an apartment of his own in Oslo, but traveled by bus from Lillestrøm to Oslo and back every day.

Kristelig Gymnasium was founded (1913) as a private *gymnas* and was then owned by five Christian mission organizations. The school was one of the many strategic educational initiatives that, among others, Ole Hallesby, a famous professor in theology at the Menighetsfakultet (Free Faculty of Theology) and a clever strategist, was involved in establishing and/or supporting in these years. Hallesby probably saw KG as a recruitment site for students to theological studies at the Menighetsfakultet.

From the very beginning, the school was intended not only to be a gymnasium but a *Christian* gymnasium, an intention that is stated in the school's statutes. In addition to the goal of providing relevant education, "It should be a main purpose to awaken and preserve the Christian life of the students." Hence, the school was not established to pursue and offer an alternative pedagogy, but focused on a Christian school environment.[1]

For an extended period of time, the school had some major financial problems, problems that were not solved until the mid-1960s, when the Norwegian government decided that private schools could also be eligible for federal financial support. KG also had to fight for years against some negative notions verbalized by some secular voices, e.g., that it was a school for those—that is, Christians—with "special opinions and limited field of vision."[2] However, Peder enjoyed the school setting and made many friends there.

All the other Greek and Latin students in his class, however, were older than Peder. The oldest was actually twenty-four years; the youngest—except Peder—was eighteen when they started in 1944. This variety in age was due to several factors, not at least to the fact that the World War II had made it difficult for some of them to attend a *gymnas* during the war. Others had been working some time for financial or other reasons before continuing their education. Hence Peder had to find his place among many students several years older than himself.

All of them, however, were eager to work their way through the curriculum and get good marks for further studies, perhaps Peder the most. The Latin and Greek classes were never large; when Peder graduated, there was a total of seventy-seven graduating students. Only six students graduated with both Latin and Greek on the diploma. Five of these then continued

---

1. Dittmann, *Kristelig Gymnasium*, 9.
2. Dittmann, *Kristelig Gymnasium*, 9.

with theological studies, and all of these ended up as ministers in the Lutheran Church of Norway, except Peder—the Methodist. A sure proof of the energy of Peder during these studies is the fact that he graduated as the best candidate of the year 1947 at that school.

In the weeks before and after graduation, the graduating students used to celebrate this event with various activities. Many of the Christian students from Kristelig Gymnasium had some special events and activities; primary among these was a series of Christian youth meetings and services in various churches and bedehus in the area both in and outside Oslo. During these activities, Peder got to know several students from other denominations. Not a few of his friends were also involved and were leading figures in these events. In retrospect, Peder regarded these weeks as incredibly "stimulating" and "rich" and rewarding times. He experienced fellowship with Christians from other denominations to an extent he had not been used to in earlier times, and he cherished these experiences and memories as he proceeded in life.

In fact, these final weeks as a graduating student from the *gymnas* represented the beginning of his encounters with practical *ecumenism*.

Congregational work in Lillestrøm

Peder was involved in the local Methodist church's work in Lillestrøm when he was a student at the *gymnas*. Later, during his studies at the Faculty of Theology, he moved out from his home on the farm and got a residence on the second floor in Torvet 1, downtown Lillestrøm, but continued his engagements in the local Methodist church. They had a growing youth association in the church from the last half of the forties, as well as an active Sunday school and other work for children. But it was somewhat problematic to carry out that kind of work during the years of World War II.

Peder's religious development in his youth was marked by the family's strong connection to the Methodist Church. He himself has said that he is not one of those who can point back to a decisive event of repentance or conversion, but there are nevertheless two events that he remembers as crucial in his Christian development.[3] One was that the Methodist Church once had a tent meeting campaign in Lillestrøm when he was ten or eleven years old, and he remembers going into the prayer room, praying for himself there. Later, as he grew up, he was repeatedly told, "You are going to be a pastor." Another case was that during a period in the *gymnas* he came under the influence of a former Methodist, Bjarne Staalstrøm (1923–2019), who

3. Borgen, interview by the author, August 17, 2017.

at that time had joined the Free Evangelical Assemblies, or De Frie Venner, as they were called in Norwegian.[4] Staalstrøm was an engaging preacher, and he gradually became a central figure in the Free Evangelical Assemblies. The influence on Peder became so strong that for a while, he wondered if he should leave school and start as an itinerant preacher. He asked his father about this, but then Omar Emil answered in his calm way: "You should probably wait until after your graduation from the *gymnas*."[5] Peder accepted his father's advice, and he never began as a traveling preacher. He continued his work in the local Methodist church in Lillestrøm as he started studying theology in Oslo. For Peder, it also meant that he was given several assignments in Lillestrøm, but he enjoyed it.

As a theological student, Peder gradually became more busy in Oslo. But when his local church in Lillestrøm celebrated its fiftieth anniversary in 1949, the small booklet published in honor of the church was written by stud.theol. Peder Borgen. The booklet also reflects that he was actively involved in the congregation's work in the anniversary year: the pictures show that he was a member of the music association, the youth association's board, and the main church board. The tall, dark, and slightly hinged fellow had now become the first theological university student having his background in the Lillestrøm Methodist church.

Peder had begun his "class journey" into academia.

As a student at the Faculty of Theology (1947–53)

At this time, theology students were supposed to start with four introductory courses: philosophy, Latin, Hebrew, and Greek. Peder, who had studied Latin and Greek at the *gymnas*, could proceed directly to the remaining two, philosophy and Hebrew, representing a total of one year of study. Many of the new theological students experienced these four subjects, which amounted to two full years of study, as a long wandering in the desert before they could enter the promised land: the study of theology proper. Moreover, those who dropped out of the theological studies usually dropped out during this preparatory period. Whether Peder also experienced it as a time in the desert is doubtful. At least he used his first year to inform himself a little more about the theological subjects, e.g., by attending some of the theological lectures at the university. In addition, he also had to serve in the military for some time before he could start with the theological subjects on a full-time basis. The theological study proper was divided into two periods of two

---

4. *De frie venner* is literally translated: the free friends.
5. Borgen, interview by the author, August 17, 2017.

years respectively: two years comprising the Old Testament, church history, and history of religions. The next two years comprised the New Testament, dogmatics and ethics, and philosophy of religion. Thus a total of six years. A final year of pastoral studies had to be added for those wanting to be pastors in the Church of Norway. Peder skipped that year, and later took some relevant topics when he studied for his PhD in the United States.

Why not study at the Free Faculty of Theology (Menighetsfakultetet)?

Peder became a student at the University of Oslo; at its Faculty of Theology (TF). This was not a choice of one among many because he had no other choice due to his lack of membership in a Lutheran church!

During most of the twentieth century, church life in Norway was incredibly polarized. The state church, the Lutheran Church of Norway, was the majority church that in the 1940s comprised over 95 percent of the population.[6] The Methodist Church of Norway had a membership of only about twelve thousand. Hence, it was a very small denomination compared to the state church, but nevertheless, it was one of the largest among the non-Lutheran denominations at this time.

Politically considered, Norway had been in a union with Denmark for over three hundred years; and then with Sweden in the years 1814–1905. Hence, in the middle of the twentieth century, Norway was relatively young as an independent nation. The first university in Norway was established in Oslo in 1811, consisting of four schools or faculties, among which the Faculty of Theology was included from the very beginning.

However, to compress a rather complicated history without digging into the complexity of its details, it might suffice to say that the development of Norwegian church life underwent several stages in the nineteenth century. On the one hand, the hegemony of the majority church was challenged by the entrance of several other denominations in Norway; on the other hand, Norwegian church life underwent several religious revivals, and the upsurge of many Christian lay movements, often in the form of mission organizations, influenced the character of Norwegian church life in many ways.[7] One of the results of these years of religious awakenings was the establishment of a free faculty of theology in Oslo, the Menighetsfakultet (MF). As signaled by its name (*menighet* = congregation), it intended to be

---

6. The population of Norway in the 1940s comprised a total of about three million. See https://www.ssb.no/a/histstat/aarbok/1946-1948.pdf.

7. See Hassing, *Religion and Power*, 105–6.

a school focusing on the life and needs of the congregations in the Church of Norway by equipping the students with a solid conservative and Lutheran confessional profile.

Hence, when Peder Borgen was about to start his academic studies, the Menighetsfakultet had established itself as the largest theological institution in terms of the number of students. Being founded in 1907, it started in 1908 as a protest institution because the leading men that established the faculty perceived the university's Faculty of Theology as representing and promoting a liberal theology that did not serve the congregations well, and which was Bible-dissolving in its consequence. The Menighetsfakultet,[8] on the other hand, wanted to represent and provide an education that was based on the Scriptures and the Lutheran Confession.[9]

The specific event that triggered the establishment of MF was the appointment of Johannes Ording as professor of systematic theology at TF in January 1906. He was perceived as very liberal, and the TF's own professor of New Testament, Sigurd Odland, resigned immediately when this appointment was made. The professors at the university were appointed by the king of Norway and his cabinet; they were thus government officials, appointed and paid by the state. The appointment created controversy right into the government offices, and the Minister of Church affairs, Christoffer Knutsen, resigned in protest too.

The Free Faculty of Theology (MF) proliferated, and already in 1921, more students were enrolling at MF than at the university Faculty of Theology. In 1949, MF had approximately 200 students, seven teachers, and two research fellows. The number of theology students decreased sharply in the following years, and in 1952 the numbers were 143 and 10 teachers, respectively, plus a research fellow at MF. However, during the years Peder was a student at TF, MF had about three times as many students as TF.

Peder paid an exploratory visit to the Menighetsfakultet and presented some questions to the dean of the faculty, the then professor of church history, Andreas Seierstad, about studying at the MF. There and then, he got the impression that the program was so broad and open that he could attend almost all lectures and most seminars, but that the exams represented a

---

8. The Menighetsfakultet has changed its English name a couple of times. First: The Free Faculty of Theology, which is the name I use in this book. Then it was changed to MF Norwegian School of Theology. The present name is MF Norwegian School of Theology, Religion and Society.

9. The background for the establishment of the Menighetsfakultet and its early history until it was granted examination rights in 1913 is given a thorough presentation in a book that was published for the faculty's fiftieth anniversary in 1958: see Nome, *Brytningstid*. For a more recent presentation of its history, see Oftestad and Røsæg, eds., *Mellom Kirke og Akademia*.

problem for non-Lutherans. As a non-Lutheran, he could not graduate from the Menighetsfakultet. This was because when receiving the diploma, the candidates had to answer in the affirmative to a question that read: "Do you promise, with God's help, to learn and live in accordance with God's Word?" They also had a similar question and promise at the Faculty of Theology, but they interpreted it as a more open statement than at MF. Although the graduation promise had no direct reference to the Lutheran confessional writings, the expression "in accordance with God's Word" was interpreted as strictly confessional by MF, that is, as an expression of understanding God's Word as they understood the Lutheran Confession did express it.[10] Not until after 1970 did MF open its doors to non-Lutherans as ordinary students.

Peder thus had to realize that he could not study theology together with the three friends he had from Kristelig Gymnasium, who began their studies at MF in the autumn of 1947. He had to find another institution, and the university's Faculty of Theology was the only real alternative in Norway. The mission school in Stavanger did not have exam rights at this time and was, for some additional reasons, not a natural alternative for Peder. Hence, he was enrolled at the university in Oslo to study at its Faculty of Theology.

However, before he started his theological studies proper, he participated in an event that had a decisive significance for his later development.

Peder Borgen at the ecumenical meeting in Amsterdam 1948

The immediate years after World War II were unique in so many ways. Everyone had to realize that there were extensive reconstructions to be carried out in many fields: political structures had, in many cases, to be reestablished; economies had to be restored; damaged societies from villages to great cities had to be rebuilt; industries and agriculture had to be recreated. Millions of people were dead, and millions were homeless in Europe. Postwar sufferings lasted for decades and are, to some extent, still among some of us. People hoped for peace; what happened was that some former allies during the war became alienated, partly competitors, and nations went into a stage of the so-called Cold War.

On the background of these issues and several other factors, the development led—perhaps inevitably—to the establishment of international organizations that sought common platforms and common goals. Consider, above all, the fact that the United Nations was established on October 24, 1945, with the aim of preventing future wars.[11] Its first leader was the

---

10. See Breistein, "Fra luthersk presteskole," 221–38, especially 229–30.

11. For a quick review, see https://en.wikipedia.org/wiki/United_Nations, then

Norwegian Trygve Lie. The North Atlantic Treaty Organization (NATO) was established in 1949, with Norway as one of its members, and with a goal of cooperation and common goals in a mutual a system of collective security, whereby its "independent member states agree to mutual defense in response to an attack by any external party."[12] Many other international organizations, treaties, and agreements were established. The overreaching hope for most of them was no more world war. Some participants were overly optimistic, others more realistic. The sentiments today are not easy to assess.

My point is: there were hopes and longings for a better future, and one of the means was to get together in structured contexts. The establishment of the World Council of Churches must also be understood in light of these post–World War II years. Ecumenism means, by definition, fellowship, or at least the search for fellowship.

In the summer of 1947, a large ecumenical Christian meeting was held in Oslo, a world youth conference for Christian youth. The conference included 1200 participants from 80 nations who came together for a 10-day gathering in Oslo.

Peder, who graduated from the *gymnas* that year, was also engaged and inspired by this conference and participated in several gatherings. One of the more important foreign participants was the Methodist pastor Philip Potter (1921–2015), who at this time represented the Christian student movement in Jamaica. He later held several key positions in the World Council of Churches and was its third general secretary (1972–84). Potter also came to mean a lot to Peder and represented a great ecumenical inspiration for him.

Peder at the establishment of the World Council of Churches

After the great youth meeting in Oslo, Peder joined an ecumenical study group, and in this group he was told that the following year, in 1948, a large ecumenical conference was to be arranged in Amsterdam, and that it would represent the occasion for the establishment of a World Council of Churches. This meeting was intended to be the climax of many years of ecumenical work and represents the beginning of a new platform for further work. For several years, work had been carried out to create greater understanding and cooperation between the various denominations. Now was the time to create a larger organization that could strengthen this work.[13]

---

https://www.britannica.com/topic/United-Nations.

12. Cf. https://en.wikipedia.org/wiki/NATO.

13. The beginning of this phase is often said to have been the great World Mission

The youth conference in Oslo helped to strengthen Peder's awareness of the international aspect of the Methodist Church. He had been very well aware that the Norwegian Methodist Church was part of a larger whole; the General Conference in the United States as the supreme conference of the Methodists in Norway also illustrated this.

However, now new perspectives opened up to Peder, and he decided to go to the ecumenical meeting in Amsterdam. No one from the Methodist Church in Norway, however, was to attend the conference. Then Peder came up with the idea that he might be able to obtain both admission and some means of travel if he was granted status as a correspondent for a Norwegian newspaper. Hence, he went to all the newspapers of importance in Oslo, but it turned out that one after the other had correspondents of their own. Finally, then, he went to *Arbeiderbladet*, a newspaper associated with the Labor movement in Norway. There he had a conversation with the editor-in-chief, Martin Tranmæl, whom he later remembered as very positive. Peder emphasized that at this ecumenical meeting social, ethical, and political issues would be addressed; hence, he argued, here *Arbeiderbladet* ought to be present. Peder himself later said that the meeting ended like this: "Okay, nice to see you, Peder Borgen," the editor said, "thanks for an interesting talk; have a good time." When Peder left the editorial office, he was somewhat frustrated: "probably yet another opportunity that obviously failed." Nevertheless, approximately one week later, he received a surprising telephone call from the switchboard at *Arbeiderbladet*: "Your Press card is ready and waiting for you at the Reception office and can be picked up here at any time."[14]

Thus, Peder was able to get ready and leave for Amsterdam. The meeting was to be held August 22 to September 5, and it was expected that there would be approximately 1400 participants, of which again approximately 450 would be official delegates and, in addition, several other representatives. All in all, one expected that churches in 135 countries would be represented. He traveled by train down to Amsterdam through parts of Germany, which then was still greatly damaged because of the war, and to Amsterdam,

---

meeting held in Edinburgh in 1910. But the two world wars slowed down the ecumenical work. The two great world conferences held in Stockholm in 1925 and in Lausanne in 1927 were nevertheless involved in driving the work forward. The same can be said of the Life and Work's conference in Oxford in 1937 and the Faith and Order's conference in Edinburgh in 1937. Both conferences decided by a large majority that these two movements should merge into a higher entity and create a "World Council of Churches." At a meeting in Utrecht in 1938, a draft constitution for such a council was provisionally adopted. But then the Second World War had come so close that most of the ecumenical endeavors came to a halt. But not completely, and by 1948 the time had come for the establishment of the World Council of Churches.

14. Borgen, interview by the author, January 10, 2017.

where he took in at a youth hostel. He brought a dark suit for the receptions, and the press card opened access for him to the various gatherings.

The opening service—an experience of surprise

Already during the opening service, he had an overwhelming experience of surprise. And it is now that the ecumenism of the Methodist Peder gets its decisive wake-up call. But at the same time, it also strengthened his own Methodist self-awareness. He retells this experience himself as follows, and we may recognize some of his favorite expressions:

> And then again I raised my head as a Methodist, because in Niuwe Kerk, where the opening service was held, there was first a procession with participants from different denominations, also from the Church of Norway, with their pipe collars. And then the service began. There were two speeches, one was held by the older, ecumenical leader John R. Mott, who gave the historical background, and the other was by a younger university leader, D. T. Niles, from Ceylon, now Sri Lanka; he had the main sermon. Both belonged to the Methodist Church! Both of the two opening preachers were from my Church! Later there were confessional gatherings, and I also met in the confessional gathering for my own Church, or church family, and got to greet several and got the impression that we were actively involved in the ecumenical work, now also within the World Council of Churches.[15]

Peder found these impressions later confirmed, and the contact he managed to establish with the youth department in the World Council of Churches was of great help when he, a few years later, wanted to apply for scholarships for further studies. Many more years later, however, he wrote in an article: "As a Norwegian Free Church student from the University of Oslo, it was liberating to come to this meeting and get to see the conditions in Norway in a larger context. A church that was a minority in Norway, the Methodist Church, had a solid delegation at the conference."[16]

Back in Norway, Peder wrote several articles for newspapers on his experiences at the Amsterdam meeting,[17] and not a few for the Methodist paper called *Kristelig Tidende*.[18] In *Kristelig Tidende*, Peder is mainly refer-

---

15. Borgen, interview by the author, January 10, 2017.
16. Borgen, *Vei utenfor Allfarvei*, 173–74.
17. Borgen, "Kirkene fordømmer både kommunismen og kapitalismen." *Arbeiderbladet*, September 7, 1948, 7.
18. Borgen, "Det arbeides i Amsterdam," *Kristelig Tidende* 77 (1948), 508–9 and

ring from the meetings; he does not give many comments on anything or anyone along the way, but briefly refers to what were the main issues in the various sections. However, he is most excited in one of his latest articles; one Wednesday, the various denominations had their own meetings, and he joined the Methodists and heard reports about the ecumenical work among the Methodists: "It was an inspiring moment," he wrote.

The Norwegian state church was represented by a solid delegation, and foremost among these participants was Bishop Eivind Berggrav, who had also been a member of the preparatory committee for the conference.[19] He was also a member of the Central Committee and the Executive Committee and was a leading figure both within the Church of Norway and in ecumenical work in Norway and abroad. But Peder wrote little about the work of Berggrav; his interest was more focused on the ecumenical movement as such and the role of his own church in it. The fact that he did not focus on the Church of Norway and its role was probably also a result of his young age and his limited knowledge of what was going on within the majority church concerning its ecumenical thinking and work at this time.

However, that the result of this meeting and his experiences of its ecumenical role was important to him, and his interest in ecumenism, is beyond any doubt; it also gave him an essential ecumenical inspiration to see what role Methodist participants and churches played during this particular meeting and in the ecumenical movement in general. The feeling of minority he previously had in the Norwegian church context was adjusted by this overwhelming encounter with the worldwide ecumenical work. He never forgot the fact that churches from the Methodist family were central in the establishment of the World Council of Churches in 1948.[20]

The Faculty of Theology in the postwar years

In 1947, the Faculty of Theology[21] at the University of Oslo had six teachers[22] and well under a hundred students. During the years Peder was a student

---

516; Borgen, "Metodister i Amsterdam," *Kristelig Tidende* 77 (1948), 549 and 555.

19. On Berggrav's life and work, see the biography by Heiene, *Eivind Berggrav*.

20. See, e.g., Borgen, *Vei utenfor Allfarvei*, 169–87.

21. It may be a little confusing to USA readers to call it a "faculty," as that is usually a term for the teaching and administrative staff as such in a USA context. Hence a more familiar term would perhaps have been "department of." However, in a Norwegian context the appropriate term is *fakultet* (from the German *Fakultät*); hence I prefer "faculty" in my text.

22. These were: Harris Birkeland, dosent in the Old Testament; Nils Alstrup Dahl, professor in the New Testament; Einar Molland, professor in church history; Sigmund

there, approximately only ten candidates graduated each year. This number should indicate that there were about sixty students in the theoretical part of the theological study (called theoreticum), and approximately ten enrolled in the pastoral studies, which at that time represented the seventh and last year in a full theological study program and was obligatory for those who wanted to be pastors in the Church of Norway. In reality, the number of students was probably lower for the main years of study. Jacob Jervell,[23] who was three years older than Peder and a student at the Faculty in 1944–51, later called it a "mini-faculty" and a "tiny little" faculty.[24] At the time of Peder's years of study, the number of students was around forty. This low number also meant that the milieu became dense and close, for better or worse. Everyone knew every one of the students, and they could also have a close relationship with the teachers, even though the relationship between a professor and his student was different than what we find in more recent years. For instance, no one called on a professor by his[25] first name at that time.

The students at the Faculty of Theology were not required to belong to a Lutheran denomination. Hence Peder, too, was welcomed there. But that did not imply that the Faculty was non-denominational. On the contrary, it was a requirement of all the theological professors—due to their status as government officials—that they had to be members of the Church of Norway—the state church. This requirement was justified, among other things, because the Faculty was an educational institution for the Church of Norway, and a consultative body for the authorities in theological and ecclesiastical matters. The Faculty has sometimes been tempted to claim that it has a different attitude or connection to the Lutheran denomination than the Menighetsfakultet. This is correct regarding the students' connection to Lutheranism, but not regarding the teachers' obligatory denominational affiliation. The issue was exemplified in the early 1970s when Dr.philos. Kari Børresen applied for a vacant position as a lecturer in the history of Christian ideas. Her application documents were promptly returned with the message that she did not meet the requirements because she was a Catholic. I will return to these issues later because at about the same time, another

---

Mowinckel, professor in the Old Testament; Hans Ording, professor in systematic theology. Herman Ludin Jansen was professor in religion, 1952–53, and Johan B. Hygen lecturer in systematic theology 1942–54 (professor 1954–78).

23. Jacob Jervell (1925–2014) was a professor in the New Testament at the Faculty of Theology 1960–1988. He is internationally well known for his studies in Luke-Acts and his commentary on *Die Apostelgeschichte* in the Meyer Series.

24. Jacob Jervell in an interview with Tor Øystein Vaaland, 2010; the interview is available at http://www.tf.uio.no/om/historie/tf200/berlin2010/jervell_1200.mp4.

25. However, all the Norwegian professors of theology at this time were male!

non-Lutheran was applying for a professorship in Christian studies at the University of Bergen, namely Peder Borgen.

The university's Faculty of Theology could probably be characterized as a "mini-faculty." However, this must be understood in context. First, it was a matter of the Faculty of Theology being a *faculty* and not a *department*. A faculty, in a Norwegian setting, usually consists of several subsections, called "departments," and the Faculty of Theology had none at this time. Therefore, it can rightly be called a "mini-faculty." Secondly, the staff was not large; six to seven teachers and approximately forty to sixty students. At the Menighetsfakultet, which had approximately 150–200 students, there were also no more than eight to ten teachers at that time.

Now, however, it is a fact that the number of teachers and students does not necessarily indicate anything about the quality of either the teachers or the students. Furthermore, it should be stated that TF had several outstanding teachers who had an excellent international reputation because of their research. Furthermore, several of the costudents of Peder Borgen later achieved significant positions in Norwegian church life.[26]

The Teachers

Sigmund Mowinckel (1884–65, professor of the Old Testament 1933–54), is probably the professor at the Faculty of Theology who won the most outstanding international reputation in his time.[27] His reputation is primarily related to studies of the Old Testament hymns and their place in the cult of Israel. He received several international awards, was an honorary doctor at several universities, and was offered professorships at several universities abroad. He initially represented the liberal wing in Norwegian church life, but in the 1930s he became actively involved in the so-called Oxford Revival and "moved more in the direction of the church center."[28] He was ordained in 1940 and conducted services in various congregations.

Nils Alstrup Dahl (1911–2001) was a professor of the New Testament at the University of Oslo from 1946 to 1965, then a professor at Yale University in the USA for fifteen years (1965–80). When he retired, he returned to

---

26. One might mention Peter Wilhelm Bøckmann, Kristen K. Bremer, Terje Ellingsen, Jacob Jervell, and Per Lønning.

27. See Hjelde, *Sigmund Mowinckel und seine Zeit*.

28. See Sigurd Hjelde, "Sigmund Mowinckel," at https://nbl.snl.no/Sigmund_Mowinckel. See also Hjelde's biography of Mowinckel, *Sigmund Mowinckel*, especially 125–35.

Norway but remained active as a researcher, writer, and inspirer of younger students for many years.

Dahl received his doctorate in the difficult circumstances of 1941 for a dissertation on *Das Volk Gottes*, a study that soon became a highly acclaimed work. He eventually published several other New Testament studies, on both the historical Jesus and Pauline theology. Dahl is also one of the Norwegian New Testament professors who has had the most significant influence internationally, not least because of his fifteen-year stay at the renowned Yale University, where he became a supervisor of a number of students and doctoral candidates.[29] His influence is justified by his publications, but also by his role as inspirer and supervisor in both the Norwegian and American contexts.

Einar Molland (1908–76) was a professor of church history for almost 40 years (1939–76). In his early days as a scholar, he published in the field of the New Testament but eventually switched to church history. He represented a different attitude than his former teachers at the Faculty as he already in 1932 gave a lecture in a student union (*Studenterforbundet*) entitled "We Believe in the Dogmas." He also explained his view of the Church of Norway in a book titled *Statskirke og Jesu Kristi kirke* (*State Church and the Church of Christ*), published in 1954. In addition to an historical analysis of questions concerning issues of a state church and religious freedom, his view of the current Norwegian church system also appeared in the concluding chapters. Peder could not follow his professor's state church enthusiasm when Molland stated:

> As things are with us today, the present State Church constitution is, in my opinion, the most practical church constitution imaginable for the work of the Church in our people. It makes it possible, more than any other system, without any problems of conscience to serve the Norwegian people with the preaching of the gospel and the administration of the sacraments.[30] (TS translation)

One of his primary arguments for this view was the consideration of the need for Christian teaching in schools. Secondly, he argued the state church system also entailed a certain conventional Christianity in the people, which, i.a., was observable in the great moments in the life of the nation. If the state church disappeared, he thought, there would also be an end to tolerance and thus to unity in the Church of Norway. Furthermore,

---

29. Cf. Johnson, who experienced Dahl as a professor at Yale in the 1970s: Johnson, *Mind in Another Place*, 78, 81, 85–86.

30. Molland, *Statskirke*, 89.

he wrote, a free church would not long remain a church *of* and *for* the people (a *folkekirke—volkskirche*).

Professor Molland also published several textbooks and studies of church history.[31] He was a teacher and researcher who was recognized far beyond the borders of Norway and was active in several committees both at home and abroad, including in several ecumenical contexts.

In the opinion of many, there was in these years a change in the Faculty of Theology's profile and place in the Norwegian church life, a change demonstrated by, among other things, these theologians' work and efforts both as teachers and church activists. The liberal attitudes in vogue in and after the struggle over liberalism and conservatism in church matters of order and dogma at the beginning of the twentieth century was replaced by a more positive ecclesiasticism, which was expressed by Mowinckel's personal piety exhibited by his involvement in the Oxford movement, by Dahl's study of *Das Volk Gottes*, and by Molland's enthusiasm of the constitution of the Norwegian state church. In a later interview about his predecessor—the more liberal NT professor Lyder Brun—N. A. Dahl said that Brun is remembered as once having uttered: "We had sleepless nights because of the dogmas, and you have added melody and sing them with joy."[32] This was not at least stated with a view to Molland's ecclesiastical optimism.

Peder Borgen as a student of theology

It was these three professors that Peder Borgen felt most attracted to during his studies. He admired the old Mowinckel, but it was Molland and Dahl he found most helpful for his own studies.

Peder uses several of his favorite expressions[33] when he talks about Molland: He thought he was a "very inspiring" lecturer and open-minded as a teacher. It was "positive" to talk to and listen to him, even though Peder had his reservations concerning Molland's state church optimism, namely, that the state church was the church structure that was by far the best—at least in the situation at that time—in Norway. Molland could be strong in his rhetoric, not at least when it came to doctoral disputations. At the same time, he was hospitable, so that they, as students, were invited to his home. The students experienced this as "inspiring." Peder eventually participated

---

31. See Molland, *Konfesjonskunnskap* (1961; revised 1976 as *Kristenhetens kirker og trossamfunn)*; and Molland, *Norges Kirkehistorie* 1–2.

32. Seim and Wyller, "Akademisk kultur," 90.

33. Borgen, interview by the author, January 10, 2017. All of the following quotations concerning Molland and Dahl are from this interview.

in a church history seminar with him and thought he got "good impulses" and remained in good standing with Einar Molland for the years to come.

Among the teachers at the Faculty of Theology, it was nevertheless Nils Alstrup Dahl with whom Peder had the most extensive contact, and it developed into a good relationship and a friendship that lasted as long as Dahl lived. After the death of Dahl in 2001, a memorial speech was to be given at the Norwegian Academy of Science and Letters in Oslo, and this task was given to Peder. He then described Dahl's life as a framework "for research of the highest international quality, and for a supervision activity that has given important impetus to new researchers over many years." And he went on to say that "he himself said that what particularly attracted him to Yale University was that he got a group of promising graduate students working on their doctorates. He wanted to plant seeds of themes and ideas that would grow into dissertations and stimulate further research." And Peder added: "As an emeritus in Norway, he continued with guidance activities, and several younger exegetes are indebted to him for his constructive comments. I myself am grateful that, while I was a student, he encouraged me to take on research in the New Testament."[34]

However, Peder's first encounter with Dahl and his teaching was not encouraging. He experienced the same thing that many other students of theology have experienced both before and later in their first meetings with scholarly biblical teaching and research:

> I was completely confused when I attended his lectures to begin with. He had a unique voice, with some fluctuations up and down, and his lectures were often a combination of his views and the fact that he also did some research for us. And it was stimulating, but not for me. I was too new and too much of a freshman.[35]

However, in the second term with Dahl, things went much better: "In the second semester with Dahl, I understood more and more of his thinking and methods, and then I became fascinated." During further conversations with Dahl, he became interested in pursuing Bible research, and he was encouraged by Dahl to do so. Initially, this led Peder to write a voluntary shorter thesis, which he submitted at the end of his studies. The curriculum provided an opportunity to submit such specialization assignments, and

---

34. Quotations are taken from Borgen's memorial speech over Nils Alstrup Dahl, held in the Norwegian Academy of Sciences and Letters (Det Norske VidenskapsAkademi), February 14, 2002. See also Borgen's comments on Dahl in Borgen, *Vei utenfor Allfarvei*, 153–68.

35. Borgen, interview by the author, January 10, 2017.

Peder chose to write an assignment within the John and Matthew research. The thesis had the theme, "The Relations between the Gospel of John and the Gospel of Matthew. A Survey of Traditions." The thesis was later revised, and parts were published as a separate article.[36]

The teachers also held devotionals at the Faculty; it was held in a seminar room where they could gather for devotion, and the one that Peder remembers as most personally in tone and content was from Mowinckel. Peder expressed himself thus in 2017:

> ... I felt—with my background in a Free Church—a better contact with him than with the others who were then more ordinary. Mowinckel was influenced by the Oxford movement, so he combined, on the one hand, very impressive research while, on the other hand, he also represented some of the personal Christianity that was related to what I myself had as a background.[37]

The latter statement points to something that Peder carried with him and what influenced his mind during his first months and years at the Faculty; *the minority situation:* "I came from an environment that was not so familiar with the Faculty of Theology and perhaps not even with the Menighetsfakultet. Hence, I had a certain feeling of a handicap or a certain minority consciousness."[38] There were no other students at the Faculty with a background from any of the Norwegian minority churches when Peder was a student, and to some degree, he felt that he encountered a somewhat different form of religiosity than he was used to. But he held on to his Methodist identity.

Being a minority: a comparison of two different reactions

As part of the background that may be relevant in order to understand Peder's development, it may be interesting to look briefly at how another student of the same age and with a free church background experienced his relationship to his childhood, his church life, and its culture developing during his studies; namely, the late professor of social anthropology Arne

---

36. See Borgen, "John and the Synoptics."

37. Borgen, interview by the author, January 10, 2017. It is somewhat interesting here that Karoline Mowinckel, the professor's wife, had a background in Methodism. She is said to have been a member of the Methodist Church until eight to ten years after she became Mrs. Mowinckel (they married in 1917), but then she joined the Church of Norway. Cf. Hjelde, *Sigmund Mowinckel,* 97, note 12. Both later joined the Oxford movement.

38. Borgen, interview by the author, January 10, 2017.

Martin Klausen (1927–2018).[39] He grew up in the Evangelical Lutheran Free Church in Porsgrunn, Norway. Hence, he also had a background in a free church, even though he and his Lutheran Church were not dissenters in the same way as the Methodist Peder Borgen; Klausen was a Lutheran. He wrote in his autobiography that part of his life revolved around "a liberation from a strongly pietistic and closed environment to an unknown and exotic academic world."[40] During his time in the Norwegian *gymnas* (college), and his first year as a student at the University of Oslo, he experienced a lengthy process of liberation from his Christian childhood and early youth environment and ideals. Peder has never described his development in that way, even though most young people—including himself—went through a process of liberation in their teen years. There may be several reasons why these two men experienced these years so differently. Klausen writes that he very early got

> a perception that we (as a family) were in a way living outside ordinary society. We were something for ourselves. Cinema, theater, dance, and sports were, of course, taboo. What was most troubling, however, was the feeling of inferiority that was created through a systematic emphasis on modesty and submissiveness. We were not to think that we had anything to be proud of if not for God's grace. In ourselves, we were worth nothing.[41]

Klausen was aware of the fact that not all free church youths felt the same way, but that was how *he* felt about it. He explained his experiences by saying that his father was a submissive type, and mixed with a strong pietism, this led to a way of life withdrawn from many cultural activities: "politics and any other active participation in secular political life was looked upon as a kind of adiaphora, but in fact not really worthy of any priority."[42] Peder's father, on the other hand, was a member of the municipal council for many years, and was once about to be elected to the Norwegian Parliament (but lost by a few votes). And the international horizon was much more present in the Methodist milieus than in the other free churches in Norway.

Both Klausen and Borgen participated partially in the same student activities during their first years of study. Both tried to attend the evangelical student association, but both found themselves more comfortable in the

---

39. He was professor in social anthropology at the University of Oslo 1973–96. A bibliography of his works is to be found at: https://www.idunn.no/nat/2018/01-02/arne_martin_klausen_en_bibliografi.

40. Klausen, *Et liv i kulturkollisjon*, 25.

41. Klausen, *Et liv i kulturkollisjon*, 40.

42. Klausen, *Et liv i kulturkollisjon*, 41.

somewhat more liberal *Studenterforbundet* (Student Union); Peder because it did not have a Lutheran profile, Klausen because he there found a more open cultural attitude. In addition, Klausen eventually also found his way into the non-religious Studentersamfunnet (Student Society), and here Peder was not very active. All this probably affected their development. However, one more issue might be mentioned here; Peder chose to study his own faith through his theological studies; Klausen chose other subjects, such as geography with ethnography and history, and eventually left—in practice at least—his Christian beliefs of childhood and early youth. In addition, he married early, had children, and took a couple of years off studying, working as a high school teacher in a small town (Flekkefjord) in southern Norway before continuing his studies in 1954. At that time, Borgen had graduated and had already gone to the United States as a research fellow, but without a wife and children. That was to come several years later.

Peder also discovered something else during his early studies that was very helpful: he discovered the importance of *worldwide Methodist scholarship*. He learned that there existed relevant textbooks for the study of the New Testament written by Methodist scholars. At first, this was associated with the works of the British professor C. K. Barrett.[43] He had written solid works, and several more were published during the years that followed.[44] Barrett was also a very active Methodist as a preacher in his church.[45] Such experiences helped Peder from the beginning. And then again, he tried to distance himself from his feelings of belonging to a minority:

> I raised my head, not only as a student, but also later as a researcher, as one of those within the Methodist Church's milieus who had similar academic commitment and interests. So, I have to say that the period as a student was not really a big problem for me, neither theologically nor on a personal level. There was also no break with my work in the Methodist church at Lillestrøm, and that too was very helpful and useful.[46]

---

43. C. K. Barrett (1917–2011) was a professor at the University of Durham, and wrote commentaries on the Acts of the Apostles, the Gospel of John, the Epistle to the Romans, and 1–2 Corinthians, as well as several other studies. Barrett was ordained a Methodist priest. See Baird, *History*, 3:538–48. A bibliography of his works can be found here: https://theologicalstudies.org.uk/theo_barrett.php.

44. See, for instance, Barrett, *Holy Spirit*. Later several commentaries were published.

45. Concerning Barrett's sermons, see Witherington, *Luminescence* 1 and 2.

46. Borgen, interview by the author, January 10, 2017. Peder claimed in this interview that he used Barrett's commentary on the Gospel of John during his studies. But this is probably a mistake; Barrett's commentary on the Gospel of John was not published until 1955: Barrett, *Gospel According to St John*.

In the footsteps of Paul: a pilgrimage to Greece (1951)

In the middle of his theological studies, Peder was given the opportunity to participate as a youth delegate on a study trip and pilgrimage to Greece. The Greek Orthodox Church had invited participants from approximately thirty different denominations, as well as a youth delegation, for an anniversary trip in Paul's footsteps. The youth delegation was selected by the youth department of the World Council of Churches. The occasion was the 1900 anniversary of Paul's and Christianity's arrival in Europe. From Norway, representatives from some denominations and educational institutions participated; from the latter, two of Peder's teachers, Professor Einar Molland and Professor Nils Alstrup Dahl, participated. Peder was the only youth delegate from Norway.

On June 15, 1951, the Greek postal service issued four stamps commemorating Paul's visit to the land in 51 AD. Paul is said to have seen an altar "for an unknown god" there, but there are no remnants of such an altar anymore.

He took the train to Venice.[47] Some of the participants, then, including Peder, took part in a group trip from Venice to Athens. The actual anniversary trip lasted two weeks, from June 7. But Peder was also allowed to attend a Christian student conference in Kifissa after the pilgrimage. The travel letters he wrote home to some newspapers and magazines, and private correspondence home to the family, show that he was overexcited; not only for the ecumenical fellowship, but especially for what they saw and experienced

---

47. Borgen, "Venezia—byen uten gater og biler," *Akershus Arbeiderblad*, June 20, 1951, 3 and 6.

in the walks "in Paul's footsteps," as Peder called some his articles about his experiences in Greece.[48]

Peder had one of his greatest moments when he saw the Acropolis: "I pinched my arm and experienced that it was true. It was one of the greatest moments when I saw the Acropolis come within sight. The Acropolis is indescribable."[49] They also visited other places, such as Philippi, Saloniki, Berea, Crete, Rhodes, and Corinth.[50] The end of the anniversary pilgrimage tour was an illuminated service in the evening darkness on the Areopagus Hill. The archbishop led the service.[51]

After the anniversary trip itself, Peder continued his travel by boat; he had been hired for a trip as an auxiliary boy onboard the Fred Olsen shipping company's boat Banaderos. They sailed to Egypt (Alexandria), Turkey, and Beirut. Peder did not get to see much of Alexandria; he was set to remove rust on the boat, so he only got to know the port area, and it was a big disappointment: "What a city! Tusk traders and rascals. Bribery, dirt, and shit. It is good I do not have any money to spend," he wrote on a postcard sent to his family back home.[52]

Later, Alexandria would become the city from antiquity that Peder came to be most interested in: Alexandria was the place where the Jew Philo (of Alexandria) lived all his life (ca. 20 BCE to ca. 50 CE). From his Norwegian doctoral work and onwards, Philo, his life and work, became a central research object for Peder. However, that was not the case in 1951. He hardly knew anything about Philo at that time.

Back home, Peder focused intensively on his studies. But in such a small faculty and with so few students, he became a lone wolf in his commitment to further studies of the New Testament. Jacob Jervell was partly a parallel student, but he graduated in the spring of 1951, got some scholarships, and spent considerable time abroad (in Germany). Peter Wilhelm Bøckman (1927-2006), who later became Peder's colleague in Trondheim, was also a parallel student. But he graduated later and was not primarily interested in the NT. His interests were within the fields of systematics and ethics. The later church historian and minister Terje Ellingsen (1928-2018)

---

48. He published some "travel letters" in several newspapers: see Borgen, "I Paulus' fotspor. Fra Paulus jubileet i Hellas," 1 and 4; Borgen, "Med båt og buss i Paulus' fotspor," 6; Borgen, "I Paulus' fotspor. Saloniki og Aten," 1, 5, and 6; Borgen, "Med båt og buss i Paulus fotspor 2," 1 and 5.

49. Private postcard to his family, dated Aten, June 11, 1951. Borgen, "Et møte på Akropolis," 105.

50. Borgen, "Pilgrimsferden går videre," 436–37 and 440.

51. Borgen, "Et møte på Akropolis," *Vår Ungdom* 10–11 (1951) 105.

52. Private postcard sent to his parents, dated Alexandria, July 15, 1951.

was also a student at the Faculty at this time. In a conversation in the spring of 2018, at the age of ninety, he stated that he remembered Peder Borgen well: "He was really quite ambitious," he said. And he continued: "He liked to emphasize the place of the Methodist Church in Norway. But he was also ecumenically minded and had, in fact, been present at the great ecumenical meeting in Amsterdam in 1948." Ellingsen's own research interests were in church history even then.

The spring term of 1953 was the final exam term for Peder, and he graduated together with eight other students. The assignment in the New Testament exam, which was one of the two final main exams, was: "The idea of judgment in the Synoptic Gospels, with particular reference to the question of the fate of the condemned." The candidates could hardly complain that the topic was not central or relevant: on Sunday, January 25, the same year, the conservative Professor Ole Hallesby (from Menighetsfakultetet) had given his (in)famous speech on the danger of hell.[53] The speech was broadcasted via radio, and for a long time afterward there was a debate in all media—and certainly also among the students at the Faculty—about the understanding of hell and the fate of the dead. But at the same time, it was an exam topic that contained enough elements to serve as a basis for separating the clever ones from the others. Peder got his *Laudabilis* for his NT exam paper, and *Laudabilis* as the main grade.

So, what to do now? Peder had acquired an excellent exam and was motivated to apply for scholarships for further studies.

It should turn out not to be that simple. He was not a Lutheran!

But he applied. And he got scholarships.

However, not from Norwegian sources.

Later that summer he traveled to the United States of America.

---

53. Cf. https://en.wikipedia.org/wiki/Ole_Hallesby?msclkid=9d94f5c3d10411ec88b5f91b78c84fbd.

3

Further Studies on Luke and Eschatology (USA, 1953–56)

PHD STUDIES

PEDER GRADUATED FROM THE University of Oslo in the spring of 1953, and having obtained good grades, he believed that he had both laid a foundation for and had a strong motivation for further studies. However, how could he get the opportunity to do so? The Faculty of Theology did not have many scholarships to offer, and for Peder, as a Methodist, it was even more difficult.

To Germany or the USA?

At this time, Norwegian research fellows in theology most often went to Germany; it was considered the place where it was most interesting to study and where the most exciting and new ideas emerged. The German universities had many internationally renowned theological professors, and much of the development in biblical research took place in Germany. There was, however, already a certain shift towards England and not at least towards the United States and their universities and theological seminars as relevant and exciting places for further studies. Peder wanted to get to know American conditions better. He had less knowledge of the German language and university life. Later, he expanded this horizon considerably through participation in many research congresses at universities in Germany, the Netherlands, Belgium, and other European countries. It is, however, probably also his Norwegian Methodist background that influenced his decisions here, related to American Methodism as it was both historically and present. In addition, the Methodist Peder had to apply for scholarships where such applications from a non-Lutheran were welcome, and then the United States, in particular, was relevant.

In the postwar period, there was increased contact between Norway and the United States. Peder orientated himself and applied to the American Fulbright Fund, to the World Council of Churches in Switzerland, and to a program within the Methodist Church (USA) called Crusade Scholarships. And he received scholarships from all three. Through the Church World Council scholarship, he was admitted to Drew University, Madison, New Jersey, which was affiliated with the Methodist Church. The university was particularly known for its theological faculty and was in the process of strengthening and further developing graduate studies, including their doctoral programs leading to the American degree Doctor of Philosophy (PhD).

At Drew University

When he enrolled at the university, the school management wanted him to study there for six months for an assessment so they could place him on the right level in their system. But that would have almost ruined his chances of completing the doctoral program in the barely three years he could stay in the USA because he had scholarships covering his expenses for a maximum of three years. However, he had been foresighted enough to get a statement from foreign student advisor at the American summer school in Oslo. And because of the information provided in these papers, the authorities at Drew could more easily understand his grades from the University of Oslo and could place him according to his level achieved in Oslo. Nevertheless, he still had to pass some language tests. Peder was not entirely happy with this start: "a psychologically bad start. I only had a three-year scholarship."[1]

In advance, Peder had gathered some information about the theological school at Drew and its teachers. But before he arrived, the professor of the New Testament with whom he had been looking forward to working with, Clarence Tucker Craig (1895–1953), died at only fifty-eight years old. Thus, they had to bring in professors from outside who gave lectures and seminars as guest teachers. Among these were Henry Cadbury, John Knox,

1. Borgen, interview by the author, January 10, 2017.

Vincent Taylor, and Morten Enslin, all professors who were or eventually became reputable scholars. After six months, Howard C. Kee (1920–2017) came in from Yale University as Drew's new professor, and he was Peder's supervisor throughout his studies. Kee was only eight years older than Peder, but it turned out that he was a "coming man" in American New Testament research, and he became a friend with whom Peder kept in touch for many years.[2]

It soon turned out that the American programs of advanced studies were quite different from what Peder was familiar with in Norway. Anyone who wanted to take a doctoral degree in the Norwegian system had to work mainly on their own. He—only male theologians had received a theological doctorate at this time[3]—had to work very much alone, not having any permanent supervisor or any program or supervision seminars or exams to pass. Preferably, they should work as independently as possible and then, after some years, present a completed dissertation that was to be submitted for assessment at the university. Then it was subjected to a strict assessment by a committee that decided whether it was worthy or not of being defended in a public disputation.

In the United States, this was completely different. Here one had to apply and was eventually accepted into a program; one had to take exams in various subjects and then write a dissertation under the supervision of a professor. In Norway, a similar system was introduced in the mid-1980s.

Peder, who had graduated from college with an emphasis on Greek and Latin, had, therefore, less knowledge of modern languages such as English, German, and French, and when starting at Drew, he felt he should have been more proficient in English. And he, who usually was not a very quiet person, struggled a little at the beginning at Drew:

> I was relatively quiet compared to the American students in the various seminars and classes. That was partly due to the fact that traditions were different, partly because I wanted to work my way into the new conditions before I let go in discussions, etc. The American students are very free and quick to raise questions. So they found that I was a little quiet and cautious, but

---

2. When Howard C. Kee was honored by a Festschrift in 1988, Peder was both one of the editors and a contributor. See Neusner et al., eds., *Social World of Formative Christianity and Judaism*.

3. Turid Karlsen Seim (1945–2016) was the first woman who obtained a theological PhD degree in Norway (1990). She was a professor in New Testament studies at the University of Oslo from 1991 to 2015.

based on the papers I submitted, the Faculty found that I was eligible to go on.[4]

Peder used the time well in the USA. He also took several practical-theological subjects to meet the requirements of the Methodist Annual Conference in Norway regarding practical-theological studies. Hence, he could be ordained as a deacon when he returned home in 1956 and as an elder the following year. In addition, he accepted a scholarship to a summer course in political and ecclesiastical work: one summer, he was a foreign overseas guest at a youth camp in Iowa; another year, he attended a summer school on foreign policy at The American University in Washington, DC, with visits, i.a., in the Pentagon, the Senate, and other key places, and he had two weeks at the United Nations headquarters and followed the work there.

Peder had not only become a church ecumenist in 1948; he had also become international in his attitudes. And his stay in the United States from 1953 to 1956 strengthened his international interests. When it became relevant a few years later (1972) to take a stand for or against the EEC (European Union), Peder signed a petition for "Yes to the EEC from Norwegian researchers." It was entirely in line with his international orientation.

"Eschatology and Heilsgeschichte in Luke-Acts"

However, most of his time at Drew Peder had to spend on his doctoral studies and the writing of his PhD dissertation. He chose to write about a topic in Luke-Acts research that was hotly debated at the time. The subject was created by the fact that he, like so many other New Testament scholars at this time, was concerned with the relationship between future eschatology and present eschatology, and then not present eschatology in general, but how modern eschatology tried to get a shift from future eschatology to salvation history as a solution to the delay or the problem that the end did not come.

A typical research project of the 1950s

Hence Peder worked on the Gospel of Luke and the Acts of the Apostles, and presented the focus of his work thus:

> The task of the present study is to analyze the changes which took place when the perspective of an imminent end could not be kept any longer (sometimes referred to as "the eschatological

---

4. Borgen, interview by the author, January 10, 2017.

problem"), and when such concepts as Jesus' life, death, and resurrection, mission and the rejection by the Jews became interpreted within the context of Heilsgeschichte, with its long perspective of time and its periodic scheme.[5]

Peder's methodological approach was primarily what is called redaction criticism (in German: die redaktionsgeschichtliche Methode); that is, he did not so much focus on what really happened or in what was said concerning the historical Jesus, but rather he examined more how the author of the Gospel of Luke and the Acts of the Apostles used his traditions, how he acted as editor of the sources and traditions he might have had. Hence, he worked with the question of whether the author—whether it was doctor Luke or not—had a particular theology that he wanted to present to his readers. The result was a three-hundred-page typewritten dissertation entitled: "Eschatology and Heilsgeschichte in Luke-Acts."

Peder's approach was strongly influenced by popular trends in Luke-Acts research at the time. And he was not alone in working on these issues. He knew the fear that another researcher should appear, having written a dissertation so close to his subject that it almost was destroyed or made superfluous. In 1954, one year after Peder had begun his PhD studies in the United States, the German Hans Conzelmann published a study addressing issues very close to Peder's topic, namely Conzelmann's work: *Die Mitte der Zeit. Studien zur Theologie des Lukas*.[6]

Peder thus had to distinguish and delimit his work vis-à-vis this dissertation of Conzelmann, but at the same time, he also had to use it as a kind of conversation partner along the way. Nevertheless, it is plausible that the close connection between Conzelmann's book and Peder's dissertation was a decisive reason why the latter was never printed and published as a book.

The very completion of his dissertation was an enormous exercise of courage and strength, and he was helped by several of his costudents in writing out the work that was to be submitted. But he finished it in a very short time—compared to what was usual for an American PhD dissertation; he was able to return to Norway with his PhD degree as early as March 1956. On Saturday, March 10, he arrived at Oslo airport by plane from New York, and he spent a couple of weeks at home in Lillestrøm before he started in a temporary position as a pastor in the Stavanger Methodist Church.

Back home in Norway, he discussed his dissertation with his former teacher Nils Alstrup Dahl: should he perhaps continue to work on it in order to present it to a publisher? Dahl, however, did not encourage that.

---

5. Borgen, *Eschatology and Heilsgeschichte*, ix–x.
6. Conzelmann, *Die Mitte der Zeit*.

Instead, he said: "Put it aside now, Peder, and try to expand your knowledge of the Jewish background material because if you can get a broader base of knowledge there, you will be more fit for later research." Peder followed this advice, and the dissertation was never published. However, he edited some of the material he had been working on and later published it in an article.[7]

---

7. Borgen, interview by the author, January 10, 2017. See here Borgen, "Von Paulus zu Lukas." English version: Borgen, "From Paul to Luke."

4

Borgen as a Pastor (1956–58)

THE REASON WHY PEDER Borgen returned home from the USA as early as March was not only because his scholarship was about to run dry, but also because he had been asked to accept a three-month-long temporary position as a pastor in the Stavanger Methodist Church. In fact, he had no other job to take up when returning home, and he was mentally prepared to start as a pastor in a local Methodist church in Norway.

A STAND-IN AT STAVANGER METHODIST CHURCH

The Stavanger Methodist Church was a very resourceful congregation, and Peder Borgen was to act as a substitute for their pastor, Trygve Karlsen (pastor in Stavanger 1952–62). Karlsen was elected as a delegate to the Methodist General Conference in the USA and wanted to spend some extra time visiting some Norwegian-American Methodist churches. Peder thus acted as a substitute in Stavanger from just before Easter until the end of June.

Starting his ministry as a substitute pastor in a resourceful congregation was a good experience, and he received help in many ways to fill the role of pastor. He especially got to work with the pastor of the Methodist church in the neighboring town of Sandnes, Reidar Skarung (1927–2017), and he enjoyed the fact that the congregation had good resources in song and music.

Pastor Karlsen returned from the USA at the beginning of June. Not long after, it was time for the Methodist Church's Annual Conference in Immanuel Church in Oslo. This conference was essential to Peder in particular as he was ordained a deacon, and he was asked where he wanted to start as a pastor after the summer holidays. Peder had not received any information in advance about where he was to serve, but at the conference, he was given two alternatives by the bishop, Odd Hagen: Kristiansund in the western part of Norway or Harstad in the far north. Borgen reflected on this choice thus: "Kristiansund was then in the situation that they were to build a new church, and I had had nothing to do with church buildings so far and did not find myself able to go to a congregation where they were to build a church. Too little experience with that kind of practical work. Hence, Harstad became the place to start my parish work."[1]

PASTOR IN HARSTAD METHODIST CHURCH

It was as an excited Methodist pastor who traveled north to Harstad in 1956. He had enjoyed working in Stavanger and had experienced a congregation that had great resources and which had received him well. This made him bold in facing the work in Harstad. However, at the same time, he knew that the work there would be different and significantly quite different from the life he had had in the United States as a research fellow. Now he was to be the leading pastor in a small local church; the extent to which there were opportunities for further New Testament studies was uncertain.

In addition to the local congregation of the majority church, the Church of Norway, there was a Baptist church in Harstad, established in 1908, and a Pentecostal church. In addition, the Catholic Church had had a congregation there since 1893, and the Salvation Army had its premises and activity. Of the city's population of about 4000, approximately 160 were registered as not being members of the majority church at a census in 1960. Most congregations probably also had members who did not live in Harstad municipality but in the neighboring communities.

Harstad is located far north in Norway, in Troms (now Troms and Finnmark) county, and was a rather small town in the 1950s. The Harstad Methodist Church was officially founded in 1918. The church had a large church building built in 1922. The main church room had 190 seats, but much of the basement floor was rented out. From the very beginning, the congregation worked closely with Kvæfjord Methodist Church. In fact, a prayer house/chapel was consecrated in Kvæfjord as early as 1901, but the formal establishment of a Methodist church in the vicinity took place in Harstad in 1918 with twenty-one members. In 1923-67, however, Kvæfjord constituted a local Methodist congregation; in the early years, it had

---

1. Borgen, interview by the author, February 14, 2017.

a pastor too, but during most of this period, however, they shared pastors with Harstad.

"We will go to the House of the Lord."

On Sunday, August 19, Peder Borgen gave his inaugural sermon in Harstad Methodist Church, and as a starting point for the sermon, he linked to a text from the book of Psalms 122:1: "I rejoice in those who say to me: We will go to the house of the Lord."

This sermon was like a program speech for him and the congregation. Those sitting in the pews should not doubt that the new pastor had expectations for his new ministry and for them as the local congregation. The house of the Lord was not a hiding place but a place of equipment and encouragement for service.[2]

One month after he had arrived in the city, he was interviewed by the local newspaper, *Harstad Tidende*. The journalist found that Borgen was "a decent and straightforward fellow whom the Methodist church will surely benefit greatly from." In the interview, Peder otherwise strongly emphasized that it is wrong to believe that the church should be a spectator; it must be active in society and relevant to society: "Our greatest task is precisely to get in touch with all groups in society."[3]

However, the first impression of the local Methodist congregation was not one of the most uplifting. The congregation was small; its heyday was in the past, and most of the parishioners were older, in part much older than the new pastor. There could be twenty to twenty-five people attending the Sunday services, and he quickly found out that it was not easy to have a gathering on Sunday evenings; only a handful would attend these. He also quickly discovered that at the age of twenty-eight, he was definitely the youngest member to attend the services.

In Stavanger, he had been almost like a guest speaker. As a substitute, he was to be there only for two to three months, and both the congregation and he knew that it was all but a short period for him as a young and inexperienced pastor. Therefore, in Stavanger, he could depend on goodwill and forbearance and enjoy good support from the Methodist pastor in the neighboring city of Sandnes, Reidar Skarung.

---

2. Typewritten script, August 19, 1956, Harstad. Text. Ps. 122.1. Now in the Borgen archive, National Library (Nasjonalbiblioteket), Oslo.

3. "Slå bro over kløften mellom kirke og arbeidsliv," *Harstad Tidende*, September 11, 1956.

In Harstad, it was different. There he came to take over as *the* parish pastor. He was to be there for two to five years, as was the customary tenure, and had to take a stand on tracks left by his predecessors. However, he realized that it did not mean he could not play on his personal abilities and possibilities. Nevertheless, the transition from Stavanger was great, and the difference in resources was quite noticeable. He soon realized that he had to do most of the work himself.

The several practical-theological subjects Peder had studied when in the USA pursuing his PhD studies were now of great help to him. He had learned to think strategically about how to set up work as a new pastor in a congregation. He eventually sought contact with various groups in the city and then, to a large extent, also groups that had no traditional ties to the Methodist Church, from amateur theater to women's societies, and set up a bold but effective plan for his work:

> I used the resources I had brought with me from the United States. And I had one main idea for each year; I made up for myself a primary goal for each year for a three-year-long period: First year: Get known; the Second year: Take initiatives; the Third year: time for harvesting. I found that strategy very helpful to me.[4]

The youth club

A church with many older members often implies that the children and youth work are weak or, in the worst case, completely down. There was a relatively good Sunday school, some Scout work, but few alternatives for smaller children. Mia Linnsund had been the leader of a girl group of teenagers when her husband, Jonny Linnsund, was pastor in the congregation before Peder took over. The girls were not entirely happy that he did not bring a wife who could continue as their leader!

But Peder eventually arranged it so that a youth club was started for both boys and girls. At first, they had access to a slightly smaller hall on the ground floor, but it soon became too small. The congregation had a large basement where most of its space was rented out. Hence Peder freed up a part so that it could be used as a youth room, and thus they were able to arrange a youth evening on Saturdays: "'Stop by' evenings, a hit among Harstad's youth" was the title of an article in *Harstad Tidende* just before

---

4. Borgen, interview by the author, February 14, 2017.

Christmas in 1957.[5] In these evenings they had various games, a small cafeteria, singing, competitions, interviews, and a devotional—an "appeal," as they called it. The young people of Harstad were hungry for entertainment and places of gatherings, and the club received great interest and support.[6]

In addition to the usual congregational work with services, meetings, committee meetings, talks, and visits, Peder was also responsible for the regular congregational paper (*menighetsblad*). He expanded the framework for this publication, gave it the name *Sentrumsnytt*, and thus tried to address the city's entire population. The circulation was increased to two thousand so that a copy could go to every household in the city.

Peder also tried to make several contacts outside his church's conventional and traditional frameworks. He contacted the local amateur theater and got to use some of his interest in drama, and he was invited to talk about Christian drama and theater. He had been in contact with drama groups both in Oslo and at Drew University in the USA. He also sought out various political and social gatherings, e.g., political groups such as the young people's groups on both the right and the left sides of the political range, and offered lectures on relevant topics. In several such contexts, it was popular that he had something that was not yet quite common at this time: color slides from the United States. He had had a friend during his stay in the United States—a Japanese Methodist pastor from Hawaii—who was a skilled photographer and even participated in photo competitions. Peder received a number of slideshows from him, which he used in Harstad for all they were worth.

At the edge of the world?

In this way, he soon managed to fulfill his first subgoal: to get to know the city and become known in the city. But he was and remained a "southerner," coming from the south of Norway, a stranger both to northern Norway's specific dialects and cultural aspects. Once, he took a taxi to the Methodist church in Kvæfjord. The taxi driver asked what he had been doing before he came to Harstad. Peder told him about his theological studies in Oslo and

5. Hall-Hofsø, "Lørdagsmoro i Metodistkirken." *Harstad Tidende*, Saturday, December 14, 1957, 9.

6. Hall-Hofsø, *Da byen var Harstad*; cf. 62: "In my memories, four luminous names appear, four people who more than anyone else in Harstad gave the so-called disorganized youth a place to be. In addition to Pastor Peder Borgen who started the first youth club in the basement of the Methodist Church and Pastor Harald Larsen who further developed the club, the couple Leon and Gudrun Leonardsen shines in a very special light." See also Hall-Hofsø, "Den glemte ungdomsklubben," 13.

his PhD studies in the USA. Then the taxi driver looked at him, shook his head, and said: "With that education, you should have been something else than a pastor in the Methodist church in Harstad and Kvæfjord." Peder then aired his protests and told the driver that the Methodist Church in Norway was part of something much larger and more significant; it was part of an international church and that this area was an outpost of that large church. This larger perspective was a perspective that gave meaning to the more minor and perhaps more trivial aspects of being in the far north, in a small local church, struggling for its survival.

After his first year of service in Harstad, in the summer of 1957, Peder was ordained a pastor, or, as it is called in the jargon of the Methodist Church, "ordained as an elder." It happened at the Annual Conference's closing service on Sunday, June 30, in Bergen First Methodist Church. The ordinator was Bishop Odd Hagen, with overseer Zander Bratland, chairman of the Methodist Church's main board E. Anker Nilsen, and the African-American Methodist bishop Willis J. King.[7]

As a Methodist pastor, Peder also had the pleasure of inscribing some new members in the congregation: not many, admittedly, but some, and each one counts both in the small and in the larger context. Moreover, the youth club worked and grew in popularity. For a time, he was also a substitute teacher of Christian knowledge in primary school, a task that traditionally and because of the prevailing law should not have been possible for a non-Lutheran.

Money, money . . .

In the midst of all this, he struggled with himself. In retrospect, he could say: "I was a little feverish . . . I was almost a little intense inside myself, and there was an inner cry in me about having to struggle with a church where resources were so limited when it came to leaders, and I also missed my studies and research, I must say." The church's finances also represented a problem. The free churches had no support from the state, nor any form of refunding the church taxes. Such an arrangement was not established in an orderly form until 1969. The activities in the free churches and other denominations were run entirely by resources provided by their members and possibly other private sponsors.

In October of the first year, they had a special week focusing on economic resources in various ways and with the help of various activities. He thought it was a tough week: "Mentally, this week was very hard, and I can

---

7. See (anonymous), "Metodistenes årskonferanse, " 2.

hardly manage another such week. Am I called to be a beggar? The result concerning the income of money was good, but as a human being, I was poorer and more exhausted than I have ever been," he wrote in a letter to his parents.[8] The pastor's salary was a big part of what had to be collected by the help of such activities: "This was very difficult for me. Not that I got poorly paid, but the way some of it was collected. It was difficult because it was collected with direct reference to the pastor's salary. Moreover, without saying anything more about it . . . I cried at home once in the evening, in such a context."[9] It helped a little that he later arranged for distributions under the auspices of the congregation. But sometimes, he felt that there were too many raffle activities around as well.[10]

But he did not give up studying

Nevertheless, when Peder started his second year in Harstad, he was still optimistic. At the beginning of September, he wrote in a letter: "Now, at the start of a new year in Harstad, I am in good shape and ready to take the problems that might come. At the same time, I look forward to the years to come. They will be very exciting if the conditions are as they seem to be."[11] Did he foresee some possibilities for further studies? It might have been written between the lines.

However that might be, he did not give up his theological studies: in the evenings, he worked with his books, theological journals, and he used the phone. He had several telephone calls, not least to Professor Nils Alstrup Dahl in Oslo, about advice for further research arrangements and any opportunities to apply for scholarships for further research. Professor Dahl still believed that he should leave the American PhD dissertation and not try to improve it but rather expand his competence in Judaism in New Testament times as a background for further work with New Testament texts. But to be able to do so, Peder was dependent upon further scholarships. There were no opportunities for him to apply for job positions in theology in the public educational system in Norway; as a "dissenter"/non-Lutheran, he was not legally qualified. He had experienced this situation some years

---

8. Letter to his parents, dated October 16, 1956; now in the Borgen archive, National Library (Nasjonalbiblioteket), Oslo.

9. Borgen, interview by the author, February 14, 2017.

10. "The whole year is characterized by raffles to keep the boat afloat. I feel like a lottery director—next to being a fundraiser." Letter to his parents on April 16, 1957. Letter now in the Borgen archive, National Library, Oslo.

11. Letter by Borgen, dated September 1, 1957.

ago too. Therefore, he needed scholarships, but there were not many available in Norway. In fact, there were only two possibilities: a scholarship from the Faculty of Theology at the University of Oslo and a scholarship from the Research Council of Norway (NAVF).

Professor Einar Molland, who was a church historian, but who himself had started as a researcher in the New Testament field,[12] wanted Peder to apply in church history, and then more specifically in the field of Reformation church history; more specifically, of Augustana Variata—a variant of the Augsburg Confession (1530)—which Philip Melanchthon had edited in 1540 and 1542. Nevertheless, Peder's interests were still in the field of the New Testament, and both Professor Molland and Professor Nils A. Dahl encouraged him to apply.

But still not a Lutheran . . .

Then he applied for a scholarship; he applied both to the Faculty of Theology and the Research Council of Norway. As for the former, he was told orally that he was the strongest applicant. However, since he was not a member of the Church of Norway, that is, not a Lutheran, the university sought legal advice, and the conclusion was that an award of that particular scholarship had as a requirement that the recipient was a member of a Lutheran church. It was also a prerequisite that the research fellow should give one lecture a week at the Faculty, and such lecturing was closed to non-Lutherans.

Thus, that road was closed to the Methodist Peder—again.

A change of church membership was not relevant.

The application was withdrawn.

However, the scholarship made available by the NAVF did not have such a clause. Peder maintained the application submitted to the NAVF and was awarded a three-year research scholarship, which was later extended by another year. Hence, he finalized his ministry in Harstad in the summer of 1958 and returned to Oslo, now as a research fellow, ready for work at the Department of Religious History, Faculty of History and Philosophy.

---

12. See Molland, *Das paulinische Evangelion*, and his collection of articles, Molland, *Opuscula Patristica*.

5

Searching for Bread from Heaven: Research Fellow (1958–62)

IN AUGUST 1958, PEDER Borgen returned to the University of Oslo, starting his advanced studies in the New Testament. His institutional affiliation was primarily to the Department of Religious History, where Herman Ludin Jansen was the professor (1905-86, professor 1953-75).[1] Five years had passed since Borgen graduated from the Faculty of Theology as a Candidatus Theologiae and received scholarships for further studies in the United States in order to obtain a PhD degree. Then he had worked as a Methodist pastor in Harstad for two years. Now, however, he was ready for further studies, intending to obtain the Norwegian degree called "doctor theologiae" (abbreviated dr.theol.). He eventually rented a small apartment at Nils Bays street 7 in Oslo. However, he often returned home to Lillestrøm, his family, and the local Methodist church.

As a research fellow, it was primarily Professor N. A. Dahl whom Peder discussed his work with; even though Dahl had no official role as supervisor, he functioned very much as a mentor for Borgen during these years.

---

1. Peder Borgen initiated and edited a Festschrift published for Ludin Jansen on his eightieth birthday in 1985: See Borgen, ed., *Many and the One*.

A DISSERTATION COMES INTO BEING

The scholarship gave Peder good opportunities for further studies. Initially, the main topic was relatively open; the application did not contain a specific and detailed topic for a dissertation but rather a broad research area to be studied. And then, the focus was supposed to be gradually narrowed down to a specific topic, resulting in a dissertation that could be submitted for assessment for the dr.theol. degree. Non-Norwegian readers must remember that there was no doctoral *program* in Norway in these years: no courses to be followed, no papers to be submitted. The doctoral students were supposed to work mainly by themselves and then submit a full-blown dissertation at the end of their scholarship period.[2]

The theme of his application

Borgen formulated the focus of his application thus: "To examine the interpretive history of Old Testament passages in Judaism and early Christianity, with special reference to Psalms 110 and 2. In addition, to prepare for the publication of some studies already begun in the New Testament."[3] In applying to NAVF, one initially applied for three years, but one had to submit a new application with a report on how the work proceeded each year along the way. Borgen's first application was for the academic year 1958–59. It is evident that he followed the advice of Professor N. A. Dahl to familiarize himself somewhat more broadly with the New Testament's historical background with a view to shed light on some specific NT texts and themes. Such a background orientation would, in principle, include both the Jewish background and the Greco-Roman world and culture.

Gradually, the focus, and thus the applications, became more precise, and thus Philo of Alexandria, Palestinian midrash, and the Gospel of John became more central in his work, and finally, the focus was narrowed down to the miracle of the manna and the Gospel of John chapter 6.

---

2. That is, if they had obtained a scholarship. As very few scholarships were available, some persons worked on a dissertation in their spare time and submitted their work to the university when they thought it was good enough to be considered acceptable for a public disputation.

3. From *Sammendrag av søknad for budsjettåret 1/7-58–30/6-1959*. Now in Borgen's private archive.

Eureka!

Sometimes a new and illuminating idea and focus of a dissertation are apparent to a doctoral student almost from the beginning; in other cases, he or she must work hard to define and delimit the particular theme to be investigated. Peder worked on his studies, and for some time, his crucial task was to find a sufficiently limited area for further investigation; that is, a topic that could be narrowed down to a doctoral dissertation.

Early in his studies, as he was on travel, he had to spend some evening hours at the central railway station in Copenhagen. He picked up his Novum Testamentum (Latin term for the New Testament) and started reading. Much later, he described what happened as he was reading:

> Interestingly, an important observation was made in the waiting room at the Main Railroad Station in Copenhagen. I had to wait for some time on a train and sitting on a bench I looked at the text of John 6 in my Greek New Testament. I noticed that words from the Old Testament quotation were also found in the subsequent verses. I picked up a pencil and underscored the repeated words and learned how each word and phrase was interpreted. The last word in the Old Testament quotation in Joh 6:31: "to eat," was added in v. 49, and it was then in the center of the exposition in vv. 49–58. Thus, an element of a systematically structured exposition can be traced.[4]

The last part of John 6 contains or represents a quotation, but it is difficult to say exactly where the quotation is taken from, but it probably relates to Exodus 16:4, 15, and possibly also to Nehemiah 9:15 and Psalm 7:24. With these observations made, Borgen could later—having left the railroad station and able to continue his studies at home—expand his focus thus:

> With these observations made, I searched for examples of parallel expository activity, in the Jewish midrashim, and particularly in the expository writings of Philo of Alexandria. It can also be examined how various biblical traditions may be alluded to and also may be woven into the exposition. In this way it is seen how a received and given text is applied and used in a meaningful

---

4. The description given here is taken from Paul N. Anderson's foreword to the third edition of Borgen's dissertation, *Bread from Heaven*, xi–xii; Borgen's dissertation was originally published in the series Supplements to Novum Testamentum 10 (Leiden: Brill, 1965, reprinted 1985). Anderson notes that he is able to provide this story because it was shared by Borgen in personal correspondence, dated September 2016. The same story was also given to me in an interview with Borgen, February 14, 2017.

way in new situations to new persons and groups. On this basis received and applied aspects of meanings are brought together.[5]

This is mainly what is investigated and argued in his doctoral dissertation.[6] Peder Borgen had experienced his *eureka*! ("I have found!").[7] Thus, it eventually turned out, as he continued working on and expanding the hypothesis, that Philo provided some even better parallels than the Rabbinica. He would then examine these further and see if they contained features he had to take up to see if the use of the Old Testament in such writings could shed light on John 6. The dissertation was eventually entitled *Bread from Heaven*.

After his *eureka* discovery, he continued to work on both the writings of the rabbis and Philo. In his view, the Gospel of John not only becomes a collection of words and actions of Jesus (cf. John 20: 30–31; 21: 24–25, cp. Luke 1: 1–4), but it also becomes exegesis, scriptural interpretation.[8] Jesus' life and message are interpreted in the Gospel scriptures in the light of the Old Testament. Such observations, according to Borgen, also confirm the hypothesis that the Gospel of John belongs in a Jewish context.

The Rabbinica, Philo of Alexandria, and John

Borgen's American PhD was a study of the Lukan writings; now, he had to carry out precisely what Professor Dahl had advised him to do: study works relevant to the background of the New Testament. He found he had to study rabbinic literature and Philo of Alexandria as relevant material to understand the Gospel of John.

The Rabbinica

The Jews had an extensive oral tradition, representing *interpretations* of the Mosaic Law, *edifying accounts* that contained actualizations of the Law, and

---

5. Borgen, *Bread from Heaven*, xii (foreword by Paul N. Anderson).

6. Peder has described these discoveries, and the working hypotheses he applied, in some articles that were published as early as during his years as a research fellow; see here Borgen, "Unity and Discourse in John 6," and Borgen, "Brød fra himmel og fra jord." See also Borgen, "Observations on the Midrashic Character of John 6."

7. *Eureka*: a statement attributed to the Greek scientist Archimedes (ca. 287–212 BC). When he immersed his body in a hot tub, he discovered the law of buoyancy of bodies in water. In his joy at the discovery, he is said to have run naked out into the street shouting "*Eureka*."

8. See Borgen, "Johannesprologen som eksegese."

some other material used to substantiate interpretations of the Law. The first was called *Halaka*; the term comes from the verb *HaLaK*, which means "to walk, live," and thus indicates "rules of living." The edifying narratives are called *Aggada* (or *Haggada*), which comes from a verb meaning "to tell." Recent research tends to downwrite the differences between the two.

By Rabbinica, or the rabbinic writings, is meant several Jewish writings that—in the form we have them now—were created during the approximately first six centuries CE. These books contain many different traditions. Some of these may go back to oral traditions before the New Testament writings were created, while others date from the same period as the NT. Others are much younger. Particularly well-known and relevant are the so-called *Targums*, paraphrasing translations of biblical scriptures into Aramaic, and *midrash*. Then we have the *Mishnah*, usually considered the earliest authoritative collection of Jewish oral law. And not to forget the great collections called *Talmud*; the Palestinian or Jerusalem Talmud (fifth century CE), and the Babylonian Talmud (sixth century CE). These two collections are interpretations of the Mishnah, also based on oral traditions.

Philo, a Jew from the Egyptian Alexandria

The other group of writings that Peder had to learn more about was the writings of Philo of Alexandria. At the time of Philo, there were probably more Jews living outside the land of Israel than in their homeland. But both in the Diaspora in general and in the city of Alexandria, the Jews represented a minority, even though they were a relatively large minority group in Alexandria. The Jews of Alexandria were not only a minority in numbers, but they also belonged to a monotheistic religion and as such were clearly in the minority religiously in the society of that time.

Philo was a Jewish Bible interpreter (exegete), theologian, philosopher, and politician, and lived all his life in Alexandria, Egypt.[9] Philo's year of birth and death, however, are no longer known, but he probably lived in the period approximately from 20 BCE to 50 CE.

Philo's literary output is enormous. We have preserved over forty of his works, and through hints in his writings and comments by some church fathers, we can assume that his production must at least have included another twenty works. As a philosopher and theologian, Philo was influenced

---

9. Peder Borgen himself has written several introductions to Philo of Alexandria; see his "Philo, Diasporajøde fra Aleksandria," "Filo fra Aleksandria," "Philo of Alexandria," "Philo of Alexandria: A Critical," and *Philo of Alexandria: An Exegete for His Time.*

by several currents; Platonic, Stoic, and Pythagorean ideas are especially prominent in his works. Nevertheless, most of his writings must be read and understood as interpretations of the Law of Moses.

Borgen later published many articles about Philo and his life and work, or articles in which Philo played a significant role. Looking back on Borgen's personal life, one might even find some similarities between himself and Philo. Both belonged to a religious "denomination" that was a minority in their local communities; both groups were discriminated against, and both fought to assert their rights in a pluralistic society. In other words, Philo was not only helpful in understanding interpretative methods in the Gospel of John. Borgen became fascinated by Philo; in some areas, Borgen even shared a personal destiny with Philo.

The Gospel of John

The Gospel of John, like the other three New Testament gospels, is about the life and preaching of Jesus. But if one proceeds from the first three gospels to the fourth, the Gospel of John, one will immediately realize that the last mentioned is remarkably different. Borgen published three articles in international journals on the Gospel of John during his time as a research fellow. Two of these are about his discoveries in the sixth chapter of the gospel.[10] The third was about another well-known problem in gospel research; namely, how should one understand the relationship between the origin of the Gospel of John and those of Matthew, Mark, and Luke, also called the Synoptic Gospels.[11]

Different views and theories have been asserted throughout the history of research on how to consider the question of the Gospel of John's relationship to the other three gospels: One might mention *the supplementary theory* (the Gospel of John supplements the Synoptics), *the theory of independence* (John is quite independent of the Synoptics), and *the theory of interpretation* or *theory of suppression* (John interprets and/or suppresses the Synoptics). Peder addressed this in an article published in 1959,[12] and he also continued to work on these issues later, right up to his retirement. The article from 1959 is a study focused on the relationship between the Gospel of John and the Synoptic Gospels in the account (s) of the sufferings of Jesus. Peder's thesis here is that the Gospel of John is mainly based on an

---

10. Borgen, "Unity of the Discourse in John"; Borgen, "Observations on the Midrashic Character of John 6."

11. Borgen, "John and the Synoptics."

12. Borgen, "John and the Synoptics."

independent tradition. However, some Synoptic pericopes (a professional term for text segments in the three first gospels) or parts of pericopes have been assimilated into this tradition. Different elements from different Synoptic narratives have been merged within these pericopes or in parts of the pericopes. As the Gospel of John seems to depend on the Synoptic Gospels only in certain pericopes, these likely represent oral traditions brought to John in a form where they were already merged. This feature may explain the relatively great freedom that the Gospel of John shows in its use of such traditions.

An intermezzo: a trip to the Soviet Union, spring 1959

We are to leave his research for a while. It turns out that Peder was not an ascetic who devoted all his time and energy only to studies in Philo, the Rabbinica, and John. He became engaged in several other activities too. Accordingly, before we continue with his doctoral studies, we must have a look at an exciting travel to the Soviet Union in 1959, his ecumenical interest and activities—and the fact that he met a girl named Inger.

Early in his time as a research fellow in Oslo, Peder met a couple of research fellows from the United States: Karen Bruce was a research fellow in sociology with the Sami in Finnmark as her field of interest; the others were Graydon Snyder and his wife, Lois. Graydon Snyder (1930 2016) was working on his American DTh. thesis at Princeton Theological Seminary, and had received a Fulbright scholarship to study for a time in Norway.[13]

The Soviet Union

The American scholars wanted to go to Russia and invited Peder to join them on their trip.[14] At the end of April 1959, they left for Russia in a Volkswagen Beetle. Moscow was their primary goal as they were to visit an American student there. In addition, they wanted to see and experience church life in Russia. For Peder, the trip also became an extension of his ecumenical horizon.

---

13. Snyder later became a well-known and recognized scholar with a special interest in the early Christian church. He was a professor of the New Testament at Bethany Theological Seminary in Richmond, Indiana, from 1959 to 1987. He then was professor and dean at Chicago Theological Seminary from 1987 to 1994. He published a number of books and articles. See further here: http://www.legacy.com/obituaries/fortwayne/obituary.aspx?pid=180178618.

14. According to Borgen, "Crossing of the Red Sea," 77, note 1.

Starting out from Oslo, they drove to Stockholm; then by boat to Turku, Finland; then by car to Helsinki and into the Soviet Union. At the Soviet border, they got another passenger, a "guide" (read: a Russian inspector), so the small Volkswagon Beetle became uncomfortably full. In the Soviet Union, they traveled via Leningrad, where they stayed one day. The return trip went via Poland (Warsaw), to German Sassnitz, and from there by ferry over to Trelleborg in Sweden.

Peder's journalistic interests led him, after they had returned home, to publish several articles in which he recounted their experiences "behind the Iron Curtain."[15] It was relevant reading stuff for many because it was not very common to go on a tourist trip to Russia in those years. One experience demonstrating the unusualness of traveling to the Soviet Union was the time spent applying for the necessary papers. Due to the Russian bureaucracy providing these necessary travel documents, everything took a long time.

They spent several days in Moscow and got to experience May 1 there, among other things. While Prime Minister Nikita Khrushchev and his men stood on the balcony watching the impressive military parade that filled the Red Square, Peder and his entourage stood on the outskirts gathering impressions from all the people there. They experienced a bustling Russian people's life that unfolded in the shadow of the Red Square and its parades.

Church life in the Soviet Union (Moscow)

The guide they were given claimed that only older people went to the churches in the Soviet Union, and if they saw some younger people participating, he alleged it was something their parents had forced them to do. However, Peder and the three Americans were allowed to attend the midnight mass the night between Easter Eve and Easter Sunday in a large cathedral. The church was crowded, and outside there were so many people that the streets were blocked, and the police had to use a loudspeaker and a car to keep order. But the number of churches in the city was not large, even though the population had increased in recent years. They managed, however, to get in touch with some younger people, and then they got a different version than the official one: there were also many young people who sought to the churches.

It was a prerequisite that the evangelical churches were not allowed to stand out as separate denominations in the Soviet Union at this time. In

---

15. Borgen, "Med bil bak jernteppet," *Vårt Land*, May 19, 1959; "Inntrykk fra kirkelivet i Sovjet-unionen i dag," *Aftenposten*, May 26 and 27, 1959.

practice, many churches were baptistic or leaned in that direction. When it came to development opportunities for the churches, the people they met were not very optimistic. This pessimism had partly economic reasons and was partly due to the relationship with the state and its prevailing ideology. In order to have peace, most Christians and their congregations withdrew from any public political activities and let the state take care of its own affairs. Hence, the Christian faith was kept in a private sphere without providing any critical political or theological focus on the actions of the state. This condition became part of their survival strategy as minorities. In addition, the economy made it difficult for non-Orthodox congregations in particular to train priests and leaders. Thus, the lack of leaders became urgent, and the danger of isolation was great. Peder wrote that they experienced the churches' attitudes as follows: "When the churches thus lack independent thinking and initiative in social and cultural life, it is close to not only accepting but even without further ado approving what is happening in these areas."[16] As a Methodist, he found this withdrawal from society understandable but nevertheless regrettable.

In Moscow, they also had another unexpected experience that turned out to be profitable when they left the country. In Moscow, they got a new guide, Karl Zimjonovich Tzyn, and it turned out that he was born in Norway in 1915 and had lived there until 1927, when the family moved back to the Soviet Union.[17] Tzyn was trained as a history teacher and was employed by Intourist as a guide. Since he had lived in Norway and thus knew Norwegian, they developed a very good relationship with him. He arranged it so that each of them was able to buy a genuine Russian icon, and when they left for Norway, he assisted them all the way to the border. There was no actual check of luggage on departure, and Peder thought it was not at least due to Tzyn's presence. Thus, Peder brought his icon safely home, which was not a common procedure at this time.

It turned out later that year that this icon was to play an important role when he met a student named Inger Solveig Duesund.

Ecumenical commitment

It was the *theologian* Peder Borgen, who was both politically and ecclesiastically interested and engaged, who traveled to Russia in 1959. After the great

16. "Inntrykk fra kirkelivet," *Aftenposten*, May 27, 1959; Borgen, "Med bil bak jernteppet," *Vårt Land*, May 19, 1959, 2 and 8.

17. Jevne, Per, "Karl Zimjonovitsj: Russisk skøyte-ekspert," *Uke-Adressa*, October 31, 1987, 16–17.

youth conference that was arranged in Oslo in 1947, Peder had been engaged in ecumenical work, and his ecumenical interest and commitment grew even greater after the founding of the World Council of Churches (see above).

Peder and Peter Wilhelm

In the coming years, especially in the late 1950s, Peder established a good relationship with a person who would later become his professor colleague in Trondheim, namely, Peter Wilhelm Bøckman (1927–2006). Together they agreed that it was time to establish an institute that could promote ecumenical contact between the various churches in Norway.

Actually, it's a little odd that they developed such a good relationship, because they were indeed very different personalities. Peder was an ardent Methodist, and Peter Wilhelm an equally convinced Lutheran and a defender of the Church of Norway as a state church. They were also different in temperament. But they worked together in mutual respect, both as fellows in Oslo and later as colleagues in Trondheim. Perhaps it also helped that they worked in two different fields, Peder in biblical studies and Peter Wilhelm in systematic theology with an emphasis on ethics.[18]

The Church of Norway's own ecumenical body, the Norwegian Institute for Interchurch Relations (established 1951; in 1971 renamed the Council on Ecumenical and International Relations), represented the Church of Norway when dealing with international affairs, not at least in the context of the World Council of Churches (WCC). But it did not consider it its task to conduct ecumenical and interchurch work *within* Norway. Peder and Peter Wilhelm agreed that it was unfortunate that only one denomination should represent the WCC in Norway. The WCC was an association that many different churches were involved in, including the Methodist Church. Thus, Peder Borgen and Peter Wilhelm Bøckman became engaged and established a contact group which they called Institute of Ecumenical Contact, established on October 27, 1959.

They worked closely with the youth department of the WCC, and they also had much contact with church academies in Germany, the Netherlands, and Switzerland, and it turned out that several denominations were

---

18. Peter Wilhelm Bøckman graduated from the University of Oslo in the autumn of the same year as Peder (spring 1953), and he was a research fellow in theology at the University of Oslo in 1956–59, and then a research fellow at NAVF in 1962–63, and at the University of Oslo again in 1964–67. After being employed at the University of Oslo for several years (1967–76), he became a professor at the University of Trondheim in 1976, and thus a colleague of Peder Borgen.

involved in these movements.¹⁹ Through the World Council of Churches, they got in touch with people who were interested in building some relations in Norway. Thus, they could eventually have three ecumenical conferences, all held at Stabekk near Oslo in the years of 1960-62. The new institute was the main organizer, but they collaborated with various agencies, inter alia, the Norwegian Christian Student Union, the Bible Society, the Methodist Church, and the Norwegian Baptist Society. Peter Wilhelm and Peder were the leaders of the first two conferences; the third was held after Peder had left for the United States to take up a teaching position there. Both national and international organizations and institutions supported them with funds so that the conferences could be well organized. And even though it turned out that the activities of the institute established by Borgen and Bøckman lasted for only a few years, it represented an impulse and inspiration to several people who later became active in various church contexts.

Norwegian mission and ecumenism: a minefield

The relationship between Norwegian mission and ecumenism could, at this time, sometimes appear as a kind of minefield. The reluctance was great within some of the central mission organizations towards ecumenical work, especially how it was conducted in and by the World Council of Churches.

In Norway, then and now, Lutheran mission activities were primarily carried out by independent mission organizations, not by the Church of Norway as such. In addition, most of the mission organizations were low-church and lay organizations. To Peder, this was almost a contradiction in terms.

By the time we get to 1959, the World Council of Churches had existed for eleven years, and gradually there was a growing interest in incorporating the International Mission Council (IMC) into the World Council of Churches. This question was raised in the Norwegian Mission Council (NMC), both in 1957 and 1959, but with negative conclusions. NMC would not support such an association. However, that is how it ended up anyway; the IMC was integrated into the World Council of Churches (1961). Concerning the question of whether the Norwegian Mission Council (NMC) should be included in this new context, the result was that the NMC chose to remain outside. No other country's mission council that was a member of the IMC chose such a position; everyone else joined the new association.

---

19. In this context, church academies are to be understood as forums for faith, culture, debates, and dialogues, and constitute a movement dedicated to serve the church, culture, and society from the basis of the Christiaan faith. See http://www.kirkeakademiene.no/parent-page/norwegian-church-academies/.

There was a rather intense debate about these issues in Norway in these years, but I cannot dig further into this broader debate here, but direct my spotlight on the contribution from Peder Borgen.

Borgen: church and mission belong together

Peder published his view in the Methodists' magazine *Kristelig Tidende* under the headline "Church and mission belong together." Here he argued loud and clear that "Mission and church belong together, biblically and Christianly they are one."[20] Peder points out that the Norwegian constellation with a majority church and many mission organizations that are admittedly *in* this church but not *under* it, is, in fact, a somewhat peculiar situation. The situation in most other churches, according to Borgen, is generally quite different than it is within the Church of Norway.

Here Peder puts his finger on a typical feature of the Norwegian church landscape. In reality, two different ecclesiologies collided here. Somewhat later, Peder had the opportunity to present and expand on his views in an interview in a weekly newspaper labeled *Vår Kirke*, an interview which was reprinted in *Kristelig Tidende*.[21] Here he first presents the Methodist Church as a "church of synthesis," containing elements both from the Anglican Church (liturgical features), from the Reformed churches (sanctification and active outward Christianity), and from Lutheranism (justification). Moreover, he points out that they do not have the tension between church and organizations, parish church and houses of prayer (*bedehus*). Such tension "is unthinkable in a Methodist church. There, the church idea and the mission idea will always be one and the same" (444). When asked about what he thought was the Methodist Church's most important task in Norway today, he answered that "The Methodist Church's basic task is always to be a mission church. In Norway, we can be a testimony of a type of church where congregation and mission form a unit" (477). Furthermore, when asked what the Methodist Church's ecumenical task in Norway is, the answer is "confessional awareness and openness to the outside world" (477), a view he thought could also have something to say to less ecumenically oriented circles in the country. In this context, he also expresses the wish that "all ecumenically interested people in Norway should work to establish a council that includes all evangelical churches" (477), since Norway at that time was one of the few countries in the world that did not have

---

20. Borgen, "Kirketanke og misjonstanke," *Kristelig Tidende* 88 (1959) 438.

21. "En kirke hvor menighet og misjon er ett," *Kristelig Tidende* 90 (1961) 444 and 477. References in the text are to this article.

an ecumenical church council. It took several years before such a council was established in Norway. We will return to the question of ecumenicity in Norway in a later chapter.

But now we turn to another "issue" that had already been going on for some time; she bore the name of Inger Solveig.

6

Peder and Inger

At the end of July 1961, Arve Solstad (1935–2016), a journalist (and later editor-in-chief) of the Oslo-based newspaper *Dagbladet*, decided that he should make a visit to the main university library to see if anyone was involved in studies there in the middle of a hot summer.[1] As he expected, he did not find many, but he did find some persistent ascetics in the basement, in the study room, where each researcher could be given a shielded desk. There he found a lecturer in history, Ottar Dahl (1924–2011), who prepared his autumn lectures; a lecturer in classical philology, Knut Kleve (1926–2017), who wrote his doctoral dissertation on Epicurus; the Greek scholar Aleksis Karagianis, who was working on a theme from the history of Drammen, a city close to Oslo; and the research fellow Peder Borgen, who was struggling with Philo from Alexandria, and who had just completed an article on "At the Age of Twenty in I QSa," a theme from the Dead Sea Scrolls.[2]

The journalist had his prejudices against the theologians ("Theologians are probably not the most enthusiastic supporters of spending their times in the sun," he wrote). Moreover, he got the impression that Philo, the Dead Sea Scrolls, and synagogue sermons were so much more important than summer vacation that Peder did not even hear or observe "the clatter of girls' shoes on the street outside the windows, or the summer-dressed girls who set the course for the city center."[3]

---

1. See Solstad, "Greker sliter med Drammen, "7–8.
2. See Borgen, "At the Age of Twenty."
3. Solstad, "Greker sliter med Drammen, "7–8.

However, what the journalist from Dagbladet obviously did not know was that Peder was already engaged at this time, and the wedding day was only a few months away...

INGER SOLVEIG DUESUND

In 1958, Olaf Duesund was appointed as the new parish priest to Sandsvær; that is, to the same municipality where Peder's mother, Harda, had grown up. He later became a parish pastor and provost in Kongsberg.[4]

In 1936 he married Inga Jenny Ravndal Ødegård (1908–2010). Together they had six children; the four youngest moved in with their parents at Sandsvær, while the two oldest, Inger and Ingunn, were students in Oslo and lived in an apartment there.

Inger, a Lutheran pastor's daughter

Inger Solveig (b. 1937) attended a school in community and social work, (*Norges kommunal og sosialhøgskole*) at this time. Sometime after the family had moved to Sandsvær, she visited her parents there. Sitting one day in the living room, she was flipping through what many call the *Presteboka*, a "who is who" volume providing brief biographical descriptions—with pictures—of all the pastors in the Church of Norway and other Norwegian theologians.[5] Inger Duesund thought it was a collection of rather serious-looking men. Many of them were friends and contemporaries of her father. However, she found one person who did not carry a black robe and pipe collar; he was young and had the widest smile.

However, he was a Methodist![6]

In the autumn of 1959, after Peder had been on his trip to the Soviet Union, he held a slide show in the Student Association in Oslo, and he also showed the icon he had bought in Moscow and brought with him home.

---

4. Olaf Duesund (1904–89) graduated from the Free Faculty of Theology (Menighetsfakultetet) in 1933 and was ordained in 1934. After a few years as a traveling priest in the Norwegian Israel Mission, and for a time as an auxiliary pastor in Bergen, he was employed as secretary general of the Norwegian Israel Mission in 1937, at only thirty-three years old.

5. This is, as the title says, an overview of *Priests in the Church of Norway and Other Theological Candidates*, and contains pictures and short biographies of the individual theologians. Since Peder became cand.theol. in 1953, he was registered in the edition that was published in 1958: Bolling, *Norges prester*. The next edition was published in 1974.

6. Information from my interview with her, March 14, 2017.

Inger came to this meeting with a friend, and in his causerie, Peder said that those who wanted to take a closer look and find out more about the icon could do so after the lecture. Inger was one of those who stopped; she recognized "him from the pastor's who-is-who book." But there was—apparently—no immediate follow-up contact. Later, however, they met at the student café and conversed, and then Peder asked her to go with him to the cinema . . .

When Peder was approaching the end of his four-year term as a research fellow at the University in Oslo, he was looking for a teaching position. But he still had to deal with some opposition; it was still not possible for him—as a non-Lutheran—to get a teaching position in theology at any public Norwegian teaching institution.

He, therefore, had to cross some borders again, orientating himself abroad. During the last years, however, rumors had been passed around in Methodist circles that there was a guy in Norway who would soon be available for, and interested in, a teaching position. Hence, in 1960 he was offered a professorship at three different institutions: Southern Methodist University, Perkins School of Theology, Dallas, Texas; Wesley Theological Seminary, Washington, DC; and at Theological Seminary, Sumatra, Indonesia. However, only Wesley was willing to postpone his start until 1962, and as it was important for Peder to finish his dissertation on *Bread from Heaven* before taking up a new position, this became decisive for his choice. Thus, it became Wesley, and he moved to Washington in the summer of 1962.

Inger and Peder got engaged in the middle of 1960, and on December 30, 1961, at 4:00 p.m. on the same day and place as Peder's parents, Harda and Omar Emil, got married thirty-seven years earlier, Inger and Peder were married in the Methodist church in Hvittingfoss, Sandsvær. They even had the same organist as that Peder's parents had in their wedding in 1924, namely Marta Grønvold, Harda's cousin. The Methodist pastor Gustav Søiland was the officiating pastor, and the bride's father, pastor Olaf Duesund, delivered the sermon. The wedding party was held at Duesunds, in the rectory at Efteløt in Ytre Sandsvær.

Several years later, on a day in the middle of May 2017, all of the Duesund children were gathered in the old vicarage at Efteløt to reminisce a bit together with a journalist from the local newspaper *Laagendalsposten*.[7] The large house of approximately five hundred square meters was, and is, no longer in use as a parsonage but was rented out to a Danish couple. But in Duesund's time, it functioned as a traditional rectory, with the priest's office

---

7. Martinsen, ". . . som om det var i går," *Laagendalsposten*, May 20, 2017, 13–16.

in the house. The Duesund children reminisced about farming, schooling, and children's play during the summer and winter times.

Inger and Peder reminisced about their wedding.

Therefore, the joy of reunion was even greater when they entered the main living room and saw that the Danish tenants had arranged the table as for a wedding dinner. Inger and Peder then could even better evoke the memories of their wedding day:

"I still remember some of what you said in your speech," Inger told her husband, Peder. "You said we would be fine since I was a social worker, and you were a pastor."[8]

The celebration later that year of fifty-six years of marriage was a good confirmation of what Peder had expressed in his speech.

Inger: from a Lutheran majority to Methodist minority

When Inger and Peder got married, Inger had one semester left of her education in social work, and during the months before they moved to the USA, they lived in Torvet 1 in Lillestrøm.

The fact that the Lutheran Inger Duesund was dating and later got married to the Methodist Peder Borgen meant that she eventually had to take a closer look at how she should relate to these two different denominations. She describes the problem thus:

> When I met Peder, and he belonged to the Methodist Church, I had to think carefully about this: If we were to be a couple and possibly a family, then it was important to me that we had the same church home, and that we could go to church together and with our children. But I had to think this through thoroughly because my father was a pastor in the Lutheran State Church, and that was what I had grown up with. Moreover, Peder was an ordained pastor in the Methodist church, and for him, it was not really an option to become a Lutheran. He never asked me to join the Methodist Church, so this was my own choice. I asked Peder to give me a book about what the Methodist Church stood for and what they believed in, and in what they differed from the Lutherans, and he did, and I found that it was not difficult to accept. Hence, I applied and was accepted into the Methodist Church. Still, it was a long step for me to take . . .[9]

---

8. Martinsen, ". . .som om det var i går," 14.
9. Inger Borgen, interview by the author, March 14, 2017.

What did the long step consist of for Inger? As she states, it was not dogmatic, that is, doctrinal differences, that constituted the most significant problems. She read and understood what the Methodist Church taught and practiced, "and it was not difficult to accept." Hence, she signed up and was admitted to the First Methodist Church at Grünerløkka in Oslo.

Nevertheless, she experienced something else that she had not seen as clearly in advance: "I actually experienced that I in a way was resigning a little from a/s Norway, almost as if I gave up, gave up my citizenship and signed up for a free church, or sect, or dissenter as I then became."[10] She did not experience that those closest to her reacted negatively to her conversion; they had tacitly thought it was natural. But she noticed reactions in her wider circle of friends. In the light of further reflection, she described it many years later (2017) thus:

> On the other hand, I experienced something that was a little weird to me because they wondered what it was I had now become a member of, something they did not know anything about, and which placed me somewhat as an outsider. These reactions gave me many thoughts about how it was to grow up as a member of a free church. As for myself, I experienced that I had a leg in each camp, understood a lot of the differences between the two denominations, and thought a lot and wondered a lot about this strange situation in Norway, seen from a church point of view.[11]

At this time, members of the various free churches were still called "dissenters." This term had been used in Norwegian law since 1845 and had become a fixed term in the Norwegian language. Although the term "dissenter" could initially have been a neutral term, that is, used more generally about a person who had a different opinion than the majority, it was predominantly used in Norway in contexts where one separated those who deviated from the Lutheran religious beliefs so dominant in the country, that is, in relation to the majority church, the Church of Norway. Today, the term "dissenter" is anachronistic. But this was not the case in the early 1960s, and it can still appear as a negative and discriminatory term. The free churches are now officially called "religious communities or congregations outside the Church of Norway." However, that this designation is still not perceived as adequate for everybody who is a member of a non-Lutheran free church has been evident in several ways in recent years. Some borders still remain.

---

10. Inger Borgen, interview by the author, March 14, 2017.
11. Inger Borgen, interview by the author, March 14, 2017.

For Inger, the social transition was more challenging than the theological one. She experienced something of what had followed Peder throughout his life: the feeling of being a minority, of being different; the sense of what in our time is called being "excluded," being an "outsider." Of still having to cross borders to be fully accepted.

However, she did not have much time to think further about this. After graduating in the summer of 1962, other and more exciting things were on their schedule; they were to move to the United States. And they looked forward to it; newlyweds and newly graduated as a social worker and further educated as a theologian as they were, they faced new jobs in a different country. The United States was certainly not new or foreign to either Inger or Peder. Peder had an almost three-year period as a research fellow behind him in the USA, and Inger had been an au pair in the USA for a year (1957–58), right after completing her artium/college. But still, it was the beginning of a new phase in their lives. Not everyone in the family was happy that they were going to the United States: "Now you will probably stay over there because you will have so many opportunities," said Inger's mother, Inga Jenny.[12] She was born in the United States and knew what the newlyweds were up to.

However, she was wrong. After four years, they were back in Norway.

---

12. Borgen, interview by the author, March 14, 2017.

7

Crossing into the Diaspora of the USA (1962–66)

INGER AND PEDER BORGEN traveled to the United States in the summer of 1962. Inger had completed her education as a social worker, and Peder had completed his research fellowship time at the University of Oslo. However, he had not yet completed his Norwegian doctoral dissertation. He had to take the work with him to the United States to complete it alongside his work as an assistant—later associate—professor at Wesley Theological Seminary.

Was the migration to the USA an escape from difficult conditions for dissenters in Norway? Inger was probably too new as a Methodist to think in such terms. Nor had she met any closed doors. The closed doors were Peder's experience. Was it perhaps an expression of a desire for adventures? Not really. In the 1950s, there was a steady stream of job-seeking youth moving to the United States.[1] However, in the transition to the 1960s and beyond, it gradually became considerably more challenging to obtain a work permit "over there" at all. Peder had been there before as a research fellow; now he traveled to use his education in a job opportunity he did not get in Norway.

To him, it represented a necessary border crossing—into a diaspora.

However, they did not travel to the United States with the explicit purpose of staying there indefinitely. It turned out later that Peder had been keeping an eye on the work opportunities as a New Testament scholar back

---

1. In the 1950s, the Norwegian American Line had almost 113,000 passengers on its trips to the United States. See Mørkhagen, *Farvel Norge*, 563.

home in Norway. Like many others in a diaspora situation, he did not forget his homeland but stayed in contact.

ESTABLISHING A NEW HOME IN THE UNITED STATES

Wesley Theological Seminary, of the American Episcopal Methodist Church, was located in Washington, DC, in a well-established and almost fashionable neighborhood that included several embassies: Massachusetts Avenue N.W. The seminary was established as early as 1881 but was for decades located in Westminster, Maryland, under the name Westminster Theological Seminary. When the seminary moved to Washington in the late 1950s, the name was also changed to Wesley Theological Seminary. It was by then the first seminary in the United States to have "Wesley" in its name. When Inger and Peder arrived there, the seminary comprised 325 students and had a teaching staff of 19 and an administrative staff.

Inger and Peder in Washington, fall 1962, with their new Volkswagen.

Inger's first job as a social worker

Initially, Inger thought she should use this opportunity for further studies, but that turned out to be somewhat problematic. When she contacted the university, they could not place her Norwegian social school education into their USA system but wanted to put her in line with all those coming from Asia and Africa, which they could not figure out on what level they belonged. The conclusion of the university administration was that they advised her to take American college education, a suggestion which to Inger meant that she had to take her social education over again, but now in the American system. That was not an acceptable option, so she turned her attention to the prevalent job market and eventually got a job at a private children's hospital, The Children's Convalescent Hospital. They accepted her Norwegian education, and Inger worked there until their first child, Heidi, was born in spring 1965.

Consequently, this is how Inger met the American health and social services, with her own experiences from what some Americans tend to call the "socialist" system of Norway. And it gave her some reason for further reflection. She experienced the tremendous social difference between those who had money and those who did not and between white and black people in America. It gave a newly graduated Norwegian social worker many second thoughts.

Battered children

Another issue that gave her cause for further reflection and perhaps strengthened her thoughts about getting further education in family care and family therapy was her encounter with life-weary children. She brought her interest in family care with her from Norway, where she had worked with Albert Assev, one of Norway's most famous family therapists.[2]

In her daily work, Inger experienced that they admitted several small children to the hospital who had lost their zest for life due to lack of care. She learned to know the terms and phenomenons of "battered children" and "failure to thrive" in a way she had never experienced at home in Norway. "It gave a twenty-five-year-old a lot of second thoughts."[3] In this way, Inger came straight into a field that just then received much attention in American

---

2. Albert Assev (1922–2013) helped start Norway's first family counselling office in 1957, and for more than thirty years he was the head of this office. See https://www.idunn.no/fokus/2013/04/albert_assev_-_9_juni_1922_21_sept_2013.

3. Inger Borgen, interview by the author, March 14, 2017.

social-medical circles.[4] One of the reasons for this attention was that in July the very same year an article was published that put an intense spotlight on the phenomenon called "battered-child syndrome" as a social problem.[5] It is now called "child abuse," and it has been a well-known phenomenon for several years in most societies. In the United States in the 1960s, where Inger's primary field of responsibility was to care for the parents of the children admitted to the hospital, she encountered it along with the great social differences that an American metropolis contained. She experienced meeting people who "had no money to pay for their hospital stay, no money to pay for medicines, and that municipal hospitals could lack soap, and that they lacked many different other things too."[6]

Heidi

Then came the moment when she was to give birth to her first child. Heidi was born in late May 1965 at Sibley Memorial Hospital. Moreover, Inger got to experience another phenomenon: American women did not breastfeed their children. The United States was different in this area as well:

> I received excellent care since I could go to a private hospital because I had insurance through the Seminary. But I felt lonely because I had no family and close friends nearby and because I had as my obvious intention—like all the Norwegian girls at this time—that I would breastfeed her. My surprised American doctor said: "My goodness, you Vikings, you sure hold on to old traditions." And it was a bit troublesome to handle it in America, where 'no one' was breastfeeding.[7]

Inger and Peder lived near the campus of the seminary, in an apartment at 4201 Massachusetts Avenue NW, one block from the school. After Heidi was born, Inger stayed at home—working at home—until they returned to Norway in 1966.

---

4. For a short description, see http://www.huffingtonpost.com/larry-wolff/battered-child-syndrome_b_2406348.htm: "It was only after this medical 'discovery' in 1962 that child abuse was recognized as a regular and recurring aspect of family life, not a sensational exception but a common syndrome."

5. See https://jamanetwork.com/journals/jama/article-abstract/327895.

6. Inger Borgen, interview by the author, March 14, 2017.

7. Inger Borgen, interview by the author, March 14, 2017.

Social life

Living so close to campus also meant a special closeness to the seminary for both of them. In an interview, Inger talked about what it was like to be the youngest of the professors' wives (there was only one female professor at the seminary):

> It was an enjoyable environment at the theological Seminary. I was definitely the youngest, but they thought it was nice to have a younger one; then, I was Mrs. Borgen. There was no use of the first name at the time; it was a bit solemn but very inclusive.[8]

As to church relations, they belonged to one of the largest Methodist churches in the city, the Metropolitan Methodist Church. But they preferred to attend the services on Sunday morning: "It was at a time when the ladies wore white gloves and hats when they came to church. It was a large church, with a large, beautiful choir and many people, but I did not attend much other congregational life at that time."[9] There were also many activities at the seminary. The school was central in educating pastors for the Methodist churches. In addition to the teaching of theology and the practical-theological subjects taught there, there were worship meetings every day for students and staff. For Peder, compared to his Norwegian minority background, the seminary must have seemed like being at a smorgasbord of opportunities for someone who wanted to carry out theological research and teaching in a Methodist context. However, it was a busy time, and he was also concerned about completing his Norwegian doctoral dissertation and preparing himself for his doctoral exam, the public disputation.

At this time, Martha and Ole Edvard Borgen—Ole E. was Peder's eldest brother—also lived in the United States. He had arrived already in 1956 and took his theological education there. He was ordained a pastor in the Methodist Church, and in the years 1962–65 he served at the West Side Avenue Methodist Church in Jersey City. Inger and Peder enjoyed fellowship with them during these years.[10]

---

8. Inger Borgen, interview by the author, March 14, 2017.

9. Inger Borgen, interview by the author, March 14, 2017.

10. In 1968, Ole E. Borgen received his doctorate from Drew University in New Jersey, but by then he had already returned to Europe (in 1966) as an assistant to Bishop Odd Hagen. When Bishop Hagen died in 1970, Ole Borgen was elected his successor as bishop of the bishopric of Northern Europe.

Assistant/associate professor Borgen

Peder Borgen started out in his work at the seminary as an *assistant professor* but advanced to *associate professor* after two years. As his closest colleague in the field of the New Testament he had George Wesley Buchanan (1921–2019). Together, they were responsible for nineteen courses within the New Testament field. Most students took a bachelor's degree (Bachelor of Sacred Theology), but the seminary also offered two master's degrees (Master of Sacred Theology and Master of Religious Education). In 1962, fifty-five bachelor's students and six master's students graduated.[11] The main burden of the teaching was thus on the bachelor's level. The seminary did not provide any doctoral programs.

Peder Borgen and G. W. Buchanan never developed a close collegial friendship beyond the working fellowship at the seminary. Their personal and scholarly profiles were too different. By the time Borgen came to Wesley, Buchanan was very interested in and concerned with the Synoptic problem.[12] He had collaborated with W. R. Farmer (1921–2000) and supported his views. Farmer was one of the strongest advocates of the view that Matthew was the oldest gospel and a source for Luke and then Mark.[13] This theory stands in stark contrast to the prevailing view, which still has the most followers, namely the so-called *two-source theory*.[14] Peder Borgen was not that interested in discussing this over and over again. Nevertheless, Buchanan helped Peder by reading through the manuscript of his doctoral dissertation and came up with suggestions for changes/improvements. Peder thanks him for that in the preface to his dissertation.

Buchanan was a kind of lone wolf in traditional New Testament research circles and felt a bit like that too at Wesley Seminary. He calls himself a "hound off the leash" in his autobiography, and was not always willing to adapt but was interested in several special fields of research and promoted views that were not always for the main road. However, he eventually

11. This information is gathered from *The Wesley Theological Seminary Bulletin*, Catalog Issue, 1962–63.

12. The "Synoptic problem" is about the relationship between the three Gospels Matthew, Mark, and Luke. Which is the oldest? Have they used each other, and, if so, who used whom?

13. Buchanan recalls this briefly in his autobiography; Buchanan, *Academic Hound*, 206–8. Farmer published his view in 1964: Farmer, *Synoptic Problem*.

14. The two-source theory claims that both Luke and Matthew used Mark and another source, called the Q-source, as the basis for their writings. The Q-source does not exist as a separate writing, but it is alleged to have consisted of the material that is common to Matthew and Luke beyond the material they have from Mark. This material in Matthew and Luke seems to be so similar that it must come from a common written source.

became a prolific researcher and remained at the seminary until he retired in 1990. Buchanan died late in 2019, at almost ninety-eight years old.

A different teaching program

The work of teaching at Wesley Theological Seminary took a lot of time and effort. The American teaching programs were quite different from what Peder was used to in Norway, in terms of both the organization and the implementation of the teaching itself. In Norway, theological studies were characterized by great personal choice concerning syllabus and syllabus literature, and the written exams could last up to eight hours. In addition, there were oral exams to pass, but little paper writing. In the USA, the syllabus was set up more thematically and with the syllabus literature much more precisely stated. The teaching took place, of course, via lectures, but also with much more extensive use of seminars, writing of seminar assignments, and the corresponding amount of paper reading for the teachers. Exams were several but smaller and counted together with the seminar papers towards a unifying grade.

Borgen had to build up his lectures from scratch; he had no previous lectures of his own to build on. Everything had to be built from scratch. Thus, he could not—if time was short—resort to the emergency solution that more experienced lecturers could apply, namely, to "turn the pile" and reuse lectures they had given before. Moreover, the lectures were, of course, to be held in English. Borgen had acquired a good vocabulary in his time as a research fellow in the USA, but it was nevertheless somewhat strenuous to give every single lecture in English. And even though his vocabulary was more than adequate, it could not be hidden that he had to struggle with his Norwegian-American accent. Students could sometimes say in their slightly teasing way: "Do you ever think we will be as clever as to pronounce Greek with a Norwegian accent?"[15]

Other circumstances were also different "over there" compared to what he knew from Norway: Employment conditions were different. If you did well and did the work you were assigned, the protection against dismissal was quite strong for the employees in the university sector in Norway. Employment without tenure was not a procedure in use for professors in Norwegian university settings. In the United States, he met a somewhat different situation; this included, among other things, that for those without tenure, one's complete work efforts were assessed by the employer, and if they were not satisfied, the employment relationship could be terminated.

15. Borgen, interview by the author, February 14, 2017.

The conditions considered also included whether one managed to publish satisfactorily ("publish or perish"). Furthermore, in private institutions, it was expected that everyone would serve the institution beyond the classroom by representing it in various contexts; for example, by being available for preaching at church services and similar arrangements. Inger mentions several times in her letters back home that Peder struggled with the lectures—and with his dissertation.

Looking to Norway

Inger and Peder Borgen had not traveled to the United States to stay there for good; it was a convenient solution for Peder to make a living out of his professional education. Accordingly, that he could also imagine returning to Norway is demonstrated by several issues. Already when he—still being in Norway—applied for an extension of his scholarship for a fourth and final year, he mentioned that he had been given a permanent position in the United States. And in his report for that fourth year, he said more specifically that he had been offered a position at Wesley Theological Seminary. But he also wrote, "However, I still intend to maintain a close connection with Norwegian research and hope to be able to return in the foreseeable future. In the meantime, I consider myself one of the many representatives of Norway and Norwegian scientific work abroad."[16]

Hence, he kept himself informed about the Norwegian job market and applied for positions being advertised. In 1965, he applied for a position as a lecturer at the Teacher Training Seminary[17] in Trondheim, but was asked to withdraw his application since he was not a Lutheran! In the late summer of the same year, he also applied for a professorship in religious studies at the University of Bergen. The application deadline was August 21, and the assessment committee was set up a couple of months later. The committee, however, did not deliver its recommendation until April of the following year.

However, in the spring of 1966, Borgen was given another work opportunity. In March, a letter arrived from Dean Charles Ransom at Drew University in Madison, New Jersey, asking if he would consider a position there. In the exchange of letters that followed, Peder received a specific offer and accepted it. Thus, he was able to resign from the position at Wesley and

---

16. Report for the period of January–June 1962. Now in Borgen's private home archive.

17. That is, Lærerhøgskolen, later part of the University of Trondheim.

started looking forward to beginning teaching at Drew. However, as we will see later, it did not turn out quite as they had expected.

Raymond E. Brown

Not long after Inger and Peder Borgen had established themselves in Washington, Peder became acquainted with the Catholic biblical scholar Raymond E. Brown (1928-1998).[18] By the time Peder got in contact with him, he had established himself as a renowned Bible scholar. Brown was then writing a large two-volume commentary on the Gospel of John. The first volume was published in 1966, and he there refers several times with recognition to articles by Borgen and to what had then been published as his doctoral dissertation.[19]

For Borgen, it was a great encouragement to be contacted by Professor Brown, and the two soon developed a close friendship both professionally and personally. Brown came to Wesley and lectured to Borgen's students, and Borgen also had similar visits back to Brown in Baltimore. Via Brown, he also became an associate member of the biblical scientific society the Catholic Biblical Association of America.[20] Later he also joined the Society of Biblical Literature (SBL).[21] Both of these large societies organized international biblical conferences. Membership in the societies and participation in the various conferences were prerequisites for establishing and developing personal friendships within the research communities and for one's development and orientation within recent research results and trends. Much of the time at the conferences was and is spent on such networking. Ever since these years in the USA, Peder Borgen was always a frequent guest at national and international biblical conferences and often encouraged younger researchers to participate. When Borgen had been established as a professor in Trondheim, Brown visited him there too. Brown was also one who later encouraged Borgen to apply for hosting a large international

---

18. Brown was a professor at St. Mary's Seminary in Baltimore from 1959 to 1971, and later at Union Theological Seminary in New York from 1971 to 1990. For an assessment of Brown's achievements as a biblical scholar, one might refer to Baird, *History of New Testament Research*, 3:395–423.

19. See Brown, *Gospel According to John (I–XII)* (1966). The second volume was published in 1970.

20. See https://catholicbiblical.org. Cf. further Baird, *History of New Testament Research* 3:448–51.

21. See https://www.sbl-site.org. Cf. Baird, *History of New Testament Research* 3:445–48.

biblical congress (SNTS) in Trondheim. The conference was successfully arranged in 1985, and Brown was one of the participants (see later).

"I have a dream": 1963 and 2009

The 1960s was a time of many social and political challenges both within the United States and internationally. The Vietnam War had been going on since 1955 and did not end until 1973. In October 1962, there was the famous Cuban Missile Crisis: the United States had discovered rocket silos in Cuba, and Russia sent boatloads of rockets for deployment on the island. USA President John F. Kennedy then decided to block Cuba. The Russian ships turned around at the last minute before reaching the blockade zone, and the Soviet Union entered into an agreement with the United States and withdrew the nuclear missiles. Many felt that the world had never been so close to a nuclear war. Several Norwegians working in the United States on a temporary basis returned to Norway as soon as they could for fear of a major war.

The racial problems

At the same time, there was unrest inside the United States regarding racial issues and the many racial demonstrations and riots. It had been a hundred years since President Lincoln had put an end to slavery in the United States, but blacks were still not free from discrimination. They often faced widespread discrimination in schools, universities, workplaces, and other social arenas. The worst situation was in the Southern states. There had been more than 1200 demonstrations in 200 cities for equal rights for African Americans. On August 28, 1963, ten civil rights organizations joined together for a large celebration in front of the Lincoln Monument in Washington. Several speakers attended, but what is remembered from this day is the speech of the black Baptist pastor and civil rights activist Martin Luther King Jr. (1929-68).

"I have a dream"

Between 200,000 and 250,000 people gathered in the large square in Washington. Among them was assistant professor Peder Borgen from Norway. He joined another Methodist, Pastor James L. Matheson. They had the full support of their bishop, and individually they carried a poster bearing the word "Methodists."[22] For Borgen, it was not without a certain anxiety that he

22. Fifty years later Peder was interviewed by both the local newspaper *Romerikes*

moved out into the crowds. There had been violent clashes before in similar demonstrations: "I was scared when I left for the march in the morning. Here came people who had participated in the struggle and fought for equal rights for the blacks. Would they use force, or would the call for non-violence prevail? What about the white racists in the Ku Klux Klan?"[23] These concerns were not only about how the march would proceed but also about what could happen if there were a clash, and if they would arrested both those involved and those closest to them. He was not a USA citizen and was a relatively new employee; if he was arrested, it could have consequences for his residence permit.[24] Nevertheless, the situation engaged him. "I did not realize in advance that this day would be a watershed in the fight against discrimination against blacks. However, along the way, something grew in us. It was a kind of cheer and joy." Among the more than 200,000 people in the streets, as many as 60,000 came at the urging of their Protestant denominations. "It was like a gigantic revival meeting, with Christian songs, negro-spirituals, a sense of rejoicing and joy." And Martin Luther King Jr's speech gradually resonated with the masses: *I have a dream today!*

Both Peder and James Matheson felt they were involved in something meaningful and significant. Matheson describes it thus: "It was also deadly serious when we heard King with perspiration dripping from his face declare the *I Have A Dream* Speech. It was our dream too."[25] Peder summed it up at the end of an interview in the Norwegian newspaper *Vårt Land* in 2013: "We had a strong feeling of having been involved in something big this August day in 1963. It was no longer possible to stop a fair claim based on the fact that we all are valuable, that we are all equal under God. For this, Martin Luther King gave his life, and he knew it could come."[26] It was a fight against discrimination, a phenomenon that Peder had his own firsthand experiences with.

One year later, in 1964, Martin Luther King Jr. was awarded the Nobel Peace Prize, and on May 26 of the following year the USA Senate passed the right to vote for all citizens, regardless of race. In 1967, the United States got its first two colored mayors. But the racial unrest did not end there: on April 4, 1968, Martin Luther King Jr. was shot and killed in Memphis, Tennessee. It seems that although many changes have taken place in the United States

---

Blad and the national Christian newspaper *Vårt Land* about this event: Børrestuen, "50 år gammel drøm," *Romerikes Blad*, August 28, 2013, 16; Fonn, "Talen grep, inspirerte og beveget," *Vårt Land*, August 28, 2013, 12–13.

23. Fonn, "Talen grep," 12.
24. Fonn, "Talen grep," 12.
25. Jim Matheson, in an email dated February 18, 2018.
26. Fonn, "Talen grep," 12–13.

since the 1960s, some people still think there are features in American society indicating that the country has a long way to go before Martin Luther King Jr's dream comes true.[27]

Many years later

In February 2009, Borgen had a reader's posting in *Romerikes Blad*, his local newspaper, labeled: "Incredible, but true!" The incredible had happened, he thought; the United States had elected a person of color as president. In 1963, few or no one thought it could ever happen in the United States. Nevertheless, in 2009 it was a fact. And Peder wrote: "Against this backdrop, it was an incredible experience to watch television, radio, and the press when a black man, Barack H. Obama, took the oath of office and his family moved into the White House. This fact heralds a new era in U.S. history and must be followed by positive and supportive attitudes in our country as well."[28]

It was, therefore, entirely in line with this enthusiasm that when Obama was awarded the Nobel Peace Prize later that year, Borgen came up with a new posting, this time in *Aftenposten*.[29] The Peace Prize award was criticized by many, and not a few thought it was too early to give it to Obama as he had been president for only a few months. For Peder, this was an invalid argument, and he compares what happened in 2009 with what conditions were like when Martin Luther King Jr. received the Peace Prize in 1963. At that time, the award was based on the fight for civil rights that he had led until then, but it was also a driving force for the future, like so many other awards. Therefore, "Without Obama and the people's election of him as president, King's dream at one important point would still only be a wish. This is how the Peace Prize, given to Obama, is based on realities and acts as a driving force in a process where forces must be gathered to resolve conflicts and distress, politically and socially."[30]

For Peder Borgen, Barack Obama was a worthy recipient of the Nobel Peace Prize. He participated in a torchlight procession in Oslo for the peace-winner Obama, together with his grandson Tobias, whose mother was born in the United States and is still a USA citizen.

---

27. The eighty-nine-year-old James Matheson formulated it thus in 2018 in his email to me: "I am afraid that the hope of his time here has been greatly damaged by present circumstances. We must pray for each other."

28. Borgen, "Utrolig, men sant." *Romerikes Blad*, February 1, 2009, 14.

29. Borgen, "Obama er en verdig mottager" (Obama is a worthy receiver), *Aftenposten*, morning edition, November 1, 2009, part 2, 4.

30. Borgen, "Obama er en verdig mottager," 4.

8

The *Bread from Heaven* Disputation (1966)

PEDER WORKED HARD TO keep up with his commitments. In addition to preparing the lectures, it was the work on his dissertation on *Bread from Heaven* that took time, attention, and energy. The dissertation was almost finished when Inger and Peder moved to the USA, but some final fine-tuning was missing.

He had had a strong hope of completing his dissertation in the spring of 1962, that is, before leaving for the United States. He contacted Professor Einar Molland, who suggested that the dissertation be published in the Norwegian Academy of Sciences Series, but the manuscript had to be completed by the end of May.[1] Peder prepared an almost finalized draft and had Professor Dahl read it and provide some advice. Dahl said: "Here are important new moments to be discussed, but your last chapter is strained; here you strive to be just traditional. You will most probably pass, but you will have a hard time defending the last chapter of your thesis."[2]

Later, looking back on this time, Borgen said, "My misfortune was Dahl's critique of the last chapter."[3] Consequently, Borgen was reworking it, sharpening his expressions, reformulating, making changes, looking up more relevant literature, and checking if more views should be included and

---

1. According to information presented by Borgen to Dahl in a letter, dated February 12, 1962.
2. Borgen, interview by the author, February 28, 2017.
3. Borgen, interview by the author, February 28, 2017.

if something more should be adjusted in terms of design and content. In the edition printed in 1965, the sixth and closing chapter was entitled "The Unique Vision of God in Jesus, the Son of God. John 6:31–58."[4] Nevertheless, although he had edited this chapter several times, Professor Jacob Jervell's critique at the disputation was stinging: "That chapter," he said, "should have been left out."[5]

That comment did hurt a tired doctoral candidate.

Borgen submitted the manuscript for evaluation in 1964.[6] The Faculty of Theology followed up by appointing an adjudicating committee to assess whether the dissertation was good enough—often expressed as "being worthy of . . ."—to be presented and defended in a public and oral doctoral disputation. Professor Dr.theol. Jacob Jervell, Professor Dr.theol. Nils Alstrup Dahl, both from the Faculty of Theology, and Professor Dr.theol. Sverre Aalen, from the Free Faculty of Theology (Menighetsfakultetet), were elected as members of the committee. Jervell and Aalen were to serve as opponents in the disputation. However, before the public defense of the dissertation was to be carried out, it was a requirement that the doctoral candidate should deliver two trial lectures, each forty-five minutes, one on a given topic and the other on a self-chosen topic.

However, the approval of the dissertation and the determination of the time for a disputation were delayed because the committee turned out to be rather slow-working. Professor Jervell pushed to get it through before he was to go on research leave in 1967–68. In a letter to Borgen in November 1965, he complained about his committee colleagues but stated that Peder should prepare himself for the public defense. The Faculty of Theology approved the dissertation on January 31, 1966. The disputation date was set for June 11 of the same year, with the two trial lectures to be presented on June 8 and the following day, respectively. In a letter in February,[7] Inger and Peder told his parents that they were to come home at the end of May, and that the time for the disputation had now been determined. But at the same time, it is expressed in several of their letters that Peder was tired: "I fear the struggle of the first weeks at home."[8]

The subject given for the first trial lecture was reported to Peder Borgen fourteen days before it was to be delivered. The theme was: "The so-called

4. See Borgen, *Bread from Heaven*, 147–92.
5. Jervell and Aalen, "Bread from Heaven," 228.
6. Borgen submitted the manuscript to the renowned Dutch publisher E. J. Brill in Leiden, where it was approved for publication in the series Supplements to Novum Testamentum. The book was published in late 1965.
7. Letter to his parents, dated February 4, 1966.
8. Letter to his parents, dated April 1, 1966.

Golden Rule (Matt. 7:12, Luke 6:13), its occurrence in the New Testament world and its content in the context of the Gospels."[9] As a self-chosen topic, Borgen presented: "From Paul to Luke."

THE TRIAL LECTURES

The Golden Rule

The *given* lecture is often perceived as the most demanding for the candidate. Not only must it be prepared in the run-up to the public defense, but the candidate had only fourteen days to work on it. In our context here, there is little room to present the lectures, the dissertation, or the disputation process in detail, but I might outline some prominent lines.

Borgen began by stating that the so-called Golden Rule ("Therefore, whatever you want men to do to you, do also to them"—Matthew 7:12) exists not only in the New Testament but "With other variations it appears in Chinese and Indian philosophy as well as in Greco-Roman, Jewish and Christian tradition, later also in Islam" (99). He then gave a brief overview of the most important places where it occurs before discussing whether its negative or positive form was the original, and its content in the New Testament world. He found both forms in both Greek traditions and in Jewish and Christian sources. He summed it all up in nine points or theses (110–12), where he claimed, among other things, that "The usage of the Golden Rule in Greco-Roman sources seems to stem from *Königsspiegel* and *Haustafel* traditions. In Jewish sources, it is found particularly in disciple instruction and testament traditions." Furthermore, "No great distinction can be made between the negative and the positive formulation, since both forms appear both in Greco-Roman, Hebrew and Christian origin."

Furthermore, "Both in Greek and Jewish sources, the maxim appears as an equilibrium between individuals, where one's own actions are dependent upon actions expected from others" (110). He further claimed that "In the Gospel of Matthew the Golden Rule serves as an expression of the Messianic interpretation of the will of God given by Jesus, expecting complete obedience from the disciples," while in the Gospel of Luke "we find the rule applied to one particular relationship, that towards enemies" (111). He thus finds an "approached equality between the commandment of loving one's neighbor and the Golden Rule as expressed in the Gospels."

---

9. The lecture was published in Norwegian in 1966; see Borgen, "Den såkalte gyldne regel." English edition (1983): Borgen, "Golden Rule," in *Paul Preaches Circumcision*, 99–114. Numbers in the text below are page numbers from this edition.

From Paul to Luke

The other lecture, with the short title "From Paul to Luke," has some connections with his American PhD dissertation, but has a somewhat different approach and focus.[10] Borgen took his point of departure in a well-known article by the German researcher Philip Vielhauer, who asked how and to what extent the author of the Acts of the Apostles (= Acts) took over and passed on Pauline theology, and to what extent he possibly modified it.[11]

A presupposition here is that the way an author presents Paul's theology will not only reveal his understanding of Paul but also show whether he and Paul belong together theologically. "It cannot be maintained that the Lucan writings can be viewed as a development from the Pauline letters, but in several instances, Paul nevertheless illustrates the background for the theology of Lk" (169).

In this sense, the question of Acts' image of Paul also becomes a question of the author's (= Luke's) own theology. Therefore, Peder argues, even though Luke does not have the Pauline notions of a remnant in Israel (Romans 9-11) that is to be saved, nor the sharp contrast between law and grace that we find in Paul, yet both he and Paul testify to the Jews' double reaction to Jesus and the gospel. And both emphasize that the hardening of Israel serves the salvation of the Gentiles.

Regarding the use of Acts, Borgen emphasized that in a comparison of the epistles of Paul with Luke, one must not only use the passages in Acts that are directly about Paul, but the letters must be seen in relation to the entire Lukan scriptures. And although one can see that Luke modifies material from Mark (it is assumed here that Luke has had the Gospel of Mark as one of his sources), these are not necessarily changes made by Luke alone, but are based on traditions that Paul also witnessed. Concerning the interim period—and here Borgen draws upon his unpublished PhD dissertation from 1956—he says, "More clearly than Mk, Lk as well as Paul interprets the time of the Gentiles on the basis of an idea of an eschatological interim period which connects historical events with the end. Lk thus interprets the delay of the Parousia within the framework of an eschatological perspective which is already evidenced in Paul's writings" (182).

---

10. Published as Borgen, "Von Paulus zu Lukas,"; updated and published in English in 1969 as Borgen, "From Paul to Luke."

11. Vielhauer, "Zum Paulinismus,"; I have here used the English version: Vielhauer, "On the Paulinism."

THE MAIN THOUGHTS IN *BREAD FROM HEAVEN*

The dissertation is subtitled "An Exegetical Study of the Concept of Manna in the Gospel of John and the Writings of Philo." It is thus the Gospel of John and Philo that are emphasized, while the Jewish-rabbinic material comes in as a supporting tradition.

A central focus is various extra-biblical accounts of the manna from heaven that the people of Israel received during their wanderings in the wilderness from Egypt to Canaan (Exodus 16). There are several reproductions or retellings of this story, and in many of these, the story of the manna has been adapted and used in new contexts. These are adaptations Borgen is looking for to find out if they can shed light on the Gospel of John's use of the story of the manna in its rendering of Jesus' miracles in the wilderness (John 6). Borgen believes that these different accounts are indeed *actualizations* of the manna narrative into new contexts, and that these actualizations might say something about the situation in which they were created and the theology of which they are bearers—a typical form-critical point of view.

It is a central part of Borgen's conclusion that both Philo and the author of the Gospel of John (6:31–58) paraphrased words from the Old Testament and wove these together with parts from the Aggada about the manna in the desert.[12] The aggadic fragments can be identified with a reasonably high degree of certainty. The interpretations of the Old Testament are then presented in a way that makes Borgen think it can be characterized as a *homiletic pattern*. He also argues that such a pattern can be found in Philo's texts and in Palestinian midrashim too. He finds clear parallels between Philo, John 6, and Palestinian midrash in terms of exegetical method, patterns, and terminology. This finding does not mean that the Gospel of John is dependent on Philo but that he was a parallel phenomenon. Philo's place or room for his writings was the Jewish synagogue in Alexandria, while the Gospel of John seems to have belonged to, came into being, and was used in a context that can be called a "school" within the young church, most likely from the time when the break with Judaism was a fact.[13]

After two rather technical chapters —which are almost impossible to paraphrase or popularize—where he develops and justifies his hypothesis of a "homiletic pattern" and the use of midrashic methods, patterns, and terminology (chapters 2–3), Borgen discusses in more detail two texts by Philo (*De Mutatione* 253–263 and *Legum allegoriae III*, 162–168), and John 6:31–58. Here he tries to comment on various aspects found in these texts,

---

12. Borgen, *Bread from Heaven*, 1–3.
13. Borgen, *Bread from Heaven*, 3.

and which he illuminates with features from the situation he believes the texts were created in, and which they reflect.

In chapter 4, then, he analyzes *Mut.* 253–263 and finds a central point in that words for "manna" are replaced by words such as "virtue" and "wisdom," which belong in an educational setting: in other words, Philo has interpreted Exodus 16:4 and fragments from the Aggada about bread from heaven into his contemporary situation where there were conflicts between how to assess "philosophy" and the "encyclical education," i.e., the more elementary knowledge. Some rejected the elementary acquisition of knowledge, while others valued it highly. Philo, on the other hand, emphasizes the encyclical education is a lower education, a kind of bastard education which the Jews have in common with their surroundings, while the true philosophy is really and primarily to be found in Jewish philosophy, in the Jewish Torah. Thus "encyclical education" becomes an education on the borderline between the low and the high, a kind of "adiaphoron," which is neither good nor bad, a kind of necessary evil to be mastered in order to advance to the true wisdom one finds by studying the Law—the Torah. Philo thus interprets Exodus 16:4 in the light of and with the help of Greek educational ideals, but at the same time, he also changes these to explain Judaism's attitude to the encyclica. Furthermore, this adoption of Greek ideas also represents a specific transformation of Judaism in the light of the Greek educational traditions.[14]

In chapter 5, the relevant section from *Leg. All. III*—the allegorical interpretations of the Law of Moses—is analyzed. While the previous text was about the relationship between wisdom (in the Law) and elementary education (the encyclical education), this text is about the use of higher education. *Leg. All. III* 162–168 criticizes the abuse of education. Philo emphasizes here, as the philosophical schools do too, that political and social careers are not the purpose of education. The goal, on the other hand, is "virtue," which must be valued for its own part. Hence, this text also reflects conditions in his contemporary Alexandria. Education was the path to advance socially and politically, and it was necessary if one wanted to make advancements in the urban community of Alexandria. Philo had close

14. There are other sources that also show that the relationship with the Greek education in Alexandria was a problem for the Jews there, partly because it was linked to the right to obtain civil rights. But Borgen also goes a step further by showing that the term "manna" in this text is also linked to the Sabbath, and thus indicates its connection to the Sabbath teaching in the synagogues. Israel will be the people who are taught by the Sabbath teaching in the Law they have from Moses. The encyclical education is not rejected, but the Law of Moses is placed at the center as the highest wisdom, God's own manna for his people. On the problem of education in Alexandria, see also Mendelson, *Secular Education.*

relatives who had chosen this path and who thus partook of the Alexandrian luxury but also its dangers, not least the danger of apostasy from Judaism—the true wisdom. The homily in this text thus presupposes a time when the Jews had the opportunity for social advancement in Alexandria, and Philo saw the dangers in this. Philo's own adaptation of this is characterized by his knowledge of both Stoic and Platonic philosophy, but also by his ability to transform parts of this knowledge into Judaism and thus facilitate the value of Judaism for his contemporaries in their current life situation. Judaism—as Philo understands it—is in harmony with the cosmic laws and principles and is realized and accessible in the laws and principles of the Jewish nation. The Torah is the true manna from heaven.

In the last chapter, Borgen discusses six different aspects of the text of John 6:31–58 in light of the previous five chapters of the dissertation. Because Borgen takes up these topics in several later studies, I will briefly present the subject matter comprised by this chapter.

The first issue he mentions is the pinpointing that just as Philo and other Jewish material link the understanding of the manna to the revelation of the Law at Sinai, this link is also found in John (6:33, 51; 6:35, 45–46, 48; 5:37–47).[15] John thus follows a line that was also used by Philo and is hinted at in Palestinian Aggada. The revelation of God at Sinai is behind John 6:45–46 and provides a key to the text.

The second feature he highlights is the relationship between the manna—the bread—and wisdom.[16] The bread is identified with wisdom. In Jewish wisdom traditions, there are expressions such as "coming," "eating and drinking," and "hunger and thirst" related to wisdom, and these issues we also find in John 6. Fragments from biblical and aggadic traditions about wisdom are linked in John 6 to eucharistic traditions. In this way eating and drinking the elements of the Eucharist will also be eating and drinking wisdom and the Torah.

The third aspect discussed is one that Borgen has returned to in several other studies, namely what he calls "the commissioned agent," "the trusted and authorized envoy."[17] According to Jewish halakhic material, it is assumed that an envoy identifies with the person who sent him. It is also stated that the sender authorized the person who was sent by transferring his own rights to him. We encounter this too in John 6, and then about Jesus as the messenger (6:38–39, 44, 57). Borgen further believes that in rabbinic material, this has been developed into what he calls a "juridical mysticism,"

---

15. Borgen, *Bread from Heaven*, 147–54.
16. Borgen, *Bread from Heaven*, 154–58.
17. Borgen, *Bread from Heaven*, 158–64.

where the emissary not only derives his authority and function from the sender, but also his qualities. This, Borgen believes, may be behind John 5:26; 6:57; and 6:40; a legal mysticism is thus introduced in Christology.

The fourth feature from John 6 that Borgen discusses is the relationship of the bread to eternal life.[18] The bread's connection to the Torah, wisdom, and the principle of dispatch provided the basis for the understanding of the bread as life-giving. "The bread of life" is a phrase that is repeated in John 6 (6:33, 35, 48, cf. vv. 51-58). Here he also discusses present and futuristic eschatology in the Gospel of John.

What is the relationship between the bread from heaven that was given once in the past and the bread of God that is given in the present? That is the focus of the fifth section of this last chapter. The answer is that John places the events of the past in the external sphere and the present bread from heaven in the spiritual sphere, and Borgen finds that the midrash-like exposition in John 6:31-32 is based on such a distinction.

In the last section,[19] Borgen further discusses what he believes is the occurrence of anti-docetic agitation in John 6; he calls those who are argued against "docetic spiritualists." In contrast to those who reject Jesus, John, according to Borgen, describes the chosen Israelites and the disciples as those who understood that the bread from heaven was truly identical with Jesus, come in the flesh. Thus, John 6, again according to Borgen, reflects the current situation of the "Johannine church" as a church facing Gnostic docetism. Borgen later left this view of the presence of an anti-docetic motive in John 6.[20]

THE PUBLIC DISPUTATION

The disputation took place in the central aula of the University. Most of the Methodist pastors in Oslo were attending the session.[21] It was the first time in the history of Norwegian Methodism that one of their own was to defend a dissertation for the degree of dr.theol. In fact, it was also the first time a non-Lutheran theologian was to defend his doctoral dissertation for that degree.

---

18. Borgen, *Bread from Heaven*, 165-179.
19. Borgen, *Bread from Heaven*, 179-92.
20. See Borgen, *The Gospel of John: More Light*, 197.
21. See Kristelig Tidende 26-27 (1966) 372 and 370.

Peder Borgen at his disputation. In those days, the doctoral candidates usually wore a "waist dress." Nowadays, the dress code is much more relaxed, as there is hardly any code at all.

Professor Jacob Jervell was appointed to act as the first examiner—or "opponent" as s/he is called in Norway—followed by Professor Sverre Aalen. The opponents' main task was to subject the dissertation to a critical review, to raise questions to the doctoral candidate about things they thought were unclear or poorly substantiated, and possibly to point out interpretations and positions that they thought arguable, if not even wrong. In addition, the other member of the committee, or even other qualified persons present in the auditorium, could ask to be allowed to speak as *opponent ex auditorio*, and raise questions or comment on the doctoral dissertation.[22] During the disputation, there was thus a form of a conversation between the opponents and the doctoral candidate, and it could sometimes be quite intense, not at least for the candidate. It was expected that the doctoral candidate should explain and defend himself. In this particular case, we have the opponents' arguments available in print as a journal article.[23] We do not, however, have the doctoral candidate's responses documented.

The discussion between Professor Jervell and Borgen lasted for almost three hours[24]; the published edition of Jervell's contribution, however,

22. The dean, who oversaw the disputation, was the one to be asked to be allowed such additional questions or comments.

23. See Jervell and Aalen, "Bread from Heaven." Numbers in my text are page numbers referring to this publication.

24. (Anonymous), "Maratondebatt om brød fra himmelen. Metodistprest blir doctor theologiae." *Aftenposten*, June 13, 1966, 5.

extends to only approximately seventeen pages. Usually, it would take less than an hour to read these aloud. This fact demonstrates that there must have been an extensive discussion between the opponent and the doctoral candidate. Reading the opponent's written comments can be compared to listening to one of two participants in a telephone conversation; one hears the one part asking, but not the answers.

To anyone who reads professor Jervell's arguments, and who does not know how the conversation between the doctoral candidate and the opponent proceeded, the disputation appears as an intense opposition. Professor Jervell, who was sometimes able to be quite arrogant and sharp, did, for example, claim that the doctoral candidate's knowledge of scholarly literature "is satisfactory without revealing a learned mind," but at the same time later admitted that the relevant "Literature in the subject area is quite unmanageable," and that "The most relevant material is included" (230). He further said that neither "in methodological terms nor as a collection of material does the dissertation represent anything new" (228). In retrospect, considering the reception the dissertation has received among other scholars, that statement may seem somewhat exaggerated. Concerning language skills, Jervell claimed that "The quotations from Greek and Hebrew are largely commendably accurate" (229). It must have made Professor Aalen jump a little in his chair because when he came up with his opposition, he claimed that the doctoral candidate "has not convinced me that he is so linguistically and grammatically familiar with the Hebrew texts he quotes from, that he is able to read and treat them satisfactorily" (245). The doctoral candidate Borgen may have partly agreed with this because he often uses translations of Hebrew texts. But at the same time, in the context of the dissertation, it must have seemed hard-hitting. Nevertheless, it is the opponents' task to read with the eyes of an eagle.

Most interesting are the opponents' views of the general and central theses in the dissertation. Professor Jervell believed that "the doctoral candidate has succeeded in proving a haggadic manna tradition common to Philo and Palestinian learning" (232), but was more uncertain whether there is evidence that Philo was *dependent* on Palestinian traditions. Another critical part of Borgen's thesis is that the interpretation of the Old Testament texts about the manna in Philo and John 6 follows a specific homiletical pattern. Jervell pointed out that there are not preserved any actual sermons from Hellenistic-Jewish literature that can be used as evidence. The question is, however, whether that is necessary; Borgen tries to argue via the existence of common style patterns. Jervell disagreed that Philo's *Leg. All. III* 162–168 could be considered a homily. He is also skeptical about whether John 6:31–58 is a homily, but he is a bit vague in his conclusions here. The main problems for Jervell seem to be that there is so much discussion or exegetical debate in the text, and that there is no clear evidence that this feature has belonged to the homilies. Then one should instead call it a midrash. Jervell was also not convinced that there is a connection between the Gospel of John and early Jewish mysticism.

Professor Aalen focused a lot on grammatical questions and problems. Concerning the dissertation's central thesis that John 6 is a midrash-like interpretation of a verse from Exodus 16, he is not convinced. But he adds: "In my opinion, the author has succeeded in proving or at least making it probable that a certain homiletical midrash form has formed patterns for the section Joh. 6:31–58 when it comes to major features," but not that the passage is a midrash to the manna verses in Exodus (246). He believes that this is the central thesis of the dissertation but that it has failed. He is also not convinced by the argument about the "mysterious" elements that Borgen believes he can find in John 6.

Aalen's comments exemplify a general disagreement with the doctoral candidate's central thesis. However, such are the discussions within the scholarly debates of research. Aalen emphasizes that "here one can talk about different views" (260). The doctoral candidate's idea has a certain plausibility; it explains to a certain extent the current text segment in Johannes, Aalen says. He sees this as a merit and a positive result of the dissertation as such.

The committee had decided that the dissertation was "worthy of being defended." Thus, the first and primary eye of the needle was passed. Although some complex discussions were part of the later disputation, the commission approved the disputation and the trial lectures. On June 17, candidatus theologiae Peder Borgen, PhD, was made a *doctor theologiae* by the University of Oslo.

Some early reception of *Bread from Heaven*

It is not possible, nor appropriate in a biography like the present volume, to deal comprehensively with the reception history of Borgen's dissertation. A few issues might nevertheless be mentioned as indicating how it was received.

In looking back, Paul N. Anderson says in his foreword to the 2017 reissue of the volume that

> The responses to Borgen's monograph were strongly favorable from the beginning, albeit with a few questions here and there. Virtually all of the major reviews directly following its

publication heralded it as a major contribution in elucidating the Jewish background and operation of the Fourth Gospel . . . overall the reviews felt the work was compelling.[25]

This view is confirmed if we check some older and newer commentaries on the Gospel of John, and some more recent and comprehensive presentations of research on that Gospel and its sixth chapter.

One of the first, and probably *the* first commentator to comment on Borgen's study was his friend R. E. Brown. In his commentary on the Gospel of John in the Anchor Bible Series,[26] published as early as 1966, Brown refers several times to Borgen's works.[27] Dealing with 6:25-34, Brown states that "Borgen . . . has shown that this is a good example of typical Jewish exegesis."[28] Furthermore, Brown says that "Peder Borgen has contributed some interesting insights into the composition of this discourse, including vss. 51-58."[29] Brown does not, however, concur with Borgen's view that 6:51-58 was originally united to verses 35-50, a view Borgen announced as early as 1959.[30]

Hence, due to the publication of Brown's great commentary as early as within a year after Borgen's book was published, Borgen's views got a flying start in the scholarly world, and he followed up with several studies in the years to come.[31] The positive evaluation of Brown was followed up in many other commentaries,[32] so that when Craig S. Keener had his two-volume commentary published in 2003, he could state: "So convincingly did Borgen array various sources that the shifts in methodology since that time have not undercut his basic argument, which has continued to retain support."[33]

---

25. Anderson, "Foreword," xxviii.

26. Brown, *Gospel According to John (I-XII)*.

27. He refers to Borgen, "Unity of Discourse"; Borgen, "Observations"; and Borgen, *Bread from Heaven*, published in 1959, 1963, and 1965 respectively.

28. Brown, *Gospel According to John (I-XII)*, 262 (referring to Borgen, "Observations," 233-34); see also 270 and 271.

29. Brown, *Gospel According to John (I-XII)*, 277. On p. 294 he states that "We find Borgen's studies of midrashic technique most persuasive."

30. Brown, *Gospel According to John (I-XII)*, 294; cf. Borgen, "Unity of Discourse."

31. Most of these are gathered in his 1983 collection of articles on John: Borgen, *Logos was the true Light*. See also his collection of articles published in 1987; Borgen, *Philo, John and Paul*, 75-204.

32. Cf. for instance, Beutler, *Das Johannesevangelium*, 221, 224. Thyen, *Das Johannesevangelium*, 350-51.

33. Keener, *Gospel of John*, 1:679.

Turning to the early and major volume of review of the Gospel of John, we find a similar assessment of Borgen's *Bread from Heaven*.[34] Robert Kysar is appreciative but also somewhat cautious: He calls Borgen's argument for "the exegetical-homiletic" form of the pericope "a valuable contribution to our understanding of the intellectual milieu of the evangelist."[35] But he also finds Borgen's suggestion "that the Jewish milieu of the evangelist was one influenced by a mysticism—a suggestion which if explored more fully and demonstrated more persuasively might shed a great deal of light on the interpretation of the gospel."[36] Hence, he also says that the problem with Borgen's view "is to show that such a gnostic Jewish mysticism existed during the first century; more evidence to that effect is required if Borgen's theory is to carry the day."[37] It might seem that Kysar here is emphasizing "gnostic mysticism" more than Borgen does, as he speaks primarily of "mysticism" or "Jewish mysticism."[38]

In retrospect, we can see that this dissertation was and remained Peder Borgen's opus magnum as a New Testament scholar. In this dissertation, we find many of the issues Borgen came to follow up on in his further research. He repeatedly returned to this dissertation in later works and elaborated upon various aspects of his study. In retrospect, we can also say that it is most often this study that Borgen is remembered for today. It is still the case that—even though it is over fifty-five years since it was published for the first time—it is quoted and discussed in studies of the bread from heaven in John 6. Among colleagues, there are still those who know him as "Bread-from-Heaven Borgen."

In 2017, *Bread from Heaven* was published in a third edition, and this time in a series that aims "to make available in printed, accessible form a selection of the most influential books on the Johannine writings in the modern era for the benefit of scholars and students alike."[39] Not many doctoral dissertations are published in several editions; some are not published

---

34. Kysar, *Fourth Evangelist*.
35. Kysar, *Fourth Evangelist*, 125.
36. Kysar, *Fourth Evangelist*, 125.
37. Kysar, *Fourth Evangelist*, 125. Cf. also Painter, *Quest for the Messiah*, 271–72.

38. The debate on John has continued, and Borgen's viewpoints are still discussed, as these studies indicate: Anderson, *Christology of the Fourth Gospel*, especially 52–61 etc.; Culpepper, *Critical Readings of John 6*, in which Borgen's "John 6: Tradition, Interpretation and Composition" is included (95–114); Hylen, *Allusion and Meaning in John 6*, 28–31, see also 102–17; Culpepper and Anderson, *John and Judaism*, 7–71, 296–97, and 303–4, to mention some.

39. See Borgen, *Bread from Heaven* (2017). Here quoted from the publisher's description of the series.

at all beyond the copies required to be made available for the public disputation itself. The fact that *Bread from Heaven* was reprinted in 1981 and republished in 2017 in a series of "classic works" demonstrates that it is still considered a work useful to know and discuss for Bible scholars of today.

Time-out (1966–67) and a break-up from the USA

His years at Wesley Theological Seminary as a teacher and researcher and his work on the doctoral dissertation had their price. The trial lectures and the disputation were also demanding. And this is not about hard currency but strength, energy, and mental surplus.

Peder Borgen became simply exhausted. Burned out.

That Peder had hit the wall became apparent in the days and weeks after the disputation. Inger, Peder, and little Heidi stayed in Norway during the summer but then returned to the USA; they were to move from Washington to Drew University in Madison, New Jersey, where Borgen had been hired for a professorship. The commencing in his new position was scheduled for the early autumn of 1966. Drew was the university where he had obtained his PhD in 1953–56; now he was going back there as an associate professor.

However, they never moved up to New Jersey and Drew.

When they returned to the United States again, it became more than clear that he was not able to take up any work there, and he soon received a sick leave from his doctor. Inger had to take responsibility for most things, in addition to the fact that she had a one-year-old girl to take care of. She describes this situation thus:

> I probably did not have any prerequisites for understanding how hard the disputation was to Peder, and all the efforts of strength that it represented. Hence, when he became exhausted, I could not know how exhausted he was or how far down he was, but it scared me... We, the people around him in Washington, had to take action and sort out his office, arrange for a return home to Norway, and work our way through all the paperwork needed...[40]

Moreover, they decided to go back home to Norway. Inger had to take responsibility and cares for the travel:

---

40. This, and following quotations, are taken from an interview with Inger Borgen, made by me on March 14, 2017. In 1966, Peder Borgen's eldest brother, Ole E., was still at Drew University studying for his own PhD. He helped with the move to Norway.

I was worried about how seriously 'this wall' had hit him in the head. I was responsible for a one-year-old baby, but I knew that in Norway, we were safe because there was a system, and many people who wanted to take care of us; hence we decided to move back home to Norway.

Adding a written note from a doctor in Washington, Borgen had to write to Drew University and say that he would return to Norway for further medical help: "... in consultation with Dr. Harold W. Wylie, he has recommended me to return to Norway for medical reasons."[41] Nothing is said in this letter indicating that he is resigning. On the contrary, the letter is a message that Dr. Wylie had recommended a two-month break: "a two-month moratorium on my professional activities while I receive further medical treatment."

Back home in Lillestrøm, he had some consultations with a local doctor, and Borgen then realized that it was best to resign from the position at Drew. No more than a week after returning home, he therefore sent a new letter to Drew announcing that he was retiring: "Based on the recommendations of these physicians, and facing medical treatment for some time, I find it right to submit my resignation as Associate Professor of New Testament at Drew University."[42]

It is difficult to comprehend how drastic it must have been for Peder Borgen to resign from the position at Drew. In an earlier letter to his parents, he had expressed that he was looking forward to starting up there, partly because he thought they had a different and better attitude to the Bible and Bible research there. And there were better professional terms and opportunities at Drew than at Wesley. Now he found himself having to retire. It also shows how exhausted he must have felt when he returned to Norway. He had resigned from the position at Wesley and now also resigned from the position at Drew. He was thus without a permanent position, and the future was open and uncertain for the newly made Dr.theol.

In Norway, both families were waiting with open arms to receive them, and Inger and Peder decided to settle down in Lillestrøm. There was an apartment available for them at Torvet 1, Peder's childhood home in the center of Lillestrøm. "Peder's father said that when you are able to do so, you can help a little in the shop while you recover, and then I could also sit

---

41. Letter dated August 29, 1966, sent from Lillestrøm to Drew University Theological School.

42. Letter dated September 8, 1966, and sent to Drew University Theological School. A small consolation in this context was that even though Peder had to resign from the position, it happened with a certificate that he was still in "good standing" at Drew University.

back and know that now we are in everyone's care here at home," said Inger many years later.[43]

The family stayed there until the summer of the following year. Peder eventually got help from a psychiatrist, who understood what had happened to him and helped him see that he could not prey on himself, but that life is also about apportioning both the physical and mental forces. And it helped, along with some further treatment, slowly but surely.

Peder tried to gain strength for new efforts. He had, as mentioned earlier, already in the summer of 1965—while they were in the United States—applied for a professorship in religious studies in Bergen. The assessment committee had submitted its recommendation in April 1966.[44] However, Peder Borgen was not their primary priority but was ranked number 2, which indicated that he would not get the position. However, could other possibilities be available?

In the following spring, the Peder Borgen family was again ready to move, but this time to Bergen. And thus began a new chapter in their lives.

Peder Borgen did not, however, become a full professor—not yet.

---

43. Inger Borgen, interview by the author, March 14, 2017.

44. This means that when Peder went to Norway in June 1966, he probably knew about the report from the evaluation committee in Bergen. He must have considered it as most probable that he would not get the position in Bergen as he left for the USA in the late summer of 1966.

9

Borgen in Bergen (1967–73)

IT TOOK SEVERAL MONTHS for Peder to recover from his fatigue. Jacob Jervell, his first opponent at the disputation, who was now on study leave in Rome, was informed that Peder had returned to Norway as a convalescent. Already in September, he wrote a letter telling him that he also had a similar reaction after his disputation in 1959: "But two months of sloppy life was enough to get recovery."[1]

It took a little longer for Peder to recuperate, but in a reply letter to Jervell in January 1967, he says, among other things, "I am now, so to speak, back in good old shape."[2]

Moreover, on April 1, the very same year, he started up in a new job as a lecturer at the University of Bergen. How could it be that he got a position at the University of Bergen, given that he was not a Lutheran?

APPLYING FOR A PROFESSORSHIP IN BERGEN

Peder Borgen had already, while he was in the USA, kept himself updated about the job market in Norway. He had also, probably in 1965,[3] applied

---

1. Private letter from Jacob Jervell to Peder Borgen, Rome, dated September 26, 1966. Now in the Borgen archive in the National Library. Jervell had defended his own dissertation on December 10, 1959.
2. Private letter from Peder Borgen to Jacob Jervell, dated January 17, 1967. Now in the National Library's Borgen archive.
3. I write "probably in 1965." Borgen himself writes in an article published in 2004

for a position in Christian studies at the Department of Religious Studies at the Norwegian College of Teaching in Trondheim (NLHT). But in March 1966, he received a friendly message from the dean of the department, Professor Åge Holter, saying that Borgen, as a non-Lutheran, put them in a somewhat tricky situation, and Holter (more than) indirectly encouraged Borgen to withdraw the application. They had, in fact, presented the issue to the Ministry of Education, and the Ministry had stated that it was "uncertain whether the legislation today can provide a basis for hiring a non-Lutheran lecturer in Christian studies, even at a university."[4]

Borgen revoked the application.

The professorship he did not get

Then, when a professorship in religious studies at the University of Bergen was announced in June 1965, he applied again. This position was a new one at the university, in order to establish the field of religious studies there. Christian knowledge was, however, to be included in the department's academic profile and work, and the announcement stated that the professorship should "form an academic background for this." When the application deadline for the applicants expired on August 21, it turned out that there were five applicants. The committee's recommendation was available already at the end of April 1966, and it was clear from the priority they set up that Peder would hardly get the position. The committee nominated Borgen as number 2, after Dr.theol. Alv Kragerud.[5] The other three applicants

---

(Borgen, "Ute-økumenikk," 280, republished in Borgen, *Vei utenfor Allfarvei*, 186, note 90) that it happened in 1964. D. Rian also mentions the application but does not give any date. In 1964, a temporary commitment was announced (*Norsk Lysingsblad* no. 72, March 25, 1964), valid from August 1 to the end of that year, but with the possibility of extension until August 1965. I doubt that Peder applied for this. (See Borgen, *Vei utenfor Allfarvei*, 185, note 90; Almås and Rian, *Kristendomsfag*, 18.) According to *Norsk Lysingsblad* no. 43 (February 20, 1965), a lectureship was announced in 1965 with an application deadline of March 15 the same year. This was a permanent position, and it was probably this one he applied for.

4. Letter from Åge Holter to Peder Borgen, dated Trondheim, March 21, 1966. Now in the National Library's Borgen archive.

5. Alv Kragerud (1932–2010) came to Bergen from a position as associate professor of religious studies at the Department of Religious History in Oslo, a position he had held since 1963. He had taken an outstanding theological exam (cand.theol.) at the University of Oslo (1954) at the age of twenty-two. After that he was a priest in Sweden for a few years; at the same time, he began to pursue more advanced studies in the New Testament. During these years, he worked especially with the Gospel of John, and in 1958 defended his dissertation at the University of Hamburg for the theological doctorate (Kragerud, *Der Lieblingsjunger*). Then he turned to the history of religion, and in

were not declared professionally competent for the position. Alv Kragerud had a doctorate from Germany (1959), and right after he was appointed in the spring of 1967, he defended his second dissertation, now for the Norwegian PhD (dr.philos.) in Oslo. The assessment committee also gave Peder Borgen competence approval for a professorship,[6] but Alv Kragerud received a stronger overall assessment.[7] This difference in assessment was most probably because Kragerud had a dissertation in religious studies (*religionsvitenskap*), while both of Borgen's doctorates were in biblical/New Testament studies.

Hence, in the end, on April 28, 1967, Kragerud was appointed to the position by the king-in-council. A university professor at this time was appointed by the king-in-council, and the person concerned was thereby made a government official (*embetsmann*).[8]

Borgen receives a lectureship

On April 1, Peder Borgen joined a lectureship in the Department of Religious Studies at the University of Bergen.[9] The Methodist paper *Kristelig*

1960 he became a university fellow in Oslo. In 1967 he obtained his PhD/dr.philos. degree there with a dissertation on the Gnostic work *Pistis Sophia* (Kragerud, *Die Hymnen des Pistis Sophia*). With this dissertation, which was also included in the material submitted for the professorship in Bergen, he established his religious-scientific competence.

6. When one reads the committee's assessments and the list of works that were submitted for assessment, it may come as a bit of a surprise that Borgen did not submit his American PhD dissertation from 1956. Most probably this was because he did not expect that this dissertation would strengthen his religious-scientific competence since it is primarily a New Testament dissertation.

7. The evaluation committee consisted of Prof. Geo Widengren, Uppsala, Prof. H. Ludin Jansen, Oslo, and Prof. E. Molland, Oslo. Widengren gave Borgen competence "Only with the greatest doubt..."; Ludin Jansen wrote in his statement that the competence "cannot be characterized as particularly strong." The theology professor Molland was the one who was most positive. The two historians of religion, Widengren and Ludin Jansen, respectively, said of Kragerud that he "must . . . be awarded strong competence for a professorship in religious studies" (Widengren), and "I declare him to be extremely competent" (Jansen).

8. An *embetsmann* was by definition a higher civil servant appointed by the king. This practice ended in 1989; from then on, the professors at the universities were no longer government officials. See more on this below.

9. I have not been able to find any announcement of this position, and thus no job description. It may have been a call of a more internal nature. Cf. Kragerud, "Universitetslektor," *Dagen*, April 20, 1967, 1 and 8. Kragerud presents Borgen, but does not say anything particular concerning the employment of him in light of Borgen's denominational affiliation.

Tidende congratulated him in an interview as early as February 17, but expressed some astonishment that he was to take up a position in *religious studies*; was he not a theologian? Borgen made it clear, however, that "The Department's task is to conduct versatile religious research. However, my area will be biblical studies with the main emphasis on the New Testament. And that is exactly what I have worked with so far." Hence, the leading teachers in the department were to be Alv Kragerud as the professor and Borgen as a lecturer. In addition, a couple of others were hired as assistant lecturers. *Kristelig Tidende* made a point of the fact that Kragerud was a Lutheran, an assistant lecturer a Catholic, and Borgen a Methodist. The magazine congratulated Borgen on the position and expressed—with a slightly hidden enthusiasm—that we "do not doubt that he will be a worthy free church representative at the University in Bergen." This statement reveals that they were very well aware of the significance that Borgen got this teaching position even though he was not a Lutheran. Or better; that he was *not* a Lutheran was a central part of the reason for their enthusiasm.

The appointment was, however, viewed in light of the prevailing Norwegian law, somewhat problematic. Nevertheless, the university may have considered it a test case concerning academic freedom.[10] As early as the autumn of 1970, a new such test case appeared at the University of Bergen, but we will return to this later.

The department had already been in operation for a few months with temporary staffing. Kragerud had worked there since the autumn of 1966. However, the number of students was currently low, and the study plans had not been completed and approved either. From April 1, Borgen lectured on the Sermon on the Mount and Norwegian church history, with three hours in each subject for two to three students, respectively. In addition, he had conferences and tutoring sessions. However, the number of students increased rapidly; already from the autumn of there were twenty-five students. The institute was organized into two sections, one focusing on religious studies, the other responsible for Christian knowledge. Borgen was in the latter section, but Kragerud as the professor had primary academic responsibility for both sections.

---

10. Borgen himself subscribed to this opinion as he writes in a private note (dated 1997/88!) that "This appointment was against the Norwegian law, but the University regarded it as a test case of academic freedom."

A PROBLEMATIC SIBLINGSHIP

Christian knowledge vis-à-vis religious studies

In the Norwegian context, the two fields of studies labeled "religious studies" (Norwegian: *religionsvitenskap*) and "Christian knowledge" (Norwegian: *kristendomskunnskap*) may be characterized as siblings. But as among many other siblings, the relationship is not always easy and straightforward; there can sometimes be a bit of an argument about how to understand each other and about one's distinctive features, duties, and rights. This situation has, at least, been the case in the relationship between religious studies and Christian knowledge in Norwegian academic circles. It is, therefore, quite natural that both Peder Borgen and Alf Kragerud not before long published their presentations of how they understood their fields of study and their relationships.

In May, Peder Borgen published an article in the newspaper *Dagen* on Christian knowledge and its place and role in a university setting.[11] The article might be read as a programmatic statement for his work within the Department of Religious Studies, and it focuses strongly on the subject of Christian knowledge and its place within the university as a public educational institution. It would, eventually, turn out to be a substantial controversy about Christian knowledge in the department in the years to come until its fellowship with religious studies was broken up, and it was to become a separate department in 1985. But seen in its local context in 1967, the article indeed should be considered a programmatic statement with an address to other readers, those outside the university.

One of the tasks of a university is to train teachers for high school and college teaching, and here Christianity belongs as a relevant teaching subject. Accordingly, it should also be a university subject, Borgen argues. He further writes that it is essential to state clearly that Christianity belongs to the world of research and science and is not to be isolated from other sectors of human life. Furthermore, at this time in Norway, the teaching of Christianity in the general school system was confined to the evangelical Lutheran doctrine, and Borgen, therefore, points out that it is "objectively justified to give Lutheran doctrine and ethics a special place in the university's relevant curriculums." On the other hand, when society is getting increasingly pluralistic, other denominations and the ecumenical movement must also be subjected to thorough treatment. "It should therefore be in the interest of the churches to encourage qualified members to fill positions

---

11. Borgen, "Kristendomskunnskap som universitetsfag," *Dagen*, May 11, 1967, 3. The quotations in the text below are taken from this article.

in Christian Studies within the framework of the university's disciplines within the humanities." To those who may problematize that the subject of Christianity was located in a Department of Religious Studies, he claims that knowledge of the most influential religions is vital for those who want to examine Christianity and that, on the other hand, "the subject of Christianity can also benefit from the many other disciplines of religion, such as the psychology of religion, sociology of religion, philosophy of religion, etc."

Borgen's chronicle is thus a strong defense of the establishment of the Department of Religious Studies at the university, but also equally strong for the integration of the subject of Christianity in this religious-scientific context. At the same time, he also wanted to say something to the various church groups both outside and within the Church of Norway about how the place and role of Christianity in the new department was intended.

Religious studies as science of religion

In the long run, it would turn out that this cohabiting relationship that Borgen referred to in his program article did not last. At the department's fiftieth anniversary in 2017, Professor Einar Thomassen[12] wrote that "Years of strife followed. The teachers in Religious Studies regarded Christian knowledge as a cuckoo in the Department nest that would dominate and displace genuine religious studies. It ended with a dramatic divorce in 1985, when the two fields ended up as separate departments."[13] A few years later, it ended with the closure of the Department of Christian Knowledge in 1991. Between these dates, there was a lot of strife at the university, not at least in the Department of Religious Studies, due to various influences. The department was established a year before 1968, the year of the famous—or infamous—student uprising in France, which spread to many other countries and universities. Its influences were felt in Norway as well and led to years of discussions about social ethics, socialism, liberation theology, feminism, ecology, etc., in the 1970s and 1980s. The separation of the department into sections for religious studies and Christian knowledge, respectively, was probably due to many and varied influences, of which the aftermath of 1968 was one part in a complex time. At the Department of Religious Studies in Bergen, teachers such as Gaute Gunleiksrud (1936–2008) and later Eva Lundgren (1947–) were central in the discussions in that setting.

12. Einar Thomassen (b. 1951) got his religious studies education at the University of Bergen, and became an associate professor there in 1986, professor from 1993.

13. Einar Thomassen, "50 år med religions-vitenskap i Bergen," *Bergens Tidende*, October 26, 2017, 46.

Borgen, however, did not get much involved; he left for Trondheim already in 1973, and his successor, Torgny Bohlin, mostly stayed out of the internal discussions.

However, when the department was newly established, the relationship was much more harmonious, even though, when seen in retrospect, one might see some reasons for the later schism. Alv Kragerud submitted a statement to the faculty council already on November 5, in connection with establishing the subject of Christian knowledge at the university. Here he used many of the same arguments that Borgen later presented in his article in the spring of 1967. At the same time, Kragerud points out that the subject of Christian knowledge differs from theology. The theological disciplines of theology and theological ethics must be considered relevant only as far as they have some historical and philosophical significance. That was a position that Borgen did not fully share, so there were opportunities already here for some conflicts.

Not many days after Borgen had his chronicle published about Christian knowledge, Alv Kragerud had an even larger chronicle in *Dagen* on religious studies.[14]

In the first part of this article, he explains the variety of the religious studies that were now established in Bergen and how it was constructed. In the second part, he discusses some fields that could be perceived as troublesome for some Christians.

Theology, Kragerud writes, is a study of one's religion, often with the intention of preparing people to serve the religion in question. The science of religion, on the other hand, is the study all religions, or perhaps more precisely the study of the characteristics of the religions at the same time as one distinguishes between the individual religions. Furthermore, the science of religion contains several subdisciplines: Within the *history of religion*, one studies the history of the particular religions, but also their present form and tries, among other things, to find out what it is that causes the religions to change. The study also places great emphasis on religious texts, the sacred texts of the respective religions. Within the subject *phenomenology of religion*, one studies the individual religions across time and place, and looks for systems with a view to creating a model of the religions' structures and functions. In *sociology of religion*, one is concerned with how religion emerges in society and how it affects and is affected by its context. In *psychology of religion*, one studies how religiosity and religion are to be

14. Kragerud, "Religionsvitenskap I," *Dagen*, May 19, 1967, 3; Kragerud, "Religionsvitenskap II," *Dagen*, May 20, 1967, 3. Two years later he gave some radio lectures on "Mennesket og Religionen" (ᵐan and Religion). These were published as a book: Kragerud, *Mennesket og Religionen*.

understood, exemplified by questions as: What is the peculiarity of the religious feeling and the religious experience? What is the relationship between healthy and sick religiosity? The last part of the curriculum in Bergen consists of *philosophy of religion*. The most crucial question in the philosophy of religion is, according to Kragerud: What is religion? Is it a separate way of thinking? Or is it a particular kind of sensitivity? Is it moral, or maybe it is a mixture of all this? Kragerud believes that the philosophy of religion has shown that "religion is a separate, independent part of normal human equipment. Because of that, it has given religion a letter of freedom that it has often missed." Thus, "Science of religion is the science of Religion." It is not a science about God, but the science of the belief in God.

These two articles demonstrate that it was essential to present these studies to potential students and other, perhaps more critical target groups. Moreover, the articles are to be read in the context of a more extensive debate, or larger "discourse," as it would be called in the academic jargon, namely, in the debate about the role and place of both these studies in the Norwegian educational system, from primary school all the way up to the university levels.

Hence, from the spring of 1967, Peder Borgen was at work in his new academic duties in Bergen. Now he had got a teaching position at a Norwegian university. And he began his work with as much zeal and fervor as he possible could master. However, he did not forget what he had been through a few months ago. The clash with the wall in the preceding summer did not leave its hold on him. When well established in Bergen, he got in touch with a psychiatrist with whom he then worked by way of some talk therapy sessions in the following year and a half. She was a great help to him. He felt she understood him: "She was marvelous," he later said.[15] He got to talk through a lot of what needed further processing. Years of tension and stress were unleashed, and he came through strengthened and emboldened. The experiences of both the crisis and the needed therapy he carried with him onwards as a resource; they affected him but were also helpful in avoiding overwork later in life.

Borgen did not get the professorship he applied for in Bergen, but he nevertheless received a positive assessment of his competence and was declared competent for a professorship. In the short term, it paid off financially as he became an "associate professor with promotion." In the longer term, it gave him the courage and guts to continue his professional work and to apply for another professorship later. He also made it clear that he was happy with the role he had taken on; on the one hand, the opportunities

---

15. In a private conversation in 1917; exact date not registered.

to work with Christian knowledge in a Norwegian context, on the other hand, of being in Bergen and in a new department.[16]

Working in the department

The study of Christian knowledge thus became Borgen's primary responsibility. Kragerud, as the department's only professor, had the overall responsibility, but as a professor in religious studies, he was primarily responsible for teaching the more explicit religious science subjects. In addition, there were some assistant teachers in both subjects at work.

The study topics were gathered into three various study programs. In terms of content, it was emphasized that "The subject Christian Knowledge emphasizes a presentation of Christianity in its uniqueness, and at the same time paying due attention to its interaction with the spiritual life in general in history and the present. In this way, Christian knowledge was given a context at the university level that corresponded to the subject context of the Christian subject in the general school system."[17] The basic Christian knowledge program (called *Grunnfag*) was given the following structure: *religious history background* (general religious knowledge, oriental history of religion, late antiquity philosophy); *Old Testament* (history, history of religion, history of Old Testament literature, exegesis, and some cursory text reading); *New Testament* (history, history of religion, history of literature and exegesis) and *history and the present* (church history, various denominations, and systematics). In general, it was a fairly traditional scheme, while within the individual subjects, there were more electives than at comparable Norwegian institutions. Another component, called *Mellomfag*, could be added. Then the Norwegian system added a third component, called *Hovedfag*: about two years of studies, including a dissertation of eighty to one hundred pages. This was long before the programs of bachelor's and master's studies were introduced in Norway; that did not happen until 2003. The *Hovedfag*, however, could be compared to the later master's.

In many ways, the first year (*Grunnfag*) became like a miniature study of theology. Initially, that was intended to be a strength of the subject of Christian knowledge. Still, others eventually thought it revealed that the subject had not cut its ties to theology sufficiently and thus not

---

16. In an interview in *Dagen* in the spring of 1967, he expressed great joy of being in Bergen: (anonymous), "Kristendom på universitetsplan—et nødvendig og naturlig krav," *Dagen*, May 5, 1967, 1 and 8.

17. Borgen, in a private written presentation, dated April 28, 1967. Now in the Borgen archives in the National Archive.

gained an apparent distinctiveness of its own. The subject's relationship to religious studies also became an Achilles heel for several years, not at least in Bergen.

Borgen as a recruitment agent

New study programs often require certain recruitment efforts and PR; the student Per Magne Aadnanes had taken a course in history in the year 1966–67, and for a while he wondered what subject he should continue with. He was interested in the study of Christianity, but also in the history of ideas; hence he contacted Borgen. In him, he experienced meeting an eager *recruitment agent*. Aadnanes describes it thus:

> Peder Borgen turned out to be an exquisitely friendly and accommodating man and quite clearly eager to "hijack" as many students as possible for this new study. He presented and explained the study plan to me in a familiar, almost comradely tone. In a marvelous way, he managed to give me a feeling of being particularly interesting, as if he saw a potential in me as a student and academic I myself had not been aware of before.[18]

Aadnanes felt comfortable having Borgen as a teacher, and Borgen was close to persuading him to take a master's degree in Christian knowledge. But majoring in the history of ideas was, at last, more tempting to Aadnanes. Borgen, however, argued strongly for his master's degree: "It was the always equally creative and ambitious Borgen . . . And now he used all his charm to hijack students for this (the master program)."[19]

Although Borgen brought in several assistant teachers, comprising systematics and ethics, church history, and parts of the Old Testament, he did a lot of work himself. He taught the New Testament and hermeneutics. "Borgen must have been a real 'workhorse,' who in this demanding phase was able to carry most of the basic teaching load alone," Aadnanes wrote in his autobiography several years later.[20] In the religious science subjects, Kragerud and his assistant teacher(s) lectured on religious studies. There was a great deal of work pressure on all the teachers in the first years, which may have affected the lack of collegial fellowship within the department.

---

18. Aadnanes, *Litt av eit puslespel*, 174.
19. Aadnanes, *Litt av eit puslespel*, 175.
20. Aadnanes, *Litt av eit puslespel*, 175.

AS A METHODIST IN BERGEN

When Peder Borgen began his work as a lecturer at the Department of Religious Studies on April 1, 1967, Inger Borgen remained in Lillestrøm. But she joined him in Bergen by the end of the summer, and after a while, they moved into a house in Rådal, a suburb to Bergen. Inger was expecting, and at the end of October, the two-year-old Heidi got a little sister. She was named Ingunn Elisabeth. Inger made a conscious choice to be at home with the children and was not in permanent paid work during the years in Bergen. However, she was involved in the Methodist Church's voluntary work, e.g., as a Sunday school teacher in the Central Church (Centralkirken), which was located in the center of Bergen.

Gradually, it also became possible for her to use her education in professional contexts. She got in touch with the Family Welfare Office and for a while had a part-time job there on Saturdays. She also arranged courses in the evenings, gave lectures in groups for young families, and wrote articles for a magazine for parents, *Vi Foreldre*. When the Methodists established a seminary for clergy education in Bergen, she became the leader of its support group. However, she did not accept a permanent job outside the home until they moved to Trondheim (1973). But then she took some further education in family therapy. At the same time, she also received assignments within the Methodist Church both locally and internationally (see next chapter).

Church commitments

Hence Peder could concentrate on the work in the department. However, it soon turned out that he also got involved in other duties and tasks. A few weeks after starting at the university, he gave his first sermon in the Methodist church in downtown Bergen, the Central Methodist Church. This church was also to become their regular worship church on Sundays. As parents of small children, it was not easy to participate as a couple in events downtown in the middle of the week, even though Peder participated in several meetings on different weekdays.

A review of the advertisements in the Christian newspaper *Dagen* shows that he participated in several different religious meetings during the years he lived in Bergen. When Alv Kragerud wrote a presentation of his colleague in *Dagen*, he wrote, among other things, that "Borgen is one of the few who combine research with a strong commitment to church work."[21]

---

21. Kragerud, "Universitetslektor i kristendomskunnskap," *Dagen*, April 20, 1967, 1 and 8.

For Peder himself, it was quite normal to be an active contributor in Bergen's Methodist circles and other circles and in ecumenical work, not least in the ecumenical prayer weeks.

He was also introduced to a larger audience through devotionals on Norwegian Radio Broadcasting (NRK).[22] In January 1968, he had some short devotionals on Saturdays called "Scripture readings." At that time, it was easier for non-Lutherans to get to participate in these than in the more ordinary radio devotionals. But the program overviews of NRK from the same year show that he also had some of the ordinary morning radio devotions in October. However, most of the religious radio programs these years focused on, and drew contributions from, the majority church, the (Lutheran) Church of Norway.

Ecumenical commitments

Peder Borgen retained his ecumenical interest, which he had cherished since the founding meeting of the World Council of Churches. Hence, during his stay in Bergen, he sometimes also preached in some other free churches.

But his ecumenical interest also led him to be active in the annual prayer weeks for Christian unity, both as a preacher and as an active member of the preparatory committees, and thus as one of those who signed the annual petitions for participation in the prayer weeks. Ecumenical themes were also repeated in several of his other speeches and sermons, such as "Different, but One," "Church Underway," and "Ecumenical Tendencies and Problems in World Methodism." The latter was a topic he lectured on at meetings for pastors of the Methodist Church, but he was also invited to give lectures on this subject at the Faculty of Theology in Oslo, at the invitation of Prof Nils Bloch-Hoell.[23]

In these lectures, he posed three questions: 1. Should Methodism aim at confessional or interconfessional gathering and renewal? 2. Should Methodism aim to form national church units or a church with an international structure? 3. Does Methodism have a theological contribution to make in interchurch contexts, or is it in danger of being absorbed by other denominations and the ecumenical movement?

Borgen commented on the several mergers of Methodist churches both in Europe and in the United States. The Norwegian church was—and is—a part of the United Methodist Church since 1968. Borgen was not blind

22. There was only one national broadcasting company at that time. It provided only one radio station and one TV station.

23. Published as Borgen, "Ekumeniske tendenser."

to claims and attitudes towards the Methodist Church in Norway that it was "a cultural import or religious import from abroad." However, he parried it by claiming that historically, the Methodist Church is no more a cultural import than the Norwegian Lutheran Church is a cultural import from Germany.[24] That was one of the reasons why he believed it was not acceptable that the majority church called itself "*The Norwegian* Church." It was not more Norwegian than the other churches.[25]

On the other hand, he is equally clear on the problems of uniting several national Methodist churches; efforts of unification are often crossed by national interests and traditions. As for the Methodist Church's role and place in Norwegian church life, he claimed that "it understands itself placed in the middle of the other free churches and the Norwegian Lutheran Church."[26] But it is Norwegian! The national roots of Methodism, he thought, should be emphasized more strongly, and he was favorable to the tendencies towards a de-Americanization of the structures of the Methodist Church. That the Annual Conference in 1970 decided to withdraw from the theological education in Sweden and restart a Methodist seminary in Norway, he also saw as a strengthening of the church's Norwegian roots. Furthermore, in these efforts, Peder Borgen was given a central role, and a Norwegian Methodist clerical education was soon to be established in Bergen!

Another aspect he points out as somewhat typically Norwegian is the following: in Norway, there were no interconfessional dialogues at this time. Norwegian Methodist efforts in the World Council of Churches (WCC) were hampered, "partly because the WCC's channels to Norway to a large extent were not ecumenical, but too confessionally limited to the Church of Norway, and partly because WCC's main channel to the Norwegian Methodist Church was via New York."[27] The Methodist Church is, admittedly, a member of the Norwegian Free Church Council, but he finds this council somewhat impeded by its fear of the Roman Catholic Church and its anxiety and unwillingness to engage in theological interdenominational talks.

24. Borgen, "Ekumeniske tendenser," 37. His argument is open to some nuances: it is a fact that the Methodists in Norway do not call their church the "Norwegian Methodist Church," but the "Methodist Church in Norway." In a most recent ecumenical report, the church is even called the "United Methodist Church in Norway." And its General Conference is still located outside Norway, in the USA.

25. Borgen never managed to come to terms with this name; and to some extent this is understandable. There are also several other free churches in Norway, even several Lutheran, but none were called Norwegian in the same way as the majority church was.

26. Borgen, "Ekumeniske tendenser," 36. By "*the* Norwegian Lutheran Church" he obviously meant the majority church.

27. Borgen, "Ekumeniske tendenser," 31.

He would have preferred a joint council for all denominations in Norway, as the Methodist Church's Annual Conference also argued for in 1969.

The article as such is a good review of the ecumenical situation in Norway in the 1970s seen from the perspective of the free non-Lutheran church, and we will have to return to the role of Borgen himself as an ecumenist in the years to come in the mainly Lutheran Norway.

Some border crossings were necessary over and over again.

Borgen and the Methodist seminary in Bergen

Those who wanted to become Methodist pastors in Norway had to receive their education at the joint Nordic seminar in Øverås near Gothenburg in Sweden (Metodistkyrkans Teologiske Seminarium Øverås). Borgen was a guest lecturer there several times.

However, what became a more lasting significance for his involvement with the Methodist Church's pastoral education was the work that was started to establish a separate Methodist pastoral education in Norway, a work that resulted in the establishment of such an educational institution in Bergen.

The seminary in Øverås was a Nordic cooperation project. There was a school board in each country but at the same time a Nordic board. The Methodist Church in Norway had been involved in this collaboration since 1924. But throughout the 1960s, Norwegian Methodists had discussed other forms of clerical education. There are several reasons for this. A contributing reason may be that in the years 1960-70, the seminary in Gothenburg had forty-one students from Norway, while there had only been thirty-five students from the three other Nordic countries, Sweden, Denmark, and Finland. However, in more recent years, there had been fewer Norwegian students in Øverås. Such figures could indicate that the education should instead be in Norway.

In 1970, the Norwegian school board made a unanimous recommendation to the Annual Conference that such an education should be linked to the teaching offered at the Department of Religious Studies at the University of Bergen. Peder Borgen, who had been involved in the preparatory work, strongly emphasized that he had undertaken this work "... after strong recommendations.... For me, this is not a question of prestige, and if there is any tug of war between Bergen and any other study centers, I will withdraw immediately," he said.[28]

28. See the report: (anonymous), "Metodistprester drøfter en alternativ utdannelse," *Vårt Land*, March 11, 1970, 6.

The Annual Conference, held in Bergen in June, favored Bergen and decided to withdraw from the Scandinavian joint seminary at Øverås. Thus, it became clear that the education of Norwegian Methodist pastors would be in Norway from the autumn of 1971, and it was to be located in Bergen. In addition to using teaching facilities at the university, a Methodist study center[29] was to be established that could take care of the additional teaching in the Methodist subjects considered necessary for those who wanted to become pastors in the Methodist Church.

What role did Peder Borgen play in this election? Even if he stated that he had done the preparatory negotiations "after strong recommendations," it does not mean that he was reluctant or uninterested. Moreover, it is natural to believe that the very fact that he was in Bergen had a particular magnetic reinforcing effect for Bergen as an appropriate place of study. Supervisor Carl Gundersen, then, also stated in an interview with the newspaper *Dagen*:

> here in Bergen, we have associate professor Peder Borgen, one of our own, who teaches religion at the University here. It would be a great advantage to have the Seminary in Bergen. The intention is not for Borgen to leave his current job, but he would be a helpful man for the Seminary in its early phases.[30]

It also turned out that Borgen became a relevant factor when a new debate arose in the latter half of the 1970s about the seminary's continued location in Norway. By then, however, Borgen had left Bergen and had taken up a new position as a professor in Trondheim. Now it was seriously discussed whether the seminary should be moved to Oslo, Trondheim, or remain in Bergen. That Trondheim was considered too was, undoubtedly, because Borgen was now located there.

Debating the future of the seminary

Not long after Borgen had left Bergen, discussions arose about moving the seminary again.

The seminary was dear to Borgen. His attitude is demonstrated not least by the commitment he demonstrated in the debate about the seminary's

---

29. See a presentation of the 1970 Annual Conference in *Kristelig Tidende* 10:99 (1970) 6–7 and 14–15.

30. See (anonymous), "Bergen aktuell som utdannelsessted for norske metodistprester," *Dagen*, April 1, 1970, 1.

future but also in a speech he gave at the one-hundredth anniversary a few years earlier.

In the early summer of 1974, the Methodist theological school's hundredth anniversary was celebrated. The Norwegian Methodist Church had started its pastoral education as early as 1874, and although there had been a few years' break, and a long period in Øverås (1924–1970), one still counted 1874 as the year of foundation; hence plans were made to celebrate the hundredth anniversary in 1974. The year may seem arbitrary since the seminary did not have a continuous history,[31] but it must be understood as an issue of legitimacy and identity-making for such an institution in its construction phase in the 1970s. At the celebration, held in Bergen on May 19, 1974, Borgen gave the keynote speech, and here he presented some of his visions for the seminary. The starting point for his speech was the Gospel of John 14:25–26, where Jesus promises the disciples the Holy Spirit, who will "teach you all things, and remind you of all things that I have said to you." Borgen strongly emphasized the importance of pastors having a good and appropriate education. This does not mean that God cannot use people without a theological education to win souls, but in the demanding position as a pastor, "it is dangerous for himself and the congregation if he does not have the necessary knowledge." In this context, it is essential that the Spirit should teach the disciples and that it is about Jesus and his words that he should teach them. Therefore, "the Spirit drives us to study the Bible to know more about him who is the mediator between God and men. The Seminary must thus be a Bible and Jesus seminar." And as the theological professor he was, but also grounded in the school's history, he emphasized that it was essential that whoever was to teach others as a pastor should also be able to "read the New Testament in Greek."

However, the seminary became involved in some problems and conflicts in the mid-1970s. These issues were both of an economic and structural nature but also influenced by person-related factors. Borgen was a member of MUO—the Methodist Church's Education and Information Council—both when he was in Bergen and after he had moved to Trondheim, and this council served as a board for the school in Bergen.[32]

In the first years in Bergen, the seminary used rented premises, but in 1973 a large building at Olaf Rye's Street 41 was purchased as premises for the school. However, during the rebuilding and restoration work, some major fungal damage was discovered in the house, which led to extra expenses

---

31. The school had a break in the years 1879–88, cf. Haddal, *Vær fra vest*, 113.

32. In 1971, E. Anker Nilsen (1904–86) was employed as a principal at the school; in 1975 Harald Larsen took over, but he stayed there for only one year and was succeeded by Paul Sundar in 1976.

in an already strained financial situation. These circumstances led to a decision at the Annual Conference in 1975 that MUO should investigate alternative solutions for further seminary operations and locations. In studying alternative solutions, both a relocation of the seminary to Trondheim or Oslo and a continued location in Bergen were discussed. MUO clearly and unequivocally promoted continued location in Bergen, while the rector argued and advocated relocation and reestablishment in Oslo. Overall, the case also suffered from poor cooperation between the rector and the board (MUO), and perhaps especially between the rector and Peder Borgen. It turned out to be one of the most critical moments in Borgen's relations with his church.

The case culminated in the negotiations at the Annual Conference in Mysen at the beginning of July 1976. On Friday, July 2, the seminary case was up for consideration. In the negotiations, Peder Borgen and several others explained the matter and "believed that the Seminary needed peace and continuity to grow and stabilize"[33] and emphasized that "coordination with the University and the congregations in Bergen was well developed." The rector, for his part, claimed that "it was pointless to invest such large amounts as is the case with O. Ryes Street 41," and argued for moving to Oslo. In addition, there had been an invitation to get reinvolved in the joint Nordic pastoral education in Øverås.

The debate gradually became one of the most intense for many years in the context of the Annual Conference. It climaxed with the presentation and voting on a proposal for a resolution from Ragnar Horn (1913–2003), a Supreme Court lawyer and Methodist layman who had a significant influence in the church. The proposal contained several points that represented a strong criticism of MUO. Among other things, it was claimed and regretted that the board's report was not good enough, and that it was doubtful whether the property had strengthened its value in the market as MUO claimed; and demands were made that a public valuation and a legitimate offer was to be obtained from relevant buyers. Furthermore, some argued that the property would probably cause the church significant financial losses in the future. The sale of the property should, therefore, be considered.

These stated opinions were de facto a scathing critique of MUO, and Borgen became very upset, to say the least.[34] He supported a counterproposal to reject the offer from Øverås, and he perceived the other submitted proposals as a no-confidence motion against the board. During the voting

33. The quotes in this paragraph are taken from *Årboken* (The Yearbook) 1976.

34. Peder most probably felt that the board had been considered completely incompetent as a board and that he did not see it possible to continue without the support of the Annual Conference. He was deeply frustrated but also angry.

session, it turned out that the alternative of reconsidering returning to Øverås was accepted.[35] Moreover, when voting over Horn's proposals, all its critical parts were adopted.[36]

The participants' reactions at the conference to this result were strong on both sides, but the most comprehensive reaction came from Peder Borgen. He announced that he would not only leave the board but would also discontinue his work as a part-time teacher at the seminary, and he even asked to be allowed to go into voluntary local relations as a pastor.[37]

In the following hours and the next day, there were many deliberations among the delegates to the Annual Conference. The voting and resulting reactions sent shock waves into the Conference; some were deeply shaken by what had happened and expressed that this was an intolerable situation.

During the negotiations concerning the executive board's additional report the following day, it was decided to take up the matter concerning the seminary again. Further negotiations took place in an extra session on the last day of the Conference, Sunday, at 4:30 p.m. The main issues in the new decision reached at that meeting were: the seminary's location was to remain in Bergen.[38] Hence, the proposals to move from Bergen and proceed on the Østerås alternative were laid to rest. The seminary remained in Bergen for many years to come. Peder Borgen continued as a part-time teacher and as a member of the MUO. However, he left the board of MUO in 1982, not in protest but more because he wanted to focus on his work as a professor in Trondheim.

It still took a long time to heal the experiences from the Annual Conference in 1976, and the seminary's aftermath was marked by what had been highlighted in these years. Peder continued as a contributor but gradually developed a somewhat restrained relationship to the Annual Conference's role in the church.[39]

The seminary remained, then, in Bergen for several years, but after about a decade, it ended with relocation. It first moved to Fyllingsdalen in

35. Sixty votes in favor, fifty-three against, and two abstentions.

36. Sixty-two votes in favor, fifty-three against, and twelve abstentions. See *Årboken* (Yearbook) 1976, 47.

37. See *Årboken* (The Yearbook) 1976, 47. In Methodist ecclesial jargon, it simply meant that he withdrew as a participant in the Annual Conference; that is, he withdrew from his status as a Pastor and his status as such within the Annual Conference, and only wanted a local and voluntary affiliation. In such a case, he would keep the ordination and could function as a pastor locally.

38. See *Årboken (1976)*.

39. Cf. Borgen, "Misjon i nytestamentlig tid og i Metodistkirken," 37. Here he reflects on the various ecclesiastical bodies of the Methodist Church and finds that it is such a complex structure that responsibility is often pulverized.

1987–88, to premises in the new Methodist suburban church being built there. Then there was a move to Oslo in 2001, where the seminary gradually collaborated with the Free Faculty of Theology (Menighetsfakultetet). The operation of the seminary is now organized so that it has a principal employed in a part-time position and who administers the Methodist subjects, that is, topics like Methodist Church order and liturgy, while the other subjects are taken from the studies offered at the Free Faculty of Theology.[40]

BORGEN'S RESEARCH IN BERGEN

The most productive phase of Peder Borgen's academic life in terms of research publications was to come a little later, from approximately the late 1970s, after having moved to Trondheim. His new position in Bergen, the impact of being new as an academic teacher in Norway, the new social environment, being a father of two, etc., demanded his primary focus there and then. Nevertheless, he produced around ten scholarly articles while in Bergen. In the USA, they might say—in a more or less serious way—"publish or perish." In Norway, there was no similar strict regime at this time, but a certain percentage of one's working hours were intended for research, and one was expected to publish. But no one checked the size or quality of your production.

His membership in some international and scholarly New Testament societies was an essential professional inspiration to Borgen. When he was a professor at Wesley Theological Seminary in Washington, DC, he became a member of the Society of Biblical Literature (SBL), a professional forum for researchers in both the Old and New Testaments. The society was formed in 1880 and is the oldest scholarly society of its kind, conducting extensive activities, including publishing books and several journals. In the beginning, the members came primarily from the United States, and the Society has divided the country into regions having their own regional meetings and gatherings. However, the essential gathering was, and still is, its Annual Meeting, which now is held in November each year.[41]

While in Bergen, he also became a member of another more European society, which had its annual meetings in Europe: Studiorum Novi

---

40. In 1947, Peder could not study at the Free Faculty of Theology because he was not a Lutheran; in 2011 and onwards, the Methodist seminary joined the Free Faculty and shared its curriculum and lectures!

41. For a brief sketch of the developments of the SBL, see Baird, *History of New Testament Research*, 3:445–48.

Testamenti Societas.⁴² While SBL is a society for which you register yourself, SNTS is more exclusive: to become a member, one must be proposed by two members and then be elected at the Annual Meeting by the members in plenum.⁴³ Borgen was proposed as a member by the Norwegian professors Sverre Aalen and Jacob Jervell and joined the Society in 1967. From then on, he was able to participate in the various meetings and could profit from the expanded field of contact such associations represented: "I had stagnated as a researcher had I not had opportunities to participate in SBL and SNTS."⁴⁴ In the years to come, he became a very eager participant in SNTS. He took part every year in their General Meetings while he was in Bergen, and sometimes also at the Annual Meetings of SBL.

Further studies: elaborations on *Bread from Heaven*

In this section, I am primarily focusing on the studies published during his stay in Bergen. However, some studies may be closely related to others published later. In such cases, it will be pertinent to comment on these too.

"God's Agent in the Fourth Gospel" (1968)

While working at Wesley Theological Seminary in the United States, he attended several of SBL's Annual Meetings. In one of these meetings, he met Erwin R. Goodenough (1893–1965) and had an hour-long conversation with him about Philo of Alexandria. Goodenough had for many years been a prominent and highly profiled scholar who had specialized in Philo and Hellenistic Judaism.⁴⁵ That this aged and reputable researcher spent some time with him made a lasting impression, and the first article Borgen published after his disputation—and while in Bergen—was a contribution to a

---

42. SNTS (Society for New Testament Studies), founded in 1938 for the furtherance of New Testament studies internationally.

43. Requirements for membership are a doctorate or equivalent, and several other publications in the field too, which is the New Testament. See https://snts.online. See also Baird, *History of New Testament Research*, 3:452–54. Baird (454) concludes his review thus: "In sum, the SNTS is the primary international association for the study of the NT. It promotes the highest quality of research and confers on its members a degree of scholarly prestige."

44. Borgen, interview by the author, November 14, 2017.

45. See Eccles, *Erwin Ramsdell Goodenough*.

book published in memory of Goodenough. The article reads: "God's Agent in the Fourth Gospel."[46]

This article is an expanded version of a section in Borgen's dissertation, *Bread from Heaven*.[47] Borgen here works with rabbinic material as a background for the Gospel of John's descriptions of Jesus as sent from God, sent as his messenger/agent. Some have wanted to see a Gnostic background as relevant to understanding this notion. Borgen, however, argues that the background should instead be sought in Jewish rabbinic material, and then Jewish material of a more mystic character, the so-called Merkabah mysticism, but in the early stages of such mysterious traditions. He summarizes his findings concerning the similarities between Halakhic principles of agency and ideas in the Gospel of John thus: "(a) a unity between the agent and his sender–(b) although the agent is subordinate, (c) the obedience of the agent to the will of the sender, (d) the task of the agent in the lawsuit, (e) his return and reporting back to the sender, and (f) his appointing of other agents as an extension of his mission in time and space."[48]

However, he also believes that he can find support for his view in texts by Philo of Alexandria. Having applied the Halakhic view of agency to the Fourth Gospel, he turns to Merkabah mysticism: "Here we find a combination of Halakah, heavenly figures and the heavenly world as is the case with the idea of agency in the Fourth Gospel."[49] Then he proceeds to Philo and finds parallels in his view of Israel, especially in Philo's *Conf.* 146 and *Leg. All.* 1.43. Finally, while Bultmann found Gnostic texts as relevant to understanding the Gospel of John, Borgen surmises that texts from Nag Hammadi provide evidence "for the fact that Jewish Merkabah traditions have influenced the gnostic movement."[50] Hence the Jewish background of the Fourth Gospel is still the most relevant.

The article is an example of how he utilized and expanded aspects from his doctoral dissertation that he had found no room to address on a broader basis in that volume.

---

46. The study as such was written in 1963–64 while he was at Wesley, but was not published until 1968, and was then republished four times. That he had this study published five times demonstrates his high evaluation of his study. See Borgen, "God's Agent in the Fourth Gospel," 137–48, reprinted in Borgen's collections of articles published in 1983 (Borgen, *Logos Was the True Light*, 121–32), in 1987 (Borgen, *Philo, John and Paul*, 171–204), and in 2014 (Borgen, *Gospel of John: More Light . . .*, 167–91). It was also included in Ashton, ed., *Interpretation of John*, 67–78 (1986). I quote from the 1983 edition. Cf. the appendix at the end of this volume.

47. See Borgen, *Bread from Heaven*, 158–64.

48. Borgen, *Logos Was the True Light*, 128.

49. Borgen, *Logos Was the True Light*, 128.

50. Borgen, *Logos Was the True Light*, 132.

As Borgen himself points out in the preface to his 1983 collection of articles on John, Jan A. Bühner further developed aspects from this early study of Borgen.[51] J. Ashton gave a full appreciation of the article when he wrote, "There is no need, when investigating the theology of Jesus' role as the agent or special representative of God to turn to Mandeism or other Gnostic systems for the source of the evangelist's idea—it is to be found ready at hand in the Jewish tradition."[52]

In 2010 Borgen participated in the Annual Meeting of the Society of Biblical Literature in Atlanta, Georgia. Here he presented a paper linked to his article from 1968 presented above but which expanded the study in several ways, especially asking questions of how this idea of agents/agency should be considered relevant for studying the historical Jesus.[53] The question might be interesting, but Borgen provides only some suggestions in his article.

Observations on the Prologue of John

Borgen continued to work on the Gospel of John during his time in Bergen and published two studies on the first chapter of this gospel. The first was published in 1970 in both Norwegian and English; the Norwegian edition was entitled "The Johannes Prologue as Exegesis" (my translation).[54] The English version is labeled "Observations on the Targumic Character of the Prologue of John." It is his central thesis that the Prologue (John 1:18–18) is an interpretation of Gen 1:1f.[55] "Thus John i.1–5 is the basic exposition

51. Bühner, *Der Gesandte und sein Weg*.
52. Ashton, *Interpretation of John*, 14.
53. This paper was published in his 2014 collection of articles, *Gospel of John*, 193–218.
54. Borgen, "Johannes-prologen som eksegese," 73–84. The English version is titled "Observations on the Targumic Character of the Prologue of John," and is reprinted in Borgen's collection of articles (1983) *Logos Was the True Light*, 13–20, and in *Philo, John and Paul*, 75–101, as "The Prologue of John—as Exposition of the Old Testament." The latter is, however, somewhat expanded. Here he also comments on some criticism from R. Alan Culpepper (93–96).
55. Borgen summarizes its view as follows: In John 1:1–5, Gen 1:1–5 is the subject of a three-part interpretation, which can be characterized as follows: a) "Logos"–"God" (vv. 1–2), b) "was created by him" (v. 3), and c) "the light" (v. 4–5). This is followed by a corresponding continuation of these points, but here the passages follow in reverse order: c) "the light" (vv. 6–9), b) "was created by him" (vv. 10–13), and a) "Logos"–"God" (vv. 14–18). Borgen further believes that he has found a parallel to this three-part pattern (a), b), c) and c) b) a) in Targum Jerusalem to Genesis 3:24 and in other Jewish sources. These parallels deal with, like the John Prologue, that which had its origin in the creation and before and which was then revealed at a later time. This, he believes, can also then explain why the coming of Jesus is mentioned three times (vv. 9, 11, and

of Gen. i.1–5, while John i.6ff elaborates upon terms and phrases from John i.1–5."⁵⁶

In late September 1970, due to an invitation by H. Riesenfeld, Borgen delivered a guest lecture at the University of Uppsala labeled "Logos Was the True Light: Contributions to the Interpretation of the Prologue of John."⁵⁷ He took his point of departure is some questions related to the unity of the passage John 1:1–18: ". . . can John I 1–18 be considered a unit, composed by the evangelist? . . . does the exegesis compel us to reckon with a reworked and supplemented source?"⁵⁸ He narrowed his focus down to a study of verses 4–5 and 6–9 on light, and he stated that his study of Jewish traditions and a closer analysis of the Prologue led to the conclusion that the theory that what we have here is a source reworked and supplemented by the evangelist was unnecessary.⁵⁹

Digitalizing Philo

The most innovative project in these years was probably the one initiated and led by Borgen related to Philo's works: he wanted to get a digitalized version of Philo's texts.⁶⁰

Computer technology was still in a kind of childhood phase in the early 1970s; perhaps one could say that it was approaching its early teens. This development was especially evident when it came to the more general use of computer technology outside the specialists' domains; PCs—personal computers—were still visions of the future. The first PCs came in the early 1980s.⁶¹

However, relevant technology was in rapid development at this time. Together with more computer-savvy people at the University of Bergen,

---

14), and opens up for a new gateway to the content of the Prologue.

56. *Logos Was the true Light*, 16, cf. 19: ". . . the structure and outline of John i.1–18 are determined by the fact that the passage is meant to be an exposition of Gen. i.1ff."

57. His lecture was published later that year in the Swedish journal *Svensk Exegetisk Årsbok*. Borgen, "Logos var det sanne lys. Momenter til tolkning av Johannesprologen," 79–95. English translation: Borgen, "Logos Was the True Light," *NovT* 14 (1972) 115–30; and in his collection of Johannine articles in 1983 (Borgen, *Logos Was the true Light*, 95–110).

58. Borgen, *Logos Was the True Light*, 98.

59. Borgen, *Logos Was the True Light*, 100.

60. The project is described (in Norwegian) in Borgen and Skarsten, "Bibelvitenskap, gresk og EDB," 37–39 and 50.

61. A brief but instructive overview of this early development can be found here: https://en.wikipedia.org/wiki/History_of_personal_computers.

Borgen managed to establish a four-year-long research project where the Greek texts of Philo of Alexandria were to be converted into computer-readable texts, funded by NAVF.[62]

In the application to NAVF, the project was entitled "Exegetical Terminology and Exegetical Style Patterns in Selected Writings by Philo from Alexandria." However, the following tasks served as subgoals: 1) to produce a machine-readable text by Philo from Alexandria's works, 2) to produce a computer-produced index verborum (glossary) for Philo's writings, and 3) to carry out an analysis of exegetical terminology and exegetical style patterns in selected writings by Philo.

The bulk of the more demanding work was undoubtedly the first part; to establish Philo's Greek texts as computer-readable text. The Greek words may have many accents and characters; most of them are above the letters, some in front, but also some below, and this represented significant challenges. Next, a so-called concordance was to be printed, that is, a list of all the occurrences of all the word forms that existed in Philo's texts.[63]

The purpose of the project was, seen in a wider context—among other things—to be able to quickly lookup patterns in Philo's texts, a task that had its own value, but which was also valuable and necessary if one were to compare Philo with other Greek texts. The New Testament was already available in electronic format, and the Philo project attracted positive attention far beyond the Norwegian research context.[64]

---

62. The project was carried on from January 1, 1970, to December 31, 1974. It was funded by NAVF (Norwegian Research Council for Science and the Humanities) and consisted of Peder Borgen as the leader and Roald Skarsten as a research fellow. In addition, several other people were involved, including two persons punching the texts into the computers and a Greek student as a proofreader.

63. See Borgen and Skarsten, "Bibelvitenskap, gresk og EDB."

64. An interview with Peder Borgen in the daily newspaper *Vårt Land* provides some insight into this; see Haddal, "Philo—ikke-kristen 'kirkefar,'" *Vårt Land* July 4 (1973) 13.

The great Philo project, initiated in Bergen, and finalized in Trondheim, was somewhat changed over the years. The end result, however, was a digitalized and tagged Greek text of Philo's works, and the publication of a *Philo Index*.

The project was not completed within the time frame they had been given; that is, the texts were punched in, and they could make printouts, but the analysis work was not completed during the projected period. When Borgen moved to Trondheim in 1973, and the project was terminated in 1974, he eventually received a printout of the texts in the form of what is called a KWIC concordance (KWIC = key words in context). It included several binders and was a good help for research in Philo's texts both for him and the research fellows he had in the 1980s and 90s.[65]

Later, this project was continued in a new NAVF project in Trondheim, also this time with Peder Borgen as leader, but now with Kåre Fuglseth as the computer scientist. At the same time, however, the development in computer technology and personal computers had advanced so fast that some of the project's subgoals from 1970 were not carried forward in their original form.

65. The first article using these texts was published in 1977, and Roald Skarsten later used this textual material in his doctoral dissertation (1987), which was an analysis of the author's identity in one of Philo's writings. See Skarsten, *Forfatterproblemet*.

It is a lasting result, however, of both the Bergen and Trondheim projects that Philo's texts are now digitally available in grammatically tagged (marked) form for anyone interested in them as they are now available in several computer programs.[66] A *Philo Index* was published in 2000; a comprehensive Philo KWIC index was published in 2005.[67]

Studies in church history

The Norwegian church historian, Prof. E. Molland had suggested that Borgen should study church history, but he chose the New Testament. However, his interest in church history appeared several times in his research career. And when his article on Hans Olsen from Bergen was published, it was dedicated to his former teacher in church history, Professor Einar Molland.[68]

Hans Olsen, or Johannes Olsonius, as he was called in Latin, was a versatile and learned man. He had worked for shorter periods both in Copenhagen and in several locations in Holland and England, and not least in Bergen. He became known as a doctor, court alchemist, linguist, theologian and mystic, book translator, and social benefactor. In 1663, he established a much-needed widows' retirement home in Bergen and was also its first manager.

Finally, the last study to be mentioned here is a minor piece that goes a little beyond the very New Testament material and into the early church history. It nevertheless has strong connections to the NT. The study deals with "Ignatius and Traditions on the Birth of Jesus."[69] Borgen examines the material contained in the Ignatian letters about the birth of Jesus and asks whether Ignatius is dependent on the accounts of Matthew and Luke, or whether he (also) has other traditional material. He concludes that it seems that Ignatius reproduces material about the virgin birth that originates from traditions representing parallel traditions to those found in the Gospels of Matthew and Luke, for they can hardly be seen as derived from the Gospels.

---

66. The text is now available in the two great Bible programs for PC/Mac on the market: Logos© (www.logos.com) and Accordance Bible Software© (www.accordancebible.com). It is also used in BibleWorks©, but that program is no longer available on the market (www.bibleworks.com). See also Seland, *Reading Philo*, especially 169–72.

67. Borgen, Fuglseth, and Skarsten, *Philo Index*. A KWIC concordance was published in 2005: Skarsten, Borgen, and Fuglseth, *Complete Works of Philo* (8 vols).

68. Borgen, "Johannes Olsonius. Theosophus et Medicus Bergensis," 1–26, reprinted in Borgen, *Vei utenfor Allfarvei*, 21–48. Borgen had lectured on Olsonius in a historical society in Bergen.

69. Borgen, "En tradisjonshistorisk analyse av materialet om Jesu fødsel hos Ignatius." English edition in Borgen, *Paul Preaches Circumcision*, 155–63.

Secondly, if it is the case that he presents parallel traditions, it shows that the boundaries of tradition for the canonical writings cannot be drawn clearly and distinctly; in other words, it becomes difficult to draw a sharp line between Scripture and tradition.

A NEW PROFESSORSHIP COMING UP

The problem of being a non-Lutheran

December 1970. Associate Professor Peder J. Borgen eagerly awaited the announcement of a new professorship at the University of Bergen. He had two doctorates, an American and a Norwegian, and had been employed at the University's Department of Religious Studies since April 1967 as an associate professor of Christian studies: Christian knowledge.

He knew the text of the announcement the university had sent to the Ministry of Church and Education in Oslo. It was also quite similar to when he applied for a professorship in religious studies at the same institution in 1965. At that time, he was acknowledged as having competence as a professor, but another person got the position due to a somewhat stronger assessment. Borgen was then hired as an associate professor/lecturer. Now he was waiting for another chance. This time, the position was also more directly related to Christian knowledge, his primary field of competence.

The announcement was published on Monday, December 28. Peder Borgen was frustrated when he discovered that the text had been changed by the ministry; a supplementary statement had been added. It made it quite clear to many what the following statement meant to Borgen and his chances of getting the new professorship: "The holder of the office must profess the State's public religion. Cf. the Act of July 21, 1894, on the Confession of the faith of State officials."

Why was that statement problematic? It demanded that any holder of that office had to be a Lutheran. Peder Borgen was still a Methodist. A "dissenter." A non-Lutheran.

He did not profess the "State's public religion" and thus could not be employed in the advertised position. Nevertheless, becoming a Lutheran was not an acceptable option for him.

It was not unknown to his colleagues at the university that he was considering applying for this new position. He was well qualified for it. It was also well known that he was a Methodist, as he was an active and a profiled one. However, now the ministry had closed the door.

The announcement text attracted attention in the university and far beyond that context. In response to inquiries to the ministry, they responded by saying that there was nothing unusual about this case and that the entire announcement was in accordance with Norwegian law. On paper, the ministry was right about that. They had brought into the light and applied an old law from 1894 that required Lutheran affiliation for state officials. And a professor was, per definition,. a state official as he was appointed by the king-in-council.

In fact, the law from 1894 had already several times represented a barrier for Peder Borgen. Because he was not a Lutheran as required by that law, he also did not receive a scholarship from the Faculty of Theology in Oslo after completing his theological degree in 1953 or after completing his PhD from the United States a few years later. After four years as a research fellow at the Norwegian Research Council for Science and the Humanities, he therefore had to cross some borders and move to the United States again (1964) to get a job as a professor in theology.

Considering these circumstances, many realized that Norway at that time actually had some form of occupational ban for non-Lutherans regarding certain positions. To understand the impact of this situation in the 1970s, we must consider some recent developments in the history of education in Norway in the preceding decades.[70]

Dissenters and public teaching positions

In the 1950s, 60s, and 70s, several things happened in school policy that left deep traces for the coming years and provided a starting point for further reforms. To understand the debate that gradually developed in Bergen concerning this professorship, one must also look at the case in light of an even older debate about the appointment of "dissenters" as teachers both in primary school and in higher education. We must go back to the middle of the nineteenth century to understand the expectations that were met by the decision of Parliament in 1969 that "dissenters"—non-Lutherans—were allowed to teach Christian knowledge in the Norwegian school system.

Until 1969, the teachers of Christian knowledge—on all levels—had to be Lutherans. A law concerning "dissenters" from 1845 (*Dissenterloven*) had given parents from non-Lutheran families the opportunity to claim an exemption for their children from Christian education. Non-Lutherans— "dissenters"—on the other hand, could not become teachers in the primary

---

70. For a more thorough presentation of the various aspects of this case, see my Norwegian article, Seland, "Lex Borgen."

school *at all* until the decisions in the National Primary School Act in 1915 and the City Schools Act in 1917. These two laws opened up for teachers to work in the public school system, but not, however, as teachers in Christian knowledge (Norwegian: *kristendomskunnskap*).

1959 is another important milestone. That year a new law was promulgated that contained several changes, but not much for the "dissenters."[71] Those who taught the subject Christian knowledge still had to be members of "the state church or a religious community that has the same doctrine as the state church" (§15.3). In other words, no "dissenters" were allowed to teach Christian knowledge in primary and secondary school.

However, ten years later, while Borgen was an associate professor at the University of Bergen, yet another new law concerning primary and lower secondary school was passed. A new provision was then introduced that opened for "dissenters" as teachers of Christian knowledge. The new law stated: "He who is to teach Christian knowledge must teach *in accordance with* the Evangelical-Lutheran Confession."[72] However, no requirements were issued for any Lutheran church membership. Furthermore, it was emphasized that teachers who did not belong to the Church of Norway or the Evangelical Lutheran Free Church were *not obliged to teach* this subject even though they had the competence needed (§ 17.3), but they were *allowed* to teach Christian knowledge. Hence, it was no longer required that the teachers in the subject should be members of the Church of Norway "or a religious community that has the same doctrine as the state church." Thus, for the first time in Norwegian history of education, it was decided in 1969 that "dissenters" could also be engaged in teaching Christian knowledge. But it was a *right*, not a *duty*.

But what about university teachers of Christian knowledge? In retrospect, it looks like Parliament had forgotten this issue. From the end of the 1950s and well into the 1960s there were only a few instances of any debate concerning this group of teachers. If the debate came up, the conclusion was most often that it was not a current issue. Few could imagine that a "dissenter" would apply for a position in Christian knowledge or theology at a university level.

---

71. Cf. *Lov om folkeskolen frå 10. april 1959. Med merknader, reglement og instruksar.* Utgitt av Kyrkje- og undervisningsdepartementet, Oslo 1959.

72. *Lov av 23. juni om grunnskolen* (Grunnskoleloven).

The Borgen case becomes a test case

Hence, the main reason why Borgen could get neither a PhD-scholarship nor a teaching position in theology or the equivalent at the Norwegian universities was a Law from 1880 on the state officials' need of a being Lutherans, a provision slightly adjusted July 21, 1894[73] [my translation]:

> In addition to members of the King's Council [Section 92 of the constitution] as well as clerical officials; the University teachers belonging to the Faculty of Theology; and state officials in general, who are required to teach Christianity, all officials and administrators employed by the elementary school [folkeskole] or of Schools for Higher Education are all required to belong to the Public State Religion.

It was not until 1951 that any serious discussions took place as to whether this law should be revised with a view to removing unnecessary conscientious objections, but this revision was primarily applied to those parts of the law that did not concern ecclesiastical matters. Some revisions were carried out in the form of a law on November 18, 1955. Nevertheless, the requirement for a confession to the "State's public religion" for university teachers or "officials who are required to teach in primary and lower secondary schools" was not discussed and was not changed. However, the debate resurfaced in a discussion that took place in the negotiations in and around the Recommendations on the Law on Religious Communities, given in 1962 by a committee set up by the state in 1957 to evaluate the laws concerning the various denominations in Norway.[74]

The 1957 committee and its discussion on the rights of the dissenters

In our context, it is primarily the discussions concerning church affiliation for teachers at a theological faculty that are of interest. Regarding university teachers, the committee of 1957 found it natural that teachers at a theological faculty had to be Lutherans because their essential task was to train priests for the Lutheran state church. The faculty professors were also used as a consultative body by the Ministry of Church and Education in

---

73. Cf. Breistein, *"Har staten bedre borgere?"*, 83–85.

74. *Innstillingen om lov om trossamfunn*, presented in 1962 by Dissenterlovkomitéen av 1957. See also Breistein, *"Har staten bedre borgere?"*, 308–47, and https://www.stortinget.no/no/Saker-og-publikasjoner/Stortingsforhandlinger/Saksside/?pid=1955-1961&mtid=24&vt=a&did=DIVL23456.

theological matters, as, e.g., participating in electing new bishops of the state church (which were then appointed by the king-in-council).

The committee, therefore, contended that "in our context, it would be inappropriate to abolish or curtail the confessional requirement. It must be reasonable for a religious community to have its priests educated by teachers who share the community's beliefs and confessions."[75]

However, the committee also made some assessments that—in retrospect—are difficult to characterize as particularly up to date or well informed. They wrote that one thought that the question of a Lutheran affiliation or not was more of a theoretical than practical relevance: the position as a university teacher in Christian knowledge/theology could only be filled by a theologian; at the Free Faculty of Theology (Menighetsfakultetet) only Lutherans were allowed to study, and the Faculty of Theology at the University of Oslo barely had any students who were not members of the state church. Therefore, the committee stated that

> There is only a slight possibility that someone who is not a member of the state church would apply, and there would be no reason for the appointing authority to take someone from outside the state church. It obviously should not be done either; and enacting legislation preventing it may not be necessary.[76]

The committee's recommendation was delivered as late as 1962. But what happened? Three years later, a "dissenter," the Methodist Peder Borgen, applied for a professorship in religious studies at the University of Bergen; he was considered competent, but the position was given to Alf Kragerud, also a theologian but a Lutheran. However, in 1967, Borgen was hired as a university lecturer at the same institution. The committee members, including the prominent Methodist Ragnar Horn, Oslo, could not have been that unfamiliar with this Borgen. Furthermore, what did they think about the usefulness of the competence requirements? Should they be overlooked and deviated from if an applicant was competent but a "dissenter," so that a Lutheran should take the lead anyway? Whatever they thought about these issues, it did not take many years before there were some non-Lutheran applicants for theological university positions: in 1970, the Catholic scholar Kari E. Børresen (1932–2016) applied for a lectureship in the history of Christianity's ideas at the Faculty of Theology, University of Oslo, but she

---

75. *Innstilling om lov om trossamfunn*, 142.
76. *Innstilling om lov om trossamfunn*, 144.

was denied assessment with reference to the law from 1894.[77] Other non-Lutherans are also said to have applied during that period.[78]

Peder Borgen and many others from the non-Lutheran free churches were engaged—sometimes provoked—by the debate about the state's relationship to the Church of Norway as a state church. And in this context, not least was the question of non-Lutheran teachers' opportunities to teach the subject of Christianity considered important, but difficult.

Borgen and the new professorship

In 1970, the Parliament (*Storting*) established a new professorship in Christian knowledge at the University of Bergen, with effect from July 1, 1971. The question was immediately raised why this old provision from 1894 had been added to the advertisement. Could it be because a "dissenter" was considered a potential applicant, or were there other reasons?

In retrospect, it is probably that the Børresen case at the Faculty of Theology earlier the same year reminded the ministry of the old law from 1894. And the ministry also knew about Borgen. In fact, as recently as both February and November 1970, questions had been raised in Parliament about this law. On February 18, the Conservative member Berte Rognerud asked the Minister of Church and Education the following question: "Will the ministry take steps to follow up the change in the law on primary and lower secondary schools that waives the requirement for a confessional obligation for teachers to also include higher education, including university level?" Minister Kjell Bondevik replied that the question was so far-reaching that the ministry had to work on it before giving a binding answer. Rognerud followed up by asking if the minister did not find it reasonable that the same guidelines regulating the elementary school should also apply to "teachers in the higher education institutions," and Bondevik answered in the affirmative.[79]

The University of Bergen contacted the ministry early in this process and asked (in early January) that the advertisement be withdrawn, and that the ministry make a change in the law so that no more requirements were set for professors than for other groups of teachers in Christian knowledge. The ministry withdrew the advertisement at the end of January 1971, and the work on an amendment of the law began.

---

77. See Borgen, "Ute-økumenikk," 277; See also Hafstad, "Det teologiske fakultet."
78. See Seland, "Lex Borgen."
79. Stortingstidende. Forhandlinger i Stortinget nr. 220. pp. 1833–34. See Seland, "Lex Borgen."

Several persons and institutions got engaged in this case. The Lutheran bishop (in Borg) Per Lønning, dr.theol and dr.philos, supported the demands for a revision;[80] the university management in Bergen had conferences with members of Parliament and ministers in the government. A group of Borgen's students went to Oslo to argue his case, and Borgen himself was invited to Parliament. He was also exchanging letters with some parliamentary representatives on the matter. For him, this case included at least two issues: Firstly, it concerned the rights of members of the free churches to be allowed to teach Christian knowledge and/or theology all the way to the top of the Norwegian educational system. It was a fight against the kind of discrimination he had encountered ever since he applied for further research opportunities after graduating in theology. Secondly, it represented an opportunity for him personally to advance in the Norwegian educational system.

The ministry's work with the law proceeded rather slowly. At the same time, not everyone in the department and faculty in Bergen were eager to have a professor in Christian knowledge. There were still tensions between the teachers of religious studies and those in Christian knowledge, as well as some other opponents. However, the work was finalized in the fall term as a new law was sanctioned on December 17, 1971, and put into force on January 1, 1972.

The new text of the law stated that anyone who teaches Christian knowledge at a state, county, or municipal high school, college, or university "shall teach in accordance with Evangelical Lutheran doctrine." But it also enshrined a similar principle as in primary school: a non-Lutheran was not obliged to teach even if one was competent. That is, it was to be a *right*, but not a *duty*. But it opened up for Borgen to apply for and be appointed to professorships in Norway. Unofficially in the university context in Bergen, the law was therefore called "Lex Borgen."[81]

Hence, the professorship in Bergen was advertised again on February 4, with an application deadline of March 20, 1972. But before this announcement was made, there had also been another position publicized that Peder Borgen found interesting, perhaps even more interesting than the one in Bergen. On January 7, a professorship in Christian knowledge was announced at the Norwegian Teacher Training College in Trondheim (Norges Lærerhøgskole), which had now (since 1968) become part of the University of Trondheim, and he was encouraged by some persons in Trondheim to apply for this position.

---

80. (Anonymous), "Lønning mot "tros-professor," *Dagen*, January 8, 1971, 1 and 8.

81. See Seland, "Lex Borgen." See also Hafstad, "Det teologiske fakultet," especially 184. Hafstad labels the new law "Lex Børresen."

Peder Borgen applied for both positions.

Professor in Bergen or Trondheim?

The position in Bergen was relatively open; it was a professorship in Christian knowledge. No specific subject area or other preferences were specified. The position in Trondheim, on the other hand, focused on "the New Testament and its world." Undoubtedly, this was a profiling that suited Peder Borgen much like a hand in glove; it was in this particular field he had been working all the time.

A total of five persons applied for the position in Bergen, and an assessment committee was established.[82] Only two applicants were found qualified for the professorship: Torgny Bohlin from Sweden and Peder Borgen. However, the further work at the university to reach a final decision took an unexpectedly long time, most probably because there was a certain discussion within the faculty about what profile—and thus which person—should be prioritized.

It all ended with Bohlin being appointed professor on November 9, 1973, almost two years after the announcement. But in the meantime, decisions had been made at a much faster speed at the University of Trondheim; their committee had finished its recommendation, and Borgen was the only one recommended. On June 15, 1973, he was appointed to the newly established professorship in Trondheim. Then Borgen withdrew his application for the position in Bergen.

Thus began a new phase in Peder Borgen's life. Three things mark this new phase: he had become a full professor at a Norwegian university; he had become the first non-Lutheran to become a professor of Christian knowledge/theology in Norway; and he was given a position that was like tailor-made for him: "the New Testament and its world."

Maybe it really was tailor-made? In any case, it suited him perfectly. In Trondheim, he and the rest of the family were to spend many good years.

He had again crossed an important border: for the first time in the history of Norway, a non-Lutheran scholar had become a professor in Christian knowledge/theology at a Norwegian university. No wonder colleagues in Bergen called the new law that made this possible "Lex Borgen."

---

82. The assessment commission consisted of Prof. Jacob Jervell, Prof. Sven Kjöllerstrøm, and Prof. Inge Lønning.

10

In the Middle of Norway: Professor in Trondheim (1973–93)

WHEN PEDER BORGEN JOINED the *University of Trondheim* in 1973, he came to an institution with a relatively long history of providing theological and religious subjects tailored for the primary and secondary schools, but it had been a university only since 1968.[1] One of its precursors was the Norwegian College of Teaching in Trondheim (NLHT), established in 1922. But the inherent department he came to, the Department of Religious Studies, did not come into being until 1964.[2]

---

1. Concerning the development of the program of Christian knowledge (*kristendomskunnskap*) at the Norwegian College of Teaching between 1922 and 1964, see Haraldsø, "Lærde prester." The Norwegian College of Teaching was initially formed to provide continuing and further education to teachers in primary and secondary schools. However, since all teacher training schools in the country in the 1970s were renamed and called "teacher colleges" (*lærerhøgskole*), the name became problematic, and in 1984 NLHT changed its name to the Norwegian College of General Sciences (Den allmennvitenskapelige høgskolen, AVH) but continued as part of the then newly established University of Trondheim.

2. The University of Trondheim was established by a decision in the Parliament (Storting) in 1968. At that time, it comprised three previously independent institutions: the Norwegian College of Teaching, the Norwegian University of Science and Technology (NTH) and the Royal Norwegian Society of Sciences and Letters, the Museum. In 1996 the university was reorganized and took the present name of the Norwegian University of Science and Technology (NTNU).

THE DEPARTMENT OF RELIGIOUS STUDIES

For many years, the teaching at the department was conducted with the help of part-time teachers. The institute was named the Department of Religious Studies, but all the teachers were theologians. It was not until 1963 that a "professorship in religious studies, with special emphasis on Christian knowledge"[3] was announced, and in the year after Åge Holter was appointed as the professor. In the following years, the number of teachers at the department grew steadily so that when Borgen arrived as its second full professor, the teaching staff consisted of six to seven persons. In 1976, Borgen's friend from the 1950s, Peter Wilhelm Böckman, joined the teaching staff as the successor of Åge Holter, who left in 1974. This group was then the colleagues Borgen was to work with for the coming twenty years.[4]

The department retained the name Department of Religious Studies during these years. However, it had no teaching position in explicit religious studies, nor was any major course offered in religious studies, only some sub-subjects within the more extensive program of Christian knowledge. It was not until new positions and appointments were made in the 1990s that a major science of religion program became fully integrated into the department. The primary subject portfolio was Christian knowledge, on levels comparable to the USA programs of bachelor's and master's.

As the need for a stronger focus on religious studies in primary and secondary schools was expanded, the department's academic character also changed as science of religion programs were established and soon became larger and larger, and the subject of Christian knowledge began to migrate out of the system. In 2003, the department merged with a smaller archeology section at the museum to form the Department of Archeology and Religious Studies.[5] Today, Christian knowledge is no longer available as a stand-alone subject in the department but is offered as a small part of various study programs within the bachelor's degree. It is not present in the master's programs. The department has now merged with philosophy and is called the Department of Philosophy and Religious Studies.

---

3. See Rian, *Kristendomsfag*, 11.
4. The teaching staff consisted of two full professors (P. W. Bøckman in systematic theology, and P. Borgen in the New Testament), and four assistant/associate professors: Dagfinn Rian in Old Testament and history of religions; Olav Hognestad in the New Testament and hermeneutics; Per Øverland in church history, and Erik Karlsaune in general sociology and sociology of religion. A part-time teacher was engaged in pedagogy of religion.
5. In the same year, the programs of bachelor's and master's degrees were introduced in Norway (the Bologna process), and in many other countries in Europe.

After he retired, Borgen, who spent more than twenty years teaching the New Testament at the University of Trondheim, often lamented these changes and development of the department in which he had spent so many happy years.

FAMILY LIFE IN TRONDHEIM

Inger Borgen and the children stayed in Bergen for a few more months for two reasons: it took some time to sell their house in Bergen, and they had not acquired a new home in Trondheim. But at Easter the following year, both problems were solved, and Inger and the girls joined Peder in Trondheim.

Inger becomes a family therapist

Heidi started in second grade at Åsvang primary school after Easter of 1974, and Ingunn started in first grade in the following autumn. Inger was thus ready to start working outside the home again. During her time in Bergen, she had had some assignments at a family counseling office (*familierådgivningskontor*) and was now ready to continue in that field, if possible. In April 1974, she thus started working at the family counseling office in Trondheim. She was employed there for twenty-five years, until they moved to Lillestrøm, and she describes this period thus: "I had twenty-five wonderfully inspiring and rewarding years in that office."[6] The family counseling office in Trondheim, which was part of the state church's family counseling, had the whole of Sør-Trøndelag county as its area, and they had offices in various locations in the county.

During these years, she also took further education as a family therapist. "We worked in teams; psychiatrists, psychologists and family therapists, and were always very concerned about staying professionally oriented, and being available to people in Sør-Trøndelag for what they might have to struggle with."[7] They were also approved as official mediators when couples were to apply for separation. Inger got to see and experience that no one has any guarantees for only "good days": "no one knows what may appear around the next turn in life."[8] As a team, they traveled to courses and congresses and had professionals come to Trondheim for further development. Inger was also, for several years, a member of the national board for the

---

6. Inger Borgen, interview by the author, March 8, 2018.
7. Inger Borgen, interview by the author, March 8, 2018.
8. Inger Borgen, interview by the author, March 8, 2018.

church's family counseling. "I look back on these years," she said later, "with immense joy and would choose the same profession if I were to start over again today."[9]

Peder, Inger, and Scientia

Peder Borgen was in his thirties when he married Inger in 1961. During his studies in Oslo, his years of PhD studies in the USA, and in his time as a pastor in Harstad, he had had many opportunities to develop some "bachelor habits." Housekeeping never became quite his thing. Inger said many years later—when living as retired in Lillestrøm—that

> we have had a fairly traditional family life in the sense that he has been the main provider, and I have been the main person in charge of the home. Hence, he has rarely been doing much work in the kitchen. But then he, in return, has had to take care of everything that has to do with the house and car and the like. For example, I have never changed tires on a car.[10]

Peder was an academic person and a scholar; to do research was both his hobby and profession; it was his life. "When I married Peder, I quickly realized what kind of type he was; he was a researcher, so I said that 'I understand that I am to go through life with you having two ladies, one named Scientia, and the other Inger.' And that is the way it has been . . ."[11] Both Peder and Inger have several times commented on their relationship throughout their lives with the help of his relationship with "Scientia."

Peder entered a period of great productivity when they moved to Trondheim. In addition to his work with various lectures and courses, several studies in Philo and the New Testament came from his hand, not least throughout the 1980s.[12] Nevertheless, he usually left his university office at the agreed time in the afternoon, strolled home over the mound from the university campus at Dragvoll, and to Theodor Petersen's Road where they lived. He also had an office at home, including an extensive library, where he could continue work after dinner. However, he did not do much work at night, although the many studies published in those years probably indicate that there were some late evenings spent at the office at home more than once.

9. Inger Borgen, interview by the author, March 8, 2018.
10. Inger Borgen, interview by the author, March 17, 2018.
11. Inger Borgen, interview by the author, March 17, 2018.
12. See the presentation of his main works in chapter 14 below.

It is a common popular notion that professors are somewhat distré. And in many cases, it may also be true, although it has also become a bit of a cliché. Inger describes her husband thus:

> he can be a little distracted at times, but it also means that we can make as much noise as we want when he is working on his studies, which we greatly appreciate. We have not had to tiptoe in the house, and there has been no hush-hush around dad. He is very historically interested, and we understand that books are the best he knows, he . . . sometimes we realized . . . well, not just sometimes, but in general, that books and studies and research are just as much work and hobby and all life, he loves it. But when we tap on his shoulder and say, 'Here we are,' he will gladly come . . .[13]

Inger and Peder had a hospitable home. Many gatherings with students and other parties were held there, not least when guest lecturers visited the department. When internationally renowned New Testament professors such as, e.g., David Flusser, Martin Hengel, Bo Reicke, Harald Riesenfeldt, Jacob Neusner, and others visited, parties were held in the Borgen residence with Inger and Peder as hosts, and colleagues and research fellows were guests together with the guest lecturers. For Peder, these gatherings were also opportunities to make contacts, maintain and expand professional and personal networks, and help others in such contexts.

Borgens and the Methodist church in Trondheim

It was obvious and self-evident to Peder Borgen that he was to be a member of the local Methodist church when he came to Trondheim. And it became his spiritual home during all the years they lived in Trondheim.

The Trondheim Methodist Church was founded in 1881, and the current church building on Cicignons Place, or Lilletorget as it is also called, was consecrated on June 21, 1925. The congregation had its heyday in the first decade after 1914. The number of members in full association was at its highest in 1924 (344). From the mid-1950s, it was approximately a hundred members lower, and in 1973 it was down to 173. When the church building was set up in the 1920s, the congregation got a proper gathering place, but at the same time, a financial burden that it had to struggle with for many years.

---

13. Inger Borgen, interview by the author, March 17, 2018.

The Methodist church in Trondheim, consecrated June 21, 1925, was the church Inger and Peder attended during their years in Trondheim.

When the Borgen family arrived, Ivar Granum (1940–) was pastoring the congregation. He was there from 1970 to 1976, when Per Braaten took over. Granum observed that Peder Borgen did not immediately engage fully in the congregational work, especially not in administrative tasks. Granum realized that Borgen wanted to prioritize his work at the university and become better acquainted with the city.[14] But he also saw that he later became a supporter and coworking member of the congregation. In the Sunday gatherings, Peder especially worked to integrate the students who attended the church. He talked to them at the church coffee gatherings and often invited them home for dinner. Sometimes he would also relieve the pastor from some stress by preaching at the Sunday services.

---

14. This description was given by Pastor Ivar Granum, in an interview, June 4, 2018.

The Methodist Inger

During the Bergen period, Inger had been at home with two small children. Now they were older, and she could get more involved; but at the same time, the Borgens were also part of the congregation as a family. Inger seems to have participated early in the congregation's various teams; she joined as a Sunday school teacher, participated in both a women's mission group and a Bible group, and was the leader of the junior youth group. After the sabbatical year of 1977–78, when the whole family was abroad, she continued in Sunday school, in the mission group, in the children's group, and joined the board of the church. Eventually, her engagement expanded also further, both nationally and internationally.[15]

During all these years, Peder was engaged in his many conference participations and his travels abroad as a guest lecturer, but when his daughters grew up, Inger tried to join him on his travels around the world.

When Peder lived in Oslo, he became involved in the annual ecumenical prayer week, held in in the beginning of the year, often in February. He continued being engaged in these events both in Bergen and Trondheim. In January, the year after he had moved to Trondheim, he gave a major lecture in the main aula of the University of Oslo, on "Thoughts in the New Testament on Christian Unity" as part of the Prayer Week for Christian Unity that year. The lecture was offered after an invitation conveyed by Professor Einar Molland, his former teacher of church history.[16]

Peder Borgen as a Methodist historian

When Peder Borgen moved to Trondheim, he had already published some articles related to the history of early Methodism in Norway. A slight hint or discovery could act as a clue that put him on the track, repeatedly hunting out more information. This procedure was applied not only within his primary field of research, the New Testament and its world, but it also worked within the history of Norwegian Methodism. His article about Johannes

---

15. In 1984 she became a member of the national board of Norwegian Family Counselling. In 1986 she was a delegate to the World Federation of Methodist and Uniting Church Women assembly in Nairobi, Kenya. In 1990 she became the president of the World Federation of Methodist and Uniting Church Women, unit Norway. For one period she was vice-president of the World Federation of Methodist and Uniting Church Women, area Europe. In 1994 she was the first lay woman who became a member of the Board of Ordained Ministry in Norway.

16. See Borgen, "Tanker i Det nye Testamente om kristen enhet." English translation: "Thoughts on Christian Unity in the New Testament," in Borgen, *"Paul Preaches Circumcision*, 131–53. See further chapter 12 in the present volume.

IN THE MIDDLE OF NORWAY: PROFESSOR IN TRONDHEIM (1973–93)

Olsonius from the years in Bergen is an example of such research.[17] During a stay in the USA, he also used the opportunity to research Norwegian Methodism by visiting the Methodist Church's headquarters at Lake Junaluska, North Carolina, where the denomination now has its central archive.[18] Borgen discovered some material that shed light on the probably first Methodist preaching activity in Norway, carried out by Hans Isaksen and Markus Nilsen, who worked as preachers paid for by the Methodist Church's mission organization in New York. The work of these early preachers helped to prepare and start the work that resulted in the establishment of a Methodist church in the Brevik-Porsgrunn-Skien area.[19] Borgen visited this organization in New York several times both as a preacher and to do research in the archives of the missionary society.[20]

In 1981 the Methodist Church in Trondheim celebrated its one-hundredth anniversary. Hence, the church appointed an ad hoc committee to present its history. Borgen was the committee's chairperson; he also wrote the chapter on the history of the years 1884–1914. The result of this work was a book of 209 pages presenting the history of the church and its various activities through the years.

The book carries the title *Kirken i Sentrum* (*The Church at the Center*). There are reasons to believe that this was a title which—even if it did not originate from Borgen himself—was at least one he must have been quite happy with. The congregation in Trondheim is located in the center of the city, but at the same time, it was entirely in line with Borgen's ecclesiology that the Methodist Church was also in the center theologically.

The anniversary book also demonstrates that by now the Borgen family was fully engaged in the congregation: Peder was on the main board, and Inger was on the mission group board, and pictures in the book show that Inger and Peder were engaged in both the junior and the youth group.[21]

---

17. See Borgen, "Johannes Olsonius," briefly presented in the preceding chapter above.

18. The archive was moved from New York to Lake Junaluska in the mid-1970s.

19. See his articles in *Kristelig Tidende* in 1976–77: Borgen, "Han knelte når han ba og bekjente at hans synder var tilgitt," *Kristelig Tidende* 27 (1976) 6–7; "Nytt lys over metodismens begynnelse i landet vårt," *Kristelig Tidende* 33/34 (1976), 9; and "Nytt lys over metodismens begynnelse i landet vårt," *Kristelig Tidende* 9/10 (1977) 2.

20. Borgen attended a church service in New York (Bethelship Church) for the first time on Sunday, June 13, 1954, while he was a research fellow at Drew University, but he also visited it in March 1983, preaching in the church on Palm Sunday.

21. At the end of the 1970s, the congregation made premises available to the Kristenfolkets Edruskapsråd, and Lilletorget Contact Center was started on the lower floor of the church. Peder Borgen also became involved here and was central in a seminar on drugs and therapy which was arranged in June 1982. The lectures from the seminar

BORGEN AS A UNIVERSITY PROFESSOR

Being a full professor at a university usually does not only involve being a teacher and researcher in his or her field of study. In addition to pursuing the teaching part, a professor is also supposed to be a driving force in his or her field by pursuing professional development, establishing and conducting research projects, tutoring students and doctoral candidates, and publishing. In general, at this time in Trondheim, the professors' work duties were divided into three parts, of which the two most prominent—teaching and research—were often equal. In addition, a much smaller administrative section included management tasks at various levels and ad hoc committees in connection with several assignments.

When Peder Borgen started at the university in 1973, and in the following years, he was consciously reluctant to take on administrative tasks.[22] It was still the experiences from his burnout in 1966 that were on his mind, and he deliberately tried to keep the balance in his new situation of life. After some time, however, it became his turn too to take on administrative challenges both outside and inside the department.[23]

Teaching, course development, and tutoring

In the department as such, he became strongly involved in the development of summer courses and continuing education courses for teachers, and he arranged professional excursions to countries that were relevant to Bible studies, crossing borders to such countries as Israel, Turkey, and Greece.[24] His colleague D. Rian highlights, for example, a two-day course (symposium) on Judaism and Christianity, which was held in the autumn of 1976. At that time, neither ecumenical contact and cooperation nor interreligious contact was particularly well developed in Norway. In Norway, there are only two Jewish synagogues, one in Oslo, and one in Trondheim. The synagogue

were published in Borgen, "Hvem er Jeppe?"

22. "I avoided as much as possible taking and getting administrative management tasks, both at the department and elsewhere," he later wrote in a private, undated note, now in Borgen's private archive.

23. He was head of the department in 1990–92; in the period 1981–84 he was vice dean at the Faculty of Humanities; and in 1984–87 he was vice-rector at AVH (Norwegian College of General Sciences). In 1981–83 he chaired a committee that reorganized the doctoral program at the university; he was a member of the library board, a member of the board of Tapir Publishing House 1977–83, and chairperson of a committee that planned the establishment of the Center for Child Research at the university 1984–87.

24. Rian, *Kristendomsfag*, 26–29.

in Trondheim, established in 1897, participated in this symposium. Their "parish magazine" described the symposium in a way that expressed both joy and yet a little wonder. They too felt that they were engaged in crossing some borders:

> On November 1 and 2, 1976, a unique symposium was held at the Department of Religious Studies in Trondheim. This event was the first symposium at that time being held at a university in Norway where lectures were given on Jewish religion and history and the relationship between Judaism and Christianity, and the topic was brought up for debate in such an impartial way and with lecturers belonging to both religions.[25]

Peder Borgen was one of the lecturers at this symposium, together with colleagues from the department and central Jewish persons such as Leo Eitinger, Oskar Mendelsohn, and Morton H. Narrowe.[26] The experiences from this course led—according to D. Rian—to the department establishing a firmer structure in its courses of continuing education: "Peder Borgen developed a concept for continuing education courses that the department has followed relatively unchanged since 1979 and until more recent times," he wrote in 2004.[27]

"to open windows between science, church, and culture."

In 2008, there was an international symposium (conference) in Oslo, where Peder Borgen (at the age of eighty) was celebrated for his many years of work as president of the board for the renowned international journal *Novum Testamentum*. In this connection, looking back on his life, he stated that "My goal has been to open windows between science, church and culture."[28] This focus is reflected in several of the subjects that he, together with the other employees at the department, set up as continuing education courses

---

25. Quoted from Rian, *Kristendomsfag*, 26.

26. Leo Eitinger (1912–1996), was a famous Norwegian professor in psychiatry. He had been a prisoner in both Auswitz and Buchenwald during World War II and became famous for his research on postwar sufferings of former prisoners of war. He was also a tireless champion of human rights. Oskar Mendelsohn (1912–193) was a Norwegian historian who especially worked with the history of the Jews in Norway. He published a great work on the history of the Jews in Norway. Morton H. Narrowe (1932–) was born in the USA, but emigrated to Sweden in 1965, where he became the main rabbi in the Jewish synagogue in Stockholm in 1975. He worked also as an author, and was especially engaged in dialogues between Christians, Jews, and Muslims.

27. Rian, *Kristendomsfag*, 27.

28. See Nordby, "Peder Borgen: Mitt mål," *Brobyggeren* 7 (2008) 14.

for teachers and other interested persons. In a row came courses such as "Religious Pluralism in Biblical Times and in Norway Today" (1979); "Man and Nature in Christianity and Science" (1980); "The Bible in the Focus of Faith, History and Literature" (1981); "Norwegian Free Churches: Emergence and Confessional Identity in Conflict with State Church" (1981); "Who Is Jeppe? Drugs, Therapy and Human Vision" (1982); "Religious Knowledge and General Education" (1985); "Biblical Themes in Literature, Film and Theater" (1987); and "Environmental Crisis and Value Choice: The Cnvironmental Crisis in a Christian Perspective and as a Challenge in Society and School" (1991). The courses were immensely popular among teachers in Trondheim and the surrounding areas.

This interest in *crossing borders* between science, church, and culture is also evident in some of his sermons. After returning home from his PhD studies in the United States, he served as a Methodist pastor in Harstad for two years (see chapter 4 above). Furthermore, up through the years, he occasionally also served his local church and others by entering the pulpit on Sunday morning, preaching the gospel.[29]

His interest in and emphasis on the relations between church and culture are evident in some of his sermons. To give just a couple of examples: On May 31, 1975, he gave a sermon (probably in Trondheim Methodist Church) on the Gospel of John 1:14 and 18:1 and had as its theme "Sent to the world." In the introduction, he asked: "How should the relationship be between us Christians and our surroundings?" And he continued: "New Testament times provides evidence of three different lines to follow. These three lines can be called *isolation, absorption,* and a *Christ-inspired solidarity* with our fellow human beings because the Church has been sent into the world."[30] The first line, *isolation*, he illustrates by the Dead Sea sect in Qumran, which retreated into isolation; *absorption* he illustrates with the Sadducees and the Prodigal Son (Luke 15). But the model for the last attitude becomes Jesus himself, both by the incarnation and by his attitudes toward the people he associated with. Furthermore, specifically for the congregations today, this means, among other things, a positive attitude towards "Youth club work, whether it happens to the music choir's drumbeat or modern rhythms and bands. It means solidarity with alcoholics. It means commitment and works in cultural life and business life to meet people in their situation . . . It also means that we let professionals in business and

---

29. In the Norwegian edition of this biography, I included a section of fifteen pages on "Borgen as a preacher." Seland, *Peder Borgen: Metodist—Økumen—Professor*, 84–98.

30. His categories here are possibly an echo of Wilson, "An Analysis of Sect Development"; a sociological analysis that was popular at this time, and which was used in studies of early Christianity.

administration in to streamline our congregations . . . it means that we become more deeply interested in following our youth in their often lonesome struggle as Christians in schools and universities . . . Jesus said: Just as you have sent me into the world, so have I sent them into the world. I do not ask that you take them out of the world, but that you keep them from evil" (John 17:18).

In another sermon from about the same time, his tone is even sharper.[31] It is a tragedy for the church, he says, that

> the church that professes Christ has to a large extent hardened and encapsulated itself so that it is unable to respond to the strong religious longing and the existential *angst* for the emptiness that the masses struggle with. . . . The result is that the tunnel out to cultural circles and academic circles has collapsed because we have assumed that the cultural world and the academic world are outside the scope of church work and dubious and dangerous; the tunnel out to many youth circles has collapsed because we so often see long hair and long beards instead of people Jesus Christ died for, and because we pretend that the Christian message has no say in the social issues that concern them. The result is that they sing songs of peace with images from the Book of Isaiah about the wolf and the lamb that will live together, while we do not allow the word of the Bible to engage us on this point. The result is too that we do not find young people from 18–25 years of age in the management on a district and national basis in our church . . .

These sermons were held in the 1970s, and they both indicate his social attitudes in the wake of the hippie movements, the student revolution in 1968, and the "Jesus Revolution" in the 1970s. Moreover, they are also in line with the Methodist emphasis on social work described in their Social Principles.

Borgen did not preach in his lectures; they were strictly academic. But in several of his sermons, one might discover a professor who draws both upon his wide reading and his experiences in the academic world. Furthermore, he laments the lack of interest in Christian congregations to draw upon the experiences and professionalism of the world at large.

However, he also discovered a need for religious information and further education in religious matters in some other cases and contexts. In an interview in 1988 on the occasion of his sixtieth birthday, Borgen put it bluntly: "In Northern Europe, we tend to displace religious needs.

---

31. Sermon on Colossians 2:9–10.

For example, going to a church service has become something special. We have become atypical and perhaps a little provincial compared to the rest of the world." Moreover, he continued: "If we look around in today's world, participating in religious activity is still a natural thing among men."[32] He had no answer as to why this had happened but believed that dialogue and contact were important for moving forward.

Some of these experiences triggered and inspired him when he—in the latter half of the 1980s—eagerly argued that the Department of Religious Studies ought to arrange courses for business people, especially those engaged in international business. Some of the colleagues feared that the business community would not be interested. The professor of social anthropology, Jan Brøgger, who had his office on the same corridor as Peder and his colleagues, and whom Peder hoped would join him in the project, thought it was a stillborn idea.[33] Nevertheless, Borgen pressed on, and five courses were set up, partly at the request of and in cooperation with the Department for Continuing Education. A collaboration was established with the University of Lund (Sweden), and together they applied for funding from the Nordic Council (Nordisk Råd). There and then, they received support under the name "export promotion measures."[34] Borgen stated in an interview with the newspaper *Dagen* that "Many from Northern Europe have a distant relationship with religious life. They are surprised when they discover how much influence religion has on daily life in other parts of the world."[35] Thus, he thought, many business people do not understand the connection between and the background of what they experience in their travels. Media-conscious as Peder Borgen has always been, he was also portrayed in a major interview in *Teknisk Ukeblad* with the headline: "Does Norwegian industry need corporate priests?"[36] Here, he presented his thoughts on religion and culture and the need for further information. And he got to talk about the significance of Shintoism in Japan, Confucianism in Korea, and various aspects of Christianity such as Calvinism in France, Methodism in England, and Haugianism in Norway. To include religion in the field of view, he thought, is to take the whole person as such seriously. Hence there is a need for a holistic attitude and approach, an approach that also includes religion.

---

32. Fordal, "Professor Peder Borgen: Vi fortrenger religiøse behov," *Aftenposten*, January 26, 1988, 18.

33. Info from K. Fuglseth, in an email to me, dated February 6, 2019.

34. Peder Borgen, in an email to the author, dated September 18, 2019.

35. Kvalbein, "Religion interesserer," *Dagen*, March 6, 1990, 9.

36. *Teknisk Vekeblad* 29 (1988) 61, 78.

Several of Borgen's colleagues in the department participated as lecturers, and the courses were well received by participants from the business community. Benjamin Brubakken, CFO at Norsk Hydro in Qatar and one of the participants, told the newspaper *Dagen* that "An introductory course in religion and culture should be mandatory for those who wants to do business in the Muslim part of the world."[37] The courses focused on different parts of our world, with topics like "Knowledge of the Arab countries and Turkey," "Courses on EU and European culture," "Courses on China—trade and culture," and "Internationalization—also a question of cultural understanding."

Research developments and mentoring

After Professor Åge Holter had left the university (1974) to become a professor at the Free Faculty of Theology in Oslo, Borgen was the only one in the department to have a doctorate. He even had two: an American PhD and a Norwegian dr.theol. Later, Olav Hognestad (1985) and Ole Gunnar Winsnes (1988) also defended their dissertations for the degree of dr.artium, the latter having a part-time position at the department for several years. Furthermore, to use the USA categories, Borgen and Böckman were the only full professors; the others were associate or assistant professors.[38]

In order to mature and grow as a young scholar, one needs to play on other and more experienced people too, and thus get some practical experience in writing, written and oral presentation, and argumentation. A part of such maturing processes is participating in the discussions provided in so-called research seminars. On the initiative of Borgen, an interdisciplinary seminar was established at the department. Here the participants presented papers; it could be a draft for an article, a special lecture, or a (sub-)chapter of a book. Their contributions were then commented on by a main respondent in session, and then by the other participants. Many got involved in this seminar over the years, not least in the 1980s, when the department had three Fulbright professors and eventually got some doctoral students too.

However, there was no fixed structured doctoral program in Borgen's first decade at the department. Those interested in obtaining a doctorate applied to various funding sources for scholarships. Perhaps most relevant were the scholarships from the Norges Almennvitenskapelige Forskningsråd

---

37. See Kvalbein, "Religion interesserer," *Dagen*, March 6, 1990, 9. See also Rian, *Kristendomsfag*, 43–44.

38. In the Norwegian context, a full professor is called "professor"; an assistant or associate professor is labeled "*amanuensis*" or "*førsteamanuensis*," never "professor."

(NAVF; now: Norwegian Research Council). But beyond that, there was little further help available and even less organized and structured mentoring codified in the form of fixed agreements. Hence, at this time, there was also some criticism leveled against this unstructured system because it turned out that many of the research fellows failed to complete their dissertation and thus did not end up with any doctorate, but instead with frustration over their failures. Therefore, demands were raised from several quarters for a more structured doctoral program with mentoring functions that could help and guide the research fellows on their tracks. Some looked to the United States, where Borgen had undergone a program and received his PhD in 1956.

Borgen then became the leader of a committee that was to study and work out plans for a new doctoral degree, and in 1984 the University of Trondheim established a new degree called the Doctor Artium (dr.art.). It comprised a course in the science of philosophy of approximately one semester, including the writing of some papers, and then the writing of a dissertation under the guidance of a professor. When the dissertation was submitted to the university, it was evaluated by a committee and, if accepted, followed up by a public and oral defense, consisting of one test lecture and a public disputation. The total workload was stipulated to be three years of full-time work. A few years later, this degree was replaced by another, the Doctor Philosophiae (PhD) degree, which showed even more clearly the relationship to the American system by its name and its inherent program.

The first person to enter the doctoral program with Borgen as the main supervisor was Torrey Seland. He was a pastor in Bakklandet parish, downtown Trondheim, from 1978 but was interested in opportunities for further studies. In the late autumn of 1979, he contacted Borgen for guidance about possible projects. He was received by an interested and benevolent professor. Already in the first conversation, he got a quick introduction to Philo of Alexandria, and information about an article Borgen was working on regarding Paul and his problems in Galatia.[39] Seland hardly knew anything about Philo yet and felt a little overwhelmed. When he returned home after the conversation, he searched through his books from his student days and finally found a few pages about Philo in a book on New Testament background issues. He would learn much more about Philo later.

Seland had a one-year scholarship from the Menighetsfakultetet in 1983 and a three-year scholarship from NAVF for 1985–87. In both periods, he had a working office at the Department of Religious Studies and worked on the Stephen episode in Acts 6–7 and the violent measures described

---

39. Published as "Paul Peaches Circumcision and Pleases Men," and later republished in his collection of articles by the same name: Borgen, *Paul Peaches Circumcision and Pleases Men*, 33–46.

there, which he tried to illuminate with texts from Philo of Alexandria. Seland defended his dissertation in March 1991.[40]

The next research fellow was Per Jarle Bekken. He too had studied theology at the Free Faculty of Theology in Oslo, and had been in contact with Borgen already in August 1983 as he was a student and had aired a desire for further studies. Bekken received a student scholarship from NAVF for the year 1985 and was a NAVF research fellow at the Department of Religious Studies in the years 1989–1992.

He was also involved in a Nordic research project on "New Perspectives on Hellenistic Judaism and the New Testament" in 1987–92. The participants met annually for joint meetings in Uppsala and SNTS meetings, e.g., in Cambridge, Dublin, and Milan. Involving Bekken as a research fellow in such a project was an expression of Borgen's strategy of encouraging research fellows to publish and participate in international settings. In 1998, Bekken defended his dissertation on Paul's use of Deuteronomy 30:12–14 in Romans, i.a., also seen in the light of Philo's use of the same Old Testament text. He is now a professor of Christian knowledge at the Faculty of Education and Arts, Nord University (formerly the University of Nordland).[41]

The third research fellow was Kåre Fuglseth. That is, he took his bachelor's and master's studies at the University of Trondheim and had Borgen as a teacher in the New Testament during these years. Fuglseth graduated as a cand.philol. in 1988. In the years 1990–93, he was engaged in a project scheduled to finalize the project of the digitalization of Philo's texts. This was the project that Roald Skarsten and Borgen had worked on in Bergen in 1970–74 (see chapter 9 above). It had been dormant for several years, but now, after diligent application work, Borgen was able to obtain external funding from NAVF to complete it. Fuglseth also continued to work on this project part-time while he was a research fellow at the Department of Religious Studies. He defended his dissertation on the Gospel of John in 2002.[42] Fuglseth has been a professor of didactics at Nord University since 2008.[43]

Kåre Fuglseth thought Borgen was a good but demanding lecturer. In his lectures, the bachelor's students were given a list of advanced articles to

---

40. Torrey Seland graduated from the Free Faculty of Theology (Menighetsfakultetet) in Oslo in the spring term of 1977. After serving as a chaplain in the army for one year, he assumed work in Bakklandet Parish, Trondheim. In 1988 he started up as an assistant professor in biblical studies at Møre and Romsdal Regional College, Volda. He remained there to 2005, from 2000 as a full professor. For further info, see http://torreys.org/cv.

41. Concerning his dissertation, see Bekken, *"The Word Is Near You"*. For further info on his work, see https://www.nord.no/en/employees/per-jarle-bekken.

42. Published in 2005 as Fuglseth, *Johannine Sectarianism*.

43. For further info, see https://www.nord.no/en/employees/kaare-sigvald-fuglseth.

read and present. Borgen had brought with him some elements from the American teaching tradition, including the practice of requiring students to read articles and books and have students present these in class and deliver papers. Otherwise, he answered the students' questions willingly: "He could answer all questions without hesitation; you got this feeling of a lecturer who knew everything and that we only managed to scratch a little at the surface of what he knew with our questions." That it was an active researcher they had as a teacher could also be experienced or deduced in this way: "I remember that he could be quite tired in the morning; then he would have sat up in the middle of the night to write an article he 'had to finish.' Always an article or two in progress."[44]

Peder's former doctoral students—here as young professors— celebrating their mentor. From right: Kåre Fuglseth, Per Jarle Bekken, Peder Borgen, and Torrey Seland.

As a supervisor, his students perceived him as a teacher who was always willing to answer questions; many lunches in the canteen were extended because he was too engaged in a professional chat (which could also serve as a mentoring chat). During my own time as a research fellow at the department, I sometimes heard from some research fellows at other departments that they had problems establishing regularly mentoring talks with their supervisors; I did not experience Borgen like that. We had our conversations, and I submitted my drafts, and he always returned them with written

44. Kåre Fuglseth, in an email to me, dated February 6, 2019. The quotes in the text from Fuglseth are from this email.

comments. In his comments, he could be challenging and demanded a lot. He only rarely said outright what he thought was not good enough and/ or what he thought should be changed or improved upon, but suggested where we should go to get more viewpoints. And then he would leave it to us to draw our conclusions from what we found. Actually, a good method of mentoring when you got used to it.

In 1987, Peter Wilhelm Böckman, Borgen's professorial colleague at the department, turned sixty, and his colleagues joined forces to publish a Festschrift in honor of the jubilee.[45] The following year it was Borgen's turn; he too received a Festschrift, edited by P. W. Böckman and Roald Kristiansen.[46] The contributors reflect Borgen's international network of contacts and professional interests.[47]

Peder Borgen thrived in international arenas

Borgen was active in relevant international arenas from early in his career. This activity was not only due to his Methodist approach and view of the church, in which he considered the church as a supranational and transnational entity, but also to his own experiences both in ecumenical work and not least as a New Testament scholar. As a research fellow at Drew University in the USA in the years 1953–56 and especially as an associate professor at Wesley Theological Seminary in the years 1962–66, he had achieved an international platform that provided him with a network of contacts that far exceeded what a research fellow and theological teacher had access to in Norway. In addition, he realized early the great benefits of participating in international scholarly societies such as the Society of Biblical Literature (SBL) and the Studiorum Novi Testamenti Societas (SNTS). It was SNTS that became his primary international arena in the years that followed. It appears that he attended its annual General Meetings every year from 1967 until 2008, then a little less often until 2018. In that year, however, he attended the meeting in Athens at the age of ninety.

Such General Meetings, as well as the Annual Meetings of the SBL, consist of lectures and seminars. In addition, many book publishers show up with their latest publications at well-discounted prices, and last but not

45. Borgen et al., *Teologi på Tidens Torg*.
46. Böckman and Kristiansen, eds., *Context*.
47. The contributors were: Peter W. Böckman, Øivind Andersen, C. K. Barrett, Ole E. Borgen, Thor Hall, Lars Hartman, Arne Hassing, Walter Klaiber, Edvin Larsson, I. Howard Marshall, Tore Meistad, Birger Olsson, Harald Riesenfeld, Vernon Robbins, Torrey Seland, Per Øverland, and Per Jarle Bekken.

least, the conferences function as social communities and places to develop one's professional network. A witty head once said that the purpose of attending was threefold: to meet colleagues, to buy new books, and—finally—to attend lectures and seminars. And he meant it in that order.

As fellows in Trondheim, we received much encouragement to participate in international conferences; Borgen was eager for the research fellows to get international experience in a greater research environment than the local university, and to build networks. However, if the research fellows were to attend the SNTS meetings, they had to be invited by someone who was a member, and Borgen regularly invited his fellows to such conferences.

Borgen himself found the Norwegian biblical and scholarly milieus narrow and small. The theological settings were dominated by the two Lutheran faculties, the Free Faculty of Theology (Menighetsfakultet) and the Faculty of Theology at the University of Oslo. In addition, there were relatively sharp fronts between these two institutions in the 1960s and for many years beyond, and there were few collaborative initiatives or common arenas where biblical scholars could meet and cooperate. They mainly worked separately on their respective islands. Borgen sought beyond Norway's borders; professional networks should not be limited by national and cultural borders. A scholar has, by definition, to cross borders, including denominational, professional, and national borders.

Fulbright professors and the 1985 SNTS General Meeting

Another initiative that Borgen became engaged in was inviting guest lecturers to the department. Here, he utilized his extensive international network and had several lecturers visiting the department. These lectures were also open to non-students, and the audiences got to meet well-known scholars such as C. K. Barrett, David Flusser, Birger Gerhardsson, Lars Hartman, Martin Hengel, Bruce J. Malina, Jacob Neusner, Bo Reicke, Harald Riesenfeldt, and others up through the years. It was also Borgen's merit that in the years 1982–85 the department was assigned three Fulbright professors from the USA, and under his leadership Trondheim became the location for the international large-scale General Meeting of the SNTS in 1985.

Aune, Robbins, and Schuler

The first Fulbright professor to come and work in the department was David E. Aune (b. 1939), a professor at Saint Xavier College in Chicago. He had just finished a significant monograph on *Prophecy in Early Christianity and the Ancient Mediterranean World* (published 1983) and was then writing on what was to become a major commentary on the Revelation of John.[48] These works contributed significantly to establishing Aune as a renowned scholar. It was thus a great asset to the department to have Aune as its first Fulbright professor for an entire year (1982–83). Aune has, as the surname suggests, strong family roots in Norway, especially in the areas around Trondheim, and he was happy to expand his knowledge of his family network while he was there. "There are so many second cousins here," he used to say. He has also been on several later visits to the Department of Religious Studies and to friends and relatives in Norway.

The next American scholar to work as a Fulbright professor at the department was Vernon K. Robbins (b. 1939), a then associate professor at Emory University in Georgia, USA. Robbins was also well on his way to establishing himself as a prominent scholar, and he later published extensively within the field of Gospel research, developing his methodological approach called *socio-rhetorical criticism*.[49] He worked in Trondheim in the academic year 1983–84. Robbins also maintained further contact with the department and Peder Borgen after his stay in Norway.

The third and final Fulbright Professor, Philip L. Shuler, stayed in Trondheim in the spring semester of 1985. He was also a Gospel researcher but did not have as many professional publications or expertise as his two predecessors.[50]

These three scholars, who all had New Testament studies as their primary field of interest and competence, and helped to put the department on the map. They enhanced the department's scholarly reputation and stimulated its competence both through their lectures, participation in the department's research seminar and not least by expanding the department's network.

---

48. The commentary was published in three volumes: Aune, *Revelation*, vols. 52a–c (1997, 1998, 1998). The first volume is dedicated to Peder and Inger Borgen, and Martin and Marianne Hengel.

49. See especially Robbins, *Jesus the Teacher*, and the more extensive presentation and elaboration of this method in Robbins, *Tapestry of Early Christian Discourse*. See further www.religion.emory.edu/faculty/robbins/: "Vernon K. Robbins is described in *Genealogies of New Testament Rhetorical Criticism* (2015) as one of 'five pioneers' of New Testament rhetorical criticism." Cf. also Stewart, "Vernon K. Robbins and His Contributions to Socio-Rhetorical Interpretation," in Porter and Dawson, eds, *Pillars in the History of Biblical Interpretation*, 3:384–408.

50. His main work was: Schuler, *Genre for the Gospels*.

The SNTS General Meeting in Trondheim (1985)

The international society Societas Novi Testamenti Studiorum, often just referred to by its abbreviation, SNTS, arranged its annual General Meeting in different cities/countries but it had never been held in Norway. Raymond E. Brown, an American Catholic Bible scholar and longtime friend of Borgen, had encouraged him to apply to host an SNTS conference in Trondheim. Borgen applied, and in the summer of 1985 the conference was set up and carried through by the University of Trondheim/Department of Religious Studies. It is so far (2022) the first and only time this conference has been held in Norway.

In advance, an offer was made to the participants for a "pre-convention tour to Western Norway—the Land of Fjords," August 16–19, from Oslo via Valdres to the Sognefjord, and on to Geiranger, Molde, and to Trondheim, which turned out to be extremely popular. Sightseeing tours were also arranged at the end of the conference, i.a., one to Røros. The conference itself was held August 19–23. About three hundred New Testament scholars participated. The conference was a success. The many letters of thanks that came in during the autumnal months testify to great enthusiasm;[51] "The best conference ever," to rephrase Juan A. Samaranch's statement after the 1994 Lillehammer Winter Olympics.

The conference was a tremendous boost for the department. Borgen had some secretarial help as a professor, but now he got a dedicated person to work with the preparations throughout the winter (Sonja Behrens), and when the appropriate time came, everyone had to show up, from the professors to the research fellows. In addition, Borgen brought in several helpers from his professional Norwegian network, including some younger theologians from Oslo. The staff consisted of a total of twenty-five people. But the one who had the overview and knew what it used to be like at such conferences was primarily Peder Borgen himself. He knew what the attendees at such conference expected: from sightseeing offers through receptions by church and political authorities to a well-oiled machinery that ensured that seminars and lectures, food service, and lodging—in short, everything—went along smoothly.

In addition, the media-conscious Borgen did not deny himself the opportunity to write a presentation in the leading newspaper in Trondheim: during the conference itself, he wrote an extensive article in *Adresseavisen* about "biblical impulses." Here he showed how there were many impulses from the Bible in general translation traditions, in literature and art, and up

---

51. These letters are now kept in the Borgen archives, National Library, Oslo.

to recent debates about ecology and technology. And in the university's own info newspaper, there was later a full review of the conference, most likely written by Borgen himself.[52] The department's historian, Dagfinn Rian, later stated that "The Congress undoubtedly meant a lot to put the Department and UNIT on the map in the professional context in question. And it meant a lot to the maintenance of the department's international network."[53]

The SNTS conference in Trondheim strengthened Borgen's position within the SNTS community, and in 1998-99 he was elected president of the society. So far, only two Norwegians have been elected president of SNTS: Nils Alstrup Dahl served as president in 1978-79 while he was a professor at Yale University in the USA (1965-80). Borgen is the only person who has been the elected president of this society while a professor at a Norwegian institution. He gave his presidential address, "Two Philonic Prayers and Their Contexts," at the 1998 General Meeting in Copenhagen.[54]

New opportunities: professor at Duke, Oslo, or Trondheim?

Borgen maintained extensive contact with colleagues and friends both inside and outside theological institutions in the United States, and he was repeatedly invited to give guest lectures over there and in Europe. In addition, he often used his travels to the United States to search in archives for information about Methodism in general and in Norway in particular: ". . . when Norwegian-Americans want to search for their roots, then they go to Norway, but Norwegian Methodists go to the United States to find their roots," he said in an interview with *Nordisk Tidende* in 1980.[55] In August of that year, he attended several conferences, visited several archives, and also delivered some guest lectures before returning home.

In March 1983, he was—by invitation—on a one-week visit at Duke University in Durham, North Carolina, to give some guest lectures there. Duke was, and is, one of the largest and most reputable private universities in the United States. While still in the USA but traveling to New York, he received on March 25 a phone call from Dennis M. Campbell, dean of the Divinity School at Duke. They were looking for someone who could

---

52. "Den første internasjonale bibelvitenskapskongress i Norge," *UNITNYTT* 7 (1985) 16–17.

53. Rian, *Kristendomsfag*, 40–41.

54. Published in 1999; cf. Borgen, "Two Philonic Prayers and Their Contexts," republished in Borgen, *Illuminations by Philo*, 69–88.

55. "Professor dr. Peder Borgen—norsk metodist med en sjelden karriere," *Nordisk Tidende*, August 21, 1980.

succeed Professor W. D. Davies (1911–2001), who was to resign, and Campbell expressed that they wanted Borgen as his successor. This exchange was followed up by a brief but hectic correspondence between Borgen and Duke University. Borgen responded on March 26 by requesting additional information about the position in order to make a more informed decision. On March 29, the head of the commission tasked with finding a successor to Davies, Professor D. Moody Smith, wrote to Borgen stating why they thought he, Peder Borgen, was the one they wanted to come to Duke. On April 1, Campbell wrote a letter in which he specified a number of current conditions concerning the professorship, such as salary conditions, research opportunities, teaching duties, etc. On May 26, Borgen wrote his final response from Trondheim and announced that he did not see himself able to accept the offered position.

In and by itself, Duke's offer was very flattering: Duke was not only a highly acclaimed institution, but Davies was also a highly praised scholar both in the United States and internationally. It was thus a great recognition of Borgen's work and reputation as a scholar and teacher that he was wanted as Davies's successor. In his first reply letter, he also stated that "Your offer appeals to me very much, and I feel drawn although the many ties to Norway, to University, family and church, are very strong."[56] In his final reply letter, he wrote about the processes of second thoughts they had gone through after he had returned to Norway. Nevertheless, the conclusion was: "we do not as a family feel that we are able to make 'the leap.'" Both he and Inger enjoyed being in the USA, but their roots in Norway were also strong; their two daughters were now fifteen and eighteen years old, and they hesitated to take them into a new life situation in a new country. At the same time, Peder also expressed that he felt obligations to the Methodist Church in Norway and its situation as a minority church. Hence, he found himself unable to accept a permanent position in the United States.

It was not easy for Borgen to respond to this offer, which from a professional point of view was both tempting and flattering. In fact, he came in a significant squeeze in many ways. On the one hand, it was the consideration for the family and his work back home in Norway. On the other hand, he had already submitted an application for a position in Norway: on February 18 of the same year, a vacancy was announced at the Faculty of Theology in Oslo—"Professor of theology with a special duty to lecture in the New Testament"—with the application deadline set to March 20 the very same year. This announcement concerned the position of Professor Ragnar Leivestad (1916–2002), who was to retire that year. Peder Borgen had submitted his

---

56. Borgen in his letter of response to the oral offer, dated March 26, 1983.

application for this position on March 8 while he was in the United States, and on June 14 he submitted the studies required by the adjudication committee to assess his qualifications for the professorship.

It turned out that a total of four persons applied for this position in Oslo.[57] It surprised some at the Faculty of Theology that Peder Borgen applied. Maybe not so much because he was a Methodist, but because rumors had reached them that he had received an offer in the United States. Not everyone was equally excited that he applied for the position at the Faculty of Theology. In addition, it was still a fact that Norwegian law stated that "Church officials and ombudsmen and teachers at the Faculty of Theology shall be a member of the Church of Norway. In exceptional cases, the King may dispense with the requirement for a teacher at the Faculty of Theology."[58] If Borgen were to be nominated for the position, he would thus have to receive a dispensation from the king in order to be permanently employed as a professor at the Faculty. Would the Faculty of Theology accept that commitment? Or to what extent would they prioritize one of their own younger researchers?

Here, too, there was a certain exchange of letters, but now between Borgen and Professor Jacob Jervell.[59] The latter was one of those who expressed surprise that Borgen applied and tried to get him to state if he really was serious about his application. Jervell justified his request on the grounds that it was his task to appoint the members of the committee to assess the applicants, and that the choice of these members depended on who the applicants were. But he also wondered what the standing was with the request from the USA, and with the upcoming SNTS conference in Trondheim (1985) if Borgen moved to Oslo. Borgen was annoyed by Jervell's request and hints and replied with a short one-liner that he maintained his application. Jervell accepted this but still expressed some astonishment.

The relationship between Jervell and Borgen was not the best. In general, they got along well as long as there was some distance. But Jervell had delivered a strong critique during Borgen's disputation, and he had repeated much of this when adjudicating Borgen's application for the professorship in Bergen in 1971-72. Borgen and Jervell never became close friends; one could sometimes get the impression that there was not room for two such distinctive personalities within the small New Testament research community in Norway. Borgen thrived best with Jervell at a reasonable distance,

---

57. The applicants were, in alphabetical order: Peder Borgen, Tord Fornberg (Sweden), Halvor Moxnes, and Jarl Henning Ulrichsen. Jacob Jervell, Bent Noack (Denmark), and Heikki Räisänen (Finland) were appointed as assessment committee.

58. The Law of September 1971, no. 107-§67.

59. Copies of the letters are now in Borgen's archives.

and that feeling was probably mutual.[60] Moreover, now it turned out that Jervell was also to join the adjudicating commission that was to evaluate the applicants for the vacancy after Leivestad. Thus, to some extent, it was predictable how the assessment of Borgen would turn out.

The problem found its solution in that only two applicants were considered competent for the professorship. In the recommendation submitted by the committee in March 1984, Peder Borgen came in second place, and an associate professor at the Faculty of Theology (TF), Halvor Moxnes, dr.theol., was awarded first place. Moxnes (1944–) was a much younger scholar but had published several studies—his age considered. He had been a student at TF and obtained his doctoral degree there in 1977.[61] Subsequently, he was appointed associate professor there and was thus one of the younger scholars prioritized by the faculty. In addition, he was more broadly oriented in his research regarding newer methods; he had made more use of newer methods and perspectives from social sciences, including social anthropology, than Borgen.

Borgen was considered by the committee to be a more traditional researcher, as he had paid little attention to the problems and advantages of the newer methods that Moxnes used in his research.

Borgen's application to the University of Oslo was a bit of a mystery to many. If appointed, he would then have become a teacher in a full theological study program, not only Christian knowledge; but those who were aware of the somewhat fragile relationship between him and Jervell wondered why he would exchange his position in Trondheim for these more problematic circumstances. In addition, it is a correct observation that he was on the threshold of essential tasks in Trondheim, initiated by himself. That it was Moxnes who was chosen for the professorship in Oslo was thus no major surprise to most people.

Nevertheless, the committee's recommendation was perceived by many as an apparent omission of Borgen, his seniority and competence taken into consideration, and some probably also questioned whether the faculty policy did not override the academic qualifications.

---

60. It is perhaps symptomatic of their mutual relationship that Borgen is not included as a contributor in the two Festschrifts that Jervell received (Berg, ed. et al., *Riv ned gjerdene*; Hellholm, ed. et al., *Mighty Minorities?*, 1985 and 1995 respectively). Nor is Jervell a contributor to any of the two Festschrifts that were presented to Borgen (Bøckman, et. al., *Context*; Aune, ed. et al., *Neotestamentica*, 1988 and 2003 respectively), nor are they on each other's lists of congratulators (Tabula Gratulatoria).

61. Moxnes, *Theology in Conflict*.

After the committee's recommendations had become known to the applicants, Borgen announced in a letter of April 26 that he withdrew his application, and Moxnes was appointed to the professorship later that year.

Hence, Borgen chose to stay in Trondheim. He was grateful for the confidence in him that was shown at Duke University but chose to remain in Norway. Both family and work conditions played a part in that decision. The latter also included that he had come a long way in the work of getting Fulbright professors to the department, he was to arrange the SNTS General Meeting in 1985, and he was in the process of establishing facilities and supervision for students in the new doctoral program at the department. In addition, he was also widely involved in Methodist initiatives, such as the International Lutheran-Methodist Dialogue Commission. He therefore chose to stay in Norway.

Borgen's travels to the United States, however, continued in the following years. In 1988 he had a sabbatical year; one year off from teaching and administration, and both he and Inger moved to the United States. They spent the spring semester at Princeton University in Mercer County, western New Jersey; the fall semester, they were at Duke University in Durham, North Carolina. Inger took the opportunity in the spring semester to study family therapy at the Ackerman Institute for the Family in New York. During the autumn semester, she accompanied Peder on several visits to places where he lectured.

That he in all these years was also active in SNTS and went to their General Meetings in July/August every year is part of the story, but it was for Peder so obvious that it is almost unnecessary to mention. What we will focus on a little more in the following is his work as a member of the Royal Norwegian Society of Sciences and Letters in Trondheim.

Borgen and the Royal Norwegian Society of Sciences and Letters

The Royal Norwegian Society of Sciences and Letters (DKNVS) was founded in Trondheim in 1760 as Norway's first scientific society. Three learned men were behind this new formation: Bishop Johan Ernst Gunnerus, Gerhard Schøning, principal at the Cathedral School, and Peter Fredrik Suhm, who lived on his wife's fortune and worked as an independent historian and author. It was almost one hundred years ahead of the establishment of the next scientific society in Norway, namely, the Norwegian Academy of Science and Letters in Christiania (= Oslo), which came into being in 1857.[62] A few others have been added in more recent times.[63]

In the Norwegian version of the history of the DKNVS, a scientific society is described as follows:

> The purpose of a scientific society is to promote scientific research through academic discussions by publishing or supporting scientific work, announcing prize assignments, providing financial support to researchers, awarding travel grants, and collaborating with similar institutions in other countries.

Peder Borgen was elected a member at the society's meeting in 1979. He gradually became increasingly involved in its activities. He was the leader of the humanities class in the years 1984–87 and was then elected vice-president (deputy chairperson) in 1990, a role he held until 1996. Then he was elected president for 1996–99.

The Royal Norwegian Society of Sciences and Letters was founded in 1760, and thus celebrated its two-hundredth anniversary in 1960. The anniversary was also marked by the issue of two Norwegian stamps in the value of forty-five and ninety øre respectively. The ninety-øre stamp is shown here. Both depicts the society's monogram.

---

62. See http://www.dnva.no/. When the Society in Trondheim celebrated its 250th anniversary in 2010, two historical representations of the Society's history were published, one in Norwegian intended for the generally historically interested reader, and one in English, intended for a more international interested readership. See Stubhaug, *Den lange linjen,* and With Andersen et al., *Æmula Lauri.*

63. Cf. *Vitenskapsakademiet i Stavanger,* and *Agder Vitenskapsakademi* in Kristiansand.

Borgen's membership and engagement in an institution such as the Royal Norwegian Society of Sciences and Letters can be seen as a natural consequence of his academic ambition and his interest in trying to cross the borders between the sciences and between the sciences and society at large.[64] When he looked back on his activity in 2008, he stated to the Methodist magazine *Brobyggeren* that "one of his goals has been to open windows between science, church, and culture."[65] And we have seen above how he could argue even in his sermons for the need of Christian and ecclesiastical insight and openness towards the more general cultural life: "the tunnel out to cultural circles and academic circles has collapsed because we have assumed that the cultural world and the academic world are outside the scope of relevant church work and even dubious and dangerous," he said in a sermon in the late 1970s.[66] His commitment at the university to arrange courses for business people was driven by the same desire to cross borders. That he was not a scholar disinterested in the patterns of ordinary life can perhaps also be illustrated by the fact that when the society celebrated its 225th anniversary in 1985, one of its celebrating activities was a gathering in the ruins of the old Gregorius church. These ruins were excavated in its present location under a bank site downtown (Trondhjem og Strindens Sparebank), and he, as the president of the society, held a short devotion there. There and then he said, among other things, that "The Bible and Christianity have from generation to generation been woven together with our general culture. If we search beneath the surface and into the ground beneath our lives, we find patterns of Biblical faith in God and confessions of Christ. Like the archaeologists digging deep down into the foundations of the city and discovering the Gregorius Church."[67] For Borgen, it was a relevant goal to find *patterns* both in his advanced research, whether that be in the works of Philo, the New Testament, or in general, and in local cultural expressions.

One of Borgen's first official assignments in the society was to give a lecture at one of its joint meetings in 1980. The topic he then chose falls, typically enough, into the suggested pattern above. It had as its subject, "Law, Inspiration and Freedom: Galatians as a Cultural-Historical Document." Here he tried to give a cultural-historical (and theological) explanation of "How did it happen that an exclusive people's religion and ethics,

64. On May 10, 1996, he was also elected to the the Royal Society of Sciences (Kungliga Vetenskaps-Societeten), Uppsala.

65. Nordby, "Peder Borgen," *Brobyggeren* 7 (2008) 14.

66. Cf. an earlier section in this chapter.

67. Quotation taken from his manuscript, now in the Borgen archives, National Library, Oslo.

in casu the Jewish people's religion and ethics, broke out of the nations' borders and became a dynamic movement out to other peoples, in the form of Christianity?"[68] Again, we here see a border-crossing focus.

The biographee and his biographer, participating at the annual festive meeting of the Royal Norwegian Society of Science and Letters in 2017.

During his years as president of the society, the city of Trondheim celebrated its one-thousandth anniversary in 1997, and the DKNVS established a major project as a gift to the city. The project was called "The City, the River, the Knowledge: An Anniversary Project in 1997," and was a remarkable success. The project was also the start of a continued expansion of knowledge dissemination and gave DKNVS a renewed place as a culturally important institution beyond its academic membership. Hence, Borgen's participation in the society helped to open new relationships with various groups and milieus.

In 1999, he was appointed as Knight First Class of the Royal Order of St. Olav for his theological research.[69] In the proposal's justification for

68. Quotation taken from his unpublished manuscript, now in the Borgen private archives.

69. The proposal was made by professors Magne Sæbø (Menighetsfakultetet), Karsten Jakobsen, Peter Wilhelm Bøckman, and Ole Gunnar Winsnes (all three from NTNU).

this award, his national and international efforts were emphasized. In the statement given by the DKNVS board, special reference was made to his interdisciplinary measures, his lively involvement in the dissemination of science, and his work to strengthen collaboration with other academies.

In the year Borgen turned seventy-five (2003), he was awarded two honors, both of which were related to his work as a professor and with which it may be appropriate to end this chapter. At the society's meeting in January, he was awarded its highest award, the Gunnerus Medal, "for his extensive and in-depth New Testament theological research, his involvement in international theological organizations, and his significant work to promote the Royal Norwegian Society of Sciences and Letters."[70] Later in the year, he received his second Festschrift.[71] Here he was hailed by nineteen internationally renowned scholars.

Peder Borgen was a professor at the University of Trondheim from 1973 until the end of 1992. Then he had a few years as a senior fellow before he and Inger moved to Lillestrøm in 1999. However, he did not even then sit down in a rocking chair. Driven by his curious restlessness, he was still engaged locally and internationally. We return to this in a later chapter.

---

70. The description is taken from the society's own (undated) description. See also a brief note in *Romerikes Blad*, March 30, 2003, 13.

71. See Aune, Seland, and Ulrichsen, *Neotestamentica et Philonica*. Contributors in this Festschrift were: James D.G. Dunn, James H. Charlesworth, Birger Gerhardsson, Andrie B. du Toit, Karl-Gustav Sandelin, Morna D. Hooker, David Hellholm, John Painter, Jarl Henning Ulrichsen, Hans Kvalbein, D. Moody Smith, Howard Clark Kee, David E. Aune, Ellen Birnbaum, David M. Hay, David T. Runia, Troels Engberg-Pedersen, Kåre Fuglseth, and Torrey Seland. As far as I know, Jacob Jervell and Peder Borgen are the only two Norwegian theological scholars who have been awarded two Festschrifts.

11

Borgen on the Issue of Church-State Relations

HAVING MOVED TO TRONDHEIM, Peder Borgen became increasingly more involved in various international activities, both in his New Testament field of research as well as in international groups and committees linked to the Methodist Church.

Worth mentioning here is his membership in the European Theological Commission, which met once a year under the leadership of the European Council of the United Methodist Church.[1] He was the head of this council from 1973 to 1977. It was also crucial that in 1979–84 he was one of two Norwegian members[2] of the Joint Commission between World Methodist Council and the Lutheran World Federation. The commission's task was to work out a text that could serve as a basis for greater recognition among Lutherans and Methodists of each other's denominations.[3] He was also a member of the World Methodist Council in 1986–91 and attended its meetings in Nairobi, Kenya, and Singapore.

---

1. See http://methodist.eu: "The EMC is a consultative council that brings together Methodist leaders from across Europe to discuss common issues facing the church, to learn and grow in understanding, to support each other and to share in fellowship and encouragement."

2. The other member was Lars Østnor, senior lecturer at the Free Faculty of Theology, who was a Lutheran representative.

3. See here Østnor, *Dialogens vei*.

In previous sections, I have touched on his ecumenical interest and participation in various forums in Norway in the early 1960s, and I will continue with this topic in the next chapter (chapter 12). But in the present chapter, I focus on his commitment to issues in the debates concerning the relationship between state and church in Norway. But first, however, it may be helpful to take a closer look at his Methodist understanding of what the church is, that is, his *ecclesiology*.

THE ECCLESIOLOGY OF BORGEN

Borgen grew up and lived most of his life in Norway, that is, in a context where the Church of Norway had been a Lutheran state church since 1537. Furthermore, as such, it was the dominating ecclesiastical institution. Non-Lutheran churches were not allowed until 1845, and the characterization of non-Lutherans as "dissenters" was still very much alive in the twentieth century. Hence, many expressions of his ecclesiology, emphases, and some of his more pointed statements must be understood in light of the dominating role of the Lutheran majority church in Norway.

In Borgen's early public statements about the state church vis-à-vis the idea of a free church, his critical attitude towards the state church is clearly expressed. Among the more pointed issues, he lists the following: one of the weaknesses of the state church, in his opinion, is that its mere existence as a *state* church makes it difficult for that church to live out its potential as a *missionary* church. The result is that the responsibility and the biblical idea of its mission are weakened. Therefore, he believes, "the very structure of the church destroys the idea that mission and testimony are a call to its members."[4] The idea and the system of a state church problematize its mission: the system as such disencourages discovering that some of its members may be part of its mission field dependent upon their personal relation to Christian faith. He also believes that the state church system has led the Lutheran Church of Norway to too easily overlook the other denominations that have worked within the country's borders for several generations. The state church becomes self-sufficient, and the other churches troublesome: "The State Church's attitude towards the free churches in Norway would be different if the Lutheran circles realistically realized that the country is a mission field, despite the statistical 96 percent of the population being church members."[5] Admittedly, these pointed views were written back in

---

4. This and the following quotations are taken from Borgen, "Misjonskirkens tid?" *Vårt Land*, January 16, 1959.

5. Today the percentage of the population who are members of the Church of

1959, but they mirror attitudes observed and held not only by Borgen, and it took some decades before the Church of Norway took steps to integrate the free churches in Norway into its ecumenical agenda. As the majority church was a territorial church, the activities of the free churches could be perceived as proselytizing.[6] It took still a couple of decades before the Church of Norway reconsidered its view of the non-Lutheran denominations in Norway.

The Methodist Church in its Norwegian context

Considering the various church models in Norway in the 1980s, one can say that the Methodist Church's ecclesial system was and is of the type that is often categorized as *synodal* (as is the Evangelical Lutheran Free Church in Norway). The Methodist Church's Annual Conference is then its synod. Other variants are the *Congregationalist* type, where each congregation is independent (such as Pentecostals and Baptists), and the *Episcopalian* (episcopal) type, which is characterized by an ecclesiastical structure with an extensive and highly developed priestly hierarchy (in Norway, most clearly represented by the Roman Catholic Church). Then the Church of Norway may be said to belong to a type we may call the *Nordic state-church model*, where state bodies have decisive influence through legislation and economics. As a synodal church, the Methodist Church considers each congregation as a local manifestation of the church as a whole. The Methodist Church is not national but international. In Norway, the congregations' joint conference—the Annual Conference—has legislative and executive authority.[7] But the Methodist Church also has a bishop, and Borgen can therefore say that the Methodist Church has a "synodal-episcopal character."[8] The condition for membership is not only baptism but baptism and the confession of believers. However, Borgen strongly rejects that this can be called having "the

---

Norway is much smaller.

6. Cf. Folkestad Breistein's comment: "As a majority church, territorial church and state church, the Church of Norway had for a long time an ambivalent attitude towards other denominations, not least because these were literally on the territory of the Church of Norway. Since new members of the Free Churches predominantly came from the Church of Norway, their activities were perceived as proselytizing." Breistein, *Fra dissens til konsensus*, 84.

7. But the *Regional Conference* is above the national Annual Conference, and at the top is the *General Conference*. The latter is most often held in the United States.

8. Borgen, "Metodismen og Norge," 24. A sketch of the various models is given on 23–25.

pure church" as an ideal.⁹ Nevertheless, he sees the synodal system as the form that best reflects New Testament motives:

> The nature of the Church is that a single church is a local manifestation of God's people as a superior entity (cf. the ecclesia in the New Testament, which designates both the people of God as a whole and the individual church). In the Methodist Church, therefore, the Annual Conference has authority as an expression of the Church's cross-national and supra-national nature, at the same time as the emphasis is placed on the local congregation with its local forms of government. This is also how the conference structure grew in early Christianity, with the meeting in Jerusalem as a first effort. Preaching, worship, sacrament administration, mission, and congregational fellowship belong together in one unit and should not be split up into parish churches and other houses of worship [Bedehus] or official churches and independent organizations.¹⁰

The context for the last statement in this quote is the fact that in Norway, mission organizations—often led by lay people—established local community buildings called a *bedehus* (prayer house). Here they came together for congregational activities such as preaching, prayers, sometimes even the last supper, and thus functioned much as a church within a church, an *ecclesiolae in ecclesia*. To Borgen, this was a contradiction in terms. Moreover, he sees several common features between the organization and structure of the Methodist Church and the structures he believes are to be found in the New Testament. On the one hand, there are many similarities between then and now regarding the place of churches in society. In the early days of New Testament times, Christianity was a minority religion; Borgen believes this is also the case in his times; the Christian faith is a minority view and in conflict with other currents. On the other hand, the picture of the church systems we see reflected in the New Testament shows that the Christian church as such was of a cross- and supranational character: "cross-national and supranational" are characteristics that we repeatedly encounter in Borgen's descriptions of the Christian church as such, of the Methodist Church, and of the church of the New Testament.¹¹

---

9. "With reference to the New Testament, the Methodist Church distances itself both from the doctrine of a pure church and from the view and practice that no one can be excluded from a church. Full membership is a testimony to the need for professing faith." Borgen, "Metodistkirken, en tverrnasjonal kirke," 31.

10. Borgen, "Metodistkirken, en tverrnasjonal kirke," 31.

11. See Borgen, "Cross-National Church for Jews and Greeks," 225–48; Borgen, "Kristne og Staten i Det nye testamente," 33–41; Borgen, "Misjon i nytestamentlig tid

Borgen pays close attention to the form of organization that the Methodist Church has and the underlying view of the church. However, he is also aware that it can have its weaknesses. Therefore, with a view to a synodal church constitution, he expresses the following observation: "Our Church emphasizes wholeness and common organization. This is of great help in times of revival because people are then taken care of, and one avoids some problems, as for example, slippings. It is also some help against divisions. In times of recession, however, centralization can intensify the decline, both because the administrative apparatus may become too large and because it can then, to an excessive extent, absorb the resources from the 'outskirts.'"[12]

The Norwegian Methodist Church as a free church

Considering the relationship with the Church of Norway and the other free churches, Borgen repeatedly claimed that the Methodist Church was in a kind of "intermediate position." In his article on ecumenical tendencies and problems in Methodism (1971), he claimed that the Methodist Church "understands itself as located in the middle between the other free churches and the Norwegian Lutheran Church."[13] However, it is a bit unclear what this delimitation to both sides is based on and how it is legitimized. In another context, he once stated it thus: "In our branch of the Methodist Church we do not see national borders or any borders between peoples as the theological basis for a "people's church" [*folkekirke*] or national Church, and in a pluralistic society it is not a proper name either."[14] Borgen thinks here of the fact that the Methodist Church in Norway is part of the worldwide United Methodist Church, and thus is different from the other free churches in Norway because they do not have any such supranational organizational affiliation. But in Norway, many others will still claim that it is natural to place the Methodist Church among the "free churches." The Methodist Church in Norway itself has also taken the consequence of this view as it accepted membership in both Dissentertinget and then, for example, the Norges Frikirkeråd (Norwegian Free Church Council), and later in its successor, Norges Kristne Råd (Norwegian Christian Council).

---

og i Metodistkirken i Europa i dag," 27–41; Borgen, "Metodistkirken, en tverr-nasjonal kirke i Norge og i andre land," 28–38.

12. Borgen, "Metodistkirken," 235.

13. See Borgen, "Ekumeniske tendenser," 36. By "the Norwegian Lutheran Church" he meant here obviously the Norwegian state church. But in several contexts, it seems that both Borgen himself and others forgot that there was more than one Lutheran church in Norway.

14. In an email to me, dated April 23, 2019.

THE FREE CHURCHES AND THE STATE-CHURCH DEBATE IN THE 1970S

The work on reforms in the Church of Norway concerning its relationship to the state as the superior and governing body was the focus of a special commission as early as in the years of 1908–11, but the debates relevant for us in this biography began in earnest in the 1960s. From then on, several commissions were at work; some established by the state, and some established by the Church of Norway itself.

The Church of Norway's internal church bodies were underdeveloped in relation to the Methodist Church's system, but in these decades intensive work was carried out to establish a strong Church of Norway with an extensive range of church bodies. The goal of these efforts was to establish a more substantial degree of democracy within the church, and to establish an organizational structure relevant to negotiations with the state. To obtain this, a development of a formal structure with relevant, functional, and autonomous bodies was necessary.[15] A Parish Council was established in each of the parishes in 1920, Diocesan Councils were established in 1933, but a National Council was not established until 1969. Then the Diocesan Synods and a General Synod were established in 1984.

But if the Church of Norway lacked a strong internal structure, it had something that the other denominations did not have, namely, its unique affiliation with the Norwegian state. It was a "state church" (*statskirke*), a term that came into use in about 1845, and which in the 1960s and beyond had long since entered the language of daily life as a term for the majority church—the Church of Norway. The Ministry of Church and Education Affairs appointed and remunerated all pastors in ecclesiastical positions, and pastors from resident chaplains and above were government officials (*embetsmenn*). However, at the same time, it must be admitted that the slow development of the internal structures of Church of Norway was to a large extent influenced, sometimes even delayed, because of the state's reluctance—and fear—of giving too much power to the national church. Politics as such has many facets; some political parties were more reluctant than others towards the reforms asked for by church leaders, which in the mid-1950 was primarily the bishops. But the call for a greater freedom and the establishment of a more varied church structure grew steadily in the last

---

15. An overview of the work of providing the Church of Norway with a relevant structure up to 1975 can be found in the report *Stat og Kirke* (1975), 6–154. See also Løvlie, *Kirke, Stat og Folk*, 37–188, and more generally Oftestad, *Den norske statsreligionen*. On the church council's origin and further history, see now Holbek, *Rådet som forandret kirken*.

decades of the twentieth century, not at least due the influence of a broad engagement within the church.

Strategies of the free churches

The other denominations were often affected by the changes in the laws established regarding the relationship of the Church of Norway to the state. They had their own bodies that functioned both as forums for discussions among themselves and externally in their relationship with the state and the majority church.

The non-Lutheran denominations sometimes made radical demands, which often led to them not being "heard" in the sense of "not taken seriously." In addition, there was the fact that "their various bills were perceived as a threat to the State Church system."[16] In particular, their proposals in the years leading up to World War II about non-denominational Christian teaching in schools aroused opposition both in the majority church and in other groups in society.

In the postwar years, the free churches changed much of their attitudes and practical proposals. Folkestad Breistein summarizes this thus:

> After World War II, the free churches retained their principles, but adjusted their strategies. They continued to work to repeal the Dissenter Law, but to implement it, they had to moderate their original objectives. *Dissentertinget* no longer primarily advocated the abolition of the State Church system or Christian education in schools. The dissenters wanted a continued Christian influence in the Norwegian society and to keep the Christian curriculum in schools . . . . Even though the idea that the churches should manage on their own without support from the State was the basis for classical free church thinking, Norwegian dissenters had to take into account that they lived in a country with a State Church system.[17]

The state church strategies in general—and especially in light of the interests and arguments from the free churches—have also been studied in recent years. Concerning the years leading up to the period we are most concerned with here (1970+), Ingunn Folkestad Breistein claims that the

> State Church strategies in the face of religious pluralism and the demands for religious freedom, the thought of the church

---

16. Breisten, *"Har Staten bedre borgere?"*, 382.
17. Breisten, *"Har Staten bedre borgere?"*, 384.

leaders ... also appears in the post-war period to have been to reject amendments on the grounds that these would weaken the State Church's position. The State Church's spokesmen still perceived the State Church's position as the only guarantor of retaining Christianity's influence in society.[18]

This is at least how it was perceived by Folkestad Breistein, who herself had her point of view from within a free church.[19]

Methodists and the state church

In the postwar period, Folkestad Breistein claims, "several of the spokesmen in the *Norwegian Free Church Council* argued that they would no longer primarily work for the abolition of the State Church."[20] However, this attitude did not apply to everyone; some still insisted that a divorce between state and church was preferable in both theory and practice. As for the Methodists, Folkestad Breistein claims that they "went the furthest in giving their support to the State Church system and continued confessional teaching in Christian knowledge in the schools."[21] A couple of interviews in *Kristelig Tidende* in 1975 also demonstrate that some key Methodists were a bit reluctant in their criticism of the Church of Norway in these days. Bishop Ole E. Borgen, the elder brother of Peder, is a bit more ambivalent. He claims that the state church system is a unique treatment of the Church of Norway and that "We must move away from the privileges that the Lutheran church receives as a State Church."[22] However, he also expresses that there will also be disadvantages in the case of separation between State and Church: he is here thinking of the teaching of Christian knowledge in the schools, which he thinks will then fall away.[23] When asked what will happen if there is a separation between state and church, the bishop answers:

18. Folkestad Breisten, 'Har Staten bedre borgere?', 386.
19. See also her somewhat harsh comment: "To the extent that the men in the State Church can be said to have promoted religious freedom, this must be understood as freedom internally in the Church of Norway. Those who have fought for greater freedom within the state church have essentially not fought for religious freedom for dissenter communities outside the state church." Folkestad Breisten, 'Har Staten bedre borgere?', 386.
20. Breisten, "Har Staten bedre borgere?", 402.
21. Breisten, "Har Staten bedre borgere?", 404.
22. "Statskirkeordningen er uten tvil en særbehandling av den lutherske kirke," *Kristelig Tidende* 23 (1975) 1.
23. "Statskirkeordningen er uten tvil en særbehandling av den lutherske kirke," *Kristelig Tidende* 23 (1975) 1.

I do not think the situation will get worse than now. Among other things, all the special rights that the Church of Norway now has will be taken away. Instead, there will be equality for all, as it has developed more and more in Sweden. The Methodist Church is not just a free church vis-à-vis the State. It is also a confessional church. These are two of the most essential features of our Church. I would like to welcome any change in the situation for the Church of Norway, if it gets a more confessional and church-like character.

In the same issue of *Kristelig Tidende*, one of the Methodist Church's two supervisors at the time, Gustav Søiland, is also interviewed. The interview was entitled: "We should not join the howling chorus that demands the State Church to be dissolved." Furthermore, he elaborates thus: "We Free Church people want to be in good contact with the Church of Norway. Therefore, we should not incite agitation and join the howling chorus that demands the State Church be dissolved. This is an issue that must not be pushed forward."[24]

Søiland also believed, like his bishop, that if there were a separation between church and state, there would be no teaching of Christian knowledge in the schools, only teaching in religion. But despite the special treatment that a state church system represented, he believed it was also important to remember that "the question of a dissolution of the State Church is really an internal Lutheran matter." Not all free churches leaders were equally positive concerning that attitude.

It is evident that there had been a development in the view of this complicated matter among the free churches since the establishment of the Dissenterting in 1902. They disagreed on much, but most agreed on one point, as Pastor Edvin Andreassen from the Free Evangelical Assemblies expressed thus: "Our task is to make sure that in the event of a separation we do not get rules of law that discriminate against the Free Churches."[25]

It was precisely at this point that Peder Borgen introduced his critique a few years later.

---

24. "Vi bør ikke være med i hylekoret som krever statskirken oppløst," *Kristelig Tidende* 23 (1975) 4.

25. See "Statskirkeordningen ubibelsk," *Kristelig Tidende* 8 (1976) 1 and 2.

BORGEN AND THE DEBATE CONCERNING THE STATE-CHURCH SYSTEM

In the part of the discussion from the 1970s referred to above, it was taken for granted by many that there were now great possibilities for a separation between state and church, and thus a dissolution of the Church of Norway's binding to the state. This was not without a foothold in both the perceived and possible reality. The public State-Church Commission of 1971, which presented its report in 1975, had—as its majority recommendation—advocated the dissolution of the Church of Norway as a state church and proposed the establishment of the majority church as a "free people's church" ("*fri folkekirke*").[26]

Peder Borgen did not come forward with any public comments before or immediately after this recommendation was presented. But that was probably simply to be expected. The recommendation applied primarily to the Church of Norway; the free churches were discussed and outlined, but no schemes were proposed that interfered restrictively with their work.

An important report from the ministry (1980)

The 1975 commission report's proposal for a transition to a free national church nevertheless attracted the attention of many. In November 1975, a circular was sent out from the ministry for a comprehensive hearing process. After the hearing statements had been received and processed by the ministry, the result was presented to Parliament (*Storting*) in a report (*Stortingsmelding*) in 1980. And then Peder Borgen came on the scene because he thought that the report to Parliament discriminated against the free churches.

The report, which was the government's report to Parliament—prepared by the Ministry of Church and Education Affairs—is in many ways clear in its proposals but also sometimes surprisingly sharp in its arguments. It demonstrates a ministry very willing to govern the church. Its conclusion was also the opposite of what the majority in the commission report of 1975 had presented. The ministry joined the minority group, stating that the state church's present relationship to the state should be maintained for the time we can reasonably foresee, but some ecclesiastical reforms should be agreed upon and granted.[27]

---

26. See NOU 1975:30 Stat og kirke, 187–207. See also Løvlie, *Kirke, stat, og folk*, 190–207.

27. *Stortingsmelding nr. 40 Om stat og kirke*, 19 (Report to the Parliament from the

Concerning the free churches, the ministry stated:

> It is important in this and any similar contexts to emphasize that the State should see it as its task to also help independent denominations to function in a good way. Gradually, the dissenting congregations have received more freedom and better working conditions. However, they have had to fight for their rights. This Report also wishes to express an understanding of the Free Churches' cause and honor their work.

Concerning the Church of Norway—the state church—the ministry further believed that a free national church would not by and in itself be a guarantor of or represent a broader and, at the same time, more profound religious devotion and true piety in the population. Nor would the ministry readily accept all criticism of the state church, which claims it is like a state-run religion, in line with other state-run and -organized institutions. Religiously, it is instead "a separate religious community with religious norms qualitatively in line with the free church communities."[28] However, the report maintains and emphasizes that "the broadest possible internal democratic way of working, the most activating way possible and the widest possible connection with and in our people"[29] are among the values that the report particularly wants to set in the center.

Peder Borgen and the state church report

Peder Borgen wanted to be ecumenically minded and active, and in 1979 he became a member of a larger international commission to investigate the relationship between the Methodist Church and Lutheran churches. State church critic and an ecumenist—is that possible? He would probably say yes. For he was a critic of the state church and its privileges more than of Lutheranism as such. And he was a critic of the laws and schemes that he thought were discriminatory.

It was the report from the Ministry of Church and Education Affairs to Parliament in 1980 that Borgen criticized several times and in various contexts. In February 1981, he had a long article in *Kristelig Tidende* where he explained his counter-perceptions;[30] not so much against the report in

---

Ministry of Church and Education).

28. *St.meld nr. 40 Om stat og kirke*, 32.

29. *St.meld nr. 40 Om stat og kirke*, 32.

30. Borgen, "Stat–kirkemeldingen er diskriminerende," *Kristelig Tidende*, February 5, 1981, 9 and 12.

general as against what he thought were discriminatory comments and attitudes towards the free churches. On March 20, the same text was sent as a letter to the Committee for Church and Education Affairs (Kirke- og undervisningskomiteen) as a statement from the Methodist Church, and it was also a central source for the message from the supervisors to the Methodist Church's Annual Conference in Kristiansand later that year. This article by Borgen in *Kristelig Tidende* is one of our primary sources for how he thought about the privileges of the majority church in the 1980s. In the present context, I will emphasize three of his arguments.

First—and this is a criticism he leveled several time—it is discriminatory to have two church laws in Norway, one for the denominations (*trossamfunn*) and another law for one particular church, named as the Church of Norway (Den norske kirke). Because the latter's own bodies placed decisive emphasis on the fact that it too was a "religious community," or a community of faith (*trossamfunn*), it would be logical that it was covered by the same law as the one covering the other denominations. However, that was not the case. There was a special law for the majority church—the Church of Norway. The arguments and reasonings for this Borgen found utterly unreasonable. It was argued, he wrote, that the Church of Norway included the predominant part of the population and that one could not ignore the historical development in a country that linked the Church of Norway to the people for centuries. Borgen had little sympathy for this historical argument. One should remove discriminatory attitudes and laws that gave one denomination explicit and implicit privileges.

Secondly, Borgen found the name as such—the Church of Norway—discriminatory. This name represented a kind of labeling that Borgen argued against several times, before and after 1981. For example, he asked several times, a little rhetorically: What about the other churches in Norway? Are they not Norwegian? Are they un-Norwegian? Maybe foreign? "This name, together with the special ecclesiastical arrangements and schemes, promotes social attitudes of a discriminatory nature by characterizing other denominations as a social fringe phenomenon."[31] Not everyone understood this argument. Perhaps one must be a free church member and thus belong to a minority to feel the weight of the fact that the majority church described (and still describes) itself as "*The* Church of Norway" (Den norske Kirke).[32]

---

31. See here also Borgen, "Religionsfrihet og statskirke," 15.

32. See now, however, also the Lutheran professor O. Skarsaune, who in his book *Etterlyst: Bergprekenens Jesus* (256–57, 300, 306–7) argues that the Church of Norway should reconsider this label and expresses hope that the feeling of arrogance which members of the free church people constantly experience might eventually disappear.

Some Methodist leaders proposed the name The Norwegian Lutheran Church as an alternative, but they then fell into the same trap as the report to Parliament because there were, and still are, more than one Lutheran church in Norway.[33] Nevertheless, this and similar alternative proposals emerged from time to time. However, Peder Borgen never managed to accept the name *The* Church of Norway as a good name for only one of the many denominations in Norway. They are all Norwegian, he thought. Therefore, this name had to be changed.

His third argument against the report from the Ministry for Church and Education is perhaps more substantial. It concerned primarily the state's attitudes and practices within administration and economics in areas involving institutions established and led by a free church. The report to Parliament, he believed, would quickly lead to discriminatory consequences of an administrative and financial nature. Some such discriminatory conditions already existed in the ways the state church system worked, he argued. Borgen mentioned some problems: that the pastors in the state church were given full access to the public registers concerning newborn children, that is, registers of birth, etc. This access was not available to other denominations. Hence it gave the Church of Norway the prerogative of being informed every time some of its members became parents; that is, the free churches were deprived of one significant way of updating their membership lists.

Furthermore: he criticized that the report stated that "the state, county and municipal authorities responsible for the social services . . . should cooperate with the church (of Norway) . . . so that the church work in important areas can continue as an integral part of the public service and be included in the plans for this business."[34] No such guidelines were at work regarding the free churches. This view, too, he found discriminating.

Conclusion: no changes for the free churches

In the free churches, the result of their protests was considered meager. None of their suggestions and/or protests were taken up and dealt with by the government. The Methodist Church's Annual Conference in the summer of 1981 was held in Kristiansand. Peder Borgen was also present. The conference had the report to Parliament up for discussion and made its decisions. The conference, inter alia, also appealed to the government to set down a committee that could investigate the situation of the free churches,

---

33. Confer here Det evangelisk-lutherske kirkesamfunn (DELK), established in 1872, and Den Evangelisk Lutherske Frikirke, established in 1877.

34. St.meld nr. 40 Om stat og kirke, 74.

and it was regretted that the recommendation from the majority in the State-Church Commission of 1971—which presented its report in 1975—that all religious communities should be treated equally, was not followed up in the report to Parliament.

However, Peder Borgen did not follow up on the state church debate in the following years. He became more involved in ecumenical work, which required much of his attention in these years. At the same time, some of the issues discussed above were also relevant in the ecumenical discussions. When the international Joint Commission between the World Methodist Council and the Lutheran World Federation—in which Borgen was a member—had its third meeting (in Oslo in October 1981), Borgen was so disappointed over the fact that the Church of Norway was to continue as a state church that he voiced his opinion in a newspaper, arguing that this situation would have "consequences for the relationship between Methodists and Lutherans in Norway."[35]

In the coming years, Borgen did not engage in extensive *public* discussions concerning the majority church's relation to the state. However, that did not indicate that he had changed his opinions. As we shall see in the next chapter, the mere existence of the Church of Norway as a majority church, enjoying extensive prerogatives from the state, was a condition he returned to in his ecumenical thinking and discussions.

35. See *Vårt Land,* October 20, 1981, 6.

12

Peder Borgen, a Struggling Ecumenist from a Minority Church

ALREADY AS A YOUNG student Borgen was taken by the idea of ecumenism, but in the Trondheim era a new emphasis of depth was added. He became more directly involved in international ecumenical work; most important was the fact that he was selected to be a member of the International Lutheran-Methodist Dialogue Commission, which in 1979–84 was to look at the doctrinal relationships between Lutheran and Methodist teachings, and the possibilities of establishing closer relationships between the two denominations. Then there also was a national committee a few years later in Norway, composed of members from the Church of Norway and the Methodist Church in Norway. While Borgen was not a member of that last-mentioned group, he was very engaged when the committee's proposals were discussed. Both of these two ecumenical commissions are dealt with in this chapter. But first, a sketch of his ecclesiology and its ramifications for his ecumenism.

"THOUGHTS ON CHRISTIAN UNITY IN THE NEW TESTAMENT"

In the year after Borgen began working in Trondheim, he gave a major lecture in the old aula at the University of Oslo as part of the ecumenical week of prayer for Christian unity. His topic was: "Thoughts on Christian Unity in the New Testament."[1]

Borgen takes his point of departure in the much-discussed question of "whether the New Testament reflects such a degree of antagonism among the Christians of the first century after Christ that we must talk about completely incompatible interpretations of Christianity and correspondingly opposed groups."[2] The differences in several details may seem significant between the different scripture groups in the NT; the epistles of Paul, the Johannine literature, the epistles of Peter, and the Epistle of James, to name the most relevant, have different accents on many common themes, and it is not always possible to harmonize them. Moreover, the question can be raised whether these differences are so significant that one cannot find any uniform ideas in the NT. Borgen, however, accepts the view that "the New Testament is held together by a basic unity . . . ,"[3] and he tries to clarify what this unity consists of, especially concerning what can be called "Christian unity." How is this unity described in the NT?

The unity is a given, but . . .

The unity of Israel, according to Borgen, was related to the belief that the one God was manifest in the one temple in Jerusalem and the one law, the Law of Moses. In the NT, we see that it is the Christian belief that unity was secured by the fact that the one God revealed himself in his Son, Jesus Christ, in the eschatological age, which was founded on his work of redemption:

> The New Testament can be read to a great extent as a revision and rejection of the Jewish idea of unity. This settlement led to a division in Israel and thus to a schism between the Christians on the one hand and the Jews of the temple and synagogue on the other hand. This is the only real schism we find in the New Testament. The other conflicts and dissimilarities described in the New Testament occur essentially within the framework of a manifest unity, apart from a few cases of incipient schism.[4]

---

1. First published in Norwegian in 1974; see Borgen, "Tanker i Det nye testamente," 1–19. Published in English in 1984 as "Thoughts on Christian Unity," 131–53.
2. Borgen, "Thoughts on Christian Unity," 132.
3. Borgen, "Thoughts on Christian Unity," 132.
4. Borgen, "Thoughts on Christian Unity," 135.

The various writings reflect different tensions among the early Christians. The Christians took over many thoughts about Israel as God's people but interpreted these in light of the belief in Jesus as the end-time Messiah. The Christians, therefore, understood themselves as the end-time people of God, the holy ones, the chosen . . . .[5]

We see that this struggle escalated when what we call early Christianity broke out of the Jewish framework and addressed non-Jewish peoples. Then it became essential to clarify the basis for such a new unity between Jewish Christians and those from the other peoples. We have clear examples of this discussion in, e.g., Galatians and Ephesians, and several other writings, including the Gospel of John. Nevertheless, Borgen believes that the church is not understood here as the new Israel in contrast to the old. No, the idea is that "the Christian Gentiles are united with the believing Jews who formed the true Israel."[6]

Borgen also deals with the Corinthian letters. Here, it was not so much the discussion with Judaism that was at the center but various issues within the congregations. There were different attitudes to and discussions about ethical and more dogmatic issues triggered and challenged by the Greco-Roman culture: "Paul also clarifies that unity in Christ does not mean standardized thinking or uniformity."[7] His use of the idea of the body in 1 Corinthians 12 demonstrates this. In summarizing, Borgen states:

> Thus, the New Testament does not seem to give us one single structure or system as the norm. However, there are certain criteria for the ideas the structures are to express, and which consequently draw up certain limits for them . . . . Since Christ and salvation include both Jews and non-Jews, the structure of God's people with its fellowship at meals must make this relationship clear . . . . The second criterion is that the structure is characterized by order, for God is not the God of disorder, but of peace (1 Cor. 14:32). The third criterion is that the differences and unique characteristics of the various services must be present, thus precluding uniformity. The fourth criterion is that structures and services may be varied in different situations because "in each of us the Spirit is manifested in one particular way, for some useful purpose" (1 Cor. 12:7). The fourth [TS: Sic] criterion is that the congregation is but a local manifestation of the people of God (cf. 1 Cor. 12:28ff.)[8]

5. Borgen, "Thoughts on Christian Unity," 138.
6. Borgen, "Thoughts on Christian Unity," 149.
7. Borgen, "Thoughts on Christian Unity," 147.
8. Borgen, "Thoughts on Christian Unity," 148. This last point is not mentioned in

I have quoted extensively from this article here because it provides relevant background to some of the questions and issues raised in the narrative to follow. Borgen's participation in ecumenical contexts is based on his Methodist understanding of what the church as a church really is. And the fact that he finds much of the ideals of Methodism in the New Testament too shines through in several of his other writings. However, at the same time, he is aware that the traditions represented by the different churches do not represent obstacles to Christian ecumenical endeavors.

Borgen's long antennas for discrimination

Borgen had an extensive sensitivity to what he considered attitudes and acts of discrimination. His background in a church that was a small minority church in the Norwegian context gave him long feelers or antennas for what could be perceived as discrimination from the state and/or the majority church. We have seen some examples of this in the previous chapter about how he was engaged by the Norwegian debate about the relations between state and church, and about the state's attitude towards the majority church and the other churches in Norway.

We will also see his skepticism in the rest of this chapter, which firstly is about Borgen's participation in the Joint Commission between World Methodist Council and the Lutheran World Federation, and then secondly about his attitudes to national and local ecumenical relations and views in the Church of Norway and the Methodist Church in Norway. His vigilance toward discrimination plays a significant role here as well.

However, before presenting the events and activities concerning the international Joint Commission, and the later national ecumenical commission, it might be relevant to get a clearer picture of how he thought about some ecumenical issues in the early 1980s. It might function as a window to Borgen's emphases and priorities in the Norwegian ecumenical context.

One part of this picture is a minor but very focused contribution he presented at a seminar in 1982. He was asked to participate in an ecumenical seminar in Trondheim on July 8–10. The context was a discussion of the topic, "Domestic Ecumenism—from a Catholic, Methodist and Baptist Point of View." Borgen delivered the mini-lecture on "from a Methodist Point of View." In many ways, this input sums up much of what he had been concerned with both in the state church debate and in ecumenical dialogues so far, and demonstrates how closely related these two themes were. At the

---

the published Norwegian version of this lecture.

same time, it also refers to some of his frustrating local and less positive ecumenical experiences.[9]

Borgen's mini-lecture lasted for only approximately twenty minutes, but he nevertheless managed to describe his positions quite clearly. After a brief sketch of the legislative changes that had taken place since 1845, he quickly turned to the then-current situation. Many problems and discriminatory conditions, he believed, still existed, and some new discriminatory features had emerged. He first pointed out that, on the one hand, it was challenging to get the Christian (mission) organizations within the state church to participate in ecumenical activities, while, on the other hand, there were several free churches that were not willing to have fellowship with the Catholics.

He was also disappointed with some attitudes within the majority church: "I hear more often caricatured criticism of the free churches in State Church circles than I hear criticism of the Church of Norway in free church circles," he said. He was here thinking about, i.a., that he in state church circles sometimes heard caricatured descriptions of the free churches as some who wanted to have "pure" congregations and that this issue was used as a negative legitimation for the national majority church. "This caricature is simply a lie." He had a concrete and recent example from Trondheim in reactions from state church representatives to a recent case where a pastor from the majority church had joined and become a pastor in the Evangelical Lutheran Free Church.

The last issue he pointed out was what he characterized as "discriminating mechanisms in the administration of the government." In municipal contexts, there was still talk of "refund of dissenter taxes" as characterizations of state and municipal pecuniary support. Furthermore, "in anniversaries and public celebrations, the state's public religion often had a monopoly on worship services." This practice is discriminatory, he said. He found the same problem when it came to using the public registers concerning the population. We recognize several of these arguments from his comments on the 1980 report to the Parliament (*Stortingsmelding*) regarding the relationship between state and church.

Finally, he came up with some concrete advice: clean up the lack of understanding, caricatures, and delusions; remove discriminatory schemes; clear up provincial attitudes; start practically by participating in local contexts such as prayer weeks, ecumenical pastoral gatherings, and theological dialogues; and practice empathic interpretations of history.

---

9. I am here able to refer to his own manuscript (in Norwegian), now kept in the Borgen archives in the National Library. All the quotations in the text are taken from this manuscript.

He expressed his own attitude thus: "On the basis of Scripture, and confident in my tradition, I am open to meeting others."

ENGAGEMENT IN INTERNATIONAL ECUMENISM (1979–84)

There should be no doubt that the establishment of the World Council of Churches in 1948 provided a basis for and inspiration for increased ecumenical contact between several different denominations in the following years. These activities gradually led to increased interest in doctrinal conversations between the churches, and the commitment grew throughout the 1960s and in the succeeding decades. When two such parties talk, it is called "bilateral talks"; when more than two are involved, it is called "multilateral." The bilateral talks received a notable boost and aimed at overcoming doctrinal disagreements that seemed divisive between two denominations. The Norwegian Lutheran professor Lars Østnor says that the upsurge in interest in such talks was related to their uniqueness and goals: they were two-way talks; they were doctrinal talks that concentrated on theological issues the churches disagreed on; and the talks were official in the sense that official bodies on both sides arranged them.[10]

The International Lutheran-Methodist Dialogue Commission

The dialogue commission in question was arranged by the World Methodist Council and the Lutheran World Federation. It was thus not a Norwegian initiative intended only for Norwegian churches, but was established from the top levels of these two international organizations. After some planning was carried out in 1977, an international discussion group of eight members from each of the two church families was established, and five joint conferences were held from 1979 to 1984. These eventually ended up in a joint closing document with a presentation of what they had come up with in these meetings and a recommendation to the two church families. This closing report was published as *The Church: Community of Grace*.

As participants from Norway, Peder Borgen was appointed by the Methodist World Council as a Methodist representative, and senior lecturer—later professor (at Menighetsfakultetet)—Lars Østnor was appointed by the Lutheran World Federation as one of the Lutheran participants. In 1990 Østnor published an extensive presentation of the work in the commission

10. Østnor, *Dialogens vei*, 10.

during these years.[11] However, it will lead us beyond our present context in this volume to dig deep into the topics discussed and the conclusions reached in and by the commission.

Peder Borgen could not attend the critical planning meeting in Epworth by the Sea (USA) in the beginning of December 1977, but Østnor was present. Among the topics proposed to be set on the agenda were the authority of the Bible, baptism, repentance, the nature of the church, sanctification, the priestly office, the general priesthood, and social, ethical issues. The possibility of linking the dialogue to the understanding of God's grace, or the work of the Spirit in the church, was also mentioned. Furthermore, it was decided to hold five talks in various locations worldwide. The actual purpose of the dialogue was finally outlined as follows:

A) To contribute to mutual understanding and respect between Methodists and Lutherans for both their similarities and their differences.

B) To help demonstrate that Lutheranism and Methodism are parts of one community in Christ and seek to stand together in their witness and service in the world.

C) To strengthen possibilities for practicing fellowship in Word and sacrament between Lutheranism and Methodism.

D) To provide theological support for church cooperation and unity according to local needs and opportunities.[12]

---

11. See Østnor, *Dialogens vei* (The Way of Dialogue). This book is, in many respects, his personal "report" and description, and was criticized as such by Borgen, but it is still a valuable presentation of how Østnor experienced these conversations.

There is no doubt that Østnor speaks as a Lutheran in this book, and something else should probably not be expected either. Criticism can therefore be levelled against using the book as a guide to the commission's work, since it only represents one party, and Borgen raised such a criticism. Borgen expressed that he thought Østnor should have consulted with a theologian from a Methodist point of view during the preparation of the book, and that the book as such should be considered Østnor's monologue about the work in the commission. Borgen also perceived the book as a defense for the dissent, which we will see later—Østnor had managed to get included in the final commission report. Østnor responded by saying that he wanted to "convey his own experiences of such an ecumenical dialogue," but that it was still not to be understood as a defense for his own views. This debate between Borgen and Østnor was conducted in 1991, in the newspaper *Vårt Land*. See Borgen, "Fra internasjonal dialog til norsk monolog," *Vårt Land* May 21, 1991, 8; Lars Østnor, "Misvisende om dialog," *Vårt Land*, June 4, 1991; Borgen, "Reel dialog i Norge?," *Vårt Land*, June 17, 1991. This small dispute in *Vårt Land* is probably somewhat colored by the fate the commission's report had received in the years between 1984 and 1991, and by the relationship between these two denominations in Norway, and not at least Borgen's disappointment with the ecumenical situation as it was in Norway in the early 1990s.

12. *The Church: Community of Grace*, 5. Østnor, *Dialogens vei*, 16. Furthermore,

Theological diversity in the commission

The Methodist delegation consisted of one participant each from Norway, Austria, the DDR (only in 1979), and Brazil, respectively, and two participants from England and three from the United States. The Lutheran delegation consisted of one each from the DDR, Liberia, West Germany, Southern India, Argentina, and Norway, respectively, and two from the United States. Hence, the commission consisted of eight Methodists and eight Lutherans from various nations, representing diverse cultural and theological traditions.

Some of the commission's meetings were marked by a factor that may seem surprising to some. It turned out that there was a somewhat remarkable theological diversity within each of the two delegations. Sometimes it seemed that the diversity *within* the two groups was even as great as between them. Lars Østnor comments thus on this issue in his book: "On the one hand, this relationship contributed to a greater understanding within the Commission of the significance of our churches' current social and cultural context and the various historical conditions under which they have emerged. However, on the other hand, the identification of our confessional identity was made more difficult."[13] Borgen believed that the diversity was greater among the Lutheran participants than among the Methodists, but both realized that the disagreements within the Methodist and Lutheran camps contributed to complicating the talks.

The actual work in the commission's meetings took place by delivering two lectures (or "papers")—one from the Methodists and one from the Lutheran group—on each of the topics to be discussed. In these sessions, they tried to clarify what was typical of the Methodist and Lutheran positions, common points, and the theological content of their disagreements. Then a report was written, and gradually a draft proposal was prepared on the subject destined to be included in the final report. The final document was primarily created in 1984 and partly under time pressure at the last and final meeting. The target group for the report was the two organizations responsible for the commission, and secondly faculties of theology and seminars, theologians and pastors, and church members in general.

---

under the theme "The Church: Community of Grace," five topics were to be explored: Biblical Authority and the Authenticity of the Church; The Gospel of Grace, The Holy Spirit in the Church, The Communion of the Saints, The Body of Christ, The Sacraments of the Gospel, and The Mission of the Church in Today's World.

13. Østnor, *Dialogens vei*, 32.

A Lutheran-Methodist dialogue group in Norway

During the preparatory meeting in 1977 and in the commission's first meeting two years later, it was aired that it was both relevant and vital if regional, national discussion groups could be established to run in parallel with the central commission's meetings and also function as support groups for the individual participants in the main commission.

The direct initiative to establish a Norwegian Lutheran-Methodist dialogue or discussion group came from Lars Østnor. In a letter to Borgen, he asked how Borgen would consider the idea of "a bilateral discussion group in this country that could work in parallel with the international dialogue and at the same time function as a backing group for us in our work in the international commission."[14] The reaction from Borgen was positive, but he emphasized that it had to be an unofficial resource group.

The group was composed of twelve participants, divided into a Methodist and a Lutheran subgroup, and had its first joint meeting on January 11, 1979, just before the commission's first meeting in Dresden. Several meetings were then held in this Norwegian group. Minutes were written from the meetings, but their unofficial character was emphasized several times, and it was also underscored that the group's function was primarily to be a backing group for Østnor and Borgen.

Although this group had such an unofficial character, it appears in the minutes that it represented a great value not only for the two delegates, Borgen and Østnor, but also for the other participants. At the same time, there was also a Lutheran-Catholic discussion group at work. Hence, one may ask whether these groups did not represent the *very first real bilateral ecumenical discussion groups* in the Norwegian church landscape.[15] In this way, they have also had value beyond being backing groups for the participants in the larger dialogue commissions.

What did the Lutheran-Methodist Dialogue Commission come up with?

The results of the discussions in the Methodist-Lutheran joint commission were published as the final report, which was named *The Church:*

---

14. Letter from Lars Østnor to Peder Borgen, dated October 24, 1978.
15. In a private conversation in 2017, Lars Østnor confirmed this suggestion of mine.

Community of Grace.¹⁶ The report is made up of ninety-four points.¹⁷ The first seven provide a retrospective summary of the work; the following seven provide background and experiences. Then comes the presentation of what they had come up with regarding the various theological topics discussed. It describes what they agree on, what they still disagree on, and it also presents to some extent what they think are the historical, cultural, and theological reasons for their continuing disagreement. Points 82–88 give "Suggestions for the Future," and points 89–94 give "Recommendations." Finally, a "Dissent" from Lars Østnor is given.

One of the purposes of the dialogue was "to assist Methodist and Lutheran churches to move towards a greater fellowship in faith, witness and service. Such fellowship finds visible expression in full sacramental communion" (point 89). It is further stated that the dialogue has brought the participants considerably closer to this goal "because we were able to discover a great amount of agreement and convergence between us" (point 90). Based on this, the following recommendations are given in point 91.1, which is quoted in full here:

> 91.1 We recommend that our churches take steps to declare and establish full fellowship of Word and sacrament; we recommend that as a first and important step our churches officially provide for pulpit exchanges and mutual hospitality at the table of the Lord. We rejoice that full fellowship of Word and sacrament is currently practiced in some of our churches.

This recommendation thus states that one recommends "that our churches take steps to declare and establish full fellowship of Word and sacrament." This is the overall recommendation. But the next statements take into account that there may still be some way to go and that several steps are needed before one has arrived at this goal. Therefore, it is said that "we recommend that as a first and important step our churches officially provide for pulpit exchanges and mutual hospitality at the table of the Lord." The latter means that one can receive the Lord's Communion in each other's churches. However, at the same time, it is also assumed that the churches take steps to move forward and declare and establish full fellowship. Moreover, the

---

16. *The Church: Community of Grace*, final report of the joint commission between the Lutheran World Federation and World Methodist Council, 1979–1984. 31 pages. Norwegian translation in Østnor, *Dialogens vei*, 100–134.

17. In our context, I cannot deal further with all the individual theological points of view that are presented, since my focus is not so much the Lutheran-Methodist Dialogue Commission as such, but *the role it played in Borgen's life* and further ecumenical work. Hence, I will here focus primarily on a few points from the Recommendations, important to Borgen, and the Dissent from Lars Østnor.

last sentence supports this: "We rejoice that full fellowship of Word and sacrament is currently practiced in some of our churches." Overall, mutual recognition of each other's teaching and administration of the sacraments is recognized on a broad basis, but one is also open to a slightly slower progression.

The personal statement by Lars Østnor

However, there was one member who dissented: the Norwegian Lutheran Lars Østnor, who thought that this main recommendation was too far-reaching:

> As a member of the Lutheran-Methodist Joint Commission I fully agree that we to a great extent have reached agreement on the theological issues which have been discussed. There is probably a wide consensus between us also with regard to some doctrinal subjects that have not been on our agenda (such as the doctrine of God, eschatology, etc.). In some of the central issues which have been discussed there is a convergence of viewpoints, but not a full consensus, as this report itself clearly indicates (for example sanctification, baptism and the eucharist. Other important subjects have not been sufficiently clarified by us and are therefore recommended for further discussion (for instance the doctrines of man, sin and grace). These topics are all of great importance for the subjects of this dialogue. The basis for church unity in the form of full pulpit and altar fellowship is according to a Lutheran understanding agreement 'concerning the teaching of the Gospel and the administration of the sacraments' (The Augsburg Confession, Article VII). There is in my opinion not yet established a sufficient theological basis between Methodist and Lutheran churches for taking such a concluding step. However, I support the recommendation of providing for pulpit exchanges and mutual hospitality at the table of the Lord, on the basis of what our churches already have in common. Further theological dialogue needs to go on in the hope that a statement of agreement will be achieved, which will make full pulpit and altar fellowship possible.[18]

Østnor thus disagrees with (he dissents from) the primary recommendation from the commission but agrees with the secondary and accepts

---

18. His dissent is characterized as a "personal statement" (in parenthesis) in the report (cf. *The Church: Community of Grace*, 28).

"pulpit exchange and mutual hospitality at the Lord's table." So far, but no longer at the present time.

It is perhaps a little remarkable that Østnor was not followed in this dissent by any of the other Lutheran members. But he was left all alone. In the dissent itself, Østnor explained theologically why he came to this conclusion, but he also gives a somewhat further theological and practical justification in his book.[19] Here he explains that three factors, in particular, made him promote his dissent. First, he felt strongly that they were still in the process of a theological clarification but that they had not reached the necessary consensus. Secondly, he had the impression that for a while, they were conducting an identification work for an idea that many already supported, namely, full fellowship of Word and sacraments. And third, he felt manipulated. Or, as he puts it: There was "a manipulation by the staff of the Lutheran World Federation. An improper attempt was made to obtain that the Commission drew far-reaching conclusions based on its work."[20] Østnor was particularly dissatisfied with Secretary-General C. H. Maus's intervention in the final process.[21] The World Council of Churches was to have a General Assembly later that year, and Maus put much effort into getting the commission's recommendation ready for this meeting. Hence, Østnor dissented.

Peder Borgen, on his side, was very dissatisfied and disappointed with this dissent. He also repeatedly pointed out that Østnor's dissent was not the dissent of the Church of Norway but his personal statement. However, it turned out later that even though it originally was not a statement by the Church of Norway, it would later become the response of that church.

Point 34 on the minority-majority relationship

Considering the state-church relationship in Norway at this time, it is interesting, but perhaps also a little weird to some, that the final report included a section that could be used directly into the *political* situation of the Norwegian churches and the current debate concerning the relationship between state and church. The commission stated, namely, in paragraph 34 of the report, that

> Methodist and Lutheran members of the commission affirm that Methodist or Lutheran churches, which are minorities in

---

19. Østnor, *Dialogens vei*, 163–64.
20. Østnor, *Dialogens vei*, 163.
21. Østnor, *Dialogens vei*, 98–99.

a situation where the other church is in a majority or privileged position, are to be recognized as fully legitimate churches and should enjoy equal rights and possibilities. We encourage a relationship to secular rule in which the church is independent, and all denominations enjoy parity before the state.[22]

One of the remarkable aspects of this statement is that it does not concern only the mutual relations of the two church families, but its second part is about the churches' relations to a third entity, namely the state. The entire commission stood behind the statement, and it aimed primarily not only at the Norwegian church landscape; the commission was internationally composed and had an international focus. But it was particularly relevant in a state-church situation like that in Norway. It is further probable that Borgen himself was active in getting this statement included in the final report, and Østnor confirms this assumption,[23] but it is also important to point out that the entire commission supported it. It was no statement of dissent. In Borgen's opinion, the statement was especially relevant for the lives of the Norwegian churches and put into words what he had worked for in many years. He argued that the relationship between the Church of Norway and the other denominations—as I have outlined it above—was particularly relevant. In an interview in *Vårt Land* in 1979 after the first ordinary meeting of the Lutheran-Methodist Dialogue Commission (in Dresden), Borgen stated that "I do hope that these conversations can have as a consequence that Methodists and Lutherans will be considered equal partners in Norway and that there can be greater understanding and trust."[24] Furthermore, in a comment on Østnor's book in 1991, he emphasized that "in the Norwegian situation," the unanimous statement from the commission's point 34 ought to be quoted.[25]

This point 34 was thus no minor issue for Borgen. But how important a role it played in his assessments was made even more apparent in his responses to the later Lutheran-Methodist Dialogue Commission in Norway and the conclusion it reached in the mid-1990s. But more on that later.

---

22. *The Church: Community of Grace*, 14.

23. Østnor, *Dialogens vei*, 162. Østnor points out here that there were also others who tried to express personal concerns, and who gained the support of the entire commission. He mentions §§ 28–29 (from the Methodist P. Stephens, England), § 34 (from the Methodist P. Borgen), and § 56 (from the Lutheran B.V. Subbamma, India).

24. Kjøllesdal, "Håper på likeverdighet i det norske kristenliv," *Vårt Land*, February 7, 1979, 13.

25. See Borgen, "Fra internasjonal dialog til norsk monolog," *Vårt Land*, May 21, 1991, 8.

The reception of the commission's recommendations

Under the leadership of Secretary-General C. H. Maus, the report was considered at the General Assembly of the Lutheran World Federation in Budapest in the summer of 1984, and hope was expressed that the final result would be in accordance with the commission's recommendations.

The reception in the Methodist Church in Norway

In an interview with *Aftenposten* in 1984, Peder Borgen said that "he thinks the final document is both honest and sober, and that the agreement is large enough to share the sacrament of communion at the Lord's table." However, the further reception was to be given by the respective church bodies within the two church families.

Borgen participated as a delegate in the meeting of the World Methodist Council in Nairobi, Kenya, in 1986. Here it was his task to present the report from the Lutheran-Methodist Dialogue Commission. In English Methodist jargon, the result was rendered as follows: "Dr. Borgen then moved that the report be received, that the recommendations be brought to the various church bodies and that the booklet be used for further study and action in the various churches . . . The Council voted to receive."[26]

The relevant Norwegian Methodist bodies dealt with the report of the commission in 1985–86. In 1986, the executive board presented the following proposal for the Annual Conference, which was then accepted:

> The United Methodist Church in Norway acknowledges the recommendations presented in the dialogue between Lutherans and Methodists as contained in the document The Church—Community of Grace, which imply:
>
> - increased exchange of ministers between our churches
> - an extended and mutual communion fellowship
> - a stronger involvement so that all churches shall be independent of and equal in parity before the state.[27]

Noticeable here is the fact that point 34 mentioned above is taken into the last statement of the decision reached by the Annual Conference. When interviewed in 1986, Borgen emphasized that "the Methodist Church

---

26. Østnor, *Dialogens vei*, 135–36.

27. Quoted from the translation given in the report "Fellowship of Grace: Report from the Conversations between Church of Norway and the United Methodist Church in Norway. No page numbering.

in Norway has by its decision wanted to contribute to the church climate in Norway being even better. We do not want a church merger, but we do want a mutual recognition of equal churches."[28] In another interview in *Aftenposten*, in the morning edition the next day, he said (commenting on the Joint Methodist-Lutheran Commission) that "We want our Lutheran friends to receive an outstretched hand." He further pointed out that in many places in Norway, there was a good relationship between the Methodist Church and other churches, and that one wanted this to also have an impact everywhere in the country. Moreover, he continued: "We encourage a relationship with the secular government where the (state) church and all denominations have equality in relation to the law." *Aftenposten* commented on the latter statement that "In this context, the international Joint Commission goes directly into the Norwegian state-church debate."[29] That comment was very pertinent.

This section (point 34) played a significant role in Peder Borgen's views and attitudes to practical Norwegian church policy both within the Church of Norway and in relation to the state as such. It represented part of his fight against discrimination. However, it is doubtful whether this section played any role in the Church of Norway's work on the recommendations from the joint commission. At least it remained silent about this point in its official statements.

The reception in the Church of Norway

In their evaluation report, the bishops of the majority church called for closer cooperation with the Methodist Church, including the exchange of preachers and closer cooperation at the local levels. Nevertheless, the bishops did not advocate complete pulpit exchanges and mutual fellowship of Word and sacrament because they felt there was insufficient agreement on some doctrinal issues. Hence, the bishops thus agreed with the dissent that Østnor had put forward in the International Lutheran-Methodist Dialogue Commission report.[30]

The Church of Norway's General Synod, a body established as late as 1984, joined the bishops' conclusions. The synod expressed a positive attitude to the document but also had some critical comments. Among other things, they thought that the commission placed too much emphasis on

---

28. (Anonymous), "Samarbeids-utspill fra Metodistkirken," *Vårt Land*, July 5, 1986, 8.

29. All quotes here are from "Oppfordring fra Metodistkirken: Alle kirkesamfunn bør stå likt overfor Staten," *Aftenposten*, morning edition, July 7, 1986, 16.

30. See Østnor, *Dialogens vei*, 140–46.

bringing out the similarities between the two denominations and that this had resulted in some downplaying of real differences in fundamental doctrinal points of view. As an overall assessment, they believed that the time had not yet come for a full fellowship of Word and sacraments, and thus no basis for taking organizational steps to implement such a fellowship. They also referred to Østnor's dissent, thus joining his personal statement.

The Methodist Church's Annual Conference called for greater fellowship here and now; the Church of Norway's General Synod responded by saying that it could happen, in its time but not yet.

Hence, looking back on this year and the receptions of the two churches, one might say that the Church of Norway parked the ecumenical train on a sidetrack for several years to come, and no one knew if or when it would start running again.

DOMESTIC ECUMENISM IN THE 1990S: "FELLOWSHIP OF GRACE"

The 1990s were busy years for Peder Borgen. In 1993, at the age of sixty-five, he resigned as an ordinary professor. However, he received a senior scholarship and became a senior researcher for 1993–97. In 1994–95, he was concerned with rescuing the Methodist congregation in Hammerfest from closure. Furthermore, in addition to pursuing his love for professional New Testament studies, he also became involved in a project concerning the First Sami National Assembly held in the Methodist church in Trondheim in 1917, which resulted in a book in 1997, written by Borgen, about this event. Moreover, he was still strongly involved in the Royal Norwegian Society of Sciences and Letters in Trondheim.

Within the Church of Norway, there was an increasingly strong ecumenical commitment. In 1982, a crucial ecumenical text from the World Council of Churches (WCC), often called the Lima Document, was published.[31]

Another ecumenical element that became important for the ecumenical debate within the Methodist Church in Norway was similar debates conducted in several other countries between Methodists and Lutherans, among others, in the USA, Germany, and Sweden. Finally, we might mention the Church of Norway's commitment regarding the so-called Porvoo

---

31. The document was not the result of a single commission, but of a lengthy work process, and consisted of three declarations, all of which were the result of a fifty-year study process under the auspices of the Faith and Order Commission.

Agreement, an agreement that had been worked on over an extended period of time.[32]

Hence, when requests for new dialogues gradually arose in Norway between the Church of Norway and the Methodist Church, it was on a slightly different background than in 1986. The ecumenical climate within the Church of Norway had undergone significant changes and provided greater openness to bi- and multilateral talks and various cooperation agreements. But since all this happened within the Church of Norway, Peder Borgen was on the sidetrack. Furthermore, when the ecumenical dialogue train started up again in 1991, and a Norwegian Lutheran-Methodist Dialogue Commission was established, he was not engaged as a member of any committee. He remained on the sidetrack as a spectator while the train got a new and younger crew. Admittedly, he came back more vigorous during the evaluation and reception period, and then he argued that what the new report (re-)presented did not provide a sufficient basis for expanded fellowship with the Church of Norway. That response was a surprise to many.

Ecumenical dialogue (1991–96)

In the spring of 1991, the Administrative Board of the United Methodist Church in Norway[33] and the Church of Norway Council on Ecumenical and International Relations appointed a Methodist-Lutheran bilateral discussion group.[34] The initiative was based in the Church of Norway. As early as December 1987, the Norwegian Theological Committee, under the Church of Norway Council on Ecumenical and International Relations, submitted a proposal to establish an official Norwegian Lutheran-Methodist discussion

---

32. In September 1996, the leaders of nine churches signed a cooperation agreement in Nidaros Cathedral: the Lutheran churches in the Nordic and Baltic countries and the Anglican churches in England, Scotland, Ireland, and Wales entered into an agreement on church fellowship. But the work on the agreement had taken place for several years. For an overview, see "Anglikansk-luthersk kirkefellesskap «Porvoo-avtalen»," at https://kirken.no/nb-NO/om-kirken/slik-styres-kirken/mellomkirkelig-rad/okumenikk-og-kirkesamarbeid/internasjonale-okumeniske-organisasjoner/porvoo-avtalen/. The Porvoo Agreement was approved by the Church of Norway's General Synod in 1994.

33. The report, in its English translation, labels the Methodist Church consistently as "The *United* Methodist Church in Norway." The Norwegian version does not contain the equivalent term.

34. The following persons were selected as members from the Methodist Church: Lars-Erik Nordby, Juel Norby, Øystein Brinch, and Helle Maria Lund, secretary. From the Church of Norway: Geir Hellemo, Steinar Moe (1991–92), Anne Grete Spæren Rørvik, and Halvor Nordhaug (secretary until June 1991), then Olav Fykse Tveit, from December 1991.

group. But the case remained dormant for a long time, awaiting a response from the Methodist Church. However, in 1991 the work started. The group's mandate was established in its first meeting: "The discussion group will determine to what extent there prevails consensus between the churches, and what practical consequences can be deduced from that background."[35]

The group did not start from scratch. It considered its work as one that built on and continued other doctrinal conversations, particularly the International Methodist-Lutheran Dialogue Commission from 1979–84, presented above.[36] Therefore, the new committee would primarily have a closer look at the theological issues that in the previous agreement, and in the debates after that had been considered unclear or inadequately discussed. Thus, one ended up with a particular discussion of the understanding of baptism and Communion in the two denominations and the view of the ecclesiastical ministry. The Porvoo Agreement (1992) gradually became known, even though it was not signed by any church in Norway until 1994, and the committee tried to get as close to it as possible. In addition, the Methodists in the group could build on the preparatory work for a Methodist study of the baptismal question, a study that ended up in a document called "By Spirit and Water."[37] Hence, the discussions in the group concentrated on topics considered decisive for mutual recognition and expanded cooperation.

The final report

The final report (1994) was divided into thirty-nine points, the last of which contained the recommendations. Thematically, it comprised a theological discussion of three aspects: baptism, the holy Communion, and ministry. Not a word about the different church orders; not a word about the relationship between the one church as a free church and the other as a state church that is, about their different relations to the state and vice versa. Thus, there is nothing like what was included in the Lutheran-Methodist Dialogue Commission report that "We encourage a relationship to secular rule in which the church is independent, and all denominations enjoy parity before the state,"[38] an item that the Methodist Church included in its reception in 1985.

The final recommendations of the dialogue group were unequivocal, suggesting an extended church fellowship that was clearer and more

---

35. "Fellowship of Grace," 1.
36. See points 4–6 in the report from 1994; cf. Nordby, *Nådens Fellesskap*, 131.
37. Lars-Erik Nordby, in an email to me, dated February 4, 2019.
38. Point 34; cf. above.

binding than the relations that already existed between the two churches. A primary basis for their understanding of church unity, and thus for their recommendations, was that "Visible church unity is not the same as complete conformity. Neither does our given unity in Christ stand in principle opposition to diversity but is to be found in diversity. Since this diversity is in accordance with the many gifts of the Holy Spirit to the Church, it is of fundamental ecclesial importance. This relationship between unity and diversity is attested to already in the New Testament" (point 38).

The group recommended that the two churches

1. recognize each other's churches as belonging to the one holy, catholic and apostolic Church of Jesus Christ, and as possessing the mission which belong to the whole people of God;
2. acknowledge that both of our churches are united in confessing the apostolic faith, as it is given to us in the Holy Scripture and expressed in the early church creeds;
3. recognize each others' baptism and administration of the sacrament of communion;
4. recognize each others' ordained ministry;
5. acknowledge that we are still two different churches, each with its own tradition, documents of doctrine and church organization, established according to the respective church's own regulations.

These recommendations, they hoped, should lead to an expanded church fellowship, which was expressed in the fact that they could worship and celebrate Communion together where those bearing the office of ordained ministry from both churches could participate together; that they welcomed members from each other's churches in line with their own members; that they stood together on the mission of the church in prayer and work, and therefore sought cooperation where it was natural; that they opened up for the exchange of each other's priests and others consecrated to church service; and that they continued with regular conversations and discussion of measures that could be implemented to make their community more visible. The report was signed during Lent in 1994 and then handed over to the two churches' respective bodies for further consideration.

The reception of the report "Fellowship of Grace"

The Methodist Church expressed that it wanted the Church of Norway to make its decisions first. It was also the Church of Norway that had taken the initiative and invited to a new dialogue with the Methodist Church. The Methodists' Annual Conference in 1994 requested that work be started on a consultation round so that the agreement could be considered at the Annual Conference the following year. However, the latter was postponed for one more year, probably not at least because the Church of Norway was not to consider the agreement until November 1995. Hence, the Methodists did not make their decisions concerning the report until the Annual Conference in 1996. In the two years between, however, there was an intense discussion regarding the report, and now Peder Borgen also joined the debate.

The reception in the Church of Norway

After the dialogue report had been dealt with in the relevant bodies within the Church of Norway, the final and positive decision of reception was made at the Church of Norway's General Synod in Bergen, November 12-17, 1995. There was no major debate at the General Synod on the agreement; the discussions were primarily carried out in the preparatory bodies. Their main decision was: "The General Synod approves the agreement between the Methodist Church in Norway and the Church of Norway, as presented in the document *Fellowship of Grace*, point 39," in which the five first subpoints represent the central points of recognition.[39]

This was the first time ever that the Church of Norway agreed to enter into a binding cooperation agreement with another denomination in Norway. It is to be noted here that the decision reached by the Church of Norway was quite in line with the recommendations set forth by the commission's dialogue report. And as in the final text of that report, church order issues or state-church issues are hardly mentioned. Contrary to what was the case in 1986, these issues were also not mentioned in the decision made by the Methodist Church in 1996.

The reception in the Methodist Church (and by Borgen)

The most intense Methodist debate on this dialogue report occurred in the autumn of 1995 and the first half of 1996. Not least, there was an intense debate in the columns of the Methodists' magazine *Kristelig Tidende* in the winter and spring of 1996 leading up to the Annual Conference. The magazine's editor opened the columns for postings, and there is hardly any other

---

39. Nordby, "Nådens Fellesskap," 135.

issue in the history of that magazine that has been so intensely debated and with such a high temperature on both sides.

But how did Peder Borgen react to the dialogue report and its proposal to approve an agreement with the Church of Norway?

He disagreed with both its arguments and its conclusions.

Borgen's position was first made known publicly by a posting in *Kristelig Tidende* in the summer of 1995: there he clearly stated that he was opposed to the Methodist Church approving the present report from the dialogue group.[40] He who had all the way argued for the agreement he participated in working out in 1979-1984 in the International Lutheran-Methodist Dialogue Commission had now turned around and vigorously opposed the new report and its proposals. But why did he change his opinion? What were his arguments for this change?

Why did Borgen change his mind?

In the previous round of discussions, the Church of Norway concluded that there was not a sufficient doctrinal basis for the agreement that was then proposed. In practice, they thus joined Østnor's dissent (see above). Borgen disliked this intensely; both because the Church of Norway thereby exalted a "personal dissent" in the international commission of 1979-84 to their main position, and then because he believed after 1986 that if there was to be a new dialogue between these two Norwegian churches, "how should one then avoid the dialogue almost becoming a Lutheran examination of the Methodist Church to find out if it is willing to change and become Lutheran?"[41]

When he then looked more closely at some of the points in the dialogue report, he thought that the answer to this question had to be that the dialogue really became an examination: the Methodist view had been modified in the report so that it could pass a Lutheran exam. First of all, he argued, this is true concerning the view of baptism, in which he believed that the Methodist doctrine of the prevenient grace of God had been weakened.[42] Second, Borgen seemed to be more satisfied with the description of

---

40. Cf. Borgen, "Angående dialogen med Den norske lutherske kirke," *Kristelig Tidende*, June 22, 1995, 10. In addition, I have used Borgen, "Faglig Vurdering og Kommentar" (unpublished); his report from pastors' gathering," Winter 1996, in *Kristelig Tidende*, February 15, 1996, 8; and his "Høringsnotat til årskonferansen," summer 1996.

41. See, i.a., Borgen, "Reell dialog i Norge?," *Vårt Land*, June 17, 1991.

42. See *Faglig vurdering og kommentar til Nådens fellesskap* (1995), 4. In addition, Borgen also thought that "it is not explicitly stated what the child's position is before baptism and in baptism." Again, he opined, the formulations became too Lutheran.

the Eucharist.[43] And third, he also found that the description of sanctification had become too Lutheran. While the Lutherans speak of an "imputed" sanctification, the Methodists speak of an "acquired" sanctification.[44]

Borgen thus believed—and he repeated these arguments in several different contexts—that the dialogue report had become too Lutheran and that the Methodist positions did not come out strong enough. On a purely dogmatic basis, therefore, he concluded that he could not, based on this report, recommend any agreement on an extended church fellowship with the Church of Norway as proposed in the report.

Concerning the Church of Norway as a state church

We have seen above that the International Lutheran-Methodist Dialogue Commission report stated that one encouraged a relationship with secular authorities where the church is independent, and all denominations are equal to the state (point 34). This was also included in the Methodist Church's decision in 1986, in which it advocated "a stronger work for all denominations to be independent of and equal in relation to the state." But the Church of Norway did not comment on this part. Nor is there any trace of this or similar arguments in the dialogue report of 1994. However, for Peder Borgen, this issue, or the aspects that belong to such a type of argumentation, gained renewed relevance in his debate against the agreement proposal in 1995-96. Let's have a brief look at how Borgen used this argument, which we here choose to call the "church order argument."

In December 1995, Borgen had completed an important document in the form of a "Professional Assessment and Commentary on the Fellowship of Grace." Here he applies most of the theological arguments that we have already encountered, but it is what I have called the "church order argument" that dominates the twenty-five-page document (5-25).[45] He

---

43. However, Borgen found the report's wording problematic when it states that "In the Lord's Supper, Christ brings his life-giving body and blood through wine and bread to all the celebrants who take part in the meal." Here it must be said, he wrote, that for those who do not receive in faith, "bread and wine are not the body and blood of Jesus." Cf. *The Church: Community of Grace*, 18-19, subpoint 54. But here it is also stated that "We are, however, convinced that such differences are less significant than the agreements between us."

44. The nuances are finetuned, but Borgen found that the report's formulation and its connection of sanctification to baptism led to a holistic understanding becoming too Lutheran. Cf. *Faglig vurdering og kommentar*, 4-5.

45. The full title is: "Faglig vurdering og kommentar til Nådens fellesskap. Rapport fra samtalen mellom Metodistkirken i Norge og Den norske kirke. Slutt rapport med forslag til avtale" (Oslo, 1994). Av Peder Borgen. Trondheim, December, 1995. The

points out that the dialogue group did not address the issue of the view of the church because it believed it was adequately addressed in the international report. Borgen objects that the two churches in question in Norway are so different that one should have taken it up for a broader discussion. The significance of these areas, he says, can be elucidated by asking whether the Methodist Church should be absorbed into the Church of Norway, and by raising the more comprehensive question of the conditions of religious freedom in Norway.

What is new here is that he addresses the issue of religious freedom—historical, practical, and actual.[46] Why did this argument become so relevant to Borgen? What had happened?

I have no other answer to this question than that Borgen's attitudes must be seen in the light of his general view of the majority church's association with the state, and thus of its special privileges, which he considered and experienced as a form of discrimination. Later, in 1996, a new church law was passed for the Church of Norway; the same year, a new funeral law was passed too, and the responsibility for the operation of the cemeteries was transferred from the municipality to the local church council of the Church of Norway. This was still on the proposal level in the spring of 1996 but was later decided as law. Borgen commented on the proposal in a way that demonstrated that he considered it as violating religious freedom. In addition, he pointed to the privileges of the majority church when it came to that church's role in occasions of state officials visiting Norway, in other major public events, and in school services (for instance, at Christmas). These privileges, he argued, demonstrate the need for a revision of the law so that the principle of religious freedom is not violated in these areas.[47]

Borgen saw here similar discriminatory attitudes as those he had encountered throughout his life. Even if the term "dissenter" was abandoned, and the 150th anniversary of the Dissenters Act of 1845 was celebrated in 1995, discrimination did not end. His conclusion regarding such attitudes he therefore formulated thus:

---

status of the document is unclear to me, but it was at least sent to the seminar in Bergen as input to their work with the dialogue report.

46. This part of his document (pp. 7–25) was originally a lecture he gave at the celebration of the 150th anniversary of the Dissenters Act in 1995. It was printed the following year as a separate article; see Borgen, "Religionsfrihet og Statskirke," 7–26.

47. To understand these arguments of Borgen, the reader should remember that when some major event in the nation, such as a visit of statesmen and -women from other countries, was to be celebrated in a church, this was always carried out in the main local church of the majority church regardless of what church the visitor(s) belonged to. Furthermore, when some national event was to be celebrated, like May 17, services in the local Church of Norway were obligatory, etc., etc.

The Methodist Church requests the Norwegian Lutheran Church to work to a greater extent for "a relationship in which all denominations are equal before the state." In this connection, one would like to point out that in our country there are still discriminatory schemes in relation to the Free churches. It is disturbing that the Norwegian Lutheran Church [TS: Sic = the Church of Norway] even aims at continuing with discriminating schemes also in the laws that are passed in our time with a view to ecclesiastical matters and the school's teaching in the future.[48]

With his former association to the state church statement from the International Lutheran-Methodist Dialogue Commission (point 34), he shows here that these conditions—in his opinion—still made it problematic with extended relations with the Church of Norway. Moreover, as he was also convinced—from his Methodist point of view—that the dogmatic, doctrinal formulations in the report were not clear enough, the result was given: the time was not yet ripe to establish full fellowship of Word and sacrament with the Church of Norway—the state church.

The final reception in the Methodist Church

The administrative board invited all the congregations, the cabinet (= the bishop and the overseers), and the seminary to give consultation statements on a possible endorsement of "Fellowship of Grace." A separate committee was set up to review the congregations' recommendations. Of fifty-one congregations, responses were received from thirty-four. Of these, nineteen again gave a positive statement, while ten were against the recommendations of the report. A few congregations, including Borgen's home congregation in Trondheim, did not take a position but sent statements with pros and cons. The parish pastor in Trondheim, Ivan Chetwynd, argued for; Peder Borgen against.

The debate in *Kristelig Tidende* also showed very divergent opinions, from the most lavish praise to the announcement that one now had to resign from the Methodist Church—now there was no purpose of being a member anymore because one had once left the Church of Norway to be a member of the Methodist Church, and now one felt let down.

However, in the final vote at the 1996 Annual Conference, there were 104 yes votes (73 percent) and 38 no votes (27 percent) to the agreement. Thus, it was also approved by the Methodist Church in Norway.

---

48. See *Faglig vurdering og kommentar*, 2 and 20.

On Sunday, January 26, 1997, the agreement was signed in a joint festive service in the cathedral in Fredrikstad, the city that fostered O. P. Petersen, the founder of Methodism in Norway. At the opening of the Methodists' Annual Conference at Mysen in 1976, Andreas Aarflot had been present as the newly appointed bishop of Borg, but did not find it appropriate to participate in the celebration of the Eucharist. In January 1997, he participated in and signed the agreement of "Fellowship of Grace," and together the two churches celebrated Holy Communion. In the evening of the same day, there was a festive meeting in the Methodist church in Sarpsborg, and Bishop Aarflot was the keynote speaker. He then said, among other things, that "We are not celebrating the return of the Methodists, but a mutual approach, in which both parties have moved. We celebrate a meeting between equal partners . . ."[49]

Was it a climate change that had taken place? Yes, undoubtedly.[50]

Epilogue

There was an early exchange of pastors in some congregations who were in urgent need of help. In 1998, Lars-Erik Nordby published an article on "The Community of Grace—a Sustainable Agreement?" And his answer was that "there are many signs that the agreement has sustainability in it."[51] In 2002, an issue of the *Journal of Theology and Church* (*Tidsskrift for Teologi og Kirke*) was dedicated to the subject "Reception of Ecumenical Agreements." Peder Borgen contributed with an article about the "The Agreement of the 'Fellowship of Grace' between the Methodist Church and the Church of Norway."[52] Borgen presented some of his own "reflections" as a conclusion to the article; here he continues to be critical of Østnor's dissent and supports the majority in the International Lutheran-Methodist Dialogue Commission of 1979–84 and what he calls their "'more open criterion" for ecclesial fellowship. He also points out that the point about a stronger work for all denominations to be independent of and equal in relation to the state should be followed up. He also questions the justification of the concept of "peoples' church" (*folkekirke*), and he still finds the name Church of Norway discriminatory.

---

49. Aarflot's speech was published in *Kristelig Tidende* 4:26 (1997) 9.

50. Lars-Erik Nordby said some years later (Nordby, "Nådens Fellesskap—en bærekraftig avtale?," 140): "As a Methodist, it is obvious that there has been a change in the Church of Norway; now we have a deal."

51. Nordby, "Nådens Fellesskap—en bærekraftig avtale?," 141. See also Haga and Tveit, "'Nådens fellesskap!'—eit grunnlag for samarbeid," 199–215.

52. Borgen, "Avtalen 'Nådens Fellesskap,'" 185–98.

Furthermore, he argues that the Methodist Church should take closer contact with several of the Christian mission organizations within the Church of Norway. And he still finds it problematic that there are different conditions for membership in the two churches. "From the Methodist Church's point of view, it must be clearly stated that baptism, faith, and confession are part of the initial phase of membership in church and congregation."[53]

Finally, he points to the resource-demanding aspects of ecumenical work and says:

> What is crucial for the future of the Methodist Church in Norway is primarily the work in the local congregations. Therefore, the main efforts should take place there. The challenge in the congregations is to grow based on a renewal of vision, activities, and beliefs. Only on that basis can the Methodist Church make significant ecumenical contributions in the future.[54]

In retrospect, it can be said that it was probably not just a climate change that contributed to the agreement with the Church of Norway; it was, to a certain extent, also marked by a generational change, not least within the Methodist Church.

Retiring

In 1997 Peder Borgen, as a Methodist pastor, applied for a transition to a retired relationship and was granted this at the Annual Conference the same year. The following year he came with a small sigh of frustration in a letter to Ragnar Horn. Horn had asked for some comments on a few points in the *Leadership Handbook* he was working on. But Peder was not very willing to comment on these: "The questions you raise interest me, but for the time being, I stay away from raising issues within our Church, as it leads to too many frustrations. I, therefore, concentrate on other tasks."[55] He then points out that he had his hands full as president of the Royal Norwegian Society of Sciences and Letters in Trondheim, and in 1997–98 he was also president of Studiorum Novi Testamenti Societas (SNTS). During 1997, he also completed—as we shall see later—the work of marking the eightieth anniversary of the First Sami National Assembly. And the same year saw the publication of his large book on Philo of Alexandria. And finally, they were soon to leave Trondheim, moving to Lillestrøm. "I therefore now focus rather on the

---

53. Borgen, "Avtalen 'Nådens Fellesskap,'" 190.
54. Borgen, "Avtalen 'Nådens Fellesskap,'" 196–97
55. Letter from Peder Borgen to Ragnar Horn, dated October 14, 1998.

challenges and opportunities that open up in an inspiring way and set aside the conditions in my own Church, where my views do not get a hearing anyway. Let me add that, of course, I go to church and have good Christian fellowship there."[56]

It seems that he was in a way withdrawing from active church politics at the national level and would prioritize local engagement. Furthermore, it is evident that his personal disappointment was great; he did not reach out with his views in the debate on "Fellowship of Grace"; he had a feeling that he was not heard.

One year later, Inger and Peder moved to Lillestrøm. There they both became active in their local congregation, Lillestrøm Methodist Church, the church where Peder had been active in his youth. Or as he himself put it in the article referred to above:

> What is crucial for the future of the Methodist Church in Norway is primarily the work in the local congregations.[57]

---

56. Letter from Peder Borgen to Ragnar Horn, dated October 14, 1998.
57. Borgen, "Avtalen 'Nådens Fellesskap,'" 196–97.

13

A Busy Senior Research Scholar (1993–99)

AT THE BEGINNING OF 1993, Peder Borgen ended his regular employment as a professor at the Department of Religious Studies, University of Trondheim. However, he did not leave the university for a quiet retirement. In fact, he did not leave the university at all at that time. Borgen turned sixty-five at the end of January 1993 and entered the status of a senior researcher. This was an arrangement provided by the Norwegian Research Council of Norway. It was awarded—for many, it was considered a reward—to some researchers after an application for support to continue and complete research projects they were involved in. The arrangement was purely financial; the Research Council was paying the difference between a retirement pension and the amount a professor would have had in an ordinary professorship. Borgen was awarded such a scholarship for five years. He retained his office at the university but was exempted from teaching and administrative tasks.

In his application, he highlighted three research fields as fundamental to his application.[1] He was to edit and coauthor two scholarly books.[2] Second, he had an agreement with the English publisher T. & T. Clark to

---

[1]. The description of Borgen's plans for the senior scholarship period is taken from his application submitted to the Research Council, dated May 5, 1992. Now in Borgen's private archives.

[2]. These were published in 1995 and 1998: Borgen and Giversen, *New Testament and Hellenistic Judaism*; and Borgen, Robbins, and Gowler, *Recruitment, Conquest and Conflict*.

write a two-volume commentary on the Revelation of John for the famous *International Critical Commentary Series*. It was a bold project for a senior scholarship period, and it eventually turned out that the assignment became too extensive. It was never completed; Peder had to throw in the towel. He had several thoughts about the project but never really got started. There is reason to believe that the Sami project, which he also started at the beginning of the scholarship period, took some inspiration from the commentary project. I will return to this Sami project below. Nevertheless, his work on the Revelation of John resulted in several articles published in the 1990s.

The third field he listed in his application was "supervision and networking." He had supervising responsibility for two doctoral students, and a third was on his way into the system.[3] Borgen wanted to continue to work with these as their supervisor, and he wanted to take them further into the networks his participation in the many conferences represented. Finally, he also mentioned that he wanted to collect some of his articles and publish them in a book about the Gospel of John.[4]

Therefore, everything was well planned for an active and productive research life as a senior fellow. However, already in the first year of this period, two things happened that he did not foresee when he wrote the application, and both of these changed much of what he was to be concerned about in the years to come: He became engaged in the fate of a congregation threatened with closure; the Methodist congregation in Hammerfest. And then, he received a phone call from a Sami journalist that opened a new field of research for him. And Peder got engaged in both in addition to what he had already planned. No wonder he had to back off from some of his planned projects.

NORTHERN NORWEGIAN METHODISM IN CRISIS

At the Methodist Church's Annual Conference in 1992, there was a proposal to arrange a seminar or conference to put Norway and Scandinavia in general on the United Methodist Church's map of Europe. One wanted solid Norwegian participation and participation from Germany; it was especially desirable to get the German Bishop Walter Klaiber to be better informed

---

3. One student eventually retracted himself from the program, but the other two completed and defended their dissertations just around the turn of the millennium: Per Jarle Bekken in 1998, and Kåre Fuglseth in 2001.

4. He never published a book dealing with the Gospel of John only, but in 1996 he published a volume that contains several articles on that Gospel (Borgen, *Early Christianity and Hellenistic Judaism*). In addition, in 1997 he published a book that is a thorough introduction to Philo's works (Borgen, *Philo of Alexandria: An Exegete for His Time*).

about the problems the geographic pattern of Norway and the rural areas in the north represented for the church. The conference accepted the proposal, and Peder Borgen joined the further committee work.

A Conference on "To the ends of Scandinavia"

The conference was held at Soltun Folkehøgskole, October 14-17, 1993. Forty to fifty persons attended, including Bishop Walter Klaiber (West Germany), president of Europe, and Bishop Hans Växby (Northern Europe).

The background for this conference was, in short, this: the Methodist congregations in northern Norway had for years experienced stagnation and partly declined. The number of members decreased steadily, and more in northern Norway than elsewhere in the country. In the north, the number of members was halved in 35 years, and in 1993-94 amounted to 258 persons with full membership, divided into eight congregations. The youth work was hard, and some congregations had no such work at all.

Borgen was invited to hold a Bible lesson at the conference. He first outlined his view of the church and then tried to concretize this into the current situation by focusing on "Mission in New Testament Times and in the Methodist Church in Europe Today."[5] The lecture was based on both his New Testament research and his insight into contemporary Judaism, as he especially knew it from Philo of Alexandria. There has been much discussion about whether the Jews ran any such activities as what we today call "mission": an outward sending of "missionaries" to get people to join Judaism. The main view today is that the Jewish communities did not conduct any such sending out of missionaries,[6] but that they promoted some propaganda in their local communities and were accepting anyone who wanted to convert to Judaism, that is—become a proselyte.[7]

Borgen believes that a similar introverted (centripetal) feature was found in today's Methodist Church as well as in Israel in the time of the early church; he sees it in the strong trends towards centralization. Speaking about Norway, Borgen argues that one might thereby undermine one's existence, even though some central congregations, such as those in Oslo,

---

5. All my references to his lecture are taken from the published version, Borgen, "Misjon i nytestamentlig tid." No page numbering.

6. Cf. Bird, *Crossing Over Land*; and McKnight, *Light Among the Nations*.

7. We can characterize an outward-looking, missionary activity as a *centrifugal movement*; it goes out from the center, out to all the others. And we can talk about an *introverted* attitude, a "come to Jerusalem" attitude, like a *centripetal* movement. In Jewish circles, the latter was a typical and dominant one, while the first Christians adopted the centrifugal one: they were sent and were to go "to the ends of the earth" (Acts 1:8).

Bergen, and Trondheim, could gain new influence by Methodists from other parts of the country moving to one of these main cities. But in the long run, this would also weaken the more rural churches, and we would get into a vicious circle; as the local congregations further out in the periphery were weakened, after a while, no one from these congregations would move to the congregations in the larger cities.

The critical issue for Borgen, therefore, was: "How can one change a centripetal attitude and dynamics to a dynamic outward (centrifugal) movement as a mission to the ends of Scandinavia?"

Borgen looks here at the situation in northern Norway, in the more peripheral parts of the country, and admits—and points with some sadness to the fact—that "in reality, our Church is not a national church in the true sense of the word. It is a coastal church for the coast from the south at the Swedish border to Bergen with some 'outpost congregations' elsewhere in the country."

There was one congregation in particular in the north that was in danger of being closed down, the congregation in Hammerfest. Proposal for closure "was on the Administrative Board's table." Borgen decided to make a personal effort to see if it was possible to save it. It became a case for him to see if an extra effort could mean something for its future.

Borgen and the case of Hammerfest

The Methodist church in Hammerfest was founded in 1890.[8] At its founding, twenty-four people attended the church, and it probably had its best time in the years from 1907–94. It was never a large congregation: after World War II, it had twenty to thirty members. But in the early 1990s, membership was in a downslide, and the congregation lost its pastor.

Hence, Borgen suggested that he could take some time to stay in Hammerfest and that a two-year plan be drawn up from the autumn of 1994. The supervisor was not completely dismissive, but clarified that he had no faith that such measures would be successful. In his view, it looked like the church had had its time in Hammerfest.

Borgen, who was now a senior researcher and able to be away from the University of Trondheim, made five visits to Hammerfest from January 1994 to October 1995. He lived in the parsonage in the church building and spent some time every day for research, reading, and writing on his laptop.

---

8. Hammerfest is said to be the northernmost town in the world with more than ten thousand inhabitants (cf. "Hammerfest" in *Wikipedia*). Its Methodist church is the northernmost Methodist church in Norway, and is located in Finnmark county.

Then he worked as a pastor: he had conversations with relevant people; he did some house visits; talked to scout parents; engaged scouts; held services; attended prayer meetings and meetings in the women's association; visited the local school; and had meetings with parish councils, meetings with employees in the municipality, with sports leaders, with the leader of the history club, and with the media. In the late spring of 1994, a new preliminary church council was formed. In the autumn, a Methodist pastor was employed in a part-time position in Hammerfest so that he also visited the congregation between Borgen's visits.

What made Borgen take these trips to Hammerfest? He wrote in a note a few years later that four issues were essential to him when he took the initiative regarding Hammerfest:

1. "For me, it was important that Hammerfest was the northernmost congregation of the Methodist Church. It marked that the Methodist Church was seriously called to be a church for the whole country and not a church essentially geographically limited to southern Norway, even with a center of gravity along the coast.
2. It was worth attempting to enter a situation where closure was threatened, and to see if one could give the place and the congregation a second chance by working on the grassroots level.
3. I had gotten a research position without teaching and administration. For shorter periods, I could therefore take my laptop with me and work away from Trondheim . . .
4. And if possible, I could take advantage of the fact that we are an international Church, and channel resources from other countries to strengthen a local initiative in Norway."[9]

We find here several themes known from his previous work. We recognize his claims that church and mission belong together; the church runs mission *as a church*. At the same time, we notice his desire to expand the Methodist Church in Norway further. For in his eyes, Norway was also a mission field. Borgen ended his note in 2009 thus: "I am thankful to God that I was able to help stop the closure of the congregation in Hammerfest and was allowed to make one of the contributions to a continuation."

What became then of the Methodist congregation in Hammerfest? It not only survived but flourished and grew, and Hammerfest still has its Methodist church today. Critics will probably point out that other congregations in the north struggled too and that some were eventually closed. Why

---

9. Private note, dated 2009. No page numbering. Now in Borgen's private archives.

then prioritize Hammerfest? For Borgen, it seems that Hammerfest became a case, perhaps a test case, on whether it could benefit from an extra effort from outside.

In November 2018, the congregation—according to its newsletter—had fifty-five confessing adult members, and seven new members had been admitted in the previous year. The congregation has a part-time pastor, and they worship every Sunday and have various other gatherings during the week. They are still dependent on contributions from a common fund to get it all going, but that is a situation several congregations are familiar with in the 2020s.

FIRST SAMI NATIONAL ASSEMBLY, 1917

During the period when Borgen provided first aid to the congregation in Hammerfest, he received another request from northern Norway. But this time it came from Karasjok, and it referred to another Norwegian minority—the Sami. It was a request that engaged him for many years to come. However, to understand the background to this request, we must briefly retrace what happened several decades earlier in Trondheim.

In February 6–9, 1917, a large meeting was arranged in the Methodist church in Trondheim. Here met approximately 150 participants, most of them were southern Sami from Nordland, Trøndelag, and Hedmark counties, but also two to three from northern Norway. It has later been called "the first Sami national meeting."[10]

At the one-hundredth anniversary in 2017, a postage stamp was issued in memory of the Sami meeting in 1917. Here is the domestic stamp with a picture of Elsa Laula Renberg, the initiator of the 1917 meeting.

---

10. See now Borgen, "Samenes første landsmøte," and https://no.wikipedia.org/wiki/Samemøtet_i_1917.

The key issues discussed at the meeting were the reindeer husbandry issue (not at least questions about the relationship between the local populaces and nomadic Sami), questions about the laws concerning the Lap people, organizational issues (how one should organize oneself), and the question of what the best school alternatives for Sami children were.

Several will claim that "the meeting led to a new impetus in the Sami movement."[11] Moreover, there was a new awareness of Sami issues in other parts of society. Later, during the fifteenth Nordic Sami Conference in Helsinki in 1992, they decided that February 6 should be Sami National Day, now celebrated every year.

The Sami's First National Assembly was thus held in the Methodist church in Trondheim. I will not go further into details about this meeting or its history of impact; my focus is instead on the consequences of its disappearance into oblivion among the Methodists in Trondheim. Peder Borgen, too, did not know about the meeting. When the Trondheim Methodist church turned one hundred years old in 1981, Borgen had chaired the committee that prepared an anniversary publication. Nevertheless, none of the contributions in the book mentioned Sami's First National Assembly. It had been forgotten, and they obviously did not find it in their sources either.[12] Hence, when Borgen received an inquiry about this meeting, he had to admit he knew nothing about it. In the following, we will look at the activity and commitment that this request triggered in the senior research fellow Peder Borgen.

An unexpected request

In early 1994, Borgen received a phone call from a journalist on Sami Radio (NRK Karasjok), Kirsten Isaksen. She could inform him that they were preparing a program in Karasjok about Sami National Day, February 6, and she wanted to know more about the Methodist church in Trondheim, where the First Sami National Assembly had been held in 1917. Borgen could tell her about the Methodist church, but he knew nothing about the Sami meeting. This first contact was by telephone; later, Isaksen came on a trip to Trondheim and followed up with Borgen. According to Borgen, Isaksen was in Trondheim on Wednesday, January 26.

The inquiry ignited Borgen's interest. He immediately started collecting material about this national meeting. Furthermore, he established a

11. Cf. https://no.wikipedia.org/wiki/Samemøtet_i_1917.

12. See Borgen, *Kirken i Sentrum*. Borgen wrote the chapter concerning the years of 1884–1914, and Dagfinn Bratland wrote about the years of 1914–25.

connection with the regional Sami Association, and during 1995 the same association and the Trondheim Methodist church appointed members to a joint committee to prepare for an anniversary celebration on February 6, 1997.[13] Borgen became chairman of this committee, and Aud Kemi Rein became the project manager. The committee called itself the "1917 Committee."

Borgen becomes a researcher of the Sami assembly

In 1994-95, Borgen was very busy working for the Methodist congregation in Hammerfest to survive and get back on its feet (see above). In 1990-96, he was vice-president of the Royal Norwegian Society of Sciences and Letters, and was elected its president in early 1997. Moreover, he was a senior fellow carrying out further research on the New Testament and its world. When he, in addition, became involved in gathering more information about the First Sami National Assembly in 1917, some interests had to suffer, and in March 1996 he sent a letter to the Research Council of Norway, applying for an unpaid period of leave from his position as a senior fellow. The application was granted, and he was then on leave from August 10, 1996, until the end of that year.[14]

From research to a published book

It is not entirely clear to me when Borgen became convinced that it ought to become a book of his collected material. But two factors, in particular, helped to bring this idea to life. First, he found no overall record of this meeting, neither of its prehistory nor its conduct. In the first instance, he also did not find any minutes from the meeting.[15] Secondly, he eventually found the minutes and several other relevant documents about the meeting. Less important was perhaps the fact that the Methodist church played a role as the meeting place, but for the Methodist Borgen, it was not insignificant, and it became more important to him as he worked his way through the material. Hence, he went ahead with his new research agenda. He arranged the material and partially provided brief comments. But the book, as it eventually became, is primarily a collection of documents with some historical comments. Therefore, it was

---

13. See Borgen, "Samenes første landsmøte," 205; also the public lecture of the same title, Skånland, August 19, 2006 (unpublished), 2

14. Granted in a letter from the Research Council, dated March 27, 1996.

15. The minutes were later found in the Ministry of Agriculture's archives in Oslo.

given the subtitle *Historisk oversikt. Dokumentasjon. Kommentar* (*Historical Overview. Documentation. Comments*).[16]

Why in the Methodist church in Trondheim?

As he dug into the historical records, he became more and more interested in *why* the Sami assembly in 1917 was held in the Methodist church in Trondheim. One of the meeting's most central initiators, Elsa Laula Renberg, had expressed that she thought the plans for such a meeting could best be promoted in a city so that it could be known in wide circles.

But why in the Methodist church? That this question was not insignificant for the Methodist Borgen is reflected in the fact that he lists several arguments for this choice, both in his book and not least in some public lectures.[17] On the one hand, the Methodist church was located in the center of the city; second, the church's inner structure was useful for larger gatherings; third, and not at least important to Borgen, the church had an open attitude to measures of a social and societal nature: "It combines the Christian experience with involvement in social issues and societal issues."[18] Fourth, it may have played a role that the local state churches were not suitable for such a meeting. But here, a political aspect comes into work too: "The State bodies, including the State Church, enforced a strict Norwegianization policy towards the Sami, and as a 'dissenter congregation,' the Methodist Church itself experienced discriminatory laws and practices. They had an element of common destiny with the Sami."[19] The Methodist Church had no history of discrimination against the Sami people and their culture.

16. See Borgen, "Samenes første landsmøte."

17. Cf. his public lecture held in Skånland, August 19, 2006; and a public lecture entitled "A Nordic People's Movement: Sami National Day, held on February 7, 2017, at a seminar in the Methodist church in Trondheim (fifteen-page manuscript now in the Borgen archives).

18. Borgen, *Samenes første landsmøte*, 47.

19. Borgen, "Hvorfor –," *Ságat* 47 (2017) 9; Borgen, "En Nordisk folkebevegelse-" (unpublished manuscript), 8, cf. 10: "The Methodist Church did not take part in the Norwegianizations that permeated public policy and activity, and which also permeated the State Church. As a minority church in Norway, the Methodist Church itself was to some extent affected by the State Church's discrimination and prejudice."
Also, Sara Ellen Anne Eira, a Sami politician, emphasized the state church's role in the Norwegianization process in a chronicle she wrote in 2017: "During the Norwegianization, the church together with the school were two of the most important tools for Norwegianizing and oppressing of the Sami" (TS trans.). Eira, "The Samenes første landsmøte og kirken," *Ságat* February 8, 2017 (available at https://www.sagat.no/mening/samenes-forste-landsmote-og-kirken-hap-om-fellesskap-og-forsoning/19.6451)

Celebrating the eightieth anniversary in 1997

The committee established in 1995 continued its work of preparation for an anniversary celebration in 1997. The committee received great encouragement: the representative (and 1917 committee member) Åsta Vangberg proposed that the Sami Parliament[20] should have a meeting in Trondheim in connection with the celebration of the eightieth anniversary in 1997, and the Sami Parliament adopted this proposal. Later it turned out that the Sami Council and the Sami Cultural Council also wanted to have meetings at the same time and place. Meanwhile, Borgen's work on the book about the First Sami National Assembly continued. He received some secretarial help but was responsible for most of the collecting, writing, and editing himself. The book was finished just in time for the anniversary. The edition was not that large, so it was quickly sold out but is now digitally available on the internet via the National Library.[21]

The actual celebration took place on the five days of February 4–8. On Tuesday the 4th, an exhibition was opened in the Methodist church, where the main attraction was Astri Aasen's paintings from the meeting in 1917.[22] In addition, there was an exhibition of several documents and other relevant artifacts. The next day there was a festive service in the Methodist church at 1900. The bishop of the Methodists, Hans Växby, gave his sermon in both Norwegian and Finnish. Liturgy, Scripture readings, and prayers were in North Sámi, South Sámi, Lule Sámi, and Norwegian. "It was touching," wrote *Kristelig Tidende*, "when everyone together prayed the Lord's Prayer in their own language."[23] But February 6 was the most important day as the National Day of the Sami. At 3:00 p.m., a memorial plaquette was unveiled on the outer wall of the Methodist church. The president of the Sami Parliament, Ole Henrik Magga, gave a short speech and unveiled the memorial. Then there was an anniversary meeting in the Methodist church. They had such a rich program that the meeting lasted almost three hours, and Magga held the main speech. Here he said, i.a., that[24]

> The meeting in 1917 came together in the middle of the darkest time in Sami history when especially the State authorities in Norway put all their means into eradicating Sami culture. From

---

20. Concerning the Sami Parliament, see https://www.sametinget.no.
21. https://www.nb.no/items/URN:NBN:no-nb_digibok_2009012004033.
22. These pictures were found during Borgen's search for information concerning the Sami assembly of 1917. The pictures are now located in the Sami Parliament.
23. *Kristelig Tidende* 4:125 (February 20, 1997), 12.
24. Cited from a copy of Magga's manuscript, now in the Borgen archives.

the end of the 19th century, Sami was banned from school. The earth was taken from us, and as if that was not enough: In order to repurchase the land, it was demanded that our language be given up . . . . Only Norwegian culture was considered culture and civilization. The Sami culture was considered inferior and was to be exterminated. Many of us who sit here have felt this policy, for it continued up to the 1960s. The consequences of this we will still notice for generations.

In his historical overview, Peder Borgen gave a glimpse of the material he had worked with; he also presented some glimpses from the 1917 meeting that are not included in his book. In the evening, there was a gala dinner in a hotel in the vicinity, arranged by the Trondheim municipality and Sør-Trøndelag county. On the menu: reindeer meat!

For Borgen, this was the culmination of months of eager and partly strenuous research into a history of which he had been completely ignorant three years prior. Now he knew what happened in his church in 1917, and the Sami, another minority in Norway, could move on with a strengthened identity. Some borders had been crossed—again.

A one-hundredth anniversary—Tråante 2017

Tråante is the South Sami name for Trondheim. Tråante 2017 was a large-scale celebration twenty years later of the one-hundredth anniversary of Sami National Day—February 6. The main organizers this time were the Sami Parliament, Sør-Trøndelag County Municipality, Nord-Trøndelag County Municipality, and Trondheim Municipality; that is, the political Norway organized the celebration, not, as in 1997, a free church—the Methodist church in Trondheim and some Sami organizations. The celebration culminated in an anniversary week but was also commemorated by several other events throughout the year. Nevertheless, the ecclesiastical element was also included in the anniversary week, namely at Nidaros Cathedral[25]— and the local Methodist church.

Peder Borgen, who had now turned eighty-nine, was partly an avid spectator and partly an avid participant throughout the week. On February 5, there was a festive service in the Methodist church. The church was designated as a historic site for the worldwide Methodist Church—United Methodist Church (UMC)—of which the Methodist Church in Norway is a part.

25. In the morning of Monday, February 6, a Sami altar was inaugurated in Nidaros Cathedral. Later the same day, there was a festive service where the king and many other representatives from official Norway were present.

The memorial plaque awarded by the United Methodist Church.

The background for this appointment was the congregation's efforts for the marginalized[26] and its role as the place for the First Sami National Assembly in 1917. A separate delegation from UMC had arrived for this service and the anniversary week. Several of these had roots in indigenous peoples in the United States, the Philippines, Nigeria, Australia, and elsewhere. On February 7, there was a seminar in the Methodist church. Peder Borgen was invited to give the opening lecture, which he did by lecturing on the topic, "A Nordic People's Movement: The National Meeting 1917 in the Methodist Church Seen in Context."[27] On the following days, there was another seminar at Evenskjer, Skånland Municipality, an international consultation on "Indigenous Peoples: From Acts of Repentance to Acts of Justice." Inger and Peder Borgen were there. Peder participated in a panel discussion on "The Sami Jubilee and the United Methodist Church in Scandinavia: Impact and Significance." The seminar lasted Wednesday to Friday, and the Borgens returned on Saturday.

26. During World War II, the Methodist congregation in Trondheim helped another minority, the Jews. Several items from the synagogue, among them Torah scrolls and other liturgical items, were hidden in the church during the war. The pastor personally helped several Jews, and in August 1942 there was even a Bar Mitzvah celebration on the upper floor, and other synagogal gatherings there. See Borgen, "Hemmelig synagoge i Metodistkirken," *Vårt Land*, December 10, 2018. See also https://trondheimumc.com/historie/.

27. A copy of the manuscript is now in the Borgen archives at the National Library, Oslo.

The anniversary week was wearying for the eighty-nine-year-old Borgen. He returned home almost exhausted; it took several weeks before he fully recovered. But he was happy. He had been able to celebrate the one-hundredth anniversary of Sami National Day; he had been able to talk about their cause, and he had talked about and for the minorities.

What was it that caught him so intensely that after a while, he actually had to apply for a short-time leave from his senior scholarship to complete a book about the Sami in 1996?

In the end, only Borgen himself can give a satisfactory answer to such questions, and I have not received any such answer. However, if we look at his previous journey of life up to 1994 and search for trajectories in his history, there are some issues that do make it easier to see and say that, yes, there are some trajectories of history in his life. Furthermore, we can see that his role as a researcher of the circumstances surrounding the Sami's first national meeting in 1917 does not represent a break with these. On the contrary, they are strengthened. I can suggest three such trajectories or patterns here.

First, Peder Borgen was an active Methodist all his life, and the First Sami National Assembly took place not only in a Methodist church but in what was his Methodist church in Trondheim. Here we can add another issue too: as a "dissenter congregation," the Methodists had experiences that made them understand the Sami situation from the inside: "as a 'dissenter congregation,' the Methodist Church itself experienced discriminatory laws and practices. They had an element of common destiny with the Sami."[28]

Second: Borgen's personal life journey. I have described in previous chapters how he, as a Methodist "dissenter," encountered obstacles that others did not encounter in scholarship applications and applications for positions. A particular form of occupational ban for "dissenters" prevailed in our general school system until 1969 and in the university sector until 1972. The discriminatory experiences that the Sami had experienced were perhaps more strongly recognized by Peder Borgen than by many other "dissenters."

Third: his studies of, among others, the Diaspora Jew Philo from Alexandria are relevant. These demonstrated to Borgen that as a Jewish migrant in the Diaspora (= Jews living outside Israel), Philo also experienced being part of a minority subjected to discrimination at various levels in the society of his times. There is, in fact, I suggest, a line from Philo via Borgen to the situation of the Sami which can be described using categories such

---

28. Borgen, "Hvorfor," *Ságat* 47 (2017), 9; Borgen, "En nordisk folkebevegelse," private manuscript, 8.

as *minority, difference, not being seen, not recognized, marginalization, discrimination,* and in the worst case, *exclusion.*

Epilogue

Peder Borgen delivered a large amount of written material from his life and work to the National Library in Oslo. This also includes material from his work with the First Sami National Assembly. On October 11, 2018, the final handover of this material was marked by a special event in the National Library. Borgen himself gave a long and thorough lecture about the First Sami National Assembly in 1917, and Kirsten Isaksen, the former journalist who contacted him in 1994, was also present and made a speech. They had both been involved in shedding light on the Sami situation both in the past and present. The circle was closed.

Now this source material is available in the library for other researchers of the times to come.

14

Biblical Studies in Trondheim: A Review

WHEN BORGEN BEGAN HIS work as a full professor in Trondheim, his conditions for doing extensive research improved considerably. In Bergen, he was a lecturer (or, in USA terms, an associate professor), with more lectures and less research possibilities than as a professor. In Trondheim, this situation changed. A professor could have up to 50 percent research time; more typical was about 40 percent of one's time reserved to do research. In addition, professors were, if possible, given a sabbatical about every seventh year. Peder Borgen had a sabbatical year in 1977–78 and 1988.[1]

BORGEN'S RESEARCH IN TRONDHEIM (1973-99)

Borgen produced and published numerous studies during his years in Trondheim; his energy was great even though he sometimes had to work some late-night hours not to transgress the publishers' deadlines too much. However, he had a help that not many have today, at least not in Norway; he had secretarial assistance. The department had a secretary who also helped the professors with their writing. The Norwegian professors of today can usually only dream of such conditions. But at the same time, they have received another secretarial aid—the PC. Today's computers are the secretaries of our time; they are not just typewriters but can keep track of a much larger amount of information than any secretary could ever hold. And Peder used

---

1. In 1977–78, the whole family spent the sabbatical partly in Egypt, Greece, Israel, and Germany. In 1988 Inger and Peder spent the sabbatical in the United States.

the PC early in his scholarly work. Vernon Robbins, a Fulbright professor at the department in 1983–84, was an avid computer user and represented a stimulus to the department being further computerized.

When considering Borgen's research after his move to Trondheim, it is possible to divide it into specific periods. I find it more advantageous, however, to group it according to topics or fields of study. In doing so, I find the following fields of interest as most worthy of attention in the present context: 1) Borgen's view of the Gospel of John, including its use of the Old Testament and relation to the Synoptic Gospels; 2) Philo as Philo, including the relevance of using Philo in New Testament studies; 3) studies in Galatians; 4) studies in the Revelation of John and Philo. In addition, he published on ecclesiology, ecumenism, and the history of Methodism, including some minor studies on early Methodist personalities.[2] In the following pages, however, the primary focus will be in the fields of the biblical interests listed above.[3]

The Gospel of John

How did the Gospel of John come into being? There is a tremendous variety in the range of answers to that question. Here we limit the range of the question thus: how did Peder Borgen consider the birth of the Fourth Gospel? Borgen never dealt extensively with this question and related issues but presented what may be considered an outline of his view in several articles published from the middle of the 1970s.

The origins of the Gospel of John

In one of his articles from 1976, Borgen gave an outline of his views on the origins of John, in the form of nine theses.[4] Here he takes his starting point in the understanding that the Gospel had its point of departure in a

---

2. Interested readers may consult the comprehensive bibliography of Borgen available in the appendix at the end of this volume.

3. It may help the reader—if s/he wants to check some of the studies referred to here—to notify that Borgen published six collections of his articles as books; see *Logos Was the True Light* (1983); *Paul Preaches Circumcision* (1983); *Philo, John and Paul* (1987); *Early Christianity and Hellenistic Judaism* (1997); *The Gospel of John: More Light* (2014); and *Illuminations by Philo* (2021). In addition, when considering Philo, Borgen published an introductory volume on Philo: *Philo of Alexandria: An Exegete for His Time* (1997). Some of his articles have been republished several times. A full overview, also indicating reprints, is given in the appendix at the end of this volume.

4. See Borgen, "John's Use of the Old Testament."

Johannine community, in which a dual activity took place: "Oral and written traditions were received and handed on, and they were subject to interpretative activity."[5] This activity was possible, ia., because there probably was a "deposit of traditions" in the community.

The evangelist, as such, took part in the interpretative activity in the community. Hence, the Gospel is a result of a process, but it also indicates that it is impossible to trace or "reconstruct comprehensive pre-Johannine theology of the sources" (86). Borgen also thinks that it is not always possible to distinguish between the evangelist's hand and his sources.

Furthermore, Borgen assumes little contact between the Synoptic Gospels and John, if any, but considers the oral and written traditions behind the Fourth Gospel to have belonged to a specific Gospel tradition. These traditions, then, he considers represented "two groups of relatively independent material, the narrative, and the discourse material" (87). At one point, he considered that there might have been some relations between the Fourth Gospel and the Synoptics, most probably in the way that there were some common traditions behind them all, but later he retracted from this position, arguing that the Gospel of John was independent of Synoptic traditions (see below).

However, in the traditions behind the Gospel of John, "some events were lifted up as points of orientation, which influenced the place and perspective given to other parts" (87). Here, the passion narrative most probably played such a role and possibly also the narratives of the beginning of Jesus' ministry and that of John the Baptist. This circumstance, Borgen surmised, gave the basis for "two independent manifestations of the gospel form, that of Mark and that of John" (87).

In his dissertation, Borgen investigates the interpretative techniques used in John 6. Moreover, he finds "the interpretative techniques applied by the Evangelist and his community for complex" (87). Some stories are used as received; others are given in an interpreted form; while some stories are formed by the community and with added key terms from traditions. Fragments from different stories may also have been reshaped together.

This interpretative activity, however, was primarily based on exegetical traditions from Old Testament expositions: "The use of the Old Testament in the Gospel indicates that learned expository methods and techniques have been employed. To a large extent, Gospel traditions have been woven together with such expositions of the Old Testament" (88).

---

5. Borgen, "John's Use of the Old Testament," 86. The following presentation is my summary of the theses of Borgen presented in this article (cf. 86–88). The numbers in my text are page number references to this article.

However, one might ask: who performed or influenced such interpretations? Borgen suggests that several persons, events, and situations influenced the interpretations, from events and conflict in the life of Jesus to problems in the Christian communities, to the renderings and interpretations by the evangelist. Furthermore, John 21 probably indicates the last edition of the Gospel as such.

The role of the Scriptures

The ways Borgen perceives the origin of the Fourth Gospel are not very extraordinary. A glance into some New Testament introductions reveals that it is relatively mainstream. However, what stands out in his presentation is the emphasis on issues of interpretation of the Old Testament as a central ingredient in shaping the traditions of the Gospel. Hence, not only the existence of the Old Testament in the early Christian communities, but even more the particular use of it in shaping the New Testament and its theology, is essential. Borgen dealt with the role of the Old Testament in John in several other articles in the years to come.[6]

For Borgen, the Old Testament was very influential in the early communities and "created many of the theological issues which were taken up in the New Testament."[7] Several of his articles can be read as examples of investigating and demonstrating the role of the Old Testament in the New Testament, as for instance, his articles on "God's Agent in the Fourth Gospel" (1968), "The Son of Man Saying in John" (1977), "The Use of Tradition in John 12.44–50" (1979), not to speak of his works on John 6.[8]

Borgen has some reservations concerning the *typological method* in understanding the use of and role of the Old Testament in the New Testament. Instead, he prefers "the more flexible concept and method of scriptural thought-models employed in the New Testament."[9] His reservations about the typological method may induce one to ask how he considers the view and methods so forcefully argued by Richard Hays. Borgen deals with

---

6. In addition to his *Bread from Heaven*, see also, especially, his "Old Testament in the Formation"; "In Accordance with the Scriptures"; "John 6: Tradition, Interpretation and Composition"l "The Son of Man Saying"; and several articles in his book *The Gospel of John: More Light*.

7. Borgen, "Old Testament in the Formation," In Borgen, *Logos Was the True Light*, 115.

8. Borgen, "Bread from Heaven: Aspects of Debates," 32–46; Borgen, "John 6: Tradition, Interpretation and Composition," See also his work on the Prologue of John, dealt with in a previous section here.

9. Borgen, "Old Testament in the Formation," 118.

this in an article on "In Accordance with the Scriptures."[10] In his first book on *Echoes of Scripture in the Letters of Paul*, Hays introduced the concept of "intertextuality," that is, "reading the letters as literary texts shaped by complex intertextual relations with Scripture."[11] Later, he also talks about a "figural" reading of the Scriptures. That this procedure has apparent affinities with the older "typological" readings of Scripture is evident from the definition of "figural reading" Hays accepts in his large volume on "Echoes of Scripture in the Gospels.": "Figural interpretation establishes a connection between two events or persons in such a way that the first signifies not only itself but also the second, while the second involves or fulfills the first . . ."[12]

Borgen, however, accepts the emphasis on the role of Scripture in Paul's hermeneutic, but on the other side, argues that the word "interpreted" should be added so that the characterization should read "echoes of *interpreted* Scripture."[13] Furthermore, based on the observation that the Scriptures not only provide guidelines for a person's way of life but are "woven into the very fabric of Jewish society and institutions . . . one might also speak about echoes of *practiced* Scriptures."[14] Consequently, one should label the kind of hermeneutic in use here as "ethnocentric hermeneutic" more than "ecclesiocentric hermeneutic," because the Jewish people met the biblical texts as applied on every level of their Jewish society.[15]

Hence, due to these emphases, Borgen is drawn in the direction of comparing the "ethnocentric hermeneutic" of John and other New Testament works and the exegesis inherent in the works of Philo. Over the years, studies of Philo were to dominate more and more in his works as he expanded his focus from the Gospel of John to Paul—especially to Paul's Letter to the Galatians—and even to the Revelation of John. But first, a few comments on his view of the relation of John to the Synoptics before we focus more on his works on Philo.

---

10. Borgen, "In Accordance with the Scriptures," 195–97.

11. Hays, *Echoes of Scripture*, xi.

12. Hays, *Echoes of Scripture*, 2, in which he quotes E. Auerbach's definition from his *Mimesis*, 73. See also Hays's explanation of such figural reading in Hays, *Reading Backwards*, 15–16.

13. Borgen, "In Accordance with the Scriptures," 196.

14. Borgen, "In Accordance with the Scriptures," 197.

15. Borgen, "In Accordance with the Scriptures," 197.

John and the Synoptics

Borgen worked on the possible relationships between the Synoptic Gospels and the Gospel of John over several decades. Not all the time, probably, but he published on the problem early in the late 1950s,[16] and returned to it in the mid-1980s at a symposium in Jerusalem on the interrelations of the Gospels.[17] Moreover, when he published his book on the Gospel of John in 2014, he included his main articles dealing with this issue and summarized how his view had developed over the years.[18]

In his 2014 introduction to his article from 1959, he states his development thus: "I grew from maintaining that John is based essentially on an independent tradition with some influence from the Synoptic Gospels to seeing John being wholly independent of the three other written Gospels."[19] The thesis he argued in that article is nevertheless intriguing:

> John is based essentially on an independent tradition. Some Synoptic pericopes or parts of pericopes have been assimilated into this tradition. Within these pericopes or fragments, various elements from several Synoptic accounts have been fused together. When John appears dependent on the Synoptics only for certain pericopes, it is probable that oral tradition brought this material to John already fused. This explains the relative freedom with which John has reproduced the Synoptic material.[20]

Then he investigated several passages in the Johannine passion narrative, comparing them to the Synoptic Gospels (the burial of Jesus, Peter's use of the sword, the scourging and mocking of Christ, the crucifixion, Jesus

---

16. Borgen, "John and the Synoptics in the Passion Narrative." According to a comment on p. 104, this article is to some degree a result of a work he had submitted to the Faculty of Theology late in his studies, labeled "Berøringene mellom Johannesevangeliet og Matteusevangeliet. En tradisjonsundersøkelse" (The Relations between the Gospel of John and the Gospel of Matthew. A Survey of Traditions).

17. The discussion between Borgen and Neirynck as well as the presentation of Borgen's paper "John and the Synoptics" obviously took place at this 1984 conference but was not published until 1990. See Borgen, "John and the Synoptics," 408–37; with a reply by F. Neirynck, "John and the Synoptics: Response to P. Borgen," 438–50, followed by Borgen, "Reply," 451–58. Then, a couple of years later: Borgen, "Independence of the Gospel of John," 1815–33. Very relevant is also Borgen, "John and the Synoptics: Can Paul Offer Help?," 80–94. The four first of these are republished in the following two books by Borgen: *Early Christianity* (121–57, 159–73, 174–82, 183–204) and *The Gospel of John: More Light* (103–19, 121–46, 147–64; debate with Neirynck not included). For the sake of convenience, I use the articles as published in the last-mentioned book.

18. See Borgen, *Gospel of John: More Light*, 103–64, 289–91.

19. Borgen, *Gospel of John: More Light*, 103.

20. Borgen, *Gospel of John: More Light*, 104.

before Pilate, from Annas to Caiaphas, and the resurrection). He concluded that "A direct literary relationship between John and the Synoptics cannot be countenanced, and yet units of Synoptic material have been added to the Johannine tradition."[21]

It was not until in the 1984 study that he took up this observation and asked if the influence should be considered as "an independent oral and/or written tradition?"[22] Then he published an article on "John and the Synoptics: Can Paul Offer Help?" (1987), and parts of this item are included in the version published in 1990.

Borgen here draws on his comparisons of 1 Corinthians 10–11 and the Gospels and argues that between mutually independent versions, there may be some close verbal agreements on various levels, from sentences to single words.[23] However, he also argues that 1 Corinthians 10–11 shows that units were received, handed on, actively used in the communities, some modified in the process, and some interpretative activities were also evident.[24]

Having investigated the traditions in 1 Corinthians 10–11, comparing them to the Gospels—a complex discussion that cannot even be condensed here—Borgen summarizes his view and clarifies the role he attributes to the material found in 1 Corinthians thus:

> The Gospel of John represents a branch of Gospel traditions which is independent of the other three written gospels. Paul's letters, especially 1 Cor, shows that already Paul had received traditions which were transmitted, had authority, and gave basis for expository comments and elaborations. This usage of traditions comes closer to John's expository character, than do the synoptic gospels and it gives support to the view that John is independent.[25]

Having thus established—in his opinion—that the variety of traditions, the application of traditions, and interpretative activities inherent in the texts indicate that the Gospel of John is independent of the Synoptic Gospels, he also adduces some other arguments in favor of that view, but now from another angle of view.

21. Borgen, *Gospel of John: More Light*, 118.
22. Borgen, *Gospel of John: More Light*, 121–46.
23. Borgen, *Gospel of John: More Light*, 123.
24. Borgen, *Gospel of John: More Light*, 123.
25. Borgen, *Gospel of John: More Light*, 165; cf. 294: "The agreements between John and the Synoptic Gospels are better understood as agreements between John and synoptic-like traditions transmitted and interpreted independently of those written gospels. Paul provides examples of such transmission and use."

In the 1990s, Borgen was also working on Philo's historical works *In Flaccum* and especially *De legatione ad Gaium*.[26] Many scholars consider the Gospel of Mark a historical model for the gospel genre, including that of John. Borgen is critical of the view that Mark had such an innovative and unique role and suggests that Philo's two historical writings mentioned above should shed light on Gospel writings such as the Gospel of John, and perhaps also the Gospel of Mark. This suggestion represents a creative idea that Borgen has asserted more strongly than most other biblical scholars: the gospel format is not unique and was not created by either Mark or John. All four of these books—Mark, John, *Flaccum,* and *Legatio*—deal with tragic events and challenges that must be met and overcome. Therefore, based on observations like this, it is not necessary to claim that John is dependent on having Mark as his model. According to Borgen, the limited but distinct biographical form that we find here is a natural way of presenting a person when his professional actions are in focus.[27]

Several of Borgen's views are included in the discussion in one of the most recent representations of the ancient biography genre as a background for the Gospels. As biography is getting more attention and even growing popularity as a relevant genre for understanding the Gospels,[28] some works of Philo may also be considered more relevant for understanding the Gospels. Time will tell whether these viewpoints of Borgen are convincing.[29]

Philo as Philo

"You might talk to Peder about whatever you want, but in just a few moments, he starts talking about Philo." This characterization is found in an interview a journalist did with Borgen in the summer of 1996.[30] "And it is not that strange," he continued, "for the Jewish philosopher Philo is a friend of Peder. Even though Philo died almost 2000 years ago, Peder associates with him daily—in the world of books." The journalist touches on several aspects of Borgen's research career in the interview. However, in the end, he ends up with Philo. Or, to be more correct: Borgen manages to bring in a few more words towards the end of the interview about both Philo, the

---

26. Borgen, "Philo's *Against Flaccus*," 41–57; and Borgen, "Application and Commitment," 86–101. Both republished in Borgen, *Illuminations by Philo*, 17–33, 34–52. See also Borgen, "Can Philo's *In Flaccum* and *Legatio* Be of Help?," 241–60.

27. Borgen, "Can Philo's *In Flaccum* and *Legatio* Be of Help?," 280.

28. See Burridge, *What Are the Gospels?*; and Bond, *Biography of Jesus*.

29. See, for example, Keener, *Christobiography*, 173.

30. Rolfsen, "Peder og Filon," *Adresseavisen*, June 15, 1996, 4.

Gospel of John chapter 6, and bread from heaven: "And he smiles all over his face. For now, he can talk about Philo again..."

This is also the case in several other interviews, both in connection with some of Borgen's anniversary days and in other circumstances. One rarely gets around Philo in the company with Borgen. And many are those who, in other contexts, talked to Borgen, and who, when the conversation was over, knew more about Philo than when the conversation began.

Philo of Alexandria

In 1974 Borgen got a two-page-long chronicle published in the major newspaper *Aftenposten* on "The Jewish Question in Alexandria in Roman Times."[31] Borgen described the conditions of the Jews in Alexandria in the first century CE, not least through the writings of Philo as a central source. However, both before and after that more popular article, Borgen published several scholarly articles and introductory review articles dealing with Philo's life and work in Alexandria. In the present context, our intention is not to describe his life and work in detail, nor to deal thoroughly with every item or issue commented on by Borgen, but to highlight some of the major issues and topics he dealt with in his studies.

His thorough review articles in three large and voluminous review volumes, two in 1984 and one in 1992, helped to present and consolidate his reputation and competence as a Philo scholar for a wide readership.[32] These works are still valuable as shorter introductions to Philo, his life, and his work. Borgen completed his introductory work concerning Philo with the publication of his book *Philo of Alexandria: An Exegete for His Time*, released in 1997.

Critical issues in Philo's Alexandria

There were great social tensions between the Jews and other groups in Alexandria in the early first century CE. This situation escalated and eventually ended in a revolt that can best be characterized as a pogrom (38–40 CE), which became decisive for the situation of the Jews in the city for a long time to come.[33]

---

31. Borgen, "Det jødiske spørsmål i Alexandria i romersk tid," *Aftenposten*, January 10, 1974, 4, and January 11, 1974, 4.

32. Borgen, "Philo of Alexandria" (CRINT II,2); Borgen, "Philo of Alexandria: Critical Issues" (ANRW II 21.1);, and Borgen, "Philo of Alexandria," (ABD 3).

33. See on this, Borgen, "Judaism in Alexandria," 1061–72.

Borgen formulates the following as his view on what was behind these conflicts in Alexandria:[34] It is likely that some of the Jews in Alexandria were satisfied with a status quo that allowed them to live in peace and granted them to follow their own laws. Others, on the other hand, wanted greater rights and more freedom, and thus opportunities to advance in society. Therefore, they also had to have a share in civil rights in the city. Some of the Jews in the city, Borgen emphasizes, also seem to have had eschatological expectations that the other nations would recognize the Law of Moses, and the Jews, God's own people, as the center of the world. Among these, Borgen further claims, there were two groups: one was willing to use power, even violence, to obtain the desired rights; the other believed that the Jews should conquer their surroundings by peaceful means, that is, by their religion, based on what they believed was their God-given law, the Law of Moses. Philo, he says, probably belonged to the latter.[35]

Philo is thus to be understood as one who exhorts his people to live in peace with their surroundings and conquer the culture by peaceful means by those Jews who obeyed the Law. Borgen also claims that Philo and his associates infiltrated the environments around the gymnasia in the city. But at the same time, Philo himself was a Torah-observant Jew and exhorted other Jews to maintain their Jewish identity so as not to be conquered by Greek culture. According to Borgen, some of Philo's writings can be understood as part of this strategy.[36]

But did Philo go too far in his "conquering" attitude toward the culture of Alexandria? Borgen believes that it was just on the brink of being too hard for Philo; he was in danger of being conquered by what he was trying to conquer. Borgen has here formed the eloquent expression "a conqueror, on the verge of being conquered."[37] When Philo claims, for example, that all that is good and great in the various philosophical schools of his day has—in fact—for a long time been found in the Jewish Scriptures, especially in the Law of Moses, it is an expression of his intention to conquer this culture. However, at the same time, he himself is so influenced by Greek philosophical ideas and terminology that one might ask if he is not stuck in what he wanted to conquer. Borgen's characterization of Philo has been characterized as "one that can hardly be bettered."[38]

34. Borgen, "Philo and the Jews in Alexandria,"; Borgen, "Philo of Alexandria. Critical Issues."

35. Concerning Borgen's view of Philo's eschatology, see Borgen, "'There Shall Come Forth a Man.'"

36. Borgen, "Philo of Alexandria. A Critical," 150–54.

37. Borgen, "Philo of Alexandria. A Critical," 150–54.

38. Runia, "Philo, Alexandrian and Jew," 16.

The introductory works published by Borgen in the early 1980s were followed up by several individual studies. In these he substantiates and expands the holistic view of Philo he presents in his review articles.[39]

Philo and the issue of Greek education

The issue of Greek education, as represented by the so-called encyclical paideia, seems to have been a burning issue in the life of Alexandria at the time of Philo.[40] Borgen commented on the issue in several articles up through the years. It began with his dissertation,[41] then he briefly commented on it in his introductory articles to Philo in the mid-1980s,[42] and then he described it in more detail in an article in 2001[43] and another as late as 2016.[44] It was apparently both the ways Philo argued, that is, how he interpreted Old Testament narratives to enlighten the issue of education, and the role of education in the Greco-Roman Alexandria that aroused the interest of Borgen.

Philo deals with this education, the encyclical paideia, in several of his works, especially in his *On Mating with the Preliminary Studies*.[45] The primary Old Testament text in this work is from Genesis 16, on Abraham, Sarah, and Hagar. Philo interprets Hagar to represent lower education, supposed to lead to virtue, admittedly a lower kind of virtue; Sarah represents the higher leading to wisdom, which to Philo is found in the Jewish Torah. Hence to Philo, encyclical education has a preparatory and subordinate role; the wisdom of the Jewish Torah is higher and is taught in the synagogues: "The basic difference between these two schools, according to Philo, is that the encyclia uses human teaching as its basis, whereas the philosophy of the laws of Moses studied in the synagogues has its basis in self-taught wisdom brought forth by nature itself."[46] This is one important emphasis in Philo's works and hence in Borgen's expositions.

---

39. See the appendix at the end of this volume.

40. As an introduction to classical education in Alexandria at the time of Philo, I might refer to Koskenniemi, "Philo and Classical Education," 102–28; and Mendelson, *Secular Education in Philo*.

41. *Bread from Heaven*, 100–127.

42. Borgen, "Philo of Alexandria," 254–56; Borgen, "Philo of Alexandria: A Critical," 115–17.

43. Borgen, "Greek Encyclical Education," 61–71.

44. Borgen, "Alternative Aims," 257–71.

45. Latin title: *De Congressu Quaerendae Eruditionis Gratia*.

46. Borgen, "Greek Encyclical Education," 67.

Secondly, Borgen emphasizes the problem of this Greek education for the Torah-observing Jews in Alexandria. On the one side is the *context* of this education, that is, the gymnasia. On the other side is the role this education played in the struggle for *social advancement* in Alexandria.[47] Philo also emphasized the danger of this education; he realized its social role but criticized those Jews who enrolled in this lower education for social profit: "all elementary lessons, for example, and what is called school-learning and philosophy itself when pursued with no motive higher than parading their superiority, or from desire of an office under our rulers." To Philo, education was for "the beautiful alone, not for the sake of something else" (*Leg. All.* 3.167). Education was essential in order to be able to climb the social ladder, but Philo warned of the dangers inherent in such behavior because it might lead to apostasy.

Philo as an exegete

Philo has been given several designations, including "'theologian,'" "philosopher," and "politician." Borgen's primary designation and characteristic is that he is an "exegete"—an interpreter. Borgen's book from 1997 demonstrates this most clearly: *Philo of Alexandria: An Exegete for His Time*.[48] But Philo was in his thinking and writings strongly influenced by religious, philosophical, and political currents in Alexandria. Not least, he was influenced by different philosophical currents such as Platonism, Stoicism, and Pythagoreanism, as well as different currents within Judaism. However, through his writings, Philo would serve the interests of the Jews in the Diaspora. Several of his writings contain much allegorical exegesis, although he maintains the literal meaning as the basic one (*Migr.* 89–93). He interprets the Law of Moses and uses "stoic, Platonic and Pythagorean thoughts to help readers live a holy life according to the divine principles," according to Borgen.[49]

However, was Philo himself a systematic philosopher and theologian, or was he an eclectic who chose or rejected according to what suited him? Some have suggested that he was an independent systematic scholar; others argue that he picked so much from other sources that he was neither

---

47. In 1982, Mendelson (*Secular Education*, 45) described Borgen as "perhaps the only contemporary scholar to consider the problem of miseducation in Philo." Mendelson, however, modifies Borgen's view a little as he emphasizes that Philo did not see virtue as the only goal of education, but tries to keep "a balance between the active and the contemplative life."

48. See also Borgen's latest book, *Illuminations by Philo*.

49. Borgen, "Philo of Alexandria," 152.

systematic nor particularly original. Borgen discusses this in a smaller article[50] and finds that although he is not a systematic philosopher, characterized by a strict scheme or form, he is also not one who simply picks flowers from others. He is a reader and interpreter of the Jews' holy law—their Torah—and in his interpretations, he uses both traditions from the fathers and current ideas from his contemporaries. It is, after all, not difficult to find that Philo the Jew is also influenced by non-Jewish philosophical thoughts, but he uses the worldviews of his contemporary world in his interpretations of the Jewish texts. That Philo uses different traditions in his writings, and that he often weaves these together in his texts, is now a general perception in Philonic research. Philo himself also states that this is exactly what he does; he relates to traditions and uses them: he will "tell the story of Moses as I have learned it, both from the sacred books . . . and from some of the elders of the nation; for I always interwove what I was told with what I read . . ." (*De vita Mosis* 1.4). Thus, his texts become new texts that are woven texts; they contain subtexts from various sources.[51]

Philo is thus to be considered as a scholar in dialogue with other interpreters in his interpretations. That he is working in dialogue with his cultural contemporaries Borgen perhaps shows most clearly in an article on "The Crossing of the Red Sea as Interpreted by Philo," with the subtitle "Biblical Event–Liturgical Model–Cultural Application."[52] Here he takes a closer look at how Philo interprets the texts about Israel crossing the Red Sea on its way from Egypt to Canaan (Exodus 13:17—15:21). Borgen argues here that Philo can interpret one and the same text on two, sometimes even three, different levels: the text has a specific and concrete level; it has a level where it is about cosmic and general principles; and it has a "divine level," a level where it concerns "the divine realm of the beyond." In this way, Philo emphasizes that the old texts (here Exodus) do not only talk about historical events, but they are about universal and cosmic principles, and they shed light on the situation of the Jews in Alexandria, and they can be applied to their current cultural situation. Philo is thus not just an exegete when he interprets specific texts and themes from the books of Exodus; Borgen strongly claims that he also applies principles from these writings when interpreting current historical events in his time, so one can say that Philo

50. Borgen, "Philo of Alexandria—a Systematic Philosopher?," 115–34.

51. This perception was central to Borgen's Norwegian doctoral dissertation (*Bread from Heaven*) with regard to both Philo's works and John 6, but is also central in several of his studies from the 1990s: "Crossing of the Red Sea," "Two Philonic Prayers," "Man's Sovereignty," "Some Hebrew and Pagan Features," and "Moses, Jesus, and the Roman Emperor."

52. Borgen, "Crossing of the Red Sea."

here applies principles from the Scriptures in a similar way as what we can find in his exegetical writings.[53]

Again, we see Borgen's interest in Philo's exegesis and the role it might play in the social world of Philo. This is an emphasis that is central in his *Bread from Heaven*,[54] and it followed him in his later career.

Borgen's interpretation of Philo has garnered great acclaim. Philo moved within different cultural currents of his times but was always an exegete and a Torah-observant Jew: an exegete for his times.[55] Some may even think that Philo and Peder Borgen are to some extent comparable.

More on Philo and early Christianity

Studies of Philo of Alexandria have been proved useful not only in understanding theological ideas and interpretations of the Old and New Testaments but also in the work of clarifying the social situation of the early Christians in their local communities, and Mediterranean cultures in general, in the world that we are used to calling the "western Diaspora." In several smaller studies, Borgen has discussed the situation of the early Christians both socially and theologically in light of, among other things, Philo's writings.

One of the major problems for the Jewish groups was how to preserve their Jewish identity in such a multicultural society. For the Christians, it was also a question of identity, as it was important to establish a Christian identity both in relation to the Jewish groups and to the Greco-Roman culture in general.

Borgen strongly emphasizes that the Christians formed their identity in close contact with Jewish communities. He illustrates this by shedding light on some subthemes, such as the transition from the Gentile to the Jewish faith, the question of the meaning and value of circumcision,[56] and finally, the problems of possible participation in pagan contexts associated with sacrifices and worship.[57]

---

53. See Borgen, "Application and Commitment"; Borgen, "Philo's *Against Flaccus*"; and Borgen, *Philo of Alexandria: An Exegete*, 149–53.

54. Cf. *Bread from Heaven*, 99–111.

55. For a further description of Philo as an exegete, readers should also consult Borgen, "Philo of Alexandria as an Exegete," 114–43, reprinted as "Philo—An Interpreter of the Laws of Moses," in Seland, ed., *Reading Philo*, 75–101; and above all, his book on Philo, *Philo of Alexandria: An Exegete*.

56. Borgen, "Catalogue of Vices"; Borgen, *Paul Preaches Circumcision*, 15–42.

57. See Borgen, "Early Church and the Hellenistic Synagogue"; Borgen, "Yes, No, How Far?"; Borgen, "Proselytes, Conquest and Mission."

What kind of relations between Philo and the Gospel of John?

To many of Borgen's colleagues at home and abroad, Borgen is probably best known as a student of the Gospel of John, then of Philo. And that is quite understandable as it was his Norwegian doctoral dissertation on John and Philo that really made him known among New Testament scholars in the mid-1960s. Furthermore, Borgen continued to publish studies on John and Philo throughout his career. The last of these was published as late as in 2003, but several other studies followed on other New Testament issues. In addition, he has also produced several other studies of the Gospel of John where he does not use much material from Philo but sheds light on other aspects of the Gospel of John, such as its relationship to the Synoptic Gospels, or its value as a source of the historical Jesus.[58]

Borgen does not think there is any direct dependency between John and Philo. The question is rather whether any of his traditions are influenced by Philo, his writings, or his ideas. These questions are still up for debate. Hence, most scholars are reluctant to draw firm and unambiguous conclusions; the sources hardly provide a basis for such solutions. In addition, although there are no direct relations between John, his traditions, and various other traditions in vogue in the Jewish Diaspora, synagogues may have been bridgeheads for many and diverse currents and traditions, including influence from Philonic thought. Consequently, although we cannot claim direct connections between Philo and the Gospel of John, or between any other New Testament writings in general, we can still talk about the influence of environments where different ideas and traditions were preserved, further processed, and developed. Furthermore, Borgen would argue that this was the case where the traditions of the Gospel of John were transmitted, and sometimes also in traditions found in the letters of Paul. Borgen argues that he finds patterns or trajectories that might illustrate and help one to understand the texts of John. This latter aspect is a feature we know from his doctoral dissertation, and he also participated further over the years in the debate about John 6.[59]

Borgen's latest book on John, published as late as 2014, is in many ways a summary of his research in the Gospel of John and Philo. The book contains a total of fifteen articles, most published earlier, but now with an introduction and summary at the end. The main title of the book is: *The Gospel*

---

58. See my description given above.

59. Borgen, "John 6"; Borgen, "John's Use of the Old Testament"; and Borgen, "Some Jewish Exegetical Traditions." See also Culpepper, ed., *Critical Readings of John 6*, which is a collection of papers presented at the Johannine Writings Seminar of the SNTS between 1991 and 1993, including Borgen, "John 6."

of John: More Light from Philo, Paul and Archeology; with the subtitle: *The Scriptures, Tradition, Exposition, Settings, Meaning*. The last words function as catchwords because it is about the fact that the Scriptures had a history; they were themselves the result of development and had a history of interpretation. They had come into being via oral traditions, originated in them, and lived with them. The themes from his doctoral dissertation in 1966 were always present in Borgen's research; various topics that he touched on in the dissertation were later expanded and developed, and he eventually included both the three Synoptic Gospels and Paul to illuminate methods and distinctive features of the interpretive practices of the first century.

Philo and the Letter to the Galatians

In the 1980s, he published a couple of studies[60] on the debate Paul carried out in his Letter to the Galatians about an accusation that he was still preaching circumcision (Galatians 5:11).[61]

Galatians 5:11 is an enigma within the letter: "But my friends, why am I still being persecuted if I am still preaching circumcision? In that case, the offense of the cross has been removed" (NRSV). How is this to be interpreted? Did Paul, in fact, preach circumcision (to Jews or Gentiles) after his call? Or does he simply refer to something else? Borgen poses the question somewhat differently: "Does Paul in the context reiterate ideas from his missionary preaching in Galatia, ideas which the opponents have misunderstood and misused in support for their circumcision campaign?"[62] In trying to understand how they could claim that he was still preaching circumcision, Borgen again—not surprisingly—turns to Philo.

The passages from Philo he draws on are especially *De Migratione Abrahami* 86–93 and *Quaestiones in Exodum* II:2. In the first, Philo states that there are some Jews stressing the symbolic value of the laws while Philo argues that they should give careful attention to both aims. He agrees, however, that "receiving circumcision does indeed portray the excision of pleasure and all passions," but that one should nevertheless not ignore the "outward observances." Likewise, in *QE* II.2, Philo says that a proselyte "is

---

60. Borgen, "Nomisme and libertinisme i Paulus' brev til galaterne"; Borgen, "Observations on the Theme 'Paul and Philo,'" (1980; reprinted in Borgen, *Paul Preaches Circumcision*, 15–32; and in Borgen, *Philo, John and Paul*, 233–54); and Borgen, "Paul Preaches Circumcision." I here use his original article from 1980.

61. In the 2000s, he published several more studies of Paul's Letter to the Galatians, but now with a focus on the interpretation of Jesus' crucifixion. These studies will be dealt with in the next chapter.

62. Borgen, "Observations on the Theme 'Paul and Philo,'" 89.

one who circumcises not his uncircumcision but his desires and sensual pleasures and the other passions of the soul." Borgen's interpretation runs thus: "Philo's understanding was thus that bodily circumcision was not the requirement for entering the Jewish community, but was one of the commandments they had to obey upon receiving status as a Jew."[63] Hence a symbolic understanding of circumcision was coupled with faithful physical observance of the rite in some Jewish circles.

Borgen then uses this understanding when reading Galatians 5:11—6:13. He finds that Galatians 3:3 supports the view that the observance of the bodily circumcision should follow and complete the ethical circumcision, but argues that in Paul's view, the completion of the ethical circumcision was not the physical circumcision as his opponents said, but the believer's crucifixion with Christ:

> When Paul preached that the heathen Galatians should depart from the desires of the flesh and enter the society of those who serve and love each other, then his opponents claimed that this was the ethical meaning of circumcision. Paul still preached circumcision, and their task was to persuade the Galatians to make bodily circumcision follow upon their ethical circumcision . . . Paul objected to this misunderstanding and misuse of his missionary preaching to the Galatians.[64]

Hence Borgen interpreted the disagreements between Paul and his opponents in light of Philo's discussions of ethical and bodily circumcision; Paul agreed that circumcision was to be interpreted in a symbolic way, but not that it was to be followed by a bodily circumcision; it was to be followed by their "crucifixion with Christ." Whether this means baptism (Romans 6:6) Borgen does not state. To Paul, according to Borgen, it meant "the new life in the community of service and love under the power of the Spirit (Gal 5:18) . . . it was a life in accordance with the Law of Christ (Gal 6:2)."[65]

---

63. Borgen, "Observations," 88.

64. Borgen, "Observations," 88.

65. Borgen, "Observations," 89. Whatever imaginative or inventive one might think Borgen's interpretation here is, it looks like it has not won support in the subsequent exegesis of Galatians 5:11. See, e.g., Martyn, who in his commentary (Martyn, *Galatians*, 476, note 30) mentions Borgen's view, but does not discuss it; Longenecker does not mention it at all (Longenecker, *Galatians*, ad loc.). Barclay (Barclay, "Paul and Philo on Circumcision," 73) calls it "unconvincing." In two more recent discussions of Galatians 5:11a, it is mentioned but not discussed at all: Campbell ("Galatians 5.11,") calls it "brilliant, but unhelpful," and Hardin ("If I Still Proclaim Circumcision," 145–63), characterizes it as "a unique example of mirror reading" (154, note 31) but does not discuss or use it.

The focus presented above is also applied by Borgen in his attempt to understand the so-called apostolic decree of Acts 15 in a study labeled the "Catalogues of Vices, the Apostolic Decree, and the Jerusalem Meeting."[66] In the six first pages of this study, Borgen repeats the main features of his understanding of Galatians 5:11 and 1:10; that is, his understanding that there were a perception in vogue that circumcision had both an ethical and a physical aspect, and that Paul was understood by some to teach ethical circumcision, and they thus expected him to follow this up by teaching the physical part.[67] Paul was, in fact, according to Borgen, drawing on Jewish proselyte traditions in which catalogues of pagan vices and physical circumcision were an integral part. Hence Borgen asks: how did Paul cope with the traditions that Gentiles had to undergo physical circumcision?[68] Borgen proceeds to Acts 15 on the premises that Paul's Letter to the Galatians may throw new light on the decree of Acts 15, and he argues that the so-called apostolic decree is not a specific decree, "but the list of vices in these verses is to be ranked together with other catalogues of vices, especially those which characterize the pagan way of life."[69] Such catalogues, he argues, were part of missionary preaching and teaching, and it was decided at the Jerusalem meeting that such preaching should continue without requiring physical circumcision. Hence, he concludes his discussion thus: ". . . there were no apostolic decree decided upon at the Jerusalem meeting. In the Christian employment of Jewish proselyte traditions exemplified at the meeting by a catalogue against pagan vices . . . the requirement of physical circumcision was taken out, and thus the gentile converts were not required to become Jews and citizens of the Jewish nation."[70]

Philo and the book of Revelation

Not many scholars in recent times have attempted to shed light on the Revelation of John with the help of Philo's writings. A bibliographical review of Philo-related studies covering the period 1987–2006[71] shows that during

66. Borgen, "Catalogues of Vices," 126–41, first published in 1988, then reprinted in Borgen, *Early Christianity*, 233–51.

67. Cf. Borgen, "Catalogues of Vices," 128: "When Gal. 5:11 and 1:10 are seen together, they give clues to the way the Judaizers claimed that Paul represented their own cause. They claimed that Paul continued . . . to preach and practice circumcision after he received his call."

68. Borgen, "Catalogues of Vices," 131.

69. Borgen, "Catalogues of Vices," 135.

70. Borgen, "Catalogues of Vices," 139.

71. See Runia, *Philo of Alexandria: An Annotated Bibliography 1987–1996*; and

this period, only seven studies were published that refer to the Revelation of John; of these, only two are directly concerned with a more detailed discussion of texts from the Revelation, and one of these is written by Borgen's student Kåre Fuglseth.[72] Unfortunately, four studies of Borgen from 1996 have not been included in this bibliography.[73]

When he became a senior researcher (1993), the plan was to write a large commentary on the Revelation of John, and he worked on this for some years. He published a few articles on the book of Revelation,[74] but it seems that he gave up working on the actual commentary in the mid-1990s. No further articles were to come from his hands after 1996 dealing with the last book of the Bible.

Borgen's first article on a topic from the Revelation of John is about "Polemic in the Book of Revelation." In Revelation 2:9 and 3:9, a couple of statements can be interpreted as being strongly anti-Jewish. The term "synagogue of Satan" is used as follows: "I also know that you are mocked by those who call themselves Jews but are not. For they are the synagogue of Satan" (2:9). Borgen takes his point of departure in these verses, asking in an article from 1993 how they are to be understood.[75]

Borgen only touches upon the works of Philo in this article but uses him more directly in articles published in 1996. Here he takes his starting point in an article from 1993 about "Heavenly Ascent in Philo,"[76] and discusses the topic "ascension to heaven" further in two other articles.[77] In the Revelation of John, it appears that John is taken up to heaven already in 4:1, and that the subsequent visions are seen and described with this as a starting point. Here Borgen can relate to several descriptions in Philo's works because he too could mention such "ascents," yes, Philo could even mention such an "ascension" he himself had had, but he was dragged down again in this world by politics and other needs that called for his efforts (*Spec. leg.* 3). Philo, however, lacks the apocalyptic scenes described in the

---

Runia, *Philo of Alexandria: An Annotated Bibliography 1997–2006*.

72. Fuglseth, "Satan's Synagoge."

73. Borgen, "Heavenly Ascent in Philo"; Borgen, "Moses, Jesus, and the Roman Emperor"; Borgen, "Emperor Worship and Persecution"; Borgen, "Illegitimate Invasion." These studies are now accessible in Borgen, *Illuminations by Philo* (2021).

74. Borgen, *Illuminations by Philo*, 235–310.

75. Borgen, "Polemic in the Book of Revelation"; republished in Borgen, *Early Christianity*, 275–291, and in Borgen, *Illuminations by Philo*, 261–76.

76. Republished in Borgen, *Illuminations by Philo*, 211–34.

77. Borgen, "Illegitimate Invasion" and "Autobiographical Ascent Reports"; both republished in *Early Christianity*, 293–307 and 309–20, and in *Illuminations by Philo*, 235–48 and 249–60.

Revelation of John. Nevertheless, Borgen still finds similarities that allow a study of such texts in Philo in order to shed light on similar features in the Book of Revelation. The following features might be mentioned here: Both Philo and John the Seer ascend to the higher heavenly realms via an "inspiration"; from the higher spheres, they gain new perspectives on what is happening/will happen on earth: Philo gains greater insight into the Law of Moses, while John, in turn, gains insight into "what is to come hereafter" (4:1). Here are both parallels and differences, and each in its own way sheds light on how Philo can be used to clarify features in the Revelation of John.

Some social issues and mission

Under this headline I gather eight studies that, in various degrees, deal with social issues and/or mission. They are all published within the years 1983 to 2000.

"The Early Church and the Hellenistic Synagogue"

In 1982 Borgen read a paper at a Nordic New Testament conference in Oslo on "The Early Church and the Hellenistic Synagogue."[78] The lecture deals with several subtopics known from other works of Borgen, of which some are dealt with above. The article deals with different problems for the Jewish Hellenistic synagogues, and for the Hellenistic synagogue and the early church. As part of his introduction, Borgen deals briefly with the older dichotomy of Palestinian and Hellenistic Judaism and/or a Palestinian Jewish church and a Hellenistic Gentile church. He rejects the old dichotomy, but nevertheless finds the term "Hellenistic" useful in signifying that "The Hellenistic synagogue means the synagogal communities in the Graeco-Roman world, where Greek is used as the main language. These communities are minority groups in a non-Jewish environment."[79] Hence the "early church" is not limited to the Jerusalem church but denotes the early church from its beginning and to the turn of the century, both in the land of Israel and in the Diaspora.

His central thesis is described thus: "The early church draws on traditions, debates and practices from Jewish proselytism, modifies them, and makes them serve a different kind of community structure. Consequently,

---

78. The study was first published in the Nordic journal *Studia Theologica* 37 (1983) 55-78; then reprinted in his book *Paul Preaches Circumcision*, 75-97; and in Borgen, *Philo, John and Paul*, 207-32.

79. Borgen, "Early Church," 55.

the Christian "proselytes" did not leave their national and ethnic society to join the Jewish nation and ethnic community."[80] Furthermore, as he finds tensions and variations within the Hellenistic synagogues, he postulates that "debates and conflicts within each Jewish community were even more crucial than the differences between Palestinian Judaism and Hellenistic Judaism."[81]

Borgen then sketches nine different fields of controversy, some of which we will know from other works mentioned or presented earlier in this volume.

First, he discusses "Conversion from paganism to synagogue/church." A central question here is if the early church's missionary preaching had its background in traditions related to Jewish proselytism. He finds a pattern of contrast (then/now) in the Christian preaching and argues that this pattern is Christianized versions of Jewish traditions related to the conversion of Gentiles to Judaism. In his expositions he draws extensively on traditions in Philo's works, but also on other Jewish literature. With regard to main themes in these traditions, he finds that the following themes are central: the transition from many gods to the one God, from other peoples to the people of God, and from pagan immorality to Jewish/Christian moral life.[82]

Then he draws on "Love of neighbour. The Golden Rule," and finds that these "commandments" were applied in both Jewish and Christian proselyte traditions.[83] Then he also applies material from his earlier discussion of the role of circumcision of the body and circumcision of the heart.[84]

Tensions were produced when some Jews wanted to deviate from the accepted rules and laws. In some cases, the relationship between the Hellenistic synagogue and the early Christian groups might take the form of various degrees of persecution. To Borgen, "These conflicts, however, should be seen as intramural controversies within the Jewish communities, in which Paul and other Christians were regarded as threats to institutional stability."[85]

In their struggle for establishing or upholding their specific identities, both Jewish and Christian communities had to consider adequate ways of relating to their pagan surroundings. Borgen finally provides a brief sketch

---

80. Borgen, "Early Church," 56.
81. Borgen, "Early Church," 57.
82. Borgen, "Early Church," 60.
83. Borgen, "Early Church," 62–64.
84. Borgen, "Early Church," 64–71; cf. his articles on Paul and circumcision, reprinted in his books *Paul Preaches Circumcision* and *Philo, John and Paul*.
85. Borgen, "Early Church," 71–72.

of the problem of participation in pagan sacrificial cults[86] by succinctly presenting some material from Josephus, Philo, rabbinic literature, and the Revelation of John and 1 Corinthians 8–10.

All in all, the early church emerged within the context of Hellenistic synagogal communities. Borgen summarizes in these articles much of his previous research, arguing the need for understanding the early Christian communities in light of comparable phenomena within the Jewish communities. Here studies of traditions, debates, and practices in Hellenistic Jewish communities are relevant for understanding the social world of the early Christians.

Proselytism and mission[87]

One set of examples in which traditions, debates, and practices played a role in both Jewish and Christian contexts is in the arena of proselytism and mission. Borgen dealt explicitly with these issues in three articles[88] in the 1990s, but some of the relevant issues are also dealt with in other related studies.[89]

The issues of Jewish proselytism and mission have been much discussed, and the question of active "mission" or proselytism is often answered negatively.[90] Much depends, however, on how one defines "proselytism" and "mission." In the following, I briefly present how Borgen dealt with these issues in his contribution at a symposium in Trondheim in 1992 on "Recruitment, Conquest, and Conflict in Judaism, Early Christianity, and the Greco-Roman World."[91]

There is no doubt that there were times in the history of Israel when proselytism by force was conducted. Borgen labels it "militant proselytism" or "mission by the sword," and in reviewing the evidence[92] he lists, i.a., the

---

86. Borgen, "Early Church," 72–74. See also Borgen, "Yes, No, How Far?," 30–59, originally published in 1994, then reprinted in Borgen, *Early Christianity*, 15–43.

87. Borgen, "Militant proselyttisme," 9–26; Borgen, "Militant and Peaceful Proselytism," 45–69; Borgen, "Proselytes, Conquest, and Mission," 57–77.

88. See Borgen, "Militant proselyttisme," 9–26; Borgen, "Militant and Peaceful Proselytism," 45–69; and Borgen, "Proselytes, Conquest, and Mission," 57–97

89. Cf. Borgen, "'There Shall Come Forth a Man,'" 341–61.

90. Cf. McKnight, *Light Among the Gentiles*, Bird, *Crossing Over Sea*. See, however, Feldman, *Jew & Gentile*, 288–382.

91. Borgen's study was published in 1998, labeled "Proselytes, Conquest, and Mission," in a volume containing contributions from both a conference in 1991 in Atlanta, Georgia, and in Trondheim, 1992, both dealing with the topic mentioned above.

92. Borgen, "Militant proselyttisme," 10–18; Borgen, "Militant and Peaceful Proselytism," 46–56. For criticism, see Bird, *Crossing Over Sea*, 55–61.

policy of Hyrcanus towards the Idumaeans (*Ant.* 13:257–258), and Aristobulus (104–103 BCE) against the Itureans (*Ant.* 13:319). Other texts are used as evidence for proselytism from fear (Esther, Judith).

Perhaps surprisingly to some, Borgen applies categories from issues of militant proselytism in Israel as background traditions for understanding Christian mission/proselytism. On the one hand, he finds the verb *anangkazo* (to force) used in some Christian texts dealing with circumcision (Galatians 2:2; 6:12); on the other hand, he says that "Christian mission in the New Testament is rooted in Jewish ideas and methods of proselytism, but they are recast on the basis of the motif of eschatology and conquest."[93] Hence Borgen summarizes his view thus:

> The sources demonstrate that some gentiles became proselytes because of attraction. In other cases, Jews actively presented their religion in gentile circles and even at times used military force to bring people into the Jewish religion. These various approaches were applied both to individuals as well as to collective groups; they were at work both in the past and present history, and they were also part of the future eschatological scenarios. Although the Christian mission did have some distinctive features, its matrix was the Jewish notions of proselytism, eschatology, and conquest.[94]

Borgen substantiates his thesis by analyzing sections of Philo's writings and material from the New Testament. Analyzing the material in Philo concerning proselytes who became Jews, he finds that the conversion of Gentiles to Judaism contains three aspects:[95] 1. *religious conversion*: a change from worshipping the many to worship the one God (see *Virt.* 102–104); 2. *ethical conversion*: change from a pagan way of life to a Jewish virtuous life (see *Virt.* 181–182): 3. *social conversion*: leaving one's family, country, and customs (see *Virt.* 102–104). These passages deal primarily with individuals, but Philo also cherishes the hope that all nations will accept the Jewish laws, or as one might phrase it, based on *De vita Moses* 2:43–4, that all nations will become Jewish proselytes. But this is a future hope, that is, part of Philo's eschatology.[96]

---

93. Borgen, "Proselytes, Conquest," 69; Borgen, "Militant and Peaceful," 59: "the military motif has been transformed by the methods of recruitment by peaceful means." Cf. 61: "The most elaborate use of ideas from militant messianism is found in the Book of Revelation."

94. Borgen, "Proselytes, Conquest," 58

95. Borgen, "Proselytes, Conquest," 63–64

96. Borgen deals with Philo's eschatology in Borgen, "'There Shall Come Forth a Man,'" 341–61, reprinted in Borgen, *Illuminations*, 105–27. For a summary, see Borgen,

Considering Christian proselytism, Borgen finds that Philo's ideas about proselytism offer "a strikingly adequate background with the threefold understanding of conversion."[97] Accordingly, in the Christian mission too, conversion consisted of religious, ethical, and social aspects and issues. The best example of how "mission" terminology is drawn from a Jewish context, especially with regard to social conversion, Borgen finds in Ephesians 2:11–22. However, there are also significant changes: "the Jewish idea of the people of God has been reshaped to mean the church of Christ into which both gentiles and Jews are to enter."[98] Hence, he can say that the Jewish idea of bringing proselytes into the Jewish nation has been changed to bringing the converts into a "cross-national community of Jews and gentiles."[99]

The question may arise how this is to be understood in light of a continuing Jewish nation and religion. However, as far as I can see, Borgen never deals with the question of how his ecclesiology relates to the question of supersessionism; the church as such is "cross-national," built upon the foundation of the apostles and prophets, Christ himself being the "cornerstone" (see Ephesians 2), but also that "Christian missionary preaching and teaching . . . clearly use Jewish traditions about the conversion of proselytes."[100] In his Bible lesson at Soltun Folkehøyskole in October 1993,[101] he even draws on Philo and his categories in profiling a theology of mission in a Norwegian context.[102] The issue of supersessionism is not present in his conception. His work paradigm is focused on expounding on how Christian exegesis and theology are influenced by Jewish traditions, debates, and practices.

Outlook

It is, admittedly, primarily as a Johannine and a Philo scholar that Borgen has made himself widely known; his work on Paul and the Revelation of John is undoubtedly less well known, nor has it had as significant impact as his studies of John and Philo. There might be several reasons for this;

"Proselytes, Conquest," 65–68.

97. Borgen, "Proselytes, Conquest," 69.

98. Borgen, "Proselytes, Conquest," 70.

99. Borgen, "Proselytes, Conquest," 70. A "cross-national community" is one of Borgen's favorite ecclesiological characterizations of the church; see, for example, Borgen, "Cross-National Church," 225–48; Borgen, "Jesus Christ, the Reception," 220–35; Borgen, "Metodistkirken, en tverrnasjonal Kirke," 28–38.

100. Borgen, "Proselytes, Conquest," 71.

101. See in chapter 13 above.

102. See Borgen, "Misjon i nytestamentlig tid," 27–41.

first, Borgen's doctoral dissertation on *Bread from Heaven* was clearly a groundbreaking work that attracted extensive attention when it was published and is still often consulted by students of John 6. Second, very many of his articles in the other fields, such as the epistles of Paul and the Revelation of John were published in so-called Festschriften or other collections of articles, and these often tend not to be as well known as contributions published in reputable journals or monograph series. Nor do the articles on Paul amount to many in view of his total production.

Another factor that may also have played a role in this regard is that in the late 1980s and beyond, New Testament research became strongly influenced by several new research perspectives and methods that Borgen did not indulge himself in nor address in his works. These include social science (sociological and social anthropological) perspectives that partly continued, and partly replaced aspects of the form-critical perspectives. However, the new methods also included text-immanent perspectives from classical rhetoric and other newer literary methods and views, such as, for example, reader-response perspectives. In addition, not a few adopted critical approaches from various other fields, such as feminist-critical readings to political perspectives, as we find them in postcolonial studies.[103] Borgen's interest was in the more textual studies in the form of studies of exegetical patterns and models and was considered by some at the end of the millennium to be somewhat traditional. He was aware of this description, and it influenced the assessment he was given when applying for a professorship at the Faculty of Theology in Oslo as early as 1984.[104] However, he found himself comfortable having found his niche and continued his studies along the lines he had applied in his *Bread from Heaven*. That is not to say there was no development in his views and interests over the years, but there were only minor changes in perspectives and methods.

In a later section in the next and final chapter, we shall comment briefly on the works he published after moving to Lillestrøm for his retirement in 1999.

---

103. For a brief review of some of these issues, see Moxnes, *Short History of the New Testament*, 159–206.

104. Cf. chapter 10 above.

15

Returning Home: Back to Lillestrøm

EARLY IN 1999: INGER and Peder Borgen were packing, and packing. Shelves upon shelves with books were put in boxes—together with everything else they wanted to bring with them of what they had collected over the years. They were to move to Lillestrøm. Back to Lillestrøm, the town of Peder's two first decades.

Peder did what his old friend Philo never did; he returned from the diaspora to his hometown. Not to Jerusalem, but to Lillestrøm. They were returning home. Back to his roots.

Peder had turned seventy the year before and had already been retired for a few years. Inger turned sixty-three in the autumn after they settled down in Lillestrøm and was working in Trondheim until they left. Well established in Lillestrøm, she worked as a family therapist at the Family Welfare Office for a few more years.

It was, in many ways, natural for them to move to Lillestrøm. They had no close family anymore in Trondheim.[1] Their daughters, Heidi and Ingunn, had long since left; they had married and established their own homes in southeastern Norway. Inger's family did not live in the Trondheim

---

1. Times had changed at the university too. In Norway, in contrast to what is the case in some other countries, working people must retire at sixty-seven, or at the latest seventy. During the 1990s several of Borgen's colleagues retired too, and the department changed its character. Not only new colleagues, but also the profile of the department changed, due to new expectations and needs. Borgen sometimes lamented that situation. He was experiencing the same development as Luke T. Johnson describes thus: "... 'the world leaves us before we leave the world,' and it certainly applies to aging academics." Johnson, *Mind in Another Place*, 173.

area either. On the other hand, all of Peder's siblings lived in Lillestrøm/Skedsmo; only he was missing there in the sibling group of four. They arrived in Lillestrøm at the end of May.

LIFE IN FAMILY AND CHURCH

Inger and Peder had lived in Lillestrøm for six months as newlyweds before they traveled to the USA. Moreover, they returned there when Peder was on sick leave in 1966–67. But beyond that, they had had their home in Washington, Bergen, and Trondheim. Now Peder's eldest brother, Ole E., and his wife, Martha, had moved back to Lillestrøm, and Peder and Inger moved there too. Ole had resigned as bishop in the Methodist Church in 1989. He then worked as a professor in systematic theology at a Methodist seminary in the USA (Asbury Seminary) until 1992. Then they returned to Lillestrøm. The youngest brother, Arne, now also lived in Lillestrøm. Arne worked in a bank and eventually established himself as a skilled icon painter. Their sister, Ester, married to Asbjørn Voldhuset, had taken over the childhood home and the farm Solhaug and lived there. Thus, the sibling group was fully present again in the Lillestrøm/Skedsmo area.

Peder was perhaps closest to his brother Ole. Both had studied in the United States; both were educated as pastors, and had worked as such. Both had earned a doctorate in the United States; Ole in systematic theology on a study of the sacraments, Peder with his New Testament dissertation on Luke. Furthermore, all four siblings were members of the Methodist church in Lillestrøm and thus shared both congregational and family fellowships.[2]

But there were also new family members. Inger and Peder's eldest daughter eventually lived in the Lillestrøm area with her family, the other in Oslo. And grandchildren and great-grandchildren came along, and with them an extended family life in which they got to know new persons, each with their own characteristics. Inger and Peder like to have their family around them and with them. Birthdays and other anniversaries are duly celebrated, some in a smaller format, others in a larger one, as it is natural and otherwise convenient. In 2011, when Inger and Peder had their golden wedding anniversary, they took the whole family—a group of fourteen people—on a trip to Israel. In 2017, the year Inger turned eighty, the same

---

2. Peder and his eldest brother, Ole, spent ten years together in Lillestrøm; then Ole died, after a long illness, in March 2009. Peder's sister, Ester, died in 2010, and her husband Asbjørn Voldhuset died four years later. The youngest person in the sibling group, Arne (b. 1933), lived for many years in Lillestrøm, but is now living in Oslo. He lost his wife, Valborg (b. 1928), abruptly in 2013.

extended family went to Trondheim for the grandchildren to experience and the children to reexperience the places where Inger and Peder had lived for twenty-five years. In 2018, when Peder turned ninety, both daughters traveled with Inger and Peder to Athens so that Peder could participate one more time at the General Meeting of Studiorum Novi Testamenti Societas (SNTS), his favorite scholarly New Testament society.

Inger is about ten years younger than Peder, so in November 2007 they merged her seventieth and his eightieth birthday celebrations and celebrated one hundred fifty years with a large party at Losby estate.

Inger and Peder's various other anniversaries have, of course, also been duly celebrated, but Peder's eighty-fifth birthday in 2013 was still something special. It was marked on January 26 with an exhibition in the Skedsmo library, Strømmen, with pictures and books from his life. The organizers were the Skedsmo municipality and Skedsmo library. The mayor opened the exhibition, and the jubilee himself held a lecture in the library on "eighty-five years and an eventful life in a challenging time." Then there was a party with invited guests.

Both Inger and Peder became active members of the local Methodist church. In September 1999, Lillestrøm Methodist Church celebrated its one-hundredth anniversary in September. Ole E. Borgen prepared the small booklet that was published for this occasion. In the program for the celebration, we can see that Ole E. participated in the anniversary service as conductor of the congregational choir; in the afternoon, Peder Borgen delivered the keynote speech at the festive anniversary dinner.

However, as in so many other congregations at this time, the Lillestrøm Methodist congregation also faced a decline in attendance. At the anniversary, the scout work and a small Sunday school were the only organized child and youth work in the congregation. In previous years, the church had profited from people moving *into* the city center, and many became active congregation members. In more recent years, the opposite was happening: people moved out to nearby smaller towns, such as Fetsund, Leirsund, Løvenstad, Kløfta, and Jessheim. It presented challenges both for those who were getting older and for the younger ones; both found it too far to go back to Lillestrøm to attend church. The membership statistics demonstrate a decrease in the number of members right after 1980, a decrease that has continued ever since. Moreover, from having a full-time pastor, their local pastor has been in a part-time position in recent years.

In 2002, Peder Borgen wrote: "What is crucial for the Methodist Church's future in Norway is first and foremost the work in the congregations. Therefore, the main efforts should take place there."[3] Inger and Peder found their place in the local church, not only as faithful worshipers but also in other contexts. Peder, for example, enjoyed some fellowship with his brothers by establishing a vocal group that performed in various congregational settings. Moreover, he got involved in several other initiatives. When various Lillestrøm congregations, for example, gathered in 2002 for a joint fundraising campaign to help the poor in Belarus and Lithuania, he was an active member of the fundraising committee.[4]

STILL MANY MORE YEARS OF RESEARCH

In the winter of 1999, more specifically, at the festive meeting on January 25 of the Royal Norwegian Society of Science and Letters, Peder Borgen was honored with the order Knight of the First Class of the Order of St. Olav.[5] For some, such an award could be seen as a worthy point of retirement from active life. Peder felt honored, but he saw it neither as a comma nor as a period in his life. He still had plans for more studies, for the ability to get engaged had not been retired.

3. Borgen, "Avtalen 'Nådens Fellesskap,'" 196–97.
4. See "Unikt samarbeid om hjelp til Øst-Europa," *Romerikes Blad*, January 2, 2004.
5. See "Ridder av første klasse," *Romerikes Blad*, April 12, 1999, 21.

As early as August that year, Inger and Peder went to Pretoria, South Africa, for the main annual conference of the Studiorum Novi Testamenti Societas (SNTS), which was held there that year. In addition, as the recently resigned president of SNTS, he attended a conference in the following days on "African Hermeneutics and Theology." Here Peder not only got to meet a country he did not know before, but he got to meet African theology, African questions on how to read the Bible (hermeneutics), and work to establish an African hermeneutics and theology for a world so different from our Western Euro-American.[6]

In 1995 he was appointed president of the Novum Testamentum in Leiden, the Netherlands. This assignment entailed editorial responsibility for a journal (*Novum Testamentum*) and a monograph series (Supplements to Novum Testamentum). The large publishing house E. J. Brill is behind this journal and many others. In 2008, the year he turned eighty, Borgen decided that it was time to resign from this relatively demanding position.[7] His departure was marked by a symposium (conference) on July 28 in Oslo. Four colleagues—Lars Hartman (Uppsala), Johan Thom (Stellenbosch), Cilliers Breytenbach (Berlin), and Maarten Menken (Utrecht)—participated with lectures. Then there was a reception by the Dutch ambassador. And in the evening dinner in the Mirror Hall in the Grand Hotel. The report in the newspaper *Skedsmonytt* emphasized that "The day was a large-scale celebration of Peder Borgen's place in the international academic environment among researchers working on the New Testament and its surroundings."[8] To outsiders, it might seem a bit strange that this was something to celebrate that much. But Borgen made it in many ways a signal that he was now entering a new phase; from now on, he no longer held any official international positions.

However, Borgen continued to do research and write articles. Almost thirty studies were published after moving to Lillestrøm, including two books. In addition to articles in his field Philo of Alexandria, and the New Testament (see below), he also wrote some studies on (Methodist) church history. Furthermore, he did some research in local history, especially about prison camps during World War II. In an earlier chapter, I have described how, as a boy during the times of war, he lined up outside the fence of such a prison camp with packed lunches for prisoners: "We were lying on the edge of the forest waiting for the armed guard to disappear. Then we ran forward

---

6. See the volume published after this conference, Getui and Ukpong, eds., *Interpreting the New Testament in Africa*.

7. See Elliott, "Vale Peder Borgen," 104–5.

8. Borgen (misprint for Bekken), "Lillestrømling bibelforsker på verdensplan," *Skedsmonytt*, December 16, 2008.

and gave the packages through the fence, or we threw them close to the fence from a distance." As tokens of gratitude, he received some woodwork that he still cherishes. Borgen later did several surveys in the local community to get an overview of the prison camps that were in use during World War II and gave some lectures presenting his findings. The material was later used in an article that is now to be found on lokalwiki.no.

During these years, he also worked on several studies on the history of Methodism. In 2001, he published an article about George Wolf (1736–1828), a merchant who was also a friend of John Wesley.[9] And he wrote an article about Methodism and the beginning of the Pentecostal movement in Norway, as well as two articles about Methodism's "founder" in Norway,[10] Ole P. Petersen, and articles about both him and bishop Odd Hagen for the Norwegian Biographical Lexicon.[11] In 2004 he published an article on ecumenism, that is, about his experiences in ecumenical settings at home and abroad.[12]

Biblical studies (1999–2021)

It is somewhat artificial to set 1999/2000 as a turning point in Borgen's research. It is not that decisive when it comes to topics, but it nevertheless represents a central point in his life as he left Trondheim and the university in 1999 when moving back to Lillestrøm. That move also meant that he left some of the research facilities he had in Trondheim. On the other hand, he had an excellent private library, and the University of Oslo and several libraries were not that far away, about half an hour by train. Hence there were some topics that he pursued before 1999, and some that he took up as new interests.

In his New Testament works, he wrote a few studies on Paul. Furthermore, he never left Philo and published on Philo and his writings too. But not much, and most of it was written in the 1990s.[13] Except for an article[14] in 2003 and his book in 2014, which contained some reprints, and a couple

---

9. Borgen, "George Wolff (1736–1828)."

10. Borgen, "Der Methodismus und die Anfänge der Pfingstbewegung in Norwegen"; Borgen, "Ole Peter Petersen fra Glemmen."

11. Borgen, "Ole Peter Petersen"; Borgen, "Odd Hagen."

12. Borgen, "Ute-økumenikk og hjemme-økumenikk."

13. See the following three studies by Borgen: "Philo's *Against Flaccus*," 41–57 (reprinted in Borgen, *Illuminations*, 17–33); "Application and Commitment," 86–101 (reprinted in Borgen, *Illuminations*, 34–52); and "Greek Encyclical Education," 61–71.

14. Borgen, "Gospel of John and Philo."

of not recently published works,[15] he published nothing new on the Gospel of John in these years. The last two books he published during this time are collections of articles that, in many ways, sum up and provide a cross-section of several of his interests throughout his life as a New Testament scholar.[16] In addition, however, he published several articles dealing with issues of the history of Methodism. Hence in this section, we will have a closer look at some of the major works published during these years in Lillestrøm.

Paul and the death of Christ

In his later years, Borgen has focused on Paul's Letter to the Galatians, and published some articles that deal with the death of Christ, especially in Galatians 3:1–14 and the death of Christ.[17] In the first of these, "Openly Portrayed as Crucified," from 2000, he takes his point of departure in the expression "that Christ died for our sins in accordance with the Scriptures" (1 Corinthians 15:3).[18] He then argues that this expression "with necessity presupposed the opposite view, that he, 'in accordance with the Scriptures,' died as a lawbreaker for his own sins."[19] Drawing then on Galatians 3:1–13, it is evident that Paul applied Deuteronomy 21:23 to interpret the death of Jesus; he became a curse. However, in Galatians 3:13, he turns this interpretation around in three ways: Jesus became a curse for us, not for his own sins. Then, Paul transferred the characterization to serve as a characterization of "us" who are under the curse of the law. Finally, "as a curse for 'us,' Christ redeemed us from the curse under the law."[20] Hence, part of the problem Paul deals with is the malfunctioning of the Law. Consequently, according to Borgen's reading, one must read these issues in light of two different jurisdictions at work: the Sinaitic and the Abrahamic:

> the fact that Christ Jesus was crucified as a cursed criminal made it evident that those who relied upon this Sinaitic law were

---

15. Borgen, *Gospel of John: More Light*, 193–218 ("Observations on God's Agent"), and 261–74 ("Appearance to Thomas").

16. See Borgen, *Gospel of John: More Light* (2014); Borgen, *Illuminations by Philo* (2021).

17. "Openly Portrayed as Crucified," 345–53 (reprinted in Borgen, *Illuminations by Philo*, 144–152); Borgen, "Crucified for His Own Sins," 17–35 (reprinted in Borgen, *Illuminations by Philo*, 153–72).

18. Cf. his study, "In Accordance with the Scriptures," 193–206.

19. Borgen, "Openly Portrayed," 144–45. I quote from the reprint in Borgen, *Illuminations*, 144–52.

20. Borgen, *Illuminations*, 147.

themselves under a curse. Thus Christ's death marked the end of the Sinaitic law and the beginning of the new era when the blessing of Abraham would come to the Gentiles and "we" could receive the promise of the Spirit (Gal 3:14).[21]

In a later article, Borgen returns to these two laws and says that they represent two opposing principles and reflect a situation of debate and conflict.[22] One should speak of two different jurisdictions, and in Galatians 3:1-14 both jurisdictions are seen at work: "One might be called 'a Sinaitic jurisdiction,' with 'works of the law as key phrase' . . . The other jurisdiction might be named the 'Abrahamic jurisdiction,' with 'faith' as a key word."[23] Hence, as a persecutor, Paul must have interpreted the crucifixion of Jesus as capital punishment for crimes committed by Jesus himself, but later, Paul came to see the death of Christ as vicarious.

In another article (2006), however, Borgen returns to the issue of Christ being executed as a criminal and asks what kind of crimes Paul possibly might have attributed to Jesus. Here Borgen ends up supporting a view set forth by many others from the earliest times, namely, that Jesus was perceived as a magician and as a blasphemer.[24] Then he proceeds to investigate what Paul might have meant by "that Christ died for *our* sins." Using Romans 1:18-32 and 7:7-8:4,[25] he works out what Paul might have understood by "our sins."

Studies in church history and early Methodism

In a preceding chapter, dealing with the life and work of Borgen in Bergen, I briefly presented his work on the learned man Johannes Olsonius, or Hans Olsen, as would be his Norwegian name. He lived from 1607 to 1684, and Borgen's description of him has as its subtitle "Theosophus and Medicus Bergensis." Borgen's study was first published in 1972.[26]

---

21. Borgen, *Illuminations*, 150.

22. See Borgen, "Perspectives for Mission," reprinted in Borgen, *Illuminations*, 131-43

23. Borgen, *Illuminations*, 136. Borgen's former student Per Jarle Bekken has elaborated on these distinctions and categories in his book *Paul's Negotiation of Abraham in Galatians 3 in the Jewish Context*.

24. Borgen, "Crucified for His Own Sins," originally published in 2006, and reprinted in Borgen, *Illuminations*, 153-72

25. Borgen deals with this text also in his "Contrite Wrongdoer."

26. Reprinted in 2009 in Borgen's collection of articles, labeled *Vei Utenfor Allfarvei*, 21-48.

Then, in 1993, he published another study within the field of church history, dealing with Georg(e) Wolff. This is a tremendous, detailed study, and Borgen worked on it several times until its last issue, published in 2009 in his collection *Vei Utenfor Allfarvei* (a title hard to translate into English but might be given as something like *Roads besides the Main Road*).

Then, a third study is also included in that volume, dealing with the "founder" of Methodism in Norway, Ole Peter Petersen. Finally, a fourth study dealing with church history is his study of "Methodism and the Initial Stages of the Pentecostal Movement in Norway," first published in German in 2005, then in English in 2009.

Peder Borgen continued to attend conferences and give lectures in various contexts even as retired. Here from one of his last public lectures, at the National Library, Oslo, October 11, 2018, at the age of ninety!

Hence, Peder Borgen, the biblical scholar and specialist in Philo of Alexandria, also worked on specialized studies in church history up through the years in both Bergen and Trondheim, and then as retired in Lillestrøm. This fact, and the published studies, reveal several characteristics: first, Borgen kept his interest in church history even through his most busy years;

second, he loved studying the development and impact of Methodism in its various contexts; and third, these studies display a scholar who also by these studies displays his preference for minority issues and the need for freedom of religion in a broad sense of that word.

George Wolff (1736–1828)

The background for this study was an invitation from Stavanger. When planning to arrange a research seminar on Norway and England before and during the Napoleonic Wars, Borgen was invited to present a paper related to Norwegian and English church life during those years. The seminar took place August 16–18, 1993. Borgen's contribution was this study on Georg Wolff (1736–1828).[27]

Georg Wolff was born in Christiania (now Oslo), in 1736, but emigrated to Great Britain as an adult. Here he built up a large business enterprise, and he thus soon belonged to the upper classes in London. Most relevant to his social status was probably also that he became the consul of Denmark-Norway in 1786.[28]

The enterprise of Wolff dealt with banking and brokerage and mediated the purchase of English goods for the Norwegian market. His company built up an extensive network of trade connections in both England and Norway.

However, Wolff was also active in society and church. From 1778 till his death, he was one of the superintendents of the Danish-Norwegian church in London, and he was active in social work within Methodist circles. Borgen mentions that Wolff, in 1779, became one of the trustees for Wesley's City Road Chapel. At about the same time, he also became a member of a Bible society, established in 1779. He was also central in the work of establishing the British and Foreign Bible Society in 1804, a Bible society that for some time also influenced the establishment of a Bible society in Norway.

Due to his wealth and social status, he supported several initiatives with his money and influence, and when the war between England and Denmark-Norway broke out in 1807, he and his son Jens Wolff had a significant impact on the conditions of the prisoners of war that were taken and kept in prison ships in London.

27. Borgen, "Georg Wolff," 49–86. The present article is an elaboration on the study presented in Stavanger in 1993; a part of this study was published in English in 2001 (Borgen, "George Wolff," 17–28). I have here used the version published in Norwegian, reprinted in Borgen, *Vei Utenfor Allfarvei*, 49–86.

28. Norway was at this time in union with Denmark; that situation ended in 1814, when Norway entered a union with Sweden, a union that was ended in 1905 when Norway became a kingdom of its own.

Borgen ends his study by underscoring Wolff as an active Methodist, and—in a typical Borgenian way—by emphasizing Methodist values thus:

> Georg Wolff's involvement in Methodism as a movement and eventually as a free church illuminates aspects of the struggle for religious freedom. At the same time, his life illuminates a movement with an ethos where there was an interplay between social and political efforts and active Christian confession. Furthermore, it is essential to note that the strong Wesleyan revival among the emerging working groups also included economically prosperous circles in society. John Wesley himself was a priest and academic, among other things, with studies in classical subjects and the writings of the Church Fathers. At the same time, he communicated with broad popular circles.[29]

Ole Peter Petersen

Ole Peter Petersen (1822–1901) is considered the founder of Methodism in Norway. When a new biographical Lexicon was to be written, Borgen was invited to write about Ole Peter Petersen.[30] The present study is a greatly expanded version of that initially brief entry in a lexicon.

Very little was known about his family, especially his father. Hence, Borgen set out to collect genealogical information about his parents, siblings, and their social context. During the research, it turned out that well-known issues such as the emerging quest for religious freedom in Norway came into focus and the poverty that induced many to emigrate to America. The first part of the article is thus characterized by an extensive search in church registries to find the various persons related to Ole Peter Petersen, and their social context.

It turned out that Ole Peter Pettersen grew up in impoverished circumstances; to this was added that his parents were not married. His father left when he was four years old, and his mother died when he was eight. As a young man, Petersen became a sailor but eventually emigrated to America in 1844, and from then on, he sailed on the American east coast. He got in contact with several congregations, and it was of great help for his development that he got in contact with the Methodist seamen's church in New

---

29. Borgen, *Vei Utenfor Allfarvei*, 85–86.

30. The *Biographical Lexicon* was published 1999–2005. The article concerned is now available on the internet: Borgen, "Ole Peter Petersen," at https://nbl.snl.no/Ole_Peter_Petersen. The present study is a much-enlarged version: Borgen, "Ole Peter Petersen," 87–128.

York, the Bethelship. In that way, he also got in contact with the Methodist Episcopal Church. In retrospect, one might say that the contact and help he received in that church is the main reason for the present Norwegian Methodist Church having an episcopal structure and it's connection to what is now called the United Methodist Church.

This study is thus, above all, a study of the family background of Ole Peter Petersen, then an investigation of his life and development as a Christian, and then as a Methodist pastor in America and in Norway. The seaman from an impoverished family background became a major impetus for establishing the Methodist Church in Norway. Accordingly, when investigating the life and work of Ole Peter Petersen, Peder Borgen was also investigating the roots of his own Methodism.

Methodism and early Pentecostalism in Norway

The character of early Methodism is also very much in focus in the next study to be mentioned here.[31] It deals primarily with the leading person in the first years of Pentecostalism in Norway, probably also best characterized as the founder of Norwegian Pentecostalism, the once Methodist pastor Thomas Ball Barrett (1862–1940).

Borgen's study aims to "follow the life and work of Thomas Ball Barrett as a pastor and leader of the Methodist Church in Norway into his pioneering initiative, which led to the founding of the Pentecostal movement and congregations in Norway."[32] In order to do that, Borgen sketches some characteristics of the developments within the Methodist Church in the decades from 1890, developments which turned out to be crucial both for Methodism and the emerging Pentecostal movement. In this connection, he also sketches three forms of organization—a state church system, an independent free church model, and societies—asking: "What is the interplay between confessional church-building and the building of societies with members

---

31. The study was originally a paper presented at a conference, organized by the Methodist Church's Commission for Church History in Tallin, August 10–15, 2004. Borgen was asked to participate and chose to present this study. It was originally written in English, then published in German as "Der Methodismus und die Anfänge der Pfingstbewegung" (2005). The original version is found as "Methodism and the Initial Stages of the Pentecostal Movement in Norway," in Borgen, *Vei Utenfor Allfarvei*, 129–151. I have used this version here.

32. Borgen, "Methodism," 129.

who come from various denominational backgrounds?"³³ One of the answers is that "revival needs to be channeled into a structured 'follow up.'"³⁴

The Norwegian Methodist Church had its most flourishing time in the decades up to 1890. Then a stagnation set in, a stagnation which was due to several causes. In his descriptions of these years, Borgen relies heavily on a dissertation by Arne Hassing.³⁵ The organizational structure changed from functioning as a channel for a dynamic movement to being more of an established church institution, including hierarchization. Furthermore, the Methodist churches got competition from several nationwide organizations (*indremisjon*; home mission organizations) and other free churches like the Baptists. In addition, an upward social and economic movement took place, and a growing secularization created new challenges. The Methodist churches also suffered from a weakening in the ability to take care of new members and introduce them to the Methodist doctrines. Drawing on Hassing's study, Borgen tries to explain the changes occurring at the turn of the century in order to describe the fertile ground for the new movement to be called Pentecostalism.

Thomas Ball Barrett (1862–1940) was born in Albasto, Cornwall, in England, but his family moved to Norway in 1867. He went to school in England for five years (1873–78). Later he studied music with the famous Norwegian composer Edvard Grieg, and Barrett was an excellent piano player. He was ordained deacon in the Methodist Church in 1889 and appointed pastor in 1889, serving in churches in Oslo, and became one of the most prominent Methodist pastors at the beginning of the twentieth century. However, working as a Methodist pastor, Barrett also felt a need for a deeper spiritual life, and when being in the United States from 1905 to 1906, he got in contact with the Azusa Street Revival in Los Angeles. Inspired by them, he had his decisive, charismatic experience in New York on October 7, 1906. He returned to Norway just in time for Christmas, and very soon he became the leader of a new charismatic movement. "From July 1907, Barrett was no longer a member of the annual conference and no longer a Methodist minister."³⁶ From that year, Barrett worked as a freelance evangelist on what Borgen calls a "non-denominational alliance basis."³⁷ In the years to come, the movement led by Barrett grew extensively and became the largest

---

33. Borgen, "Methodism," 129.
34. Borgen, "Methodism," 132.
35. Hassing, *Religion and Power*.
36. Borgen, "Methodism," 145.
37. Borgen, "Methodism," 146.

non-Lutheran denomination in Norway, several times larger than the Methodist Church, depending on how one counts.[38]

This last study, thus being mentioned here, is not one of Borgen's most well researched. It is a conference contribution in which he draws heavily on other studies, summarizing and synthesizing their results. Nevertheless, it is interesting for several reasons: it exposes his thorough knowledge of the history of Methodism in Norway, and it demonstrates his awareness of the impact of changing social structures as well as the problem of establishing adequate ecclesiastical and organizational structures. But it also illustrates—in my mind, at least—the relevance of his statement in the early 1990s:

> What is crucial for the future of the Methodist Church in Norway is primarily the work in the local congregations.[39]

---

38. Cf. https://en.wikipedia.org/wiki/Pentecostalism_in_Norway.
39. Borgen, "Avtalen 'Nådens Fellesskap,'" 196–97.

16

A Life of Border Crossings: Outlook and Conclusions

SOME CONCLUDING FLASHBACKS

PEDER BORGEN WAS—ECCLESIASTICALLY CONSIDERED—A part of a minority at a time when the dominance of the state church was pervasive in Norway. Today we can sometimes wonder how broad and dominant the position of the Church of Norway was even in the last half of the twentieth century, and how self-confident it was in its position and its connection to the state and the local municipalities. It was, admittedly, a dominant position enshrined in the constitution, and protected by several other laws and by the customs of the people, but it was also a position which by some, perhaps not least by the "dissenters," was perceived as characterized by some arrogance and lack of vision for the justification of other denominations and their rightful place in Norwegian society.

But at the same time, Peder Borgen's life and work took place during a turning point in Norwegian history. The struggle of the free churches against the domination of the state church came about at the same time as more secular forces also tried to free themselves from this dominance. On the one hand, one might say that these struggles or currents against the position of the state church ran from the same root, but they represented different branches, and the kinship was not always easy to discover. But it was there.

The twentieth century stood on the shoulders of the nineteenth-century champions and their struggles for religious freedom. We can discover these when we now in the twenty-first century are looking back from a greater distance trying to draw the broad lines that also continue into our times.

In this biography, I have emphasized the minority issues in Peder Borgen's life. This emphasis is necessary if one is to understand both his development from his youth and several of his problems regarding the work situation in Norway. But it is also important in order to understand how these experiences became integrated within his personality and shaped his steadfastness in other issues of his adult life, such as his ecclesiastical positions and attitudes in the later years of his life. The feeling of being not only a minority, but a minority for which there are social, cultural, and/or political barriers, is not just an unpleasant feeling, but a factor that can easily affect one's personal development. Some settle down and find a niche of their own in life. Others fight back and try to break the barriers, crossing some borders. Peder Borgen belongs to the latter group. He obtained a scholarship despite closed opportunities in Norway; he went abroad because there was a professional ban in Norway for "dissenters" of his type to get academic positions. He pushed for a change in the law so that a "dissenter"—sorry, a free church non-Lutheran—could also become a professor of Christian knowledge/theology in Norway. And he helped win that battle by crossing borders.

Crossing borders as class voyages

Peder Borgen's life was, in several ways, a class voyage. He continued the journey his father—the entrepreneur—had begun when he took the step from a farmer's son to being self-employed as a merchant and owner of several stores of meat products. Peder's grandfather was a farmer, and Peder's father ran a farm too as a tenant before he established himself in Lillestrøm and took the step into the class of merchants. Peder liked to emphasize that the driving force that was the basis for this change was influenced by the Haugian view of work, profession, and entrepreneurship and by the Methodist view of the need for Christian inputs in the various areas of society. That Peder then took the step further into academic work and life can thus be seen as a continuation of this class voyage begun by his father. He continued crossing some borders.

His father had some objections and second thoughts. We have encountered these a few times in this book. But Peder Borgen continued and made a bigger leap than his immediate ancestors. One might say that a natural development in a Norwegian context would have been that he had become a pastor, a Methodist pastor, and then possibly that the next generation took the step further up in the academic elite. But Peder's inner drive pushed him forward; he became a professor and established himself in his field with recognition far beyond the borders of Norway. Yes, perhaps the recognition both was and is greater abroad than in Norway; he was somehow never "discovered" in his own fatherland. To those who studied theology in Norway from approximately 1965, he was not a well-known name. For although he was a professor of New Testament theology, he did not belong to the academic Lutheran ecclesiastical elite having a position in the majority church or in a faculty of theology; he was a non-Lutheran free church member, to some a "dissenter." Furthermore, he was not working in a theological faculty, teaching prospective pastors, but remained in the field of Christian knowledge, primarily teaching prospective high school and college teachers.

Anyone who has read the previous chapters will have discovered the issues of minorities, and what it could represent in the different phases of his life.

Crossing borders as a search for patterns

Throughout his theological research, Peder Borgen was interested in *patterns*; patterns in the various texts, social currents, and life expressions he explored. This interest was present whether it concerned exegetical patterns in the texts of Philo of Alexandria, in the Gospel of John, or in other New Testament texts. And it was present when he immersed himself in topics such as ecclesiology/-ies in the New Testament, the history of Methodism, or foreign and domestic ecumenism. Or in the ways he worked when he researched the life of Johannes Olsonius in Bergen or O. P. Petersen as the founder of Methodism in Norway. And there are some noticeable trajectories extending from his interest in Philo of Alexandria to the situation of the Sami minorities in Norway.

Peder Borgen was a Methodist. No one who has ever met him, heard him, or read the previous pages should have any doubts about that. But he was proud of being a Methodist. It was and is a pride that in many ways could be perceived as a bit unconventional. Firstly, it is pretty non-Norwegian to be proud of one's church membership. Secondly, it was usually not among the free church members that pride was most conspicuous. They were more often reserved and modest, affected by the minority situation they lived in both as denominations and as individual Christians. The so-called *Law of jante*[1] has, in many ways, also had a strong effect in various congregational contexts. But Borgen was a proud Methodist. From a professional point of view, he justified this by finding that the church in the New Testament was transnational and supranational. And he believed that he could find such structures and patterns also in the Methodist Church's vision and organizational structure.

His pride could sometimes be experienced as tipping over into stubbornness and even self-preoccupation. He could be stubborn in his internal church tug-of-war as we saw happened at the annual conference in 1976, and in the church-political tug-of-war approximately twenty years later concerning the *Community of Grace*, an ecumenical agreement between the Church of Norway and the Methodist Church in Norway, an agreement of which he strongly disagreed with.

He could be resolute, almost stubborn, about his research work, that is, what he perceived as his research findings. And he could be preoccupied with his publications and the insights he thought they brought, in a way that could be perceived by some as self-centeredness; he loved to tell about what he had just published or what he was doing. *Eureka*! But at the same time: those who have not themselves experienced and know a scholar's curiosity and joy of seeing patterns that no one else has discovered may have difficulty understanding this joy. Hence, it is sometimes wrongly perceived as self-obsession. Beware of the Law of Jante.

For many, there is something unorthodox about this research joy, this enthusiasm of "see what I have found." To some Norwegians, it even sounds a little too American! And Peder Borgen spent some of his most crucial and formative years as a scholar and theologian in the United States when he was a research fellow in New Jersey in 1953–56 and a professor at Wesley Theological Seminary in Washington in 1962–66. The impressions and impulses he received there he always carried with him; the students noticed it in his positive interest in them and their studies, and in his lectures. While most of his colleagues often sat down with other teachers in the canteen, Peder could eat his lunch chatting with his students. And when he got research fellows for mentoring, he was genuinely interested in their findings and progression far beyond what one might expect. The impulses from America were present there as well. And he thrived in international forums: "It's so stimulating," he used to say.

---

1. On the Law of Jante, see https://en.wikipedia.org/wiki/Law_of_Jante: "It is used generally in colloquial speech in the Nordic countries as a sociological term to denote a social attitude of disapproval towards expressions of individuality and personal success." Its rule no. 1: "Don't think you are anything special."

Crossing borders; Peder, Philo, and the Sami

Peder was a specialist in Philo from Alexandria; in his writings and their theology, but also in Philo's social world, the Jewish Diaspora in Egypt. "You can talk to Peder about anything you want, but before you know it, he will be talking about Philo," a journalist wrote in *Adresseavisen*.[2] And many others have had similar experiences with Peder Borgen.

Not only was Peder interested in Philo, but there are also many similarities between Philo and Peder. Maybe that's why Peder found Philo so fascinating. He found Philo useful for his understanding of John 6, but he also found Philo interesting in a broader sense. We can mention some features that we have encountered previously: Philo lived—for a reason unknown to us—outside his homeland, in the Diaspora, in the "dispersion" in Egypt. But he regarded Jerusalem as his "metropolis," his mother city. Peder also had to travel and spent two periods in a diaspora, in the United States, perhaps more involuntarily than voluntarily.

Philo lived in Alexandria as part of minority communities, the Jewish synagogue congregations. And his Jewish cocitizens at times experienced great discrimination in the city, even in the form of violent persecution and curtailment of their social rights. Peder too was not unfamiliar with social discrimination.

Philo was an examiner of the Law, the Prophets, and the other scriptures. And he tried to actualize his Judaism for his contemporaries, both Jews and others. Many of his writings are just that: interpretations—actualizations—of the Law, the Torah. Peder Borgen must have been able to recognize himself within this agenda as well.

We should not exaggerate these similarities. Of course, there are also significant differences. Nevertheless, it is not to be denied; there are some commonalities between Philo and Peder that are more striking than others.

We have marked Peder's experiences—in a certain context, namely, in his church affiliation—of belonging to a minority, and some discrimination too. During his retirement, he unexpectedly encountered another minority, a Norwegian minority: the Sami. And he gained insight into their experiences of discrimination from the society at large. However, Peder has never—as far as I know—drawn any comparisons between his own experiences and the Sami. But the parallels are obvious. And his interest in the Sami has survived the decades after the 1990s. They got a place of their own in his heart.

---

2. Rolfsen, "Peder og Filon," *Adresseavisen*, June 15, 1996, 4.

Crossing borders

I have chosen *Crossing Borders* as the main title of this biographical presentation of the life and work of Peder Borgen. Borders may be found in several contexts and may be of several types; one might speak of *national* borders as well as *social* borders, and of *spatial* borders as well as *temporal* ones. And borders may be *blocked* to some persons, but *open* to others. We could go on, and definitions are numerous and characterizations diverse.

Where there are borders, there will also be some attempts of border crossings, and most often some actual crossings. At the same time, there will be some borders that are neither passable nor traversable.

When Peder Borgen entered the Faculty of Theology as a student in 1947, he crossed a social border; no one else in his family had crossed that border before him. When he was found not eligible for scholarships from the University in Oslo in 1953, he met a border that was both social, cultural, and denominational, and uncrossable to him at that time.

When he traveled to the United States, he crossed both social and national borders. Likewise, when he obtained the degree of dr.theol. in Norway (1966) and became the first non-Lutheran to be a professor in Christian knowledge (1973), and was later appointed Knight of the First Class of the Order of St. Olav (1999), he crossed social borders no other non-Lutheran theologians had crossed within the national borders of Norway.

Likewise, when he integrated the works of Philo as a central discourse partner in his New Testament studies, he was crossing borders; not alone, but not in the tracks of the many. And he has probably had more followers in this interest than he had predecessors.

Crossing Borders is thus a presentation of how some borders represented wide-ranging obstacles to the lives of many religious dissenters in Norway. However, at the same time, many values were questioned, and some borders had to be done away with. In order to set the life and work of Peder Borgen in context, *Crossing Borders* is an appropriate label to describe that life and work.

Appendix

Bibliography of Peder Borgen's Works (1956–2021)

THE BIBLIOGRAPHY DOES NOT contain articles from newspapers and periodicals but focuses on scholarly articles published in journals, Festschriften, other collections of articles, and other studies. The various items are numbered, listed chronologically, and alphabetized within every year. In addition, cross-references are added so a reader can discover if an article has been published several times, and where to locate it.

1956

01 *Eschatology and Heilsgeschichte in Luke-Acts*. PhD diss., Drew University, New Jersey, 1956. Microfilm; unpublished.

1959

02 "John and the Synoptics in the Passion Narrative." *New Testament Studies* 5 (1959) 246–59. Reprinted in 51 and 150.

03 "The Unity of the Discourse in John 6." *Zeitschrift für die neutestamentliche Wissenschaft und die Kunde der älteren Kirche* 50 (1959) 277–78. Reprinted in 51.

1960

04 "Brød fra himmel og fra jord. Om Haggada i Palestinsk Midrasj, hos Philo og i Johannesevangeliet." *Norsk Teologisk Tidsskrift* 61 (1960) 318-40.

1961

05 "At the Age of Twenty in I QSa." *Revue de Qumran* 3 (1961) 267-77. Reprinted in 53.

1963

06 "Observations on the Midrashic Character of John 6." *Zeitschrift für die neutestamentliche Wissenschaft und die Kunde der älteren Kirche* 54 (1963) 232-40. Reprinted in 51 and 69.

1965

07 *Bread from Heaven: An Exegetical Study of the Concept of Manna in the Gospel of John and the Writings of Philo*. Supplements to Novum Testamentum 10. Leiden: Brill, 1965. Reprinted as 36 and 157.

1966

08 "Den såkalte Gyldne Regel (Matt. 7:12, Luk. 6:31), dens forekomst i Det nye testamentes omverden og dens innhold i evangelienes kontekst." *Norsk Teologisk Tidsskrift* 67 (1966) 129-46. English translation in 53.

09 "Von Paulus zu Lukas. Beobachtungen zur Erhellung der Theologie der Lukasschriften." *Studia Theologica* 20 (1966) 140-57. English translation in 12 and 53.

1968

10 "God's Agent in the Fourth Gospel." In *Religions in Antiquity: E. R. Goodenough Memorial Volume*, edited by Jacob Neusner, 137–48. Leiden: Brill, 1968. Reprinted in 51, 69, and 150.

1969

11 "Eine allgemein-etische Maxime." *Temenos* 5 (1969) 37–53.

12 "From Paul to Luke: Observations Toward Clarification of the Theology of Luke-Acts." *Catholic Biblical Quarterly* 31 (1969) 168–82. German original = 09; this version reprinted in 53.

1970

13 "Johannes-prologen som eksegese." In *Skrift og Skole. Festskrift til O. Hjelde*, edited by P. Mehren et al., 73–84. Oslo: Land og Kirke, 1970. Comparable to 15; reprinted in 51.

14 "Logos var det sanne lys." *Svensk Exegetisk Årsskrift* 35 (1970) 79–95. English translation in 20, 51, and 69.

15 "Observations on the Targumic Character of the Prologue in John." *New Testament Studies* 16 (1970) 13–20. Reprinted in 51 and 69.

16 "En tradisjonshistorisk analyse av materialet om Jesu fødsel hos Ignatius." *Tidsskrift for Teologi og Kirke* 42 (1970) 37–44. English translation in 53.

1971

17 Coauthor with Roald Skarsten. "Bibelvitenskap, gresk og EDB, Maskinleselig tekst og indeks av Philo fra Alexandrias skrifter." *FORSKNINGSNYTT, fra Norges allmennvitenskapelige forskningsråd*, 3 (1971) 37–39, 50.

18 "Ekumeniske tendenser og problemer i metodismen." *Norsk Teologisk Tidsskrift* 72 (1971) 19–42.

1972

19 "Johannes Olsonius. Theosophus et Medicus Bergensis." *Norsk Teologisk Tidsskrift* 73 (1972) 1–26. Reprinted in 143.

20 "Logos Was the True Light." *Novum Testamentum* 14 (1972) 95–110. English translation of 14; reprinted in 51 .

1973

21 "Philo Judeus: Om dannelsen av verden." In *Platonisme i antikk og middelalder*, edited by Egil. A. Wyller, 113–23. Oslo: Filosofisk institutt og Klassisk institutt, Universitetet i Oslo, 1973.

1974

22 "Tanker i Det nye testamentet om kristen enhet." *Lumen* 17 (1974) 1–19. English translation in 53.

1976

23 "The Place of the Old Testament in the Formation of New Testament Theology. Response." *New Testament Studies* 23 (1976) 67–75. Reprinted in 51 and 69.

24 Coauthor with Roald Skarsten. "Questiones et Solutiones: Some Observations on the Form of Philo's Exegesis." *Studia Philonica* 4 (1976/1977) 1–16. Reprinted in 53.

1977

25 "Der Logos war das wahre Licht. Beitrage zur Deutung des Johanneischen Prologs." In *Theologie aus dem Norden*, edited by A. Fuchs, 99–117. Studien zum Neuen Testament und seiner Umwelt, ser. A, vol. 2. A. Fuchs: Linz, 1977. German translation of 14; English translation in 20 and 51.

26 "Some Jewish Exegetical Traditions as Background for Son of Man Sayings in the Fourth Gospel (Jn 3:13-14) and Context." In *L'Evangelie de Jean*, edited by M. De Jonge, 243-58. Gembloux: Leuven, 1977. See also revised version in 51 and 69.

1979

27 "Religiøs pluralisme i nytestamentlig tid." In *Religiøs pluralisme i bibelsk tid og i Norge i dag*, edited by Peder Borgen, 101-18. Trondheim: Tapir, 1979.

28 "The Use of Tradition in John 12,44-50." *New Testament Studies* 26 (1979) 49-66. Reprinted in 51 and 69.

1980

29 "Fornuftens, erfaringens og den sosiale konteksts rolle i relasjon til Skriftens autoritet." *Nordisk ekumenisk årsbok* (1980/81) 35-48. English version = 35.

30 "Helbredelsesundere i Det nye testament." In *Mennesket og naturen i kristendom og naturvitenskap*, edited by Peder Borgen, 43-64. Trondheim: Tapir, 1980. English translation in 53.

31 "Nomisme og libertinisme i Paulus brev til Galaterne." *Tidsskrift for Teologi og Kirke* 51 (1980) 257-67.

32 *Det nye testamentes omverden. Tekster i oversettelse med innledninger. Utvalgte greske tekster og ordlister*. Trondheim: Tapir, 1980.

33 "Observations on the Theme Paul and Philo: Paul's Preaching of Circumcision in Galatia (Gal 5:11) and Debates on Circumcision in Philo." In *Die Paulinische Literatur und Theologie*, edited by S. Pedersen, 85-102. Århus: Forlaget Aros, 1980. Reprinted in 53 and 69.

1981

34 "Biblical Authority and the Authenticity of the Church in Relationship to Auxiliary Keys Such as Reason, Experience, and Social Contexts." *Epworth Review* 8 (1981) 72-81. English translation of 29.

35 "Fra Bibeltolkningens historie og aktuelle debatt." In *Bibelen i brennpunktet for tro, historie og litteratur*, edited by Peder Borgen, 83-110. Trondheim: Tapir, 1981.

36 *Bread from Heaven: An Exegetical Study of the Concept of Manna in the Gospel of John and the Writings of Philo.* 2nd ed. Supplements to Novum Testamentum 10. Leiden: Brill, 1981. Reprint of 07.

37 "Grunnleggelse, motgang og fremgang 1884-1914." In *Kirken i Sentrum. Trondheim Metodistmenighet 100 år. 1881, 6. november—1981*, edited by Peder Borgen et al., 9-50. Trondheim: Tapir, 1981.

38 "Kirkebevegelse og foreningsbevegelse." In *Norske Frikirker. Framvekst og konfesjonell egenart i brytning med statskirkelighet*, edited by Per Øverland, 9-33. Trondheim: Tapir, 1981.

39 Coedited with Ole Einar Andersen et al. *Kirken i Sentrum. Trondheim Metodistmenighet 100 år. 18816-. november—1981*. Trondheim: Tapir, 1981.

40 "Miracles of Healing in the New Testament." *Studia Theologica* 24 (1981) 91-106. Norwegian original = 30; reprinted in 53.

41 "Odd Hagen." In *Kirken i Sentrum. Trondheim Metodistmenighet 100 år. 1881-6. november—1981*, edited by Peder Borgen, 184-86. Trondheim: Tapir, 1981.

42 "Synd och nåd." *Tro och Liv* 3 (1981) 29-34.

1982

43 *Dåp i Det nye testament og i konfesjonell debatt.* Oslo: Norsk Forlagsselskap, 1982.

44 Coeditor with Tore Meistad. *Hvem er Jeppe? Rusgift, terapi og menneskesyn.* Trondheim: Tapir, 1982.

45 "Hvilket menneskesyn? Hvilket livssyn?" In *'Hvem er Jeppe?' Rusgift, terapi og menneskesyn*, edited by Peder Borgen and Tore Meistad, 45-67. Trondheim: Tapir, 1982.

46 "Jesus og de fattige." *Norsk Teologisk Tidsskrift* 83 (1982) 19-32.

1983

47 "The Early Church and the Hellenistic Synagogue." *Studia Theologica* 37 (1983) 55-78. Reprinted in 53 and 69.

48 "Aristobulus—A Jewish Exegete from Alexandria." In *Paul Preaches Circumcision and Pleases Men, and Other Essays on Christian Origins*, 179-90. Trondheim: Tapir, 1983. Reprinted in 69; revised version included in 57.

49 "Bread from Heaven. Aspects of Debates on Expository Method and Form." In *Logos Was the True Light, and Other Essays on the Gospel of John*, 32-47. Trondheim: Tapir, 1983. Trondheim: Tapir, 1983. Reprinted in 69.

50 "John's Use of the Old Testament and the Problem of Sources and Traditions." In *Logos Was the True Light, and Other Essays on the Gospel of John*, 81-91. Trondheim: Tapir, 1983. Reprinted in 69.

51 *Logos Was the True Light, and Other Essays on the Gospel of John*. Trondheim: Tapir, 1983. Contents: 02, 03, 06, 10, 13, 14, 15, 20, 23, 25, 26, 28.

52 "Paul Preaches Circumcision and Pleases Men." In *Paul and Paulinism: Essays in Honour of C. K. Barrett*, edited by M. D. Hooker and S. G. Wilson, 37-46. London: SPCK, 1983. Reprinted in 53.

53 *Paul Preaches Circumcision and Pleases Men, and Other Essays on Christian Origins*. Trondheim: Tapir, 1983. Contents: republishing of 05, 08, 09, 12, 16, 22, 24, 30, 33, 40, 47, 48; not previously published is 54 below.

54 "Philo, Luke and Geography." In *Paul Preaches Circumcision and Pleases Men, and Other Essays on Christian Origins*, 59-71. Trondheim: Tapir, 1983. Reprinted in 69.

1984

55 "Etterutdanning av lærere i Universitetets regi." *Prismet* 2-3 (1984) 86-90.

56 "Filo, Diasporajøde fra Aleksandria." In *Blant skriftlærde og fariseere: Jødedommen i oldtiden*, edited by Hans Kvalbein, 43-56. Oslo: Verbum, 1984.

57 "Philo of Alexandria." In *Compendia Rerum Iudaicarum ad Novum Testamentum II,2*, edited by M. de Jonge and S. Safrai, 233-82. Minneapolis: Fortress, 1984.

58 "Philo of Alexandria: A Critical and Synthetical Survey of Research Since World War II." In *Aufstieg und Niedergang der römischen Welt II 21,1: Geschichte und Kultur Roms im Spiegel der neueren Forschung. 2, Principat. Religion: Hellenistisches Judentum in römischer Zeit: Philon und Josephus*, edited by W. Haase, 98–154. Berlin: de Gruyter, 1984.

1985

59 "Bibel—kultur—identitet." In *Religionskunnskap og allmennutdannelse*, edited by Ole G. Winsnes, 79–113. Trondheim: Tapir, 1985.

60 "The Cross-National Church for Jews and Greeks: Observations on Paul's Letter to the Galatians." In *The Many and the One: Essays on Religion in the Graeco-Roman World Presented to H. Ludin Jansen*, edited by Peder Borgen, 225–48, Trondheim: Tapir, 1985. Reprinted in 69 and 160.

61 Editor. *The Many and the One: Essays on Religion in the Graeco-Roman World Presented to H. Ludin Jansen*. Trondheim: Tapir, 1985.

1986

62 "God's Agent in the Fourth Gospel." In *The Interpretation of John*, edited by J. Ashton, 67–78. Philadelphia: Fortress, 1986. Issues in Religion and Theology 9. Reprint of 10; reprinted also in 51 and 69.

63 "Nattverdtradisjonen i 1. Kor. 10 og 11 som evangelietradisjon." *Svensk Exegetisk årsbok* 51–52 (1986/1987) 32–39.

1987

64 "Bibelske tema i litteratur, film og teater." In *Bibelske tema i litteratur, film og teater*, edited by Peter W. Bøckman, 9–22. Trondheim: Tapir, 1987.

65 "The Church as the Body of Christ." *Doxology* 4 (1987) 7–16.

66 "Creation, Logos and the Son: Observations on John 1:1–18 and 5:17–18." *Ex Audite* 3 (1987) 88–97.

67 "John and the Synoptics: Can Paul Offer Help?'" In *Tradition and Interpretation in the New Testament: Essays in honor of E. Earle Ellis for His*

60th Birthday, edited by G. W. Hawthorne, 80-94. Grand Rapids: Eerdmans, 1987.

68 "Kristne og staten i Det nye testamente." In *Teologi på tidens torg. Festskrift til Peter Wilhelm Bøckman,* edited by Peder Borgen et al., 33-41. Trondheim: Tapir, 1987.

69 *Philo, John and Paul: New Perspectives on Judaism and Early Christianity.* Brown Judaic Studies 131. Atlanta: Scholars, 1987. The author states on p. 324, "These studies are either reproductions, elaborations or modifications of essays which have been previously published": see 06, 10, 13, 14, 15, 23, 26, 28, 33, 47, 48, 49, 50, 54, 60, 62; parts of 57 and 58 are also used in the two first articles in this collection.

70 Coeditor with others. *Teologi på tidens torg. Festskrift til Peter Wilhelm Bøckman.* Trondheim: Tapir, 1987.

1988

71 "Catalogue of Vices, the Apostolic Decree, and the Jerusalem Meeting." In *The Social World of Formative Christianity and Judaism: Essays in Tribute to Howard Clark Kee,* edited by Jacob Neusner et al., 126-41. Philadelphia: Fortress, 1988. Reprinted in 103.

72 *Utredning om behovet for forskning innenfor området kulturarv-religion-sundervisning-skole.* UniTRel Studieserie 8. Trondheim: Tapir, 1988.

1989

73 "En tysk buddhist tolker kristendommen og dens historie." In *Kristendommen og religionene,* edited by Peter W. Bøckman, 45-64. Trondheim: Tapir, 1989.

74 "Undervisning i kristendom, andre religioner og livssyn." In *Skolen mot år 2000,* edited by A. Wikan and Aa. O. Aakervik, 53-69. Namsos: Pedagogisk psykologisk, 1989.

1990

75 "John and the Synoptics." In *The Interrelations of the Gospels*, edited by D. L. Dungan, 408-37. Bibliotheca Ephemeridum Theologicarum Lovaniensium 95. Leuven: Leuven University Press, 1990. Reprinted in 103 and 150.

76 "John and the Synoptics: A Reply." In *The Interrelations of the Gospels*, edited by D. L. Dungan, 451-58. Bibliotheca Ephemeridum Theologicarum Lovaniensium 95. Leuven: Leuven University Press, 1990. Reprinted in 103.

1991

77 "Metodistkirken, en tverrnasjonal kirke i Norge og i andre land." In *Norges kristne kirkesamfunn*, edited by Per Øverland, 28-38. Trondheim: Tapir, 1991.

78 "Miljø, skapelse og frelse. Nåtid og fremtid." In *Miljøkrise og verdivalg: miljøkrisen i kristent perspektiv og som utfordring i samfunn og skole*, edited by Peder Borgen, 35-56. Trondheim: Tapir, 1991.

79 "The Sabbath Controversy in John 5:1-18 and Analogous Controversy Reflected in Philo's Writings." *The Studia Philonica Annual* 3 (1991) 209-21. Reprinted in 103 and 150.

1992

80 "Filo fra Alexandria. Jødisk filosof og Jesu samtidige." *Midtøsten Forum. Tidsskrift om Midtøsten og Nord-Afrika* 1 (1992) 40-46.

81 "The Independence of the Gospel of John. Some Observations." In *The Four Gospels 1992: Festschrift Frans Neirynck*, edited by Frans van Segbroeeck et al., 1815-33. Bibliotheca Ephemeridum Theologicarum Lovaniensium. Leiden: Brill, 1992. Reprinted in 103 and 150.

82 "Judaism in Egypt.'" In *Anchor Bible Dictionary*, edited by David Noel Freedman, 3:1061-72. New York: Doubleday, 1992. Reprinted in 103.

83 "Overcoming Fears." In *Overcoming Fears between Jews and Christians*, edited by James H. Charlesworth, 109-18. New York: Crossroad, 1992.

84 "Philo of Alexandria." In *The Anchor Bible Dictionary*, edited by David Noel Freedman, 5:333-42. New York: Doubleday, 1992.

85 "Philo and the Jews in Alexandria." In *Etnicity in Hellenistic Egypt*, edited by Per Bilde et al. 122-38. Århus: Aarhus University Press, 1992.

86 "'There Shall Come Forth a Man.' Reflections on Messianic Ideas in Philo." In *The Messiah*, edited by James H. Charlesworth, 341-61. Minneapolis: Fortress, 1992. Reprinted in 160.

87 "Et visst håp for framtiden." In *Snart enige? Glimt fra samtaler mellom forskjellige kirkesamfunn*, edited by R. Tofte, 78-79. Oslo: Verbum, 1992.

1993

88 "Georg Wolff (1736-1828): Handelsmann, metodist og norsk-dansk konsul i fred og krig." In *"Dette Ukrudt fra Engellands sectrige og geile jordbund." Rapport fra forskningsseminar om Den rolle kristne dissenterbevegelser—spesielt kvekerne—spilte i norsk kulturutvikling på 1800-tallet*, edited by B. S. Utne et al., 86-101. Stavanger, 1993. See also 94, 128, and 143.

89 "Heavenly Ascent in Philo: An Examination of Selected Passages." In *The Pseudepigrapha and Early Biblical Interpretation*, edited by James H. Charlesworth and Craig A. Evans, 246-68. Journal for the Study of Pseudepigrapha Supplement Series. Sheffield: Sheffield Academic, 1993. Reprinted in 160.

90 "John 6: Tradition, Interpretation and Composition." In *From Jesus to John: Essays on Jesus and New Testament Christology in Honour of Marinus de Jonge*, edited by M. C. Boer, 268-91. Journal for the Study of the New Testament Supplement Series 84 Sheffield: JSOT, 1993. Reprinted in 103 and 113.

91 "Metodistkirken." In *Kristne kirker og trossamfunn*, edited by Peder Borgen and Brynjar Haraldsø, 231-44. Trondheim: Tapir, 1993.

92 "Polemic in the Book of Revelation." In *Anti-Semitism and Early Christianity: Issues of Polemic and Faith*, edited by Craig A. Evans and D. A. Hagner, 199-211. Minneapolis: Fortress, 1993. Reprinted in 103 and 160.

93 Coauthor with N. Bloch-Hoell. "Den reformerte kirke." In *Kristne kirker og trossamfunn*, edited by Peder Borgen and Brynjar Haraldsø, 229-42. Trondheim: Tapir, 1993.

1994

94 "Den Dansk-Norske Konsul Georg Wolff (1736-1828). Religion, Handel og Politikk i Dansk-Norsk og Engelsk miljø i London." In *Clios Tro Tjener. Festskrift til Per Fuglum*, edited by H. W. Andersen, et al., 45-75. Skriftserie fra Historisk Institutt 1. Trondheim: Historisk institutt: Universitetet i Trondheim, 1994. See also 93, 128, and in 143.

95 "Jesus Christ, the Reception of the Spirit, and a Cross-National Community." In *Jesus of Nazareth: Lord and Christ: Essays on the Historical Jesus and New Testament Christology*, edited by Joel B. Green and Max Turner, 220-35. Grand Rapids: Eerdmans, 1994. Reprinted in 103.

96 "Man's Sovereignty over Animals and Nature according to Philo of Alexandria." In *Texts and Contexts: Biblical Texts in Their Textual and Situational Contexts: Essays in Honor of Lars Hartman*, edited by Tord Fornberg et al., 361-89. Oslo: Scandinavian University Press, 1994.

97 "Militant proselyttisme og misjon." In *Ad Acta: Studier til Apostlenes Gjerninger og urkristendommens historie*, edited by Reidar Hvalvik and Hans Kvalbein, 9-26. Oslo: Verbum, 1994. Revised and English translation in 108; see also 119.

98 "Misjon i nytestamentlig tid og i Metodistkirken i Europa i dag." *Teologisk Forum* 8 (1994) 27-41.

99 "Yes, No, How Far?: The Participation of Jews and Christians in Pagan Cults." In *Paul in His Hellenistic Context*, edited by T. Engberg-Pedersen, 30-59. Edinburgh: T. & T. Clark, 1994. Reprinted in 103.

1995

100 Coeditor with Søren Giversen. *The New Testament and Hellenistic Judaism*. Aarhus: Aarhus University Press, 1995.

101 "Some Hebrew and Pagan Features in Philo's and Paul's Interpretation of Hagar and Ishmael." In *The New Testament and Hellenistic Judaism*, edited by Peder Borgen and Søren Giversen, 151-64. Aarhus: Aarhus University Press, 1995. Reprinted in 160.

1996

102 "Autobiographical Ascent Reports: Philo and John the Seer." In *Early Christianity and Hellenistic Judaism*, 309-20. Edinburgh: T. & T. Clark, 1996. Reprinted in 160.

103 *Early Christianity and Hellenistic Judaism*. Edinburgh: T. & T. Clark, 1996. Contains 71, 75, 76, 79, 81, 82, 83, 90, 92, 95, 99, 102; in addition, 106 is not previously published, and 108 is a translation of 97.

104 "Emperor Worship and Persecution in Philo's *In Flaccum* and *De Legatione ad Gaium* and Revelation of John." In *Geschichte—Tradition—Religion. Festschrift für Martin Hengel zum 70 Geburtstag*. Band III. Frühes Christentum, edited by H. Cancik et al., 493-509. Tübingen: Mohr-Siebeck, 1996. Reprinted in 160.

105 "The Gospel of John and Hellenism: Some Observations." In *Exploring the Gospel of John: In Honor of D. Moody Smith*, edited by R. Alan Culpepper et al., 98-123. Louisville: Westminster John Knox, 1996. Reprinted in 150.

106 "Illegitimate Invasion and Proper Ascent." In *Early Christianity and Hellenistic Judaism*, 293-307. Edinburgh: T. & T. Clark, 1996. Reprinted in 160.

107 "In Accordance with the Scriptures." *Early Christian Thought in Its Jewish Context*, edited by J. M. G. Barclay and J. Sweet, 193-206. Cambridge: Cambridge University Press, 1996.

108 "Militant and Peaceful Proselytism and Christian Mission." In *Early Christianity and Hellenistic Judaism*, 45-69. Edinburgh: T. & T. Clark, 1996. Draws on 97; see further 119.

109 "Moses, Jesus, and the Roman Emperor. Observations in Philo's Writings and the Revelation of John." *Novum Testamentum* 38 (1996) 145-60. Reprinted in 160.

110 "Philantropia in Philo's Writings: Some Observations." In *Biblical and Humane: Festschrift for John Priest*, edited by L. B. Elder et al., 173-88. Atlanta: Scholars, 1996.

111 "Philo of Alexandria—A Systematic Philosopher or an Eclectic Editor? An Examination of His Exposition of the Laws of Moses." *Symbolae Osloenses* 71 (1996) 15-34.

112 "Religionsfrihet og statskirke." *BAPTIST. Tidsskrift for baptistisk historie, teologi og praksis* 2 (1996) 7–26.

1997

113 "John 6: Tradition, Interpretation and Composition." In *Critical Readings of John 6*, edited by R. Alan Culpepper, 95–114. Biblical Interpretation Series 22. Leiden: Brill, 1997. Reprint of 90 and 104.

114 *Philo of Alexandria: An Exegete for His Time*. Supplements to Novum Testamentum 86. Leiden: Brill, 1997.

115 "Philo of Alexandria: Reviewing and Rewriting Biblical Material." *Studia Philonica Annual* 9 (1997) 37–53.

116 *Samenes første Landsmøte 6–9 Februar 1917. Grunnlaget for Samefolkets dag 6. Februar. Historisk oversikt. Dokumentasjon. Kommentar*. Trondheim: Tapir, 1997.

1998

117 "The Crossing of the Red Sea as Interpreted by Philo. Biblical Event—Liturgical Model—Cultural Application." In *Common Life in the Early Church: Essays Honoring Graydon F. Snyder*, edited by J. V. Hills, 77–90. Harrisburg, PA: Trinity, 1998. Reprinted in 160.

118 "George Scott—Wesleyan Missionary to Sweden: Aspects of His Preaching." In *Beyond the Boundaries: Preaching in the Wesleyan Tradition*, edited by T. Sykes, 116–25. Oxford, 1998.

119 "Proselytes, Conquest and Mission." In *Recruitment, Conquest, and Conflict: Strategies in Judaism, Early Christianity, and the Greco-Roman World*, edited by Peder Borgen et al., 57–77. Emory Studies in Early Christianity. Atlanta: Scholars, 1998.

120 Coeditor with Vernon Robbins et al. *Recruitment, Conquest, and Conflict: Strategies in Judaism, Early Christianity, and the Greco-Roman World*. Emory Studies in Early Christianity. Atlanta: Scholars, 1998.

121 "A Response to Fredriksen's 'Judaism, the Circumcision of Gentiles, and Apocalyptic Hope: Another look at Galatians 1 and 2.'" In *Recruitment, Conquest, and Conflict: Strategies in Judaism, Early Christianity, and the*

Greco-Roman World, edited by Peder Borgen and Vernon Robbins et al., 245–50. Emory Studies in Early Christianity. Atlanta: Scholars, 1998.

1999

122 "Two Philonic Prayers and Their Contexts: An Analysis of *Who Is the Heir of Divine Things (Her.)* 24–29 and *Against Flaccus (Flac.)* 170–75." *New Testament Studies* 45 (1999) 291–309. Reprinted in 160.

2000

123 "Jøder og kristne. Følelse av slektskap-opplevelse av overgrep-forståelse av skyld-dialogens vei." In *Kropp og sjel. Festskrift til professor Olav Hognestad*, edited by Th. Jørgensen et al., 195–201. Trondheim: Tapir, 2000.

124 "Openly Portrayed as Crucified: Some Observations on Gal 3:1–14." In *Christology, Controversy and Community: New Testament Essays in Honour of David R. Catchpole*, edited by D. G. Horrell et al., 345–53. Leiden: Brill: Leiden, 2000. Reprinted in 160.

125 Editor with Kåre Fuglseth and Roald Skarsten *The Philo Index: A Complete Greek Word Index to the Writings of Philo of Alexandria*. Grand Rapids: Eerdmans, 2000.

126 "Philo's *Against Flaccus* as Interpreted History." In *A Bouquet of Wisdom: Essays in Honour of Karl-Gustav Sandelin*, edited by K.-J. Illman et al., 41–57. Åbo: Åbo Akademi, 2000. Reprinted in 160.

2001

127 "Application of and Commitment to the Laws of Moses: Observations on Philo's Treatise 'On the Embassy to Gaius.'" In *The Spirit of Faith: Studies in Philo and Early Christianity in Honor of David Hay*, edited by David T. Runia and Greg E. Sterling, 86–101. Studia Philonica Annual/ Studies in Hellenistic Judaism 13. Atlanta: Scholars, 2001. Reprinted in 160.

128 "George Wolff (1736–1828): Norwegian-Born Merchant, Consul, Benevolent Methodist Layman, Close Friend of John Wesley." *Methodist History* 40 (2001) 17–28. See also 93 and 143.

129 "Greek Encyclical Education, Philosophy and the Synagogue. Observations from Philo of Alexandria's Writings." In *Libens Merito. Festskrift til Stig Strømholm på sjuttioårsdagen Sep. 16, 2001*, edited by O. Matsson et al., 62-71. Acta academiæ Regiæ Scientiarum Upsaliensis. Kungl. Uppsala: Vetenskapssamhällets Uppsala Handlingar, 2001.

130 "A Necessary and Important Step." In *Interpreting the New Testament in Africa*, edited by M. N. Getui, T. Maluleke, and J. Ukpong, 1-4. Nairobi, Kenya: Acton, 2001.

2002

131 "Avtalen 'Nådens fellesskap' mellom Metodistkirken og Den norske kirke." *Tidsskrift for Teologi og Kirke* 73 (2002) 185-98.

2003

132 "The Gospel of John and Philo of Alexandria." In *Light in a Spotless Mirror: Reflections on Wisdom Traditions in Judaism and Early Christianity*, edited by James H. Charlesworth, 77-91. London: Continuum, 2003. Reprinted in 150.

133 "Philo of Alexandria as Exegete." In *A History of Biblical Interpretation*, edited by A. J. Hauser and D. F. Watson, 1:114-43. Grand Rapids: Eerdmans, 2003. Reprinted as 155.

2004

134 "Avhandlingen das Volk Gottes. Dens økumeniske perspektiv, historiske kontekst og innflytelse." *Norsk Teologisk Tidsskrift* 105 (2004) 12-20. English translation in 143.

135 "The Contrite Wrongdoer—Condemned or Set Free by the Spirit? Romans 7:7—8:4." In *The Holy Spirit and Christian Origins: Essays in Honor of James D. G. Dunn*, edited by G. N. Stanton et al., 181-92. Grand Rapids: Eerdmans, 2004.

136 "Ute-økumenikk og hjemme-økumenikk. Hendelser og erfaringer." In *Etikk, tro og pluralisme. Festskrift til Lars Østnor*, edited by Kjell Olav Sandnes et al., 269–80. Bergen: Fagbokforlaget, 2004. Reprinted in 143.

2005

137 "Der Methodismus und die Anfänge der Pfingstbewegung in Norwegen: Eine auf Thomas Ball Barratt konzentrierte Studie mit einem kurzen Hinweis auf Erik Andersen Nordquelle." In *Der europäische Methodismus um die Wende vom 19. und 20. Jahrhundert*, edited by P. Ph. Streiff, 237–57. EmK Geschichte—Monografien 52. Freiburg: Medienwerk der Evangelisch-methodistischen Kirche, 2005. English translation in 143.

2006

138 "Crucified for His Own Sins—Crucified for Our Sins: Observations on a Pauline Perspective." In *The New Testament and Early Christian Literature in Greco-Roman Context: Studies in Honor of David E. Aune*, edited by John Fotopoulos, 17–35. Supplements to Novum Testamentum 122. Leiden: Brill, 2006. Reprinted in 160.

139 "Some Crime-and-Punishment Reports." In *Ancient Israel, Judaism, and Christianity in Contemporary Perspective: Essays in Memory of Karl-Johan Illman*, edited by Jacob Neusner et al., 56–80. Studies in Judaism. Lanham, MD: University Press of America, 2006. Reprinted in 160.

2007

140 "The Scriptures and the Words and Works of Jesus." Response by M. Labahn. In *What We Have Heard from the Beginning: The Past, Present, and Future of Johannine Studies*, edited by T. Thatcher, 39–58. Waco, TX: Baylor University Press, 2007. Reprinted in 150.

2009

141 "Odd Hagen." *Norsk biografisk leksikon*, internet edition, 2009. https://nbl.snl.no/Odd_Hagen.

142 "Ole Peter Petersen." *Norsk biografisk leksikon*, internet edition, 2009. https://nbl.snl.no/Ole_Peter_Petersen.

143 *Vei utenfor Allfarvei. Studier i skjæringspunktet mellom kirkehistorie, personalhistorie og samfunnshistorie*. Skrifter (Det Kongelige norske videnskabers selskab) 1. Trondheim: DKNVS/Tapir, 2009. Contains 19, 128, 136, 137 (= English translation), and in addition:

144 "Nils Alstrup Dahl (1811–2001), Das Volk Gottes." In *Vei utenfor Allfarvei*, 153–68. English revised and translated from 134.

145 "Ole Peter Petersen fra Glemmen (1822–1901." In *Vei utenfor Allfarvei*, 87–128.

146 "Vei utenfor allfarvei—oversikt—hovedtemaer." In *Vei utenfor Allfarvei*, 7–20.

2013

147 "On the Migration of Moses." In *Outside the Bible*, edited by L. H. Feldman et al., 1:951–58. Philadelphia: Jewish Publication Society, 2013.

2014

148 "The Appearance to Thomas: Not a Blasphemous Claim, but the Truth." In *The Gospel of John: More Light*, 261–74.

149 "Can Philo's *In Flaccum* and *Legatio ad Gaium* Be of Help?" In *The Gospel of John: More Light*, 241–60.

150 *The Gospel of John: More Light from Philo, Paul and Archaeology: The Scriptures, Tradition, Exposition, Settings, Meaning*. Supplements to Novum Testamentum 154. Leiden: Brill, 2014. Contains 02, 10, 51, 75, 79, 82, 108, 132, and 140; in addition, not previously published are 148–49, 151–54:

151 "Gospel Traditions in Paul and John: Methods and Structures. John and the Synoptics." In *The Gospel of John: More Light*, 67–77.

152 "John the Witness and the Prologue: John 1:1–34(37)." In *The Gospel of John: More Light*, 219–38.

153 "Observations on God's Agent and Agency in John's Gospel Chapters 5–10: Agency and the Quest for the Historical Jesus." In *The Gospel of John: More Light*, 193–218.

154 "Summary: John, Archaeology, Philo, Paul, Other Jewish Sources. John's Independence of the Synoptics. Where My Journey of Research Has Led." In *The Gospel of John: More Light*, 275–94.

155 "Philo—An Interpreter of the Laws of Moses." In *Reading Philo: A Handbook to Philo of Alexandria*, edited by Torrey Seland, 75–101. Grand Rapids: Eerdmans, 2014. Reprint of 133.

2016

156 "Alternative Aims and Choices in Education: Analysis of Selected Texts." In *The Studia Philonica Annual XXVIII 2016 / Studies in Hellenistic Judaism*, edited by David T. Runia and Greg E. Sterling, 257–71. Atlanta: SBL, 2016.

157 "Observations on God's Agent and Agency in John 5–9: Tradition, Exposition, and Glimpses into History." In *John, Jesus, and History*, vol. 3, *Glimpses of Jesus through the Johannine Lens*, edited by Paul N. Anderson, Felix Just, and Tom Thatcher, 423–38. Early Christianity and Its Literature 18. Atlanta: SBL, 2016. Modified version of 153.

2017

158 *Bread from Heaven: An Exegetical Study of the Concept of Manna in the Gospel of John and the Writings of Philo*. The Johannine Monograph Series. Eugene, OR: Wipf & Stock, 2017. Reprint of 07/36, with a foreword by Paul N. Anderson (ix–xxxiv) and a new preface by Peder Borgen (xxxv–xliv).

2018

159 "Perspectives for Mission: Galatians 3:1–14 in Context." In *The Church and Its Mission in the New Testament and Early Christianity: Essays in Memory of Hans Kvalbein*, edited by David E. Aune and Reidar Hvalvik, 181–92. Wissenschaftliche Untersuchungen zum Neuen Testament 404. Tübingen: Mohr Siebeck, 2018. Reprinted in 160.

2021

160 *Illuminations by Philo of Alexandria: Selected Studies on Interpretation in Philo, Paul, and the Revelation of John.* Edited by Torrey Seland. Studies in Philo of Alexandria 12. Leiden: Brill, 2021. Contains reprints of 60, 86, 89, 92, 101, 102, 104, 106, 109, 117, 122, 124, 126, 127, 138, 139, and 159.

Bibliography

UNPUBLISHED MATERIAL

Borgen, Omar Emil. *Brev til en venn*. Lillestrøm: not published but distributed in the family, 1970.
Interviews with Peder Borgen, digitalized by the author.
Kirkebok for Rakkestad døde og gravlagte 1918/Church Register for Rakkestad; deaths. https://media.digitalarkivet.no/view/4762/1
Ministerialbok for Skjeberg nr. I 10, 1898–1911. https://media.digitalarkivet.no/view/3460/22679/1
Peder Borgen Archives, The National Library, Oslo. Not available to the general public.

DIVERSE MATERIAL FROM INTERNET SITES

"Amerikansk bombeangrep på Kjeller 1943" (American/Allied bombing Lillestrøm 1943). *Lokalhistoriewiki*. https://lokalhistoriewiki.no/index.php/Amerikansk_bombeangrep_p%C3%A5_Kjeller_1943.
"Anglikansk-luthersk kirkefellesskap «Porvoo-avtalen»." April 17, 2015. https://kirken.no/nb-NO/om-kirken/slik-styres-kirken/mellomkirkelig-rad/okumenikk-og-kirkesamarbeid/internasjonale-okumeniske-organisasjoner/porvoo-avtalen/.
Battered Child Syndrome:
Kempe, C. Henry, et al. "The Battered-Child Syndrome." *JAMA* 181:1 (1962) 17-24, https://jamanetwork.com/journals/jama/article-abstract/327895.
Wolf, Larry. "The Battered-Child Syndrome: 50 Years Later." *HuffPost*, January 4, 2013. http://www.huffingtonpost.com/larry-wolff/battered-child-syndrome_b_2406348.html.
Bibliography of Arne Martin Klausen. https://www.idunn.no/nat/2018/01-02/arne_martin_klausen_en_bibliografi.
Church of Norway:
Church of Norway. https://kirken.no/nb-NO/church-of-norway/.
"Church of Norway." *Wikipedia*. https://en.wikipedia.org/wiki/Church_of_Norway.

Comments to St.meld. nr. 40 Om Stat og kirke fra Kirkerådet. https://www.nb.no/nbsok/nb/e66b1698e0de5d57d1ca17e44537b75b?lang=no#0.
Communion of Protestant Churches in Europe (CPCE). http://www.leuenberg.net.
Conference of European Churches: https://www.ceceurope.org.
Ellingsen, Karl Anders. "Menigheten i Trondheim hedret for arbeid med marginaliserte og urfolk" (Honoring the Methodist Congregation in Trondheim for Their Work with and for Marginalized and Indigenous People). February 1, 2017. http://www.metodistkirken.no/hoved/artikkel/article/1411080.
"Fellowship of Grace: Report from the Conversations between Church of Norway and the United Methodist Church in Norway." Oslo, 1994. https://kyrkja.no/globalassets/kirken.no/church-of-norway/dokumenter/fellowship_of_grace_1994.pdf.
Graydon Snyder's obituary. http://www.legacy.com/obituaries/fortwayne/obituary.aspx?pid=180178618.
Griniposten, May 8, 1945. https://digitaltmuseum.no/011024286403/grini-posten.
"Hans Nielsen Hauge." *Wikipedia*. https://en.wikipedia.org/wiki/Hans_Nielsen_Hauge.
Hjelde, S. "Sigmund Mowinckel." *Norsk biografisk leksikon*. https://nbl.snl.no/Sigmund_Mowinckel.
Høringsuttalelser—NOU 2006: 2. "Staten og Den norske kirke—tros- og livssynssamfunn." https://www.regjeringen.no/no/dokumenter/horingsuttalelser-nou-20062-staten-og-9/id437630/.
Høringsuttalelser—NOU 2006: 2. "Staten og Den norske kirke—kirkelige organisasjoner." https://www.regjeringen.no/no/dokumenter/horingsuttalelser-nou-20062-staten-og-7/id437632/.
Høringsuttalelse fra Metodistkirken i Norge. NOU 2006: 2. "Staten og Den norske kirke." https://www.regjeringen.no/globalassets/upload/kilde/kkd/hdk/2006/0021/ddd/pdfv/298514-metodistkirken_i_norge_statkirke2006.pdf.
Jacob Jervell in an interview with Tor Øystein Vaaland, 2010. http://www.tf.uio.no/om/historie/tf200/berlin2010/jervell_1200.mp4.
Lund, Jon Magne. "Ole Edvard Borgen." *Norsk biografisk leksikon*, March 26, 2009. https://nbl.snl.no/Ole_Edvard_Borgen.
———. "Peder Borgen." *Norsk biografisk leksikon*, January 30, 2013. https://nbl.snl.no/Peder_Borgen.
Methodist Church in Norway. http://www.metodistkirken.no.
Methodist Council. https://worldmethodistcouncil.org.
Moxnes, H. "Nils Alstrup Dahl." *Norsk biografisk leksikon*. 2016. https://nbl.snl.no/Nils_Alstrup_Dahl.
Norges kristne råd / Norwegian Christian Council. https://norgeskristnerad.no/english/
"Norwegian Population in the 1940s." *Statistisk sentralbyrå*. https://www.ssb.no/a/histstat/aarbok/1946-1948.pdf.
NOU 1975: 30. "Stat og Kirke." https://www.nb.no/items/URN:NBN:no-nb_digibok_2008052804002.
Porvoo Agreement. https://kirken.no/nb-NO/om-kirken/slik-styres-kirken/mellomkirkelig-rad/okumenikk-og-kirkesamarbeid/internasjonale-okumeniske-organisasjoner/porvoo-avtalen/.
"På vei mot ny kirkeordning" (On the Way to a New Church Order). https://kirken.no/nb-NO/om-kirken/slik-styres-kirken/kirkeordning/ny-kirkeordning-2020/.
Sak KM 13/97: "Urfolk i den verdensvide kirke med utgangspunkt i samisk kirkeliv." Available at http://www.kirken.no.

Sametinget (Sami Council). https://www.sametinget.no.
Stortingsmelding nr. 40 1980–81 *Om stat og kyrkje*. Available as a PDF at: https://www.nb.no/items/2a03b029e921638f5c7d9bbf9e4b6bfb?page=0&searchText=Stortingsmelding%20nr.%2040%20Om%20stat%20og%20kirke.
"Tyske fangeleire i Skedsmo" (German Prison Camps in Skedsmo). *Lokalhistoriewiki*. https://lokalhistoriewiki.no/index.php/Tyske_fangeleire_i_Skedsmo.
United Methodist Church. http://www.umc.org.
United Nations:
"United Nations." *Wikipedia*. https://en.wikipedia.org/wiki/United_Nations.
Fomerand, J., Karen Mingst, and Cecelia M. Lynch. "United Nations." *Encyclopedia Britannica*, April 7, 2022. https://www.britannica.com/topic/United-Nations.

PAMPLETS, CATALOGUES, REPORTS, ETC.

The Church: Community of Grace. Final Report of the Joint Commission between the Lutheran World Federation and World Methodist Council, 1979–1984. Lutheran World Federation World Methodist Council, 1984.
Den norske kirke og staten. Innstilling fra Det frivillige kirkeråds utredningskommisjon av 1969. Stavanger: Nomi, 1973.
Dåp, Nattverd og Embete. Limadokumentet med forord av Ivar Asheim. Kommisjonen for tro og kirkeordnings dokument nr. 111. Kirkenes Verdensråd, Geneve, 1982. Oslo: Verbum, 1982.
Festskrift ved Lillestrøms Metodistmenighets 100-årsjubileum Sep. 3, 1999. Utarbeidet av Ole E. Borgen, 1999.
NOU 1975:30 Stat og kirke. "Kirke og undervisningsdepartementet: Sivertsenutvalget." Oslo: Universitetetsforlaget, 1975.
Reform av den norske kirke. Innstilling fra Det frivillige kirkeråds reformkommisjon av 1965. Stavanger: Nomi, 1969.
Statistisk årbok 1923. Kristiania, 1924.
Wesley Theological Seminary Bulletin, April–June 1961. Wesley Theological Seminary, Washington, DC.
Wesley Theological Seminary Bulletin, Catalog Issue, 1962–1963. Wesley Theological Seminary, Washington, DC.

ARTICLES IN MAGAZINES AND NEWSPAPERS

Kristelig Tidende, Brobyggeren, and *Vår Ungdom* are Christian periodicals, here given by number, year, and page numbers. The daily newspapers are given by date, year, and page numbers. In the footnotes these articles are given in full references in order to distinguish them from articles published in books and journals. The last-mentioned are given in abbreviated forms.

ARTICLES WRITTEN BY PEDER BORGEN

"Angående dialogen med Den norske lutherske kirke." *Kristelig Tidende* 12 (1995) 10.

"Det arbeides i Amsterdam. Glimt fra Verdenskirkemøtet." *Kristelig Tidende* 77 (1948) 508–9 and 516.
"Et Bibel- og Jesus-Seminar." *Kristelig Tidende* 20 (1974) 2–3 and 7.
"Med bil bak jernteppet." *Vårt Land*, May 19, 1959, 2 and 8.
"På biltur bak jernteppet." *Kristelig Tidende* 88 (1959) 337, 340–41, and 344.
"Med båt og buss i Paulus fotspor. Reisebrev til Dagen fra Peder Borgen." *Dagen*, July 7, 195, 6.
"Med båt og buss i Paulus fotspor. 2. reisebrev til Dagen fra eder Borgen." *Dagen* July 12, 1951, 1 and 5.
"Med båt og buss i Paulus fotspor. 3dje reisebrev til Dagen fra Peder Borgen." *Dagen*, July 23, 1951, 1 and 6.
"Hvorfor ble samenes første landsmøte lagt til metodistkirken i Trondheim?" *Sagat* 47 (2017) 9. Available at: https://www.sagat.no/mening/hvorfor-ble-samenes-forste-landsmote-lagt-til-metodistkirken-i-trondheim/19.6799.
"Fra internasjonal dialog til norsk monolog." *Vårt Land*, May 21, 1991, 8.
"Inntrykk fra kirkelivet i Sovjet-Unionen i dag." *Aftenposten*, evening ed., May 26, 1959, 8.
"Inntrykk fra kirkelivet i Sovjet-samveldet." *Aftenposten*, evening ed., May 27, 1959, 8.
"Inntrykk fra kirkelivet i Sovjet-Unionen i dag." *Kristelig Tidende* 88 (1959) 384–85 and 388.
"Det jødiske spørsmål i Alexandria i romersk tid. Første artikkel." *Aftenposten* morning ed., January 10, 1974, 4.
"Det jødiske spørsmål i Alexandria i romersk tid. Annen artikkel." *Aftenposten*, morning ed., January 11, 1974, 4.
"En kirke der menighet og misjon er ett." *Kristelig Tidende* 90 (1961) 444 and 477.
"Kirkene fordømmer både kommunismen og kapitalismen." *Arbeiderbladet*, September 7, 1948, 7.
"Kirketanke og misjonstanke hører sammen." *Kristelig Tidende* 88 (1959) 438 and 446.
"Kristendomskunnskap som universitetsfag." *Dagen*, May 11, 1967, 3.
"Metodister i Amsterdam." *Kristelig Tidende* 77 (1948) 549 and 555.
"Et møte på Akropolis." *Vår Ungdom* 10–11 (1951) 105.
"Nytt lys over metodismens begynnelse i landet vårt." *Kristelig Tidende* 33/34 (1976) 9.
"Nytt lys over metodismens begynnelse i landet vårt." *Kristelig Tidende* 9/10 (1977) 2.
"I Paulus fotspor. Fra Paulus jubileet i Hellas. Reisebrev til Vårt Land fra Peder Borgen." *Vårt Land*, June 29, 1951, 1 and 4.
"I Paulus fotspor. Saloniki og Aten. Annet reisebrev til Vårt Land fra Peder Borgen." *Vårt Land*, July 13m, 1951, 1 and 5–6.
"Pilegrimsferden går videre." *Kristelig Tidende* 80 (1951) 436–37 and 440.
"Reell dialog i Norge?" *Vårt Land*, June 17, 1991, 3.
"Saloniki og Athen." *Kristelig Tidende* 80 (1951) 453–554.
"Stat-kirkemeldingen er diskriminerende." *Kristelig Tidende* 3–4 (1981) 12 og 9.
"Obama er en verdig mottager" / "Obama is a worthy recipient." *Aftenposten*, morning ed., November 1, 2009, part 2, 4.
"Utrolig, men sant." *Romerikes Blad*, February 1, 2009, 14.
"Venezia—byen uten gater og biler." *Akershus Arbeiderblad*, June 20, 1951, 3 and 6.

OTHER MAGAZINE AND NEWSPAPER ARTICLES

Anonymous. "Bergen aktuell som utdannelsessted for norske metodistprester." *Dagen*, April 1, 1970, 1.

———. "Ekumenisk på Stabekk." *Arbeiderbladet*, August 3, 1960, 8.

———. "Kristendom på universitetsplan—et nødvendig og naturlig krav." *Dagen*, May 5, 1967, 1 and 8.

———. "Lønning mot 'tros-professor': Kirken vinner bare en Pyrrhos-seier!" *Dagen*, January 8, 1971, 1 and 8.

———. "Maratondebatt om brød fra himmelen. Metodistprest blir doctor theologiae." *Aftenposten*, June 13, 1966, 5.

———. "Metodistenes årskonferanse fikk en strålende slutning." *Dagen*, July 1, 1957, 2.

———. "Metodistprester drøfter en alternativ utdannelse." *Vårt Land*, March 11, 1970, 6.

———. "Oppfordring fra Metodistkirken: Alle kirkesamfunn bør stå likt overfor Staten." *Aftenposten*, morning ed., July 7, 1986, 16

———. "Professor dr. Peder Borgen—norsk metodist med en sjelden karriere." *Nordisk Tidende*, August 8, 1980. (S.D.)

———. "Samarbeids-utspill fra Metodistkirken." *Vårt Land*, July 5, 1986, 8.

———. "Slå bro over kløften mellom kirke og arbeidsliv,. *Harstad Tidende*, September 11, 1956, n.p.

———. "Statskirkeordningen er uten tvil en særbehandling av den lutherske kirke." Interview with Ole Borgen. *Kristelig Tidende* 23 (1975) 1

———. "Uenighet om hvor seminaret skal ligge i fremtiden." *Kristelig Tidende* 18/19 (1976) 2.

———. "Vi bør ikke være med i hylekoret som krever statskirken oppløst." Interview with Harald Larsen. *Kristelig Tidende* 23 (1975) 4.

Bøckman, P. W. "Kristendomskunnskap som universitetsfag." *Morgenbladets kronikk*, September 18, 1967, 3 og 8.

Børrestuen, Espen. "50 år gammel drøm." *Romerikes Blad*, August 28, 2013, 16.

Eira, Sara Ellen Anne. "The Samenes første landsmøte og kirken—håp om fellesskap og forsoning." *Ságat*, February 8, 2017. Aavailable at https://www.sagat.no/mening/samenes-forste-landsmote-og-kirken-hap-om-fellesskap-og-forsoning/19.6451.

Fonn, Geir Ove. "Talen grep, inspirerte og beveget." *Vårt Land*, August 28, 2013, 12–13.

Fordal, Jon-Annar. "Professor Peder Borgen: Vi fortrenger religiøse behov." *Aftenposten* January 26, 1988, 18.

Haddal, Ingvar. "Philo—ikke-kristen 'kirkefar' gjennom datamaskin i Bergen. Fireårig prosjekt vekker internasjonal oppsikt." *Vårt Land*, July 4, 1973, 13.

Hall-Hofsø, B. "Den glemte ungdomsklubben i kirka." *Harstad Tidende*, May 13, 2017, 13.

———. "Med bankende hjerte for lokalkulturen." *Harstad Tidende*, March 15, 2013, n.p.

———. "Lørdagsmoro i Metodistkirken." *Harstad Tidende*, December 14, 1957, 9.

Kjøllesdal, Helge. "Håper på likeverdighet i det norske kristenliv." *Vårt Land*, February 7, 1979, 13.

Kragerud, Alv. "Religionsvitenskap I." *Dagen*, May 19, 1967, 3.

———. "Religionsvitenskap II." *Dagen*, May 20, 1967, 3.

———. "Universitetslektor i kristendomskunnskap." *Dagen*, April 20, 1967, 1 and 8.

Kvalbein, Aud. "Religion interesserer næringslivet." *Dagen*, March 6, 1990, 9.

Martinsen, Cato. "... som om det var i går." *Laagendalsposten*, May 20, 2017, 13-16.
Nordby, Lars-Erik. "Peder Borgen: Mitt mål har vært å åpne vinduer mellom vitenskap, kirke og kultur." *Brobyggeren* 7 (2008) 14.
Østnor, Lars. "Misvisende om dialog." *Vårt Land*, June 4, 1991, 3.
Rolfsen, Rolf. "Peder og Filon." *Adresseavisen*, June 15, 1996, 4.
Solstad, Arve. "Greker sliter med Drammen." *Dagbladet*, July 29, 1961, 7-8.
Thomassen, E. "50 år med religions-vitenskap i Bergen." *Bergens Tidende*, October 26, 2017, 46.

GENERAL BIBLIOGRAPHY[1]

Aadnanes, Per M. *Litt av eit puslespel. Ei vestnorsk ungdomstid*. No publisher, 2015.
Aalen, Sverre, "'Bread from Heaven.' Opposisjonsinnlegg ved Peder Borgens disputas for den teologiske doktorgrad 11. juni 1966." *Norsk Teologisk Tidsskrift* 67 (1966) 243-260.
Aarflot, A. *Trossamfunn og folkekirke. Om reformene i Den norske kirke i de siste femti år*. Oslo: Verbum, 1976.
Årboken. *Metodistkirkens årskonferanse i Norge. Holdt på Mysen 30 juni-1 juli 1976*. Konferansens offisielle protokoll. Oslo: Norsk Forlagsselskap, 1976.
Åmås, Knut Olav. "Biografiens teori og metode." In *Mitt liv var ein draum. En biografi om Olav H. Hauge*, 545-604, and notes 679-83. Oslo: Det Norske Samlaget, 2004.
Almås, K., and Dagfinn Rian, eds. *Kristendomsfag og religionsforskning i Trondheim*. UniTRel Studieserie 1. Religionsvitenskapelig institutt: NTNU, 1998.
Amundsen, L. "Det teologiske fakultet. Lærere og forskning." In *Universitetet i Oslo 1911-1961*, 1-62. Oslo: Universitetsforlaget, 1961.
Andersen, H. With, et al., eds. *Æmula Lauri: The Royal Norwegian Society of Sciences and Letters 1760-2010*. Sagamore Beach, MA: Science History, 2009.
Andersen, R. A. *Metodismen 100 år i Hammerfest. Fra livet i verdens nordligste metodistmenighet 1890-1990*. No place or date.
Anderson, Paul N. *The Christology of the Fourth Gospel: Its Unity and Disunity in the Light of John 6*. Eugene, OR: Cascade, 2010.
———. "Peder Borgen's *Bread from Heaven*—Midrashic Developments in John 6 as a Case Study in John's Unity and Disunity. A Foreword." In *Bread from Heaven: An Exegetical Study of the Concept of Manna in the Gospel of John and the Writings of Philo*, by Peder Borgen, ix-xxxiv. Johannine Monograph Series 6. Eugene, OR: Wipf & Stock, 2017.
Ashton, John. ed. *The Interpretation of John*. Issues in Religion and Theology 9. Minneapolis: Fortress, 1986.
Aune, David E. "The Influence of Roman Imperial Court Ceremonial on the Apocalypse of John." *Biblical Research* 18 (1983) 5-26.
———. *Revelation*. Word Biblical Commentary 52a-c. Dallas: Word, 1997-1998.
Aune, David E., Torrey Seland, and Jarl H. Ulrichsen, eds. *Neotestamentica et Philonica: Studies in honor of Peder Borgen*. Supplements to Novum Testamentum 106. Leiden: Brill, 2003.
Bach, Neil, *Leon Morris: One Man's Fight for Love and Truth*. Milton Keynes, UK: Paternoster, 2015.

---

1. For articles in journals and books by Peder Borgen, see Appendix.

Baird, W. *History of New Testament Research*, vol. 3, *From C. H. Dodd to Hans Dieter Betz*. Minneapolis: Fortress, 2013.
Barclay, J. M. G. "Paul and Philo on Circumcision. Romans 2.25-9 in Social and Cultural Context." *New Testament Studies* 44 (1998) 536-56.
Barrett, C. K. *The Gospel According to St. John*. London: SPCK, 1955.
———. *The Holy Spirit and the Gospel Tradition*. London: SPCK, 1947.
Bekken, Per Jarle. *Paul's Negotiation of Abraham in Galatians 3 in the Jewish Context*. Beiheft zur Zeitschrift für die neutestamentliche Wissenschaft 248. Berlin: de Gruyter, 2021.
———. *"The Word Is Near You": A Study of Deuteronomy 30:12-14 in Paul's Letter to the Romans in a Jewish Context*. Beiheft zur Zeitschrift für die neutestamentliche Wissenschaft 144. Berlin: de Gruyter, 2007.
Berg, Rolf, et al., eds. *Riv ned gjerdene! Festskrift til Jacob Jervell på 60-årsdagen 21. mai 1985*. Oslo" Land og kirke, Gyldendal, 1985.
Beutler, Johannes. *Das Johannesevangelium. Kommentar*. Freiburg: Herder, 2013.
Bird, Michael F. *Crossing Over Sea and Land: Jewish Missionary Activity in the Second Temple Period*. Peabody, MA: Hendrickson, 2010.
Bloch-Hoell, N. E. "Norsk Misjonsråd." *Norsk Tidsskrift for Misjon* 20 (1978) 209-12.
Bond, Helen. *The First Biography of Jesus: Genre and Meaning in Mark's Gospel*. Grand Rapids: Eerdmans, 2020.
Bolling, R., ed. *Norges Prester og teologiske kandidater. Sjette økede utgave av "Norges Geistlighet"*. Oslo: Hanches Forlag, 1958.
Breistein, Ingunn Folkestad. "Fra dissens til konsensus: økumeniske relasjoner og tilnærmingsmåter i Norge etter 1970." In *Kirke Kultur Politikk. Festskrift til professor dr.theol. Bernt T. Oftestad på 70-årsdagen*, edited by Birger Løvlie et al., 83-92. Trondheim: Tapir, 2012.
———. "Fra luthersk presteskole til økumenisk utdanningssted." In *Mellom kirke og akademia. Det teologiske Menighetsfakultet 100 år, 1908-2008*, edited by Bernt T. Oftestad and Nils Aksel Røsæg, 221-38. Trondheim: Tapir, 2008.
———. *"Har staten bedre borgere?": Dissenternes kamp for religiøs frihet 1891-1969*. KIFO perspektiv 14. Trondheim: Tapir, 2003.
———. "Når skilsmisse er det beste: Frikirkelige perspektiver på stat-kirke-utredningen." In *Stat, kirke og menneskerettigheter*. Oslo: Abstrakt, 2006.
Brown, R. E. *The Gospel According to John (I-XII)*. Anchor Bible 29a. Garden City, NY: Doubleday, 1966.
Buchanan, George Wesley. *An Academic Hound Off the Leash: The Autobiography of George Wesley Buchanan*. Gaithersburg: Create Space, 2014.
Burridge, Richard A. *What Are the Gospels? A Comparison with Graeco-Roman Biography*. Cambridge: Cambridge University Press, 1992.
Bühner, Jan. *Der Gesandte und sein Weg im vierten Evangelium: Die kultur- und religionsgeschichtlichen Grundlagen der johanneischen Sendungschristologie und ihre traditionsgeschichtliche Entwicklung*. Wissenschaftliche Untersuchungen zum Neuen Testament. Tübingen: Mohr Siebeck, 1975.
Bøckman, P. W., and R. E. Kristiansen, eds. *Context. Festskrift til Peder Johan Borgen*. Relieff 24. Trondheim: Tapir, 1987.
Bøckman, P. W. "Kristendomsstudiet og teologien." In *For kirke og skole. Festskrift til dosent dr. theol. Ole Modalsli på 70-årsdagen 1. april 1983*, edited by Ivar Asheim, et al., 11-23. Oslo: Universitetsforlaget, 1983.

———. "Kristendomsundervisning på universitetsnivå." In *Skrift og skole. Festskrift til Oddmund Hjelde på 60-årsdagen 15. mars 1970*, 132–48. Oslo: Forlaget Land og Kyrkje, 1970.

Campbell, Douglas A. "Galatians 5.11: Evidence of an Early Law-Observant Mission by Paul?" *New Testament Studies* 57 (2011) 325–47.

Conzelmann, Hans. *Die Mitte der Zeit. Studien zur Theologie des Lukas*. Beiträge zur historischen Theologie 17. Tübingen: Mohr Siebeck, 1954.

Culpepper, R. Alan, ed. *Critical Readings of John 6*. Biblical Interpretation Series. Leiden: Brill, 1997.

Culpepper, R. Alan, and Paul N. Anderson, eds. *John and Judaism. A Contested Relationship in Context*. Resources for Biblical Study 87. Atlanta: SBL, 2017.

Dittmann, E. *Kristelig gymnasium 50 år*. Oslo: Kristelig Gymnasium, 1963.

Eccles, R. S. *Erwin Ramsdell Goodenough: A Personal Pilgrimage*. Chico, CA: Scholars, 1985.

Elliott, J. K. "Vale Peder Borgen." *Novum Testamentum* 51 (2009) 105.

Falcetta, Alessandro. *A Biography of James Rendel Harris, 1852–1941*. London: T. & T. Clark, 2018.

Farmer, W. R. *The Synoptic Problem: A Critical Analysis*. London: MacMilan, 1964.

Feldman, Louis H. *Jew & Gentile in the Ancient World: Attitudes and Interactions from Alexander to Justinian*. Princeton, NJ: Princeton University Press, 1993.

Fuglseth, Kåre S. *Johannine Sectarianism in Perspective: A Sociological, Historical and Comparative Analysis of Temple and Social Relationships in the Gospel of John, Philo and Qumran*. Supplements to Novum Testamentum 119. Leiden: Brill, 2005.

———. "'Satans Synagoge'? Mogelege historiske og sosiologiske tolkingar av Op 2,9 og 3,9." *Tidsskrift for kyrkje, religion og samfunn* 2 (2003) 135–50.

Getui, M. N., T. Maluleke, and J. Ukpong, eds., *Interpreting the New Testament in Africa*. Nairobi, Kenya: Acton, 2001.

Grass, Tim, *F. F. Bruce: A Life. The Definitive Biography of a New Testament Scholar*. Milton Keynes, UK: Authentic Media, 2011.

Haddal, Ingvar. *Vær fra vest. Fra Metodistkirkens historie i Norge*. Oslo: Luther Forlag, 1977.

Haga, J., and Olav Fykse Tveit. "'Nådens fellesskap'!—eit grunnlag for samarbeid." *Tidsskrift for Teologi og kirke* 73 (2002) 199–215.

Hall-Hofsø, B. *Da byen var Harstad og resten var avsides—del II. Barn og ungdomsmiljø i Harstad i 1950-åra*. Harstad, 1997.

Hals, H. *Lillestrøms Historie*. 2 vols. Skedsmo: Utgitt av Skedsmo kommune, 1978.

Hammann, Konrad. *Rudolf Bultmann: A Biography*. Salem, OR: Polebridge, 2013.

Haraldsø, B. "'Lærde prester . . . færre enn de var.' Religionsundervisning og kristendomsfag ved Noregs Lærarhøgskole frå 1922 til 1964." In *Det levende Ordet. Festskrift til professor dr.theol. Åge Holter på hans syttiårsdag 19. januar 1989*, edited by Ivar Asheim et al., 97–117. Oslo: Universitetsforlaget, 1989.

Hardin, Justin K. "'If I Still Proclaim Circumcision' (Galatians 5:11a): Paul, the Law and Gentile Circumcision." *Journal for the Study of Paul and His Letters* 3.2 (2013) 145–63.

Hassing, Arne. *Religion and Power: The Case of Methodism in Norway*. Lake Janaluska, NC: United Methodist Church, 1980.

Hays, Richard B. *Echoes of Scripture in the Letters of Paul*. New Haven, CT: Yale University Press, 1989.

———. *Reading Backwards: Figural Christology and the Fourfold Gospel Witness*. Waco, TX: Baylor University Press, 2014.

Heiene, Gunnar. *Eivind Berggrav. En biografi*. Oslo: Universitetsforlaget, 1992.

Hellholm, David, et al., eds. *Mighty Minorities? Minorities in Early Christianity— Positions and Strategies: Essays in Honour of Jacob Jervell on His 70th Birthday, 21 May 1995*. Oslo: Scandinavian University Press, 1995.

Hellholm, David. "Nils Alstrup Dahl som formhistoriker." *Norsk Teologisk Tidsskrift* 105 (2004) 21–25.

Hjelde, S. Sigurd. *Mowinckel und seine Zeit*. Forschungen zum Alten Testament 50. Tübingen: Mohr Siebeck, 2006.

Holbek, Jan Arild. *Rådet som forandret Kirken. Kirkerådet gjennom 50 år*. Oslo: Verbum, 2019.

Hughes, Aaron J. *Jacob Neusner: An American Iconoclast*. New York: New York University Press, 2016.

Hylen, Susan. *Allusion and Meaning in John 6*. Beiheft zur Zeitschrift für die neutestamentliche Wissenschaft 137. Berlin: de Gruyter, 2005.

Haanes, Vidar L. "Studentliv i hundre år." In *Mellom kirke og Akademia. Det teologiske Menighetsfakultet 100 år, 1908–2008*, edited by Bernt T. Oftestad et al., 23–43. Trondheim: Tapir, 2008.

Jansen, H. Ludin. *Sannhetens Evangelium. Det nyfunne koptiske skrift, innledet, oversatt og forsynt med anmerkninger av professor H. Ludin Jansen*. Oslo: Aschehoug, 1961.

Jervell, J. "'Bread from Heaven.' Opposisjonsinnlegg ved Peder Borgens disputas for den teologiske doktorgrad 11. juni 1966." *Norsk Teologisk Tidsskrift* 67 (1966) 227–43.

Johnson, Luke Timothy. *The Mind in Another Place: My Life as a Scholar*. Grand Rapids: Eerdmans, 2022.

Jølle, H. D. "Innledning til en historiefaglig biografi." Tillegg til Jølle, H.D. *F. Nansen, Oppdageren*. Del av Avhandling levert for graden doctor philosophiae—oktober 2013. Institutt for historie og religionsvitenskap. UiT

Keener, Craig S. *Christobiography. Memory, History, and the Reliability of the Gospels*. Grand Rapids: Eerdmans, 2019.

———. *The Gospel of John: A Commentary*. Vol. 1. Peabody, MA: Hendrickson, 2003.

Klausen, Arne Martin. *Et liv i kulturkollisjon*. Oslo: Aschehoug, 1999.

Koskenniemi, Erkki. "Philo and Classical Education." In *Reading Philo: A Handbook to Philo of Alexandria*, edited by Torrey Seland, 102–28. Grand Rapids: Eerdmans, 2014.

Kragerud, A. *Die Hymnen des Pistis Sophia*. Oslo: Universitetsforlaget, 1967.

———. *Der Lieblingsjunger im Johannesevangelium. Ein exegetischer Versuch*. Oslo: Oslo Universitätsverlag, 1959.

———. *Mennesket og religionen*. Oslo: Universitetsforlaget, 1971.

Kysar, Robert, *The Fourth Evangelist and His Gospel: An Examination of Contemporary Scholarship*. Minneapolis: Augsburg, 1975.

Longenecker, Richard N. *Galatians*. Word Biblical Commentary 41. Dallas: Word, 1990.

Løvlie, B. *Kirke, stat og folk i en etterkrigstid*. Diss., Lund University, 1995.

Martyn, J. Louis. *Galatians*. Anchor Bible. New York: Doubleday, 1997.

McKnight, Scot. *A Light Among the Gentiles: Jewish Missionary Activity in the Second Temple Period*. Minneapolis: Fortress, 1991.

Mendelson, Alan, *Secular Education in Philo of Alexandria*. Cincinnati: Hebrew Union College, 1982.

Molland, E. *Konfesjonskunnskap*. 2. Rev. ed. Oslo: Forlaget Land og Kirke, 1961.
———. *Kristenhetens kirker og trossamfunn*. Oslo: Gyldendal, 1976.
———. *Norges Kirkehistorie i det 19. århundre*. Vol. 1. Oslo: Gyldendal, 1979.
———. *Opuscula Patristica*. Bibliotheca Theologica Norvegica 2. Oslo: Universitetsforlaget, 1970.
———. *Das paulinische Euangelion. Das Wort und die Sache*. Avhandlinger utgitt av Det norske Videnskaps-Akademi i Oslo. Hist-Filos Klasse, 1934, no. 3. Oslo, 1934.
———. *Statskirke og Jesu Kristi kirke*. Oslo: Forlaget Land og Kirke, 1954.
Moxnes, H. *A Short History of the New Testament*. London: I. B. Tauris, 2014.
———. *Theology in Conflict: Studies in Paul's Understanding of God in Romans*. Supplements to Novum Testamentum. Leiden: Brill, 1980.
Mørkhagen, Sverre. *Farvel Norge. Utvandringen til Amerika 1825–1975*. Oslo: Gyldendal, 2009.
Neusner, J., et al., eds. *The Social World of Formative Christianity and Judaism*. Philadelphia: Fortress, 1988.
Niehoff, Maren. *Philo of Alexandria: An Intellectual Biography*. New Haven, CT: Yale University Press, 2018.
Nilsen, E.-B. "Norges Kristne Råd—et fellesskap av kristne kirker og trossamfunn i Norge." *Norsk Tidsskrift for Misjon* 70 (2016) 39–47.
Nome, John. *Brytningstid. Menighetsfakultetet i norsk kirkeliv*. Oslo: Lutherstiftelsen, 1958.
Nordby, L.-E. "Nådens fellesskap—en bærekraftig avtale?" *Tidsskrift for Teologi og Kirke* 99 (1998) 131–42.
Oftestad, Bernt T. *Den norske statsreligionen. Fra øvrighetskirke til demokratisk statskirke*. Kristiansand: Høyskoleforlaget, 1998.
Oftestad, Bernt T., and N. A. Røsæg, eds., *Mellom kirke og akademia. Det teologiske Menighetsfakultet 100 år, 1908-2008*. Trondheim: Tapir akademisk, 2008.
Olsen, Ø. "Norge og Øverås." In *Berättelser om Øverås. Minnen, Möten och Människor. Textinsamling och urval*, edited by I. Nordieng et al., 88–95. No publisher, no date.
Osnes, E. "Norsk Misjonsråd i 25 år." *Norsk Tidsskrift for Misjon* 25 (1947) 33–39.
Østnor, Lars. *Dialogens Vei. Den internasjonale luthersk-metodistiske samtale 1979–84*. Nordisk ekumenisk skriftserie 19. Oslo/Uppsala: Økumenisk institutt—Mellomkirkelig råd for Den norske kirke, 1990.
———. "En—og samtidig splittet." In *Snart enige? Glimt fra samtaler mellom forskjellige kirkesamfunn*, edited by R. Tofte, 80–82. Oslo: Verbum, 1992.
———. "Den økumeniske bevegelse og Den norske kirke. Fra debatten i den første etterkrigstid om vårt engasjement i Kirkenes Verdensråd." In *Misjonskall og forskerglede. Festskrift til O.G. Myklebusts 70 års dag*, edited by N. Bloch-Hoell, 222–56. Oslo: Universitetsforlaget, 1975.
Øverland, Per, ed. *Norske Frikirker: framvekst og konfesjonell egenart i brytning med statskirkelighet*. Trondheim: Tapir, 1981.
———. ed. *Norges kristne kirkesamfunn*. Trondheim: Tapir, 1991.
Possing, Birgitte. *Ind i Biografien*. København: Gyldendal, 2015.
———. *Understanding Biographies: On Biographies in History and Stories in Biography*. Odense: University Press of Southern Denmark, 2017.
Rian, Dagfinn. *Kristendomsfag og religionsforskning 1964–2004*. UniRel Studieserie 32. Institutt for arkeologi og religionsvitenskap. Trondheim: NTNU, 2004.

Robbins, Vernon K. *Jesus the Teacher: A Socio-Rhetorical Interpretation of Mark*. Minneapolis: Fortress, 1984.

———. *The Tapestry of Early Christian Discourse: Rhetoric, Society and Ideology*. London: Routledge, 1996.

Runia, David T. "Philo, Alexandrian and Jew." In *Exegesis and Philosophy: Studies on Philo of Alexandria*, 1–18. Collected Studies Series. Aldershot: Variorum, 1990.

———. *Philo in Early Christian Literature: A Survey*. Compendia Rerum Iudaicarum ad Novum Testamentum, sec. 3, vol. 3. Assen: Van Gorcum, 1993.

———. *Philo of Alexandria: An Annotated Bibliography 1987–1996*. Supplements to Vigiliae Christianae 57. Leiden: Brill, 2000.

———. *Philo of Alexandria: An Annotated Bibliography 1997–2006*. Supplements to Vigiliae Christianae 109. Leiden: Brill, 2012.

Schuler, Ph. L. *A Genre for the Gospels: The Biographical Character of Matthew*. Philadelphia: Fortress, 1982.

Seierstad, Ivar. *Kristelig Gymnasiums Historie*. Oslo: Lutherstiftelsen, 1963.

———. *Kristelig Gymnasium 1913–1988. En plogspiss for friskolesaken i Norge*. Oslo: Utgitt av Kristelig Gymnasium, 1988.

Seim, T. Karlsen, and T. Wyller. "Akademisk kultur og vitenskapelig redelighet. Utdrag fra en samtale med Nils Alstrup Dahl." *Norsk Teologisk Tidsskrift* 101 (2000) 90–93.

Seland, Torrey. "Lex Borgen: Et blad i norsk skolehistorie om ikke-lutheraneres rett til å undervise i høyere utdanning." In *Tru på Vestlandet. Tradisjonar i endring*, edited by Birger Løvlie et al., 363–90. Kyrkjefag Profil 36. Oslo: Cappelen Damm Akademisk, 2020.

———. *Paulus i Polis. Paulus sosiale verden som forståelsesbakgrunn for hans liv og forkynnelse*. Kyrkjefag Profil 4. Trondheim: Tapir, 2004.

———, ed. *Reading Philo: A Handbook to Philo of Alexandria*. Grand Rapids: Eerdmans, 2014.

———. "Why Study Philo? How?" In *Reading Philo: A Handbook to Philo of Alexandria*, edited by Torrey Seland, 157–79. Grand Rapids: Eerdmans, 2014.

Seters, John van, *My Life and Career as a Biblical Scholar*. Eugene, OR: Cascade, 2018.

Skarsaune, Oskar. *Etterlyst: Bergprekenens Jesus. Har folkekirkene glemt ham?* Oslo: Luther Forlag, 2018.

Skarsten, Roald, Peder Borgen, and Kåre Fuglseth. *The Complete Works of Philo of Alexandria: A Key-Word-in-Context Concordance*. 8 vols. Piscataway, NJ: Gorgias, 2005.

Skarsten, R. *Forfatterproblemet ved De aeternitate mundi i Corpus Philonicum*. Bergen: Universitetet i Bergen, 1987.

Skre, Arnhild. *Tilnærmingar, metode, drøftingar og val: vitskapeleg etterskrift til biografien Hulda Garborg. Nasjonal strateg*. Oslo: Institutt for arkeologi, konservering og historie, Det humanistiske fakultet, Universitetet i Oslo, 2015.

Smidt, Martin, *John Wesley: A Theological Biography*. London: Epworth, 1971

Stewart, Alexander Coe. "Vernon K. Robbins and his Contributions to Socio-Rhetorical Criticism." In *Pillars in the History of Biblical Interpretation*, edited by Stanley E. Porter and Zachary K. Dawson, 3:384–408. Eugene, OR: Pickwick, 2021.

Stubhaug, A. *Den lange linjen. Historien om Videnskabsselskabet i Trondheim*. Trondheim: Tapir, 2010.

Thyen, H. *Das Johannesevangelium, 2. Auflage*. Handbuch zum Neuen Testament 6. Tübingen: Mohr Siebeck, 2015.

Tjørhom, Ola. *Kirkesamfunn i Norge: innføring i kirkekunnskap*. Oslo: Cappelen Damm Akademisk, 2018.

Tveit, Olav Fykse. "Alle gode ting er tre? Om Porvoo-avtalen, Nådens fellesskap og Leuenberg-konkordien." *Luthersk Kirketidende* 132 (1997) 64–69.

Ulvund, Frode. *Nasjonens Antiborgere. Forestillinger om religiøse minoriteter som samfunnsfiender i Norge, ca. 1814–1964*. Oslo: Cappelen Damm Akademisk, 2017.

Veiteberg, Kari. *Jacob Jervell Et portrett*. Oslo: Verbum, 2013.

Vielhauer, P. "On the Paulinism of Acts." In *Studies in Luke-Acts,* edited by Leander E. Keck and J. Louis Martyn, 33–50. London: SPCK, 1968.

———. "Zum Paulinismus der Apostelgeschichte." *Evangelische Theologie* 10 (1950–51) 1–15.

Vågen, T. "Det internasjonale misjonsråd og Kirkenes Verdensråd." *Norsk Tidsskrift for Misjon* 13 (1959) 65–69.

Wendel, Jorunn. "Metodistkirken—fra nasjonal vekkelse til internasjonal kirke." In *Kirkesamfunn i Norge. Innføring i kirkekunnskap*, edited by Ola Tjørhom, 151–68. Oslo: Cappelen Damm Akademisk, 2020.

Wilson, B. R. "An Analysis of Sect Development." *American Sociological Review* 24 (1959) 3–15.

Wisløff, C. Fr. *Norsk kirkedebatt gjennom 100 år*. Oslo: Lunde, 1979.

———. *Norsk Kirkehistorie*. Vol. 3. Oslo: Lutherstiftelsen, 1971.

Witherington, Ben, III, ed. *Luminescence: The Sermons of C. K. and Fred Barrett*. 3 vols. Eugene, OR: Cascade, 2017–2018.

www.ingramcontent.com/pod-product-compliance
Lightning Source LLC
Chambersburg PA
CBHW050616300426
44112CB00012B/1530